Star Trek: the manga
Shinsei/Shinsei

Toning (Orphans) - Hon Lam Chow
Lettering - Lucas Rivera
Development Editor - Aaron Suhr
Cover Design - Christian Lownds
Cover Artists - Makoto Nakatsuka, EJ Su (Diamond Exclusive),
Bettina Kurkoski (Convention Exclusive)

Editor - Luis Reyes
Digital Imaging Manager - Chris Buford
Pre-Production Supervisor - Lucas Rivera
Art Director - Anne Marie Horne
Production Manager - Liz Brizzi
VP of Production - Ron Klamert
Editor-in-Chief - Rob Tokar
Publisher - Mike Kiley
President and C.O.O. - John Parker
C.E.O. and Chief Creative Officer - Stuart Levy

A  Manga

TOKYOPOP Inc.
5900 Wilshire Blvd. Suite 2000
Los Angeles, CA 90036

E-mail: info@TOKYOPOP.com
Come visit us online at www.TOKYOPOP.com

ISBN: 1-59816-744-8
1-4278-0030-8 (Convention Exclusive)
1-4278-0031-6 (Diamond Exclusive)

First TOKYOPOP printing: September 2006
10 9 8 7 6 5 4 3 2 1
Printed in the USA

STAR TREK ®

新生 Shinsei Shinsei 新星

HAMBURG // LONDON // LOS ANGELES // TOKYO

TABLE OF CONTENTS

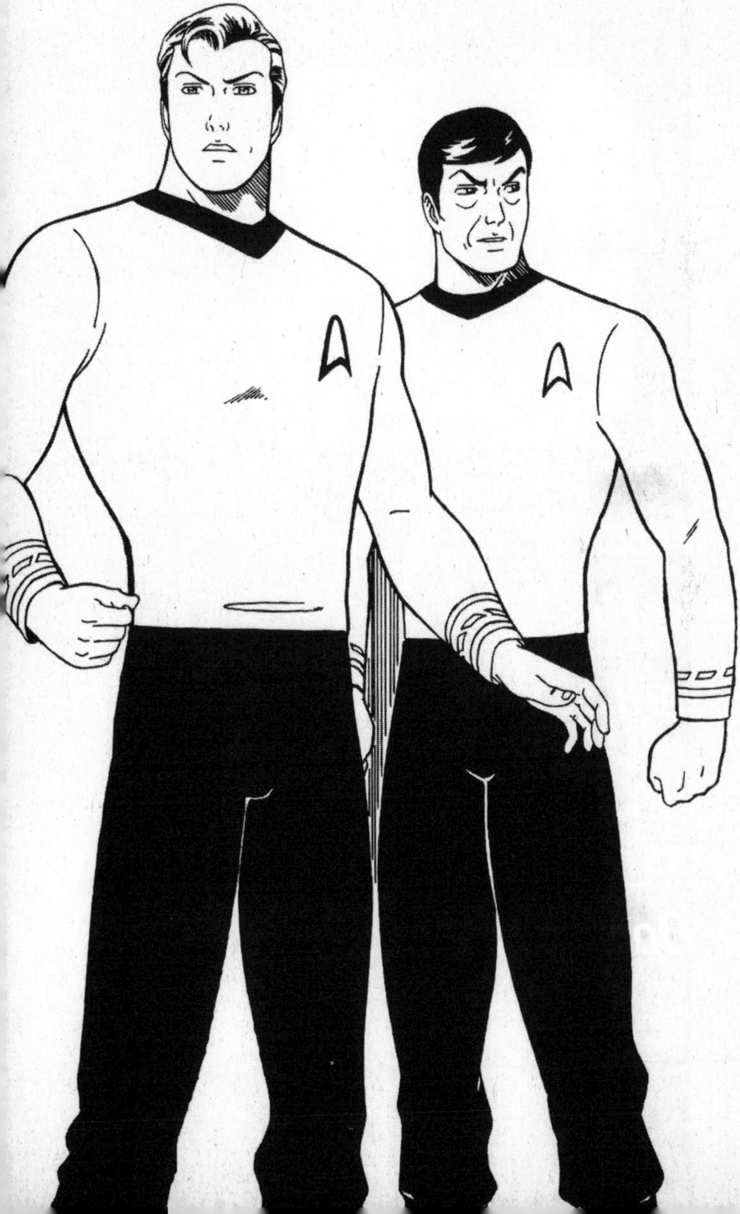

SIDE EFFECTS

STORY BY CHRIS DOWS
ART BY MAKOTO NAKATSUKA

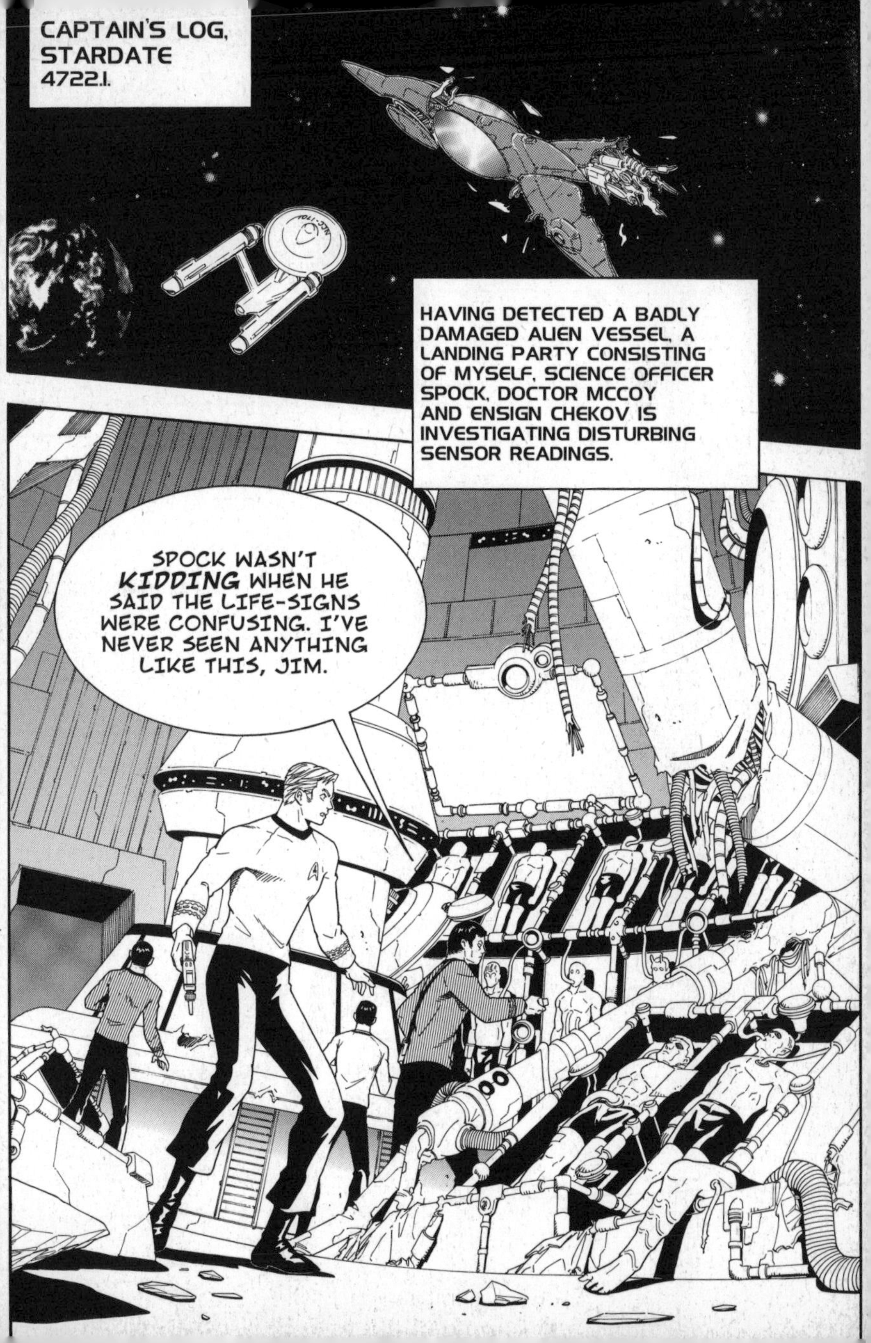
CAPTAIN'S LOG, STARDATE 4722.1.
HAVING DETECTED A BADLY DAMAGED ALIEN VESSEL, A LANDING PARTY CONSISTING OF MYSELF, SCIENCE OFFICER SPOCK, DOCTOR MCCOY AND ENSIGN CHEKOV IS INVESTIGATING DISTURBING SENSOR READINGS.
SPOCK WASN'T *KIDDING* WHEN HE SAID THE LIFE-SIGNS WERE CONFUSING. I'VE NEVER SEEN ANYTHING LIKE THIS, JIM.

THEY'RE ALL THE SAME RACE BUT HAVE COMBINATIONS OF OTHER SPECIES SPLICED INTO THEM. THIS ONE ALONE HAS TRACES OF HUMAN AND ROMULAN DNA...AND THERE'S *HUNDREDS* MORE.

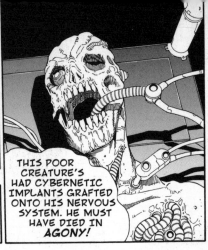

THIS POOR CREATURE'S HAD CYBERNETIC IMPLANTS GRAFTED ONTO HIS NERVOUS SYSTEM. HE MUST HAVE DIED IN *AGONY!*

DEAR LORD...

CAPTAIN...

THE SHIP'S RECORDS ARE BADLY DAMAGED, BUT IT APPEARS THIS VESSEL WAS LAUNCHED OVER TWO HUNDRED YEARS AGO.

HOW HAS IT MANAGED TO KEEP TOGETHER SO LONG?

IT HAS A SOPHISTICATED AUTOMATIC REPAIR SYSTEM, CAPTAIN. EVIDENTLY, IT HAS FAILED.

TWO HUNDRED YEARS... THESE POOR SOULS ARE SEMI-CONSCIOUS, JIM.

THEY'RE BEING KEPT ALIVE BY FEEDING TUBES AND *CIRCUITRY.* THEIR SUFFERING *HAS TO STOP!*

ENTERPRISE TO CAPTAIN KIRK.

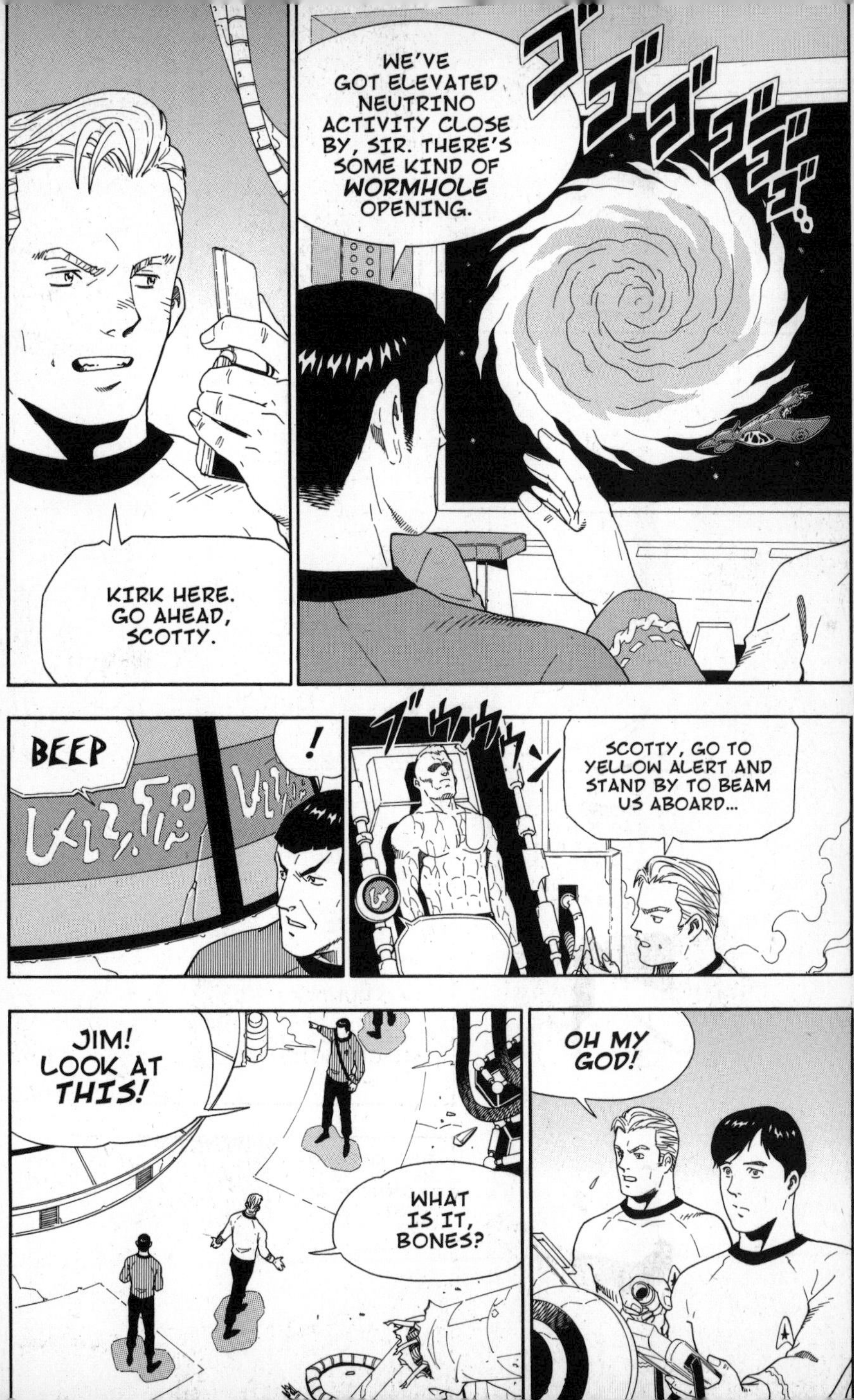
KIRK HERE. GO AHEAD, SCOTTY.
WE'VE GOT ELEVATED NEUTRINO ACTIVITY CLOSE BY, SIR. THERE'S SOME KIND OF WORMHOLE OPENING.
BEEP
!
SCOTTY, GO TO YELLOW ALERT AND STAND BY TO BEAM US ABOARD...
JIM! LOOK AT THIS!
WHAT IS IT, BONES?
OH MY GOD!

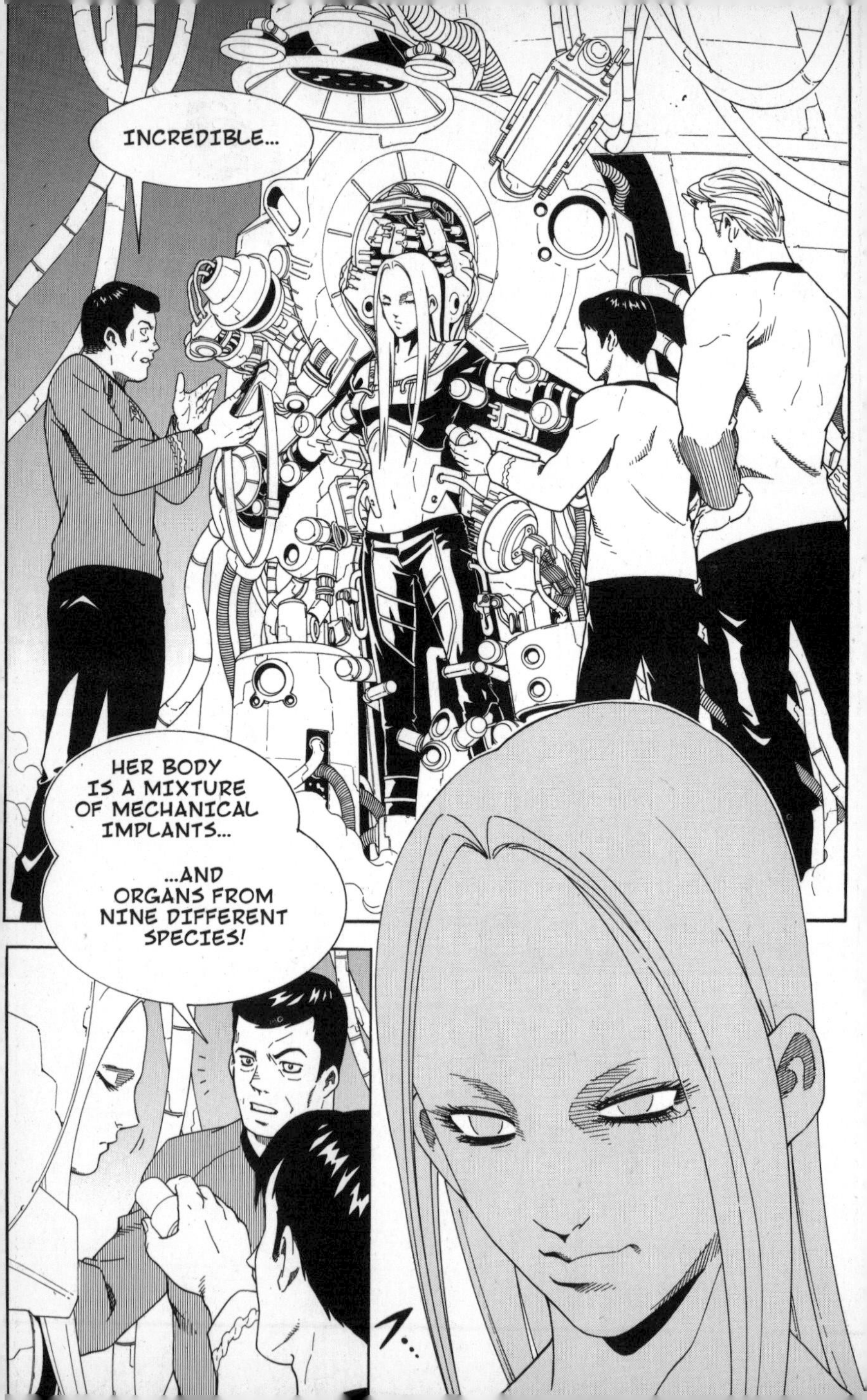
INCREDIBLE...
HER BODY IS A MIXTURE OF MECHANICAL IMPLANTS...
...AND ORGANS FROM NINE DIFFERENT SPECIES!

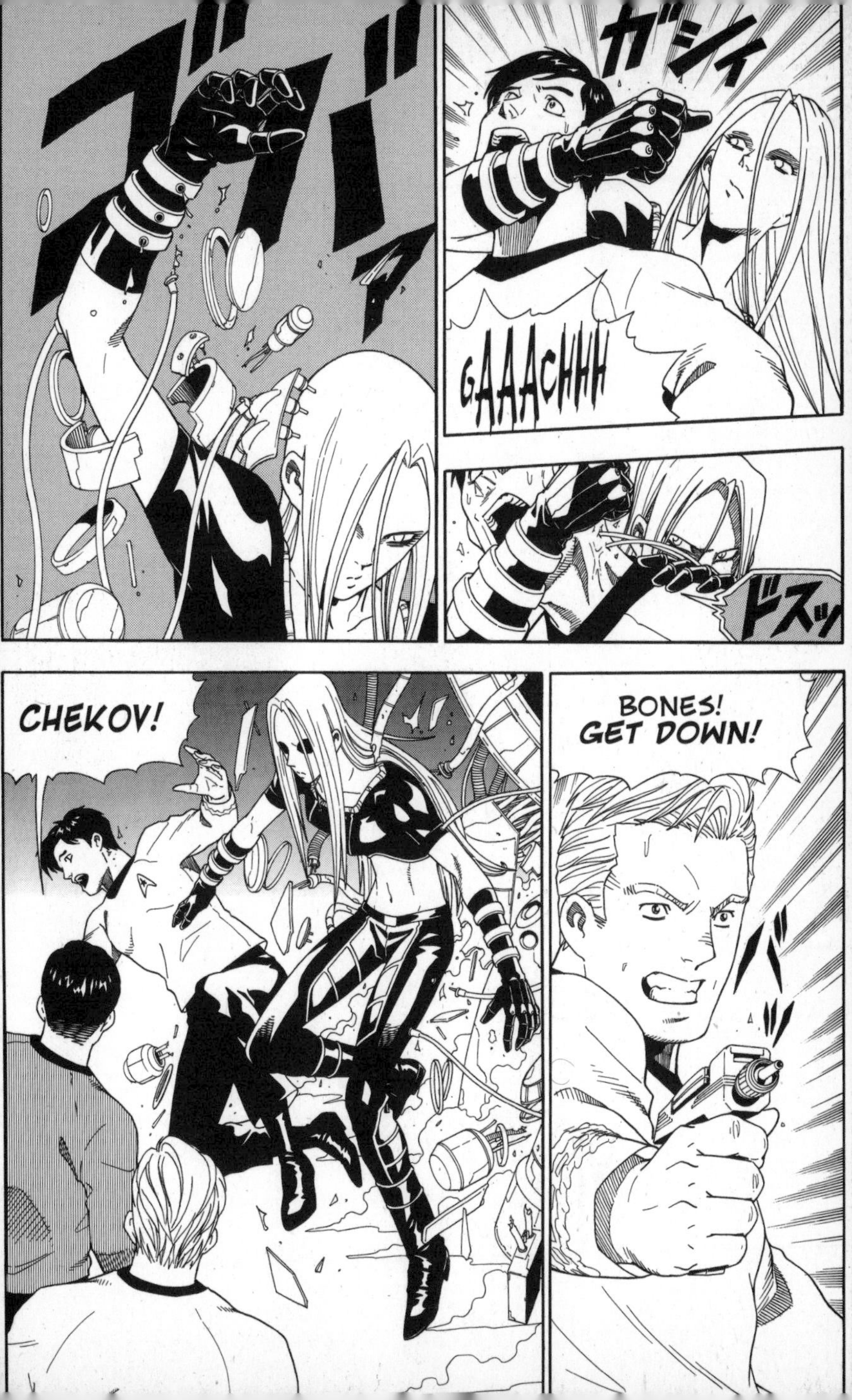

ガシィ
GAAACHHH
ドスッ
CHEKOV!
BONES!
GET DOWN!

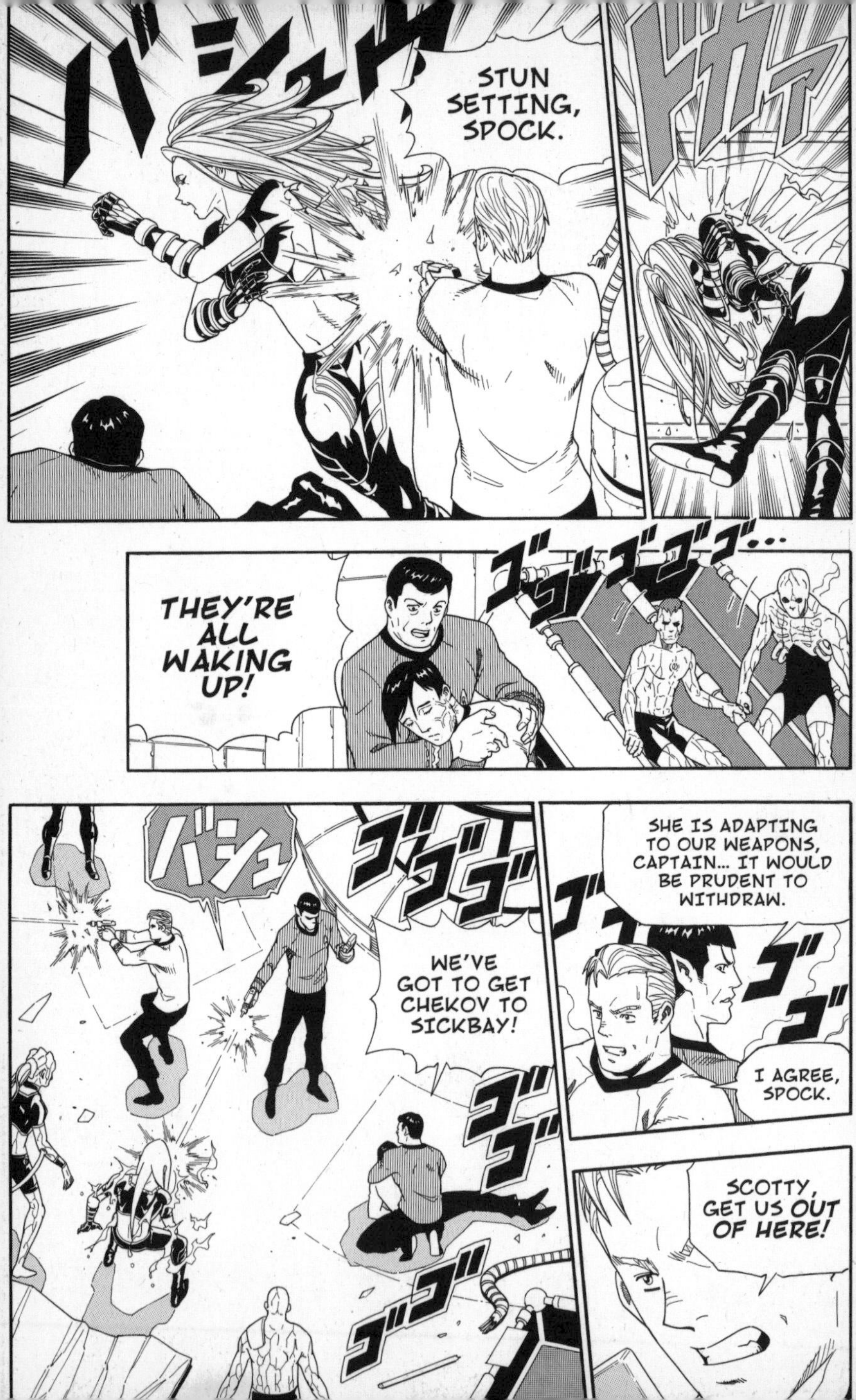

STUN SETTING, SPOCK.
THEY'RE ALL WAKING UP!
バシュ
WE'VE GOT TO GET CHEKOV TO SICKBAY!
SHE IS ADAPTING TO OUR WEAPONS, CAPTAIN... IT WOULD BE PRUDENT TO WITHDRAW.
I AGREE, SPOCK.
SCOTTY, GET US OUT OF HERE!

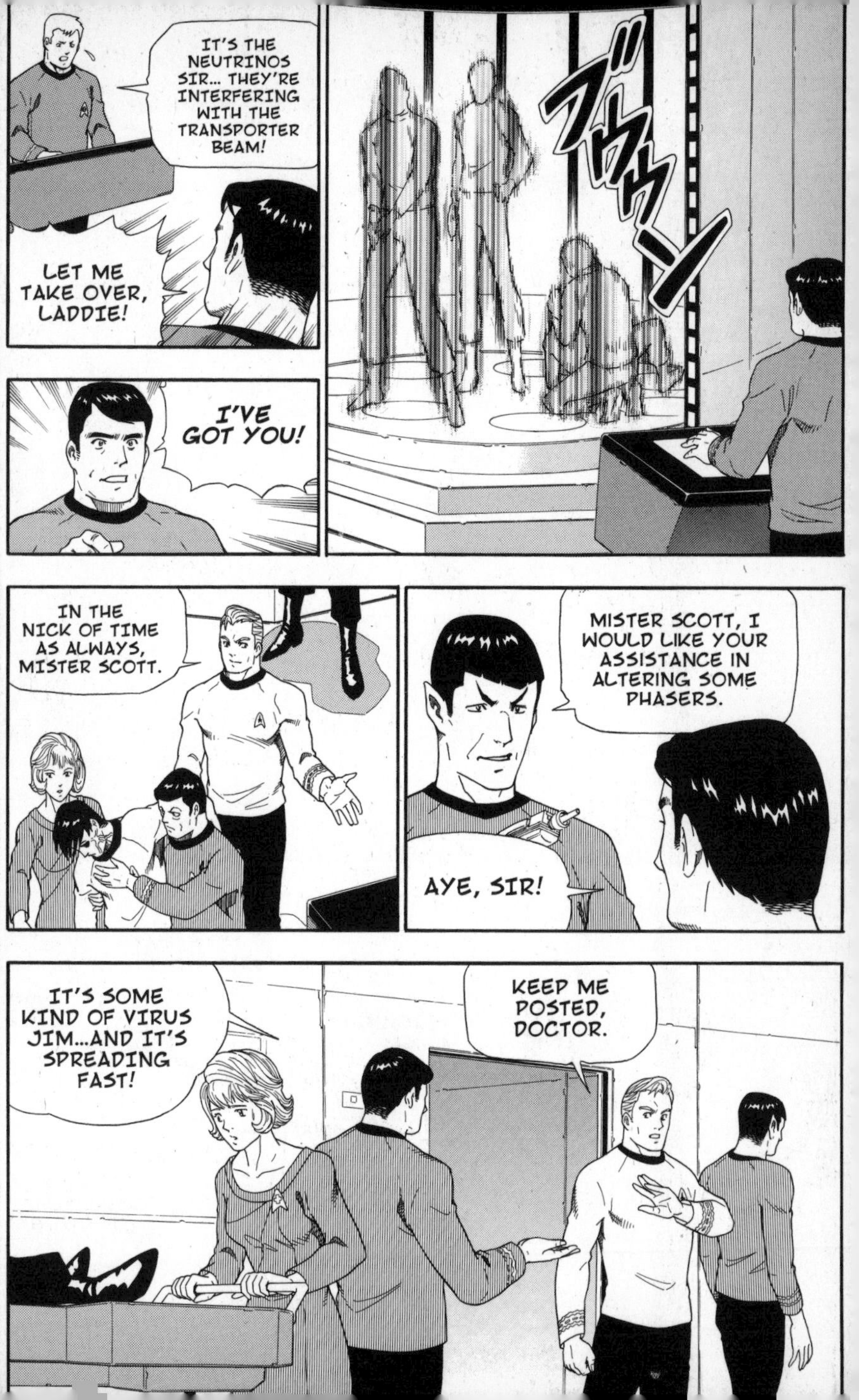
IT'S THE NEUTRINOS SIR... THEY'RE INTERFERING WITH THE TRANSPORTER BEAM!
LET ME TAKE OVER, LADDIE!
I'VE GOT YOU!
ブヴゥーン
IN THE NICK OF TIME AS ALWAYS, MISTER SCOTT.
MISTER SCOTT, I WOULD LIKE YOUR ASSISTANCE IN ALTERING SOME PHASERS.
AYE, SIR!
IT'S SOME KIND OF VIRUS JIM...AND IT'S SPREADING FAST!
KEEP ME POSTED, DOCTOR.

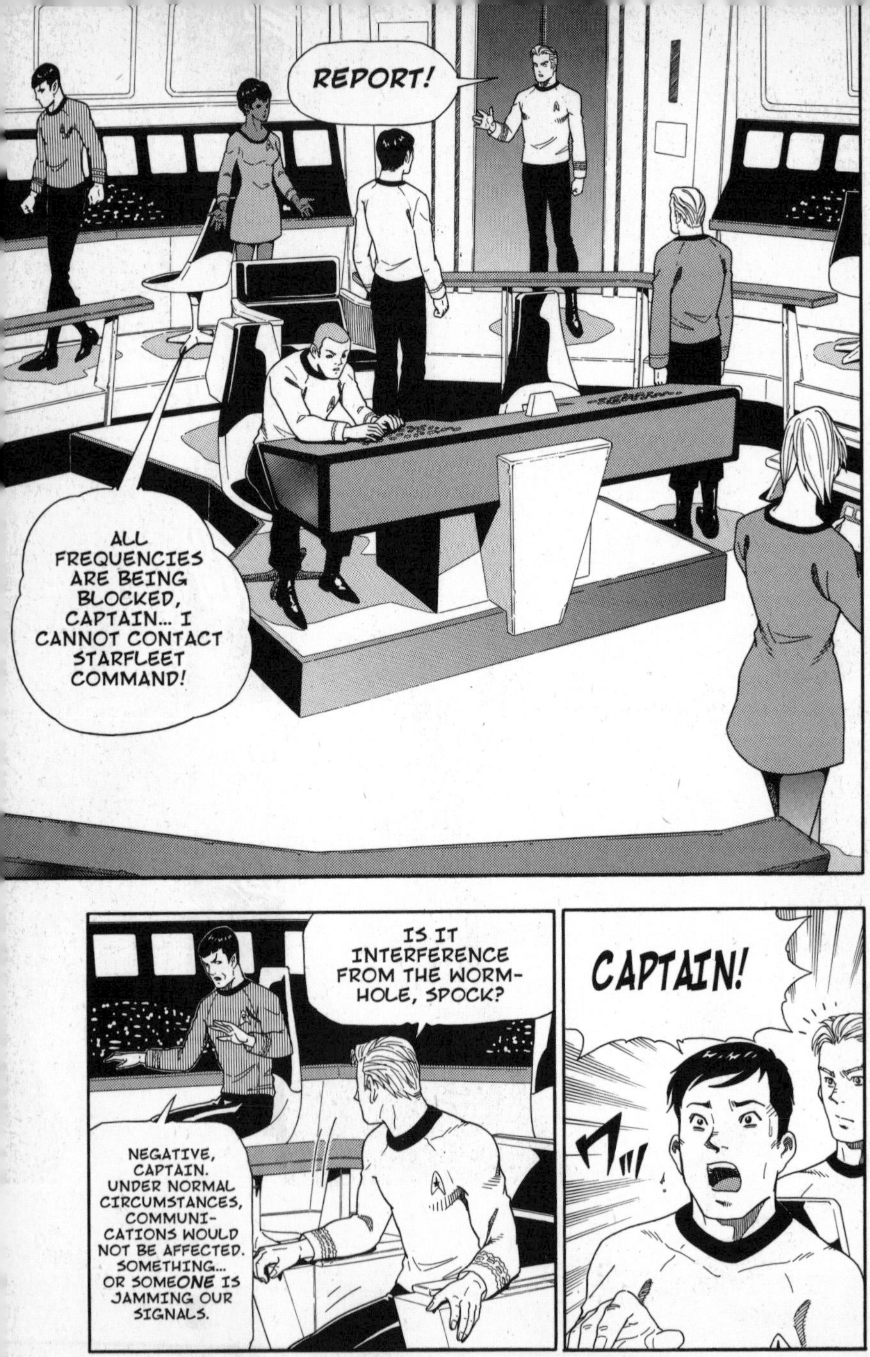
REPORT!
ALL FREQUENCIES ARE BEING BLOCKED, CAPTAIN... I CANNOT CONTACT STARFLEET COMMAND!
IS IT INTERFERENCE FROM THE WORM-HOLE, SPOCK?
NEGATIVE, CAPTAIN. UNDER NORMAL CIRCUMSTANCES, COMMUNI-CATIONS WOULD NOT BE AFFECTED. SOMETHING... OR SOMEONE IS JAMMING OUR SIGNALS.
CAPTAIN!

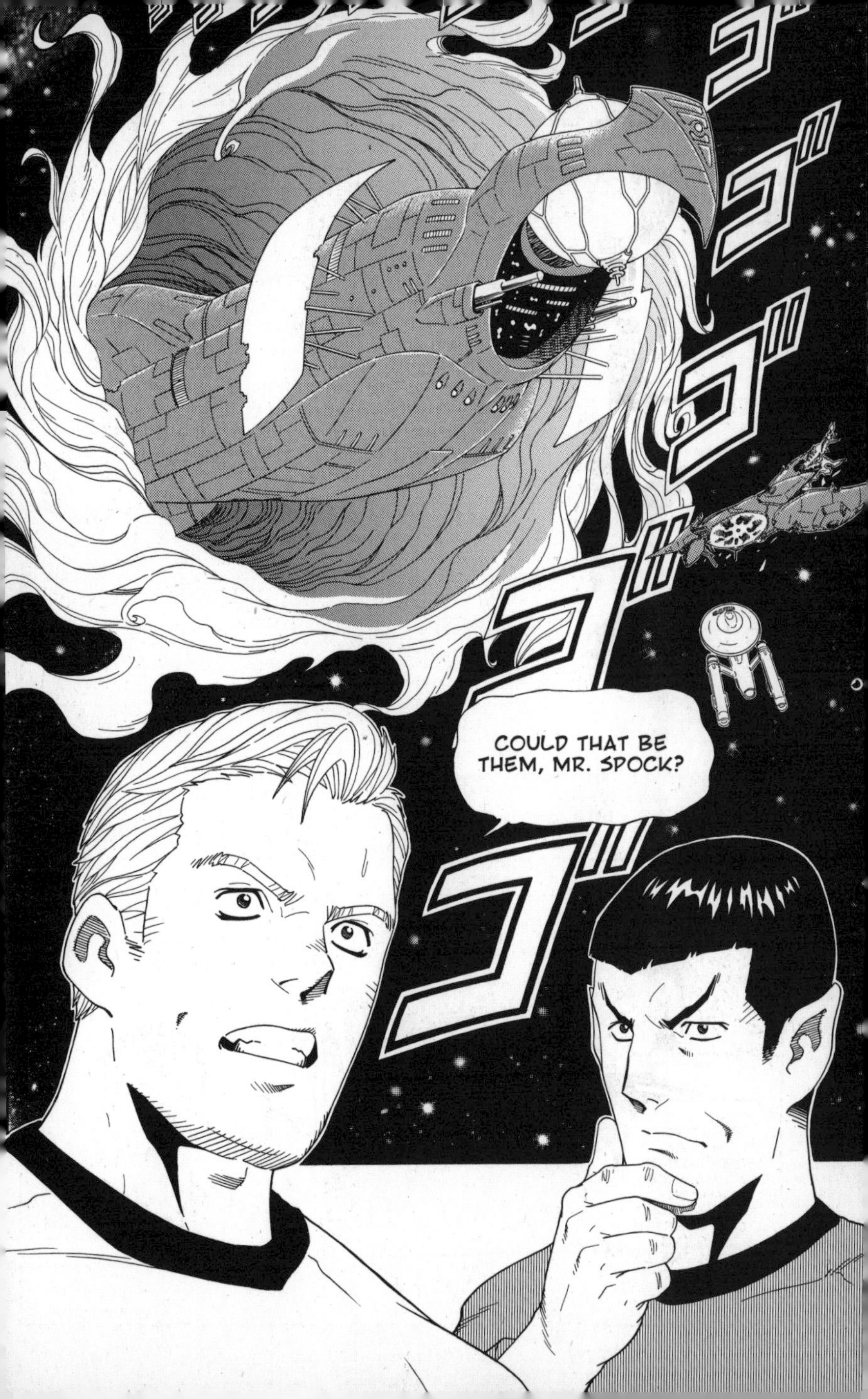
COULD THAT BE THEM, MR. SPOCK?

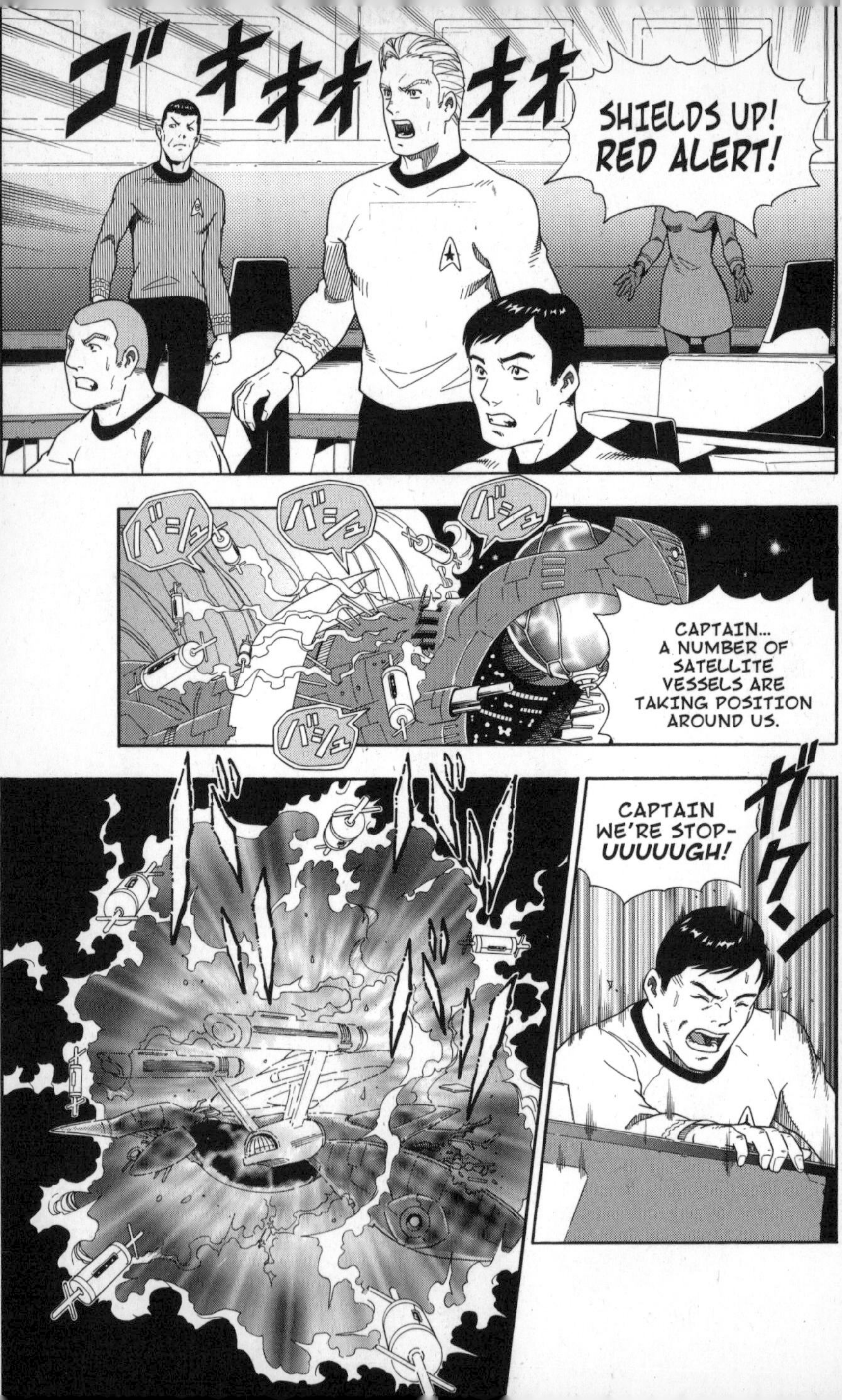
ゴオオオオオ
SHIELDS UP! RED ALERT!
バシュ
バシュ
バシュ
バシュ
CAPTAIN... A NUMBER OF SATELLITE VESSELS ARE TAKING POSITION AROUND US.
CAPTAIN WE'RE STOP-UUUUUGH!
ガク!

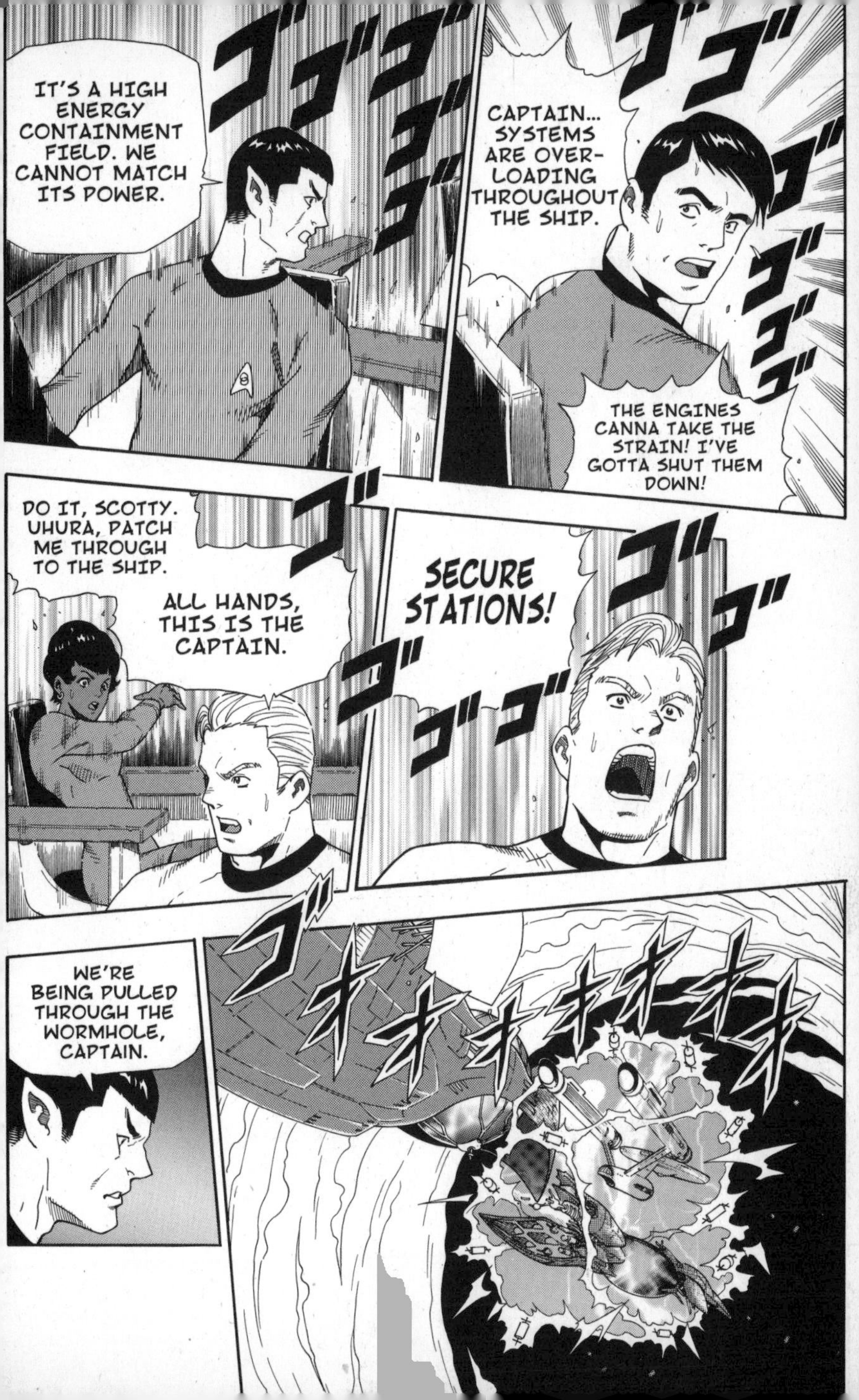
IT'S A HIGH ENERGY CONTAINMENT FIELD. WE CANNOT MATCH ITS POWER.
CAPTAIN... SYSTEMS ARE OVER-LOADING THROUGHOUT THE SHIP.
THE ENGINES CANNA TAKE THE STRAIN! I'VE GOTTA SHUT THEM DOWN!
DO IT, SCOTTY. UHURA, PATCH ME THROUGH TO THE SHIP.
ALL HANDS, THIS IS THE CAPTAIN.
SECURE STATIONS!
WE'RE BEING PULLED THROUGH THE WORMHOLE, CAPTAIN.

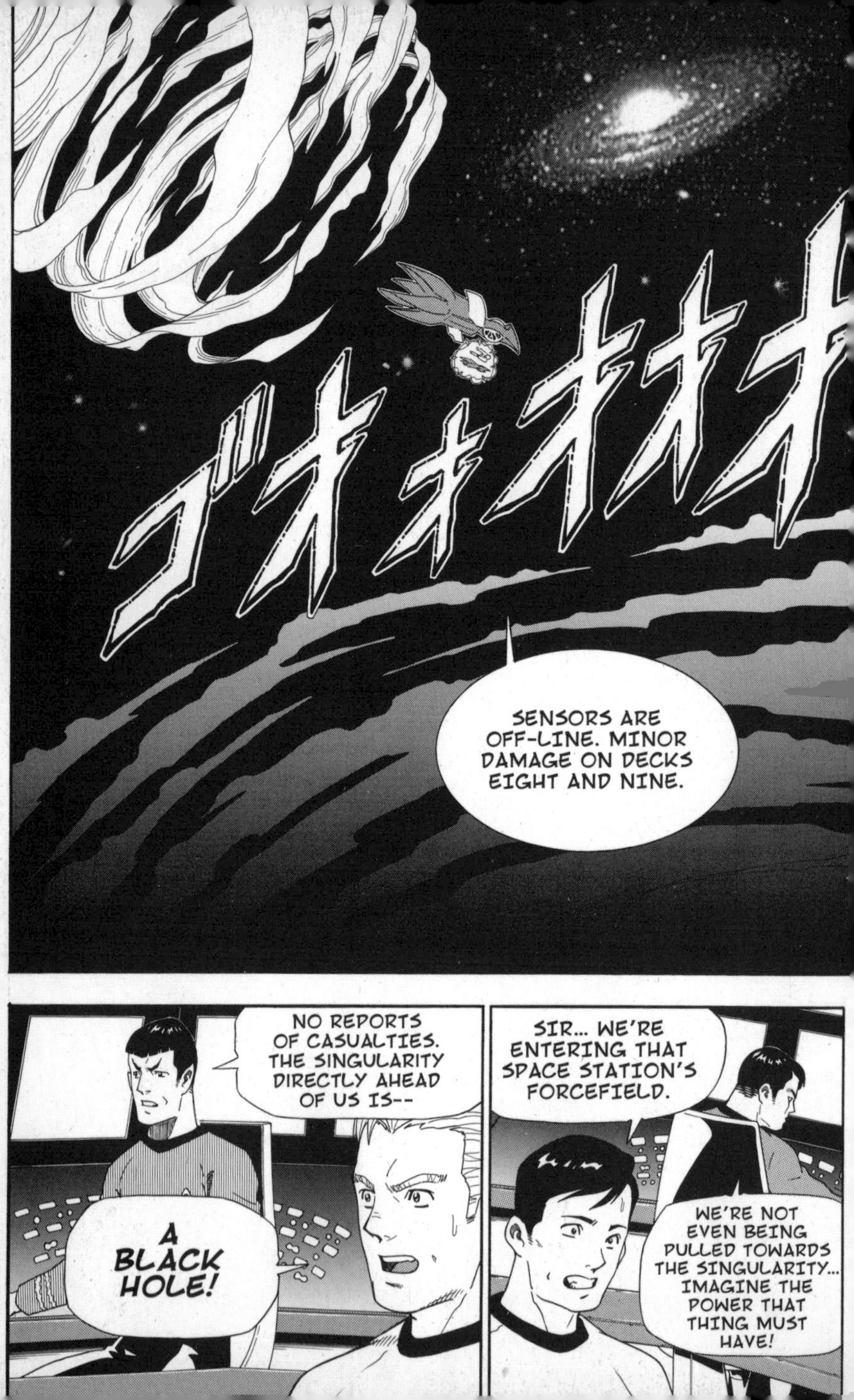
ゴオォオオオ
SENSORS ARE OFF-LINE. MINOR DAMAGE ON DECKS EIGHT AND NINE.
NO REPORTS OF CASUALTIES. THE SINGULARITY DIRECTLY AHEAD OF US IS--
A BLACK HOLE!
SIR... WE'RE ENTERING THAT SPACE STATION'S FORCEFIELD.
WE'RE NOT EVEN BEING PULLED TOWARDS THE SINGULARITY... IMAGINE THE POWER THAT THING MUST HAVE!

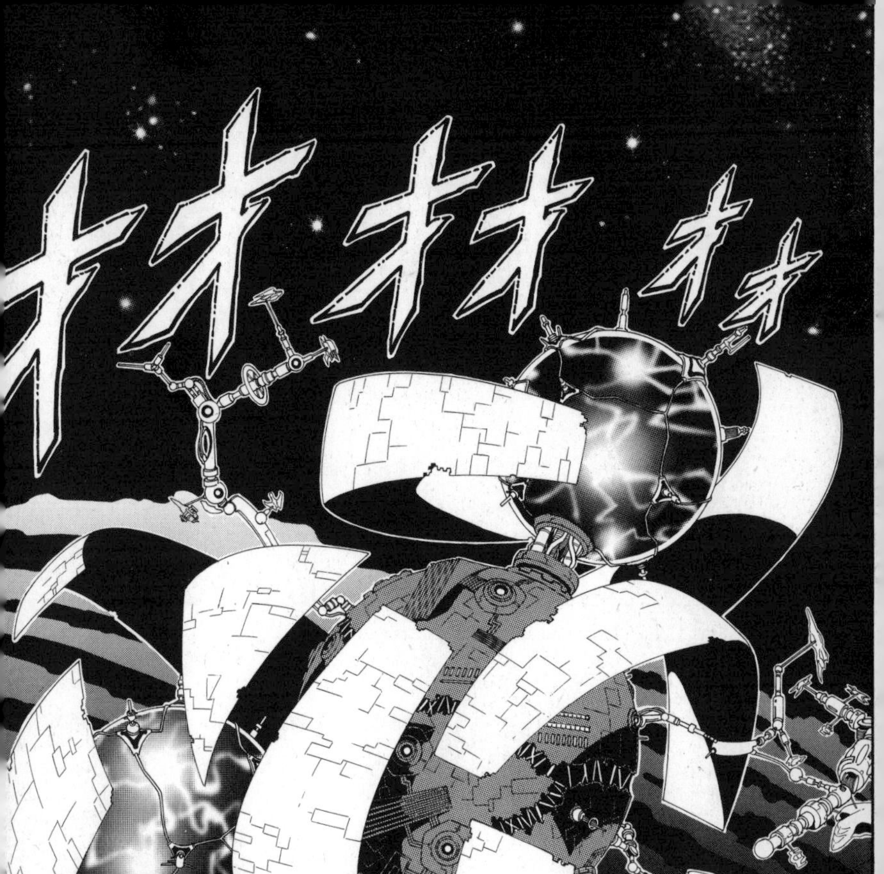
オオオオォォ

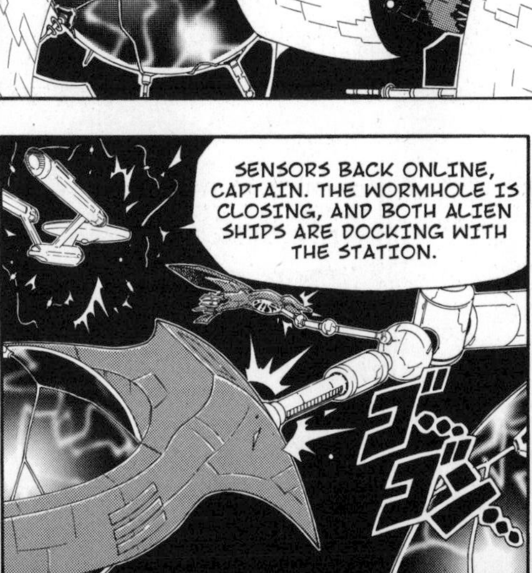
SENSORS BACK ONLINE, CAPTAIN. THE WORMHOLE IS CLOSING, AND BOTH ALIEN SHIPS ARE DOCKING WITH THE STATION.
ゴゴン

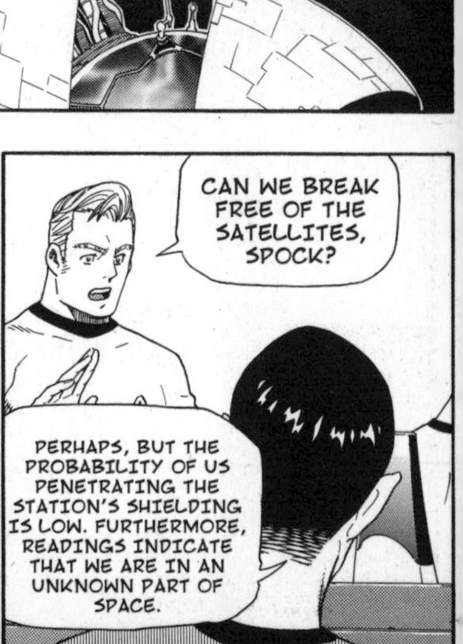
CAN WE BREAK FREE OF THE SATELLITES, SPOCK?
PERHAPS, BUT THE PROBABILITY OF US PENETRATING THE STATION'S SHIELDING IS LOW. FURTHERMORE, READINGS INDICATE THAT WE ARE IN AN UNKNOWN PART OF SPACE.

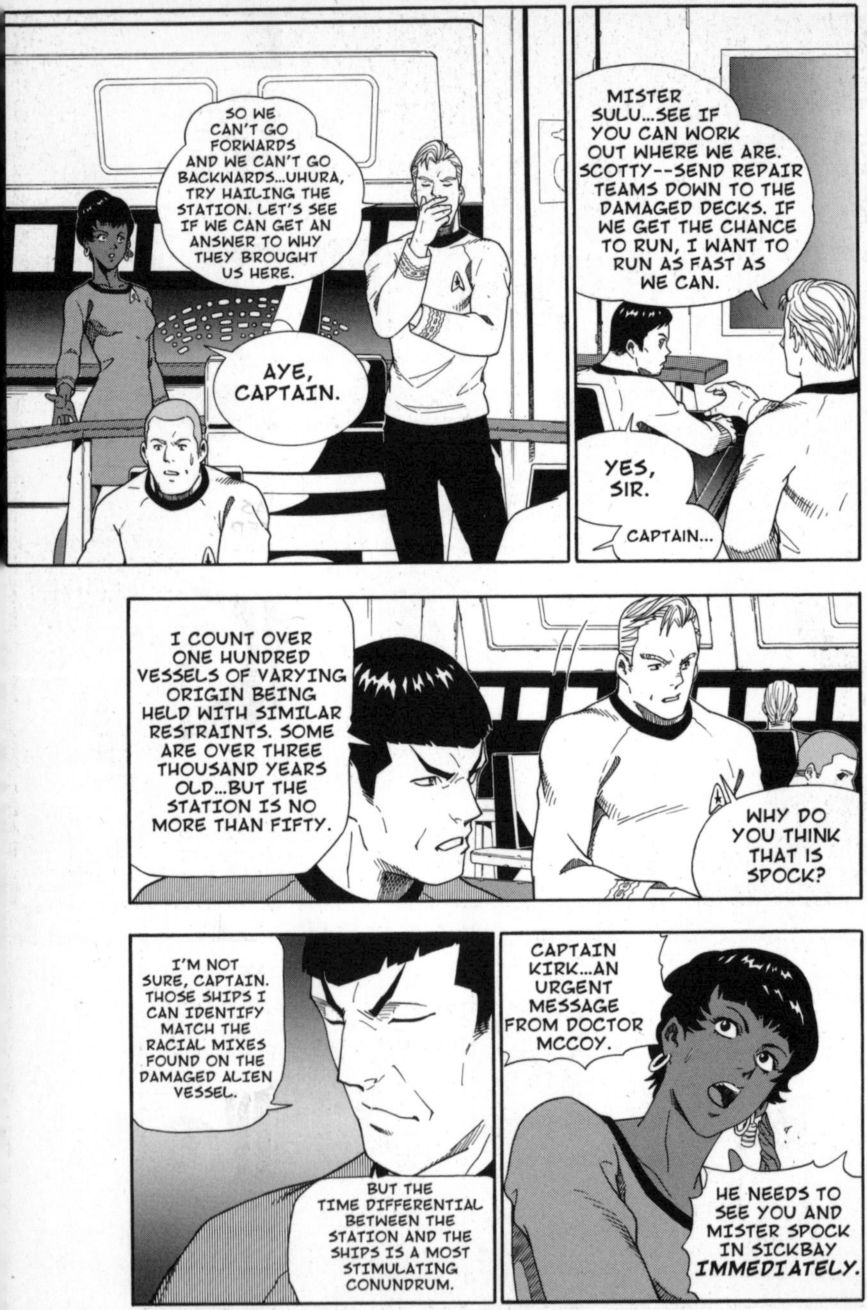
SO WE CAN'T GO FORWARDS AND WE CAN'T GO BACKWARDS...UHURA, TRY HAILING THE STATION. LET'S SEE IF WE CAN GET AN ANSWER TO WHY THEY BROUGHT US HERE.
AYE, CAPTAIN.
MISTER SULU...SEE IF YOU CAN WORK OUT WHERE WE ARE. SCOTTY--SEND REPAIR TEAMS DOWN TO THE DAMAGED DECKS. IF WE GET THE CHANCE TO RUN, I WANT TO RUN AS FAST AS WE CAN.
YES, SIR.
CAPTAIN...
I COUNT OVER ONE HUNDRED VESSELS OF VARYING ORIGIN BEING HELD WITH SIMILAR RESTRAINTS. SOME ARE OVER THREE THOUSAND YEARS OLD...BUT THE STATION IS NO MORE THAN FIFTY.
WHY DO YOU THINK THAT IS SPOCK?
I'M NOT SURE, CAPTAIN. THOSE SHIPS I CAN IDENTIFY MATCH THE RACIAL MIXES FOUND ON THE DAMAGED ALIEN VESSEL.
BUT THE TIME DIFFERENTIAL BETWEEN THE STATION AND THE SHIPS IS A MOST STIMULATING CONUNDRUM.
CAPTAIN KIRK...AN URGENT MESSAGE FROM DOCTOR MCCOY.
HE NEEDS TO SEE YOU AND MISTER SPOCK IN SICKBAY *IMMEDIATELY*.

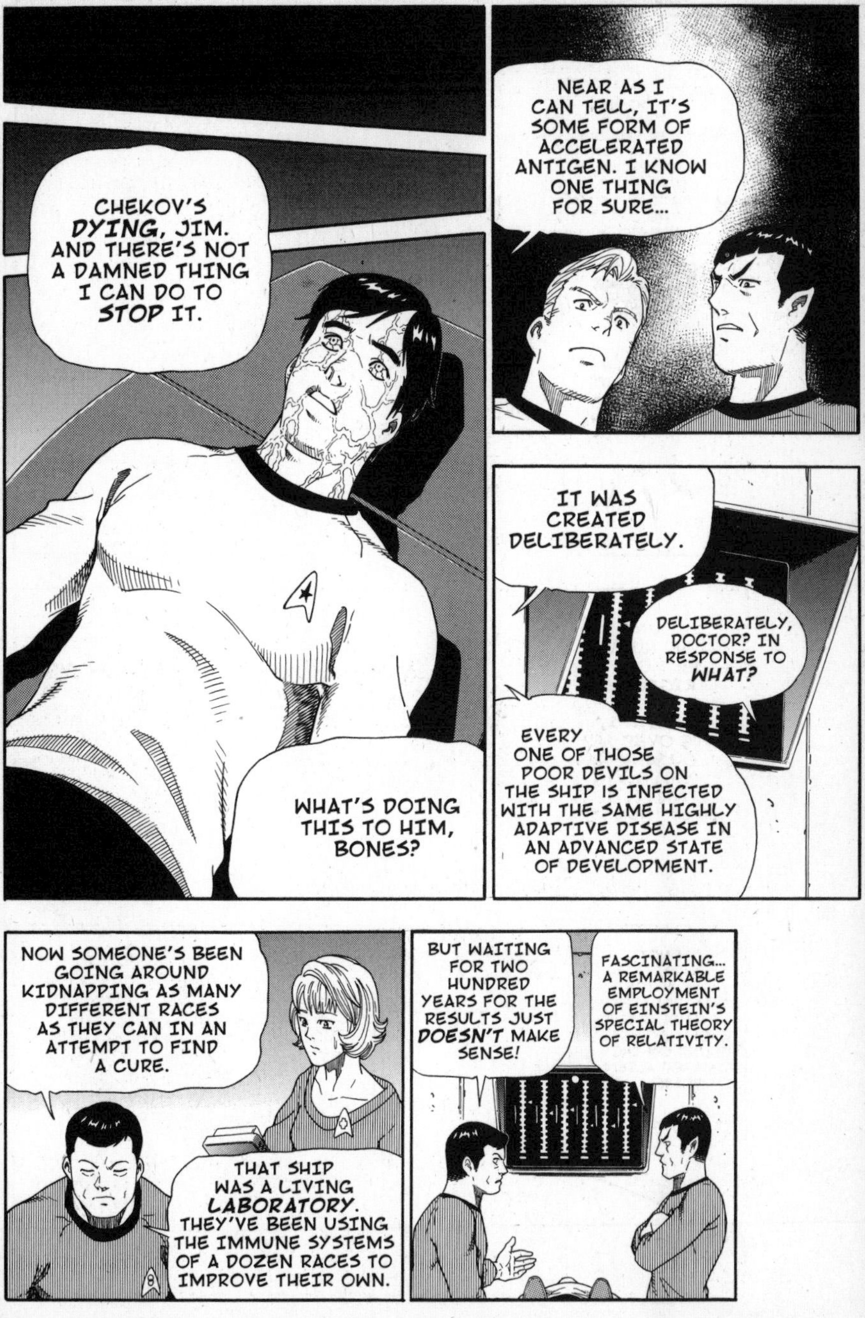

CHEKOV'S DYING, JIM. AND THERE'S NOT A DAMNED THING I CAN DO TO STOP IT.
WHAT'S DOING THIS TO HIM, BONES?
NEAR AS I CAN TELL, IT'S SOME FORM OF ACCELERATED ANTIGEN. I KNOW ONE THING FOR SURE...
IT WAS CREATED DELIBERATELY.
DELIBERATELY, DOCTOR? IN RESPONSE TO WHAT?
EVERY ONE OF THOSE POOR DEVILS ON THE SHIP IS INFECTED WITH THE SAME HIGHLY ADAPTIVE DISEASE IN AN ADVANCED STATE OF DEVELOPMENT.
NOW SOMEONE'S BEEN GOING AROUND KIDNAPPING AS MANY DIFFERENT RACES AS THEY CAN IN AN ATTEMPT TO FIND A CURE.
THAT SHIP WAS A LIVING LABORATORY. THEY'VE BEEN USING THE IMMUNE SYSTEMS OF A DOZEN RACES TO IMPROVE THEIR OWN.
BUT WAITING FOR TWO HUNDRED YEARS FOR THE RESULTS JUST DOESN'T MAKE SENSE!
FASCINATING... A REMARKABLE EMPLOYMENT OF EINSTEIN'S SPECIAL THEORY OF RELATIVITY.

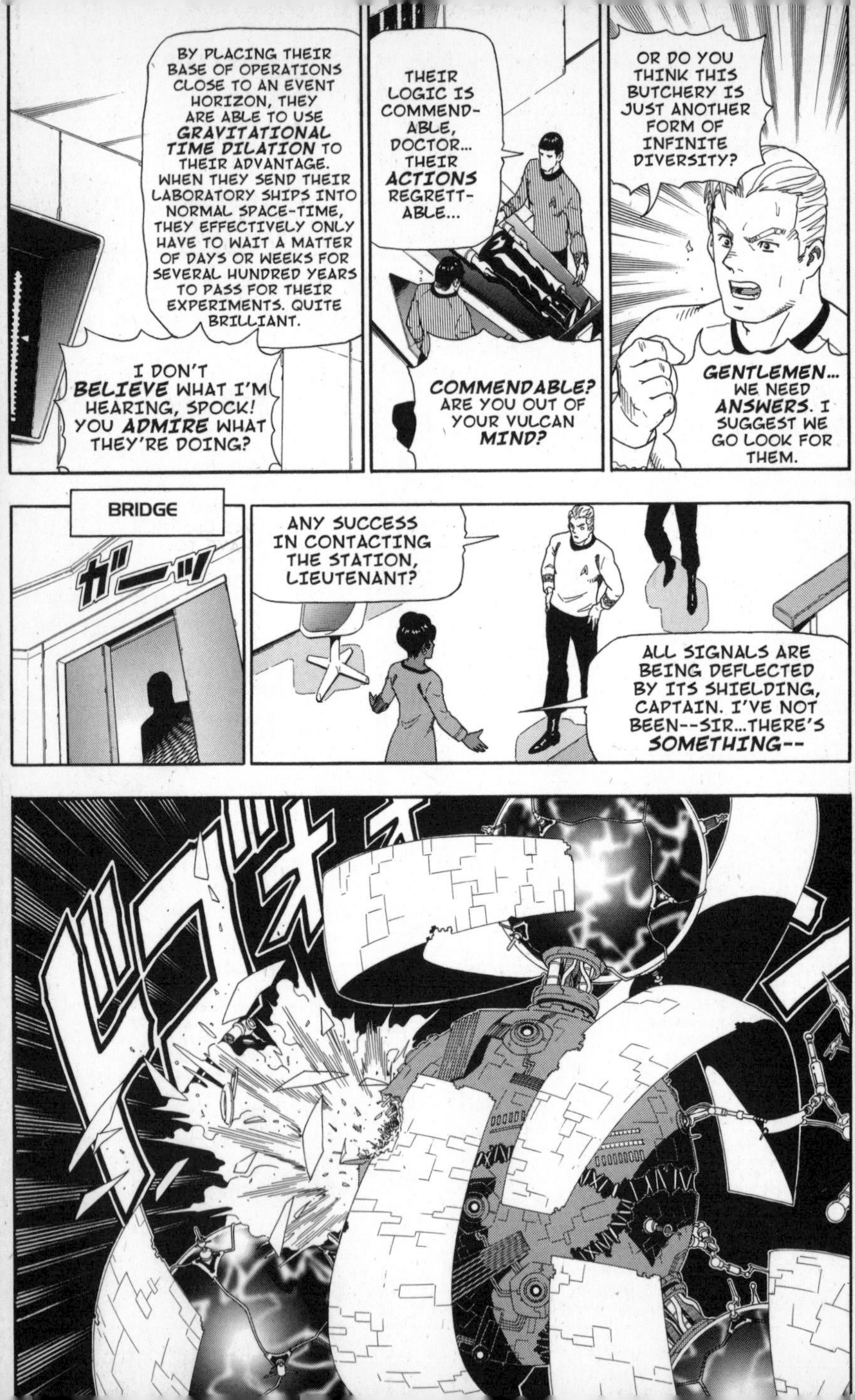
BY PLACING THEIR BASE OF OPERATIONS CLOSE TO AN EVENT HORIZON, THEY ARE ABLE TO USE **GRAVITATIONAL TIME DILATION** TO THEIR ADVANTAGE. WHEN THEY SEND THEIR LABORATORY SHIPS INTO NORMAL SPACE-TIME, THEY EFFECTIVELY ONLY HAVE TO WAIT A MATTER OF DAYS OR WEEKS FOR SEVERAL HUNDRED YEARS TO PASS FOR THEIR EXPERIMENTS. QUITE BRILLIANT.
I DON'T **BELIEVE** WHAT I'M HEARING, SPOCK! YOU **ADMIRE** WHAT THEY'RE DOING?
THEIR LOGIC IS COMMENDABLE, DOCTOR... THEIR **ACTIONS** REGRETTABLE...
COMMENDABLE? ARE YOU OUT OF YOUR VULCAN **MIND?**
OR DO YOU THINK THIS BUTCHERY IS JUST ANOTHER FORM OF INFINITE DIVERSITY?
GENTLEMEN... WE NEED **ANSWERS**. I SUGGEST WE GO LOOK FOR THEM.
BRIDGE
ガーッ
ANY SUCCESS IN CONTACTING THE STATION, LIEUTENANT?
ALL SIGNALS ARE BEING DEFLECTED BY ITS SHIELDING, CAPTAIN. I'VE NOT BEEN--SIR...THERE'S **SOMETHING--**

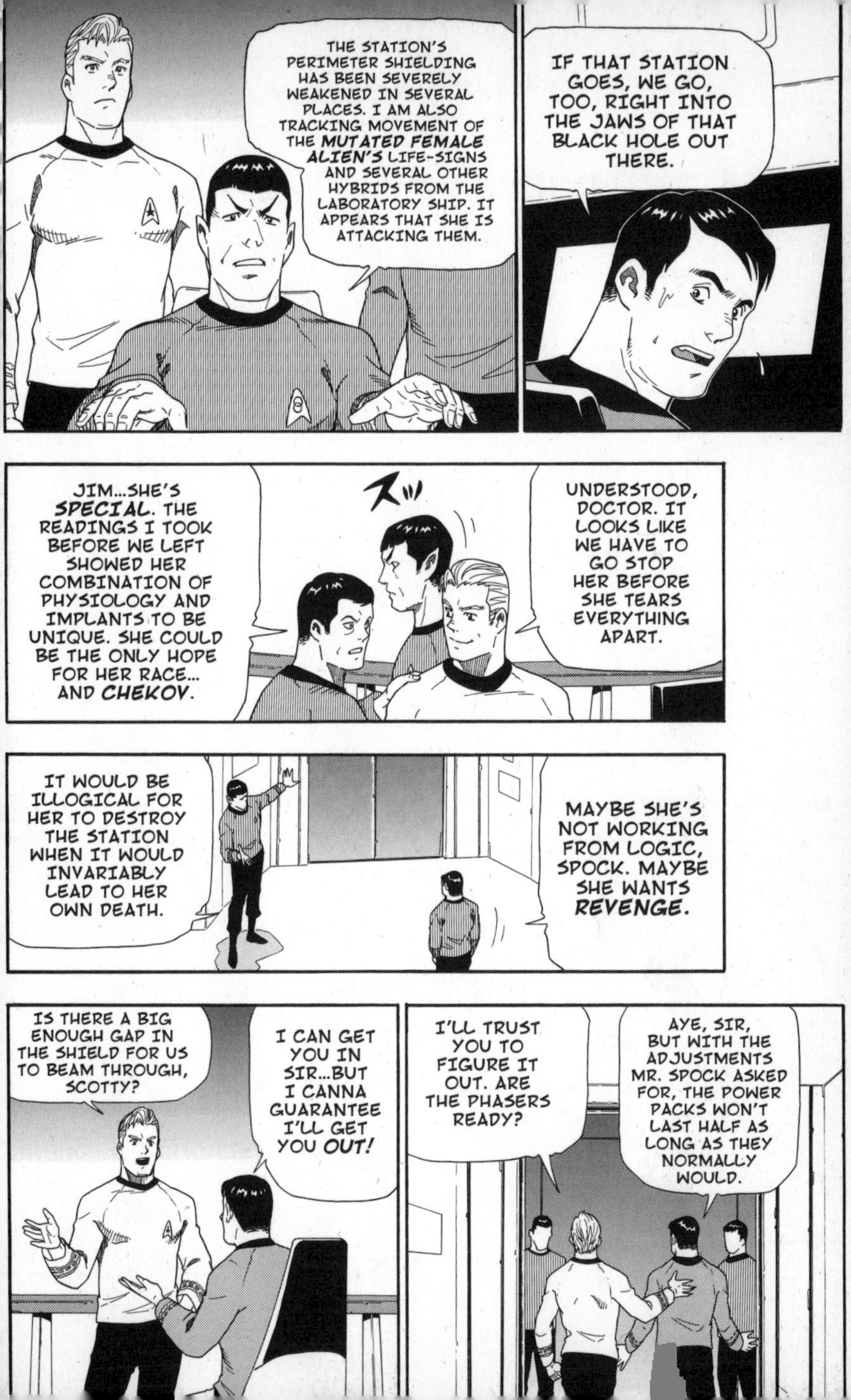
THE STATION'S PERIMETER SHIELDING HAS BEEN SEVERELY WEAKENED IN SEVERAL PLACES. I AM ALSO TRACKING MOVEMENT OF THE ***MUTATED FEMALE ALIEN'S*** LIFE-SIGNS AND SEVERAL OTHER HYBRIDS FROM THE LABORATORY SHIP. IT APPEARS THAT SHE IS ATTACKING THEM.
IF THAT STATION GOES, WE GO, TOO, RIGHT INTO THE JAWS OF THAT BLACK HOLE OUT THERE.
JIM...SHE'S ***SPECIAL***. THE READINGS I TOOK BEFORE WE LEFT SHOWED HER COMBINATION OF PHYSIOLOGY AND IMPLANTS TO BE UNIQUE. SHE COULD BE THE ONLY HOPE FOR HER RACE... AND ***CHEKOV***.
UNDERSTOOD, DOCTOR. IT LOOKS LIKE WE HAVE TO GO STOP HER BEFORE SHE TEARS EVERYTHING APART.
IT WOULD BE ILLOGICAL FOR HER TO DESTROY THE STATION WHEN IT WOULD INVARIABLY LEAD TO HER OWN DEATH.
MAYBE SHE'S NOT WORKING FROM LOGIC, SPOCK. MAYBE SHE WANTS ***REVENGE***.
IS THERE A BIG ENOUGH GAP IN THE SHIELD FOR US TO BEAM THROUGH, SCOTTY?
I CAN GET YOU IN SIR...BUT I CANNA GUARANTEE I'LL GET YOU ***OUT!***
I'LL TRUST YOU TO FIGURE IT OUT. ARE THE PHASERS READY?
AYE, SIR, BUT WITH THE ADJUSTMENTS MR. SPOCK ASKED FOR, THE POWER PACKS WON'T LAST HALF AS LONG AS THEY NORMALLY WOULD.

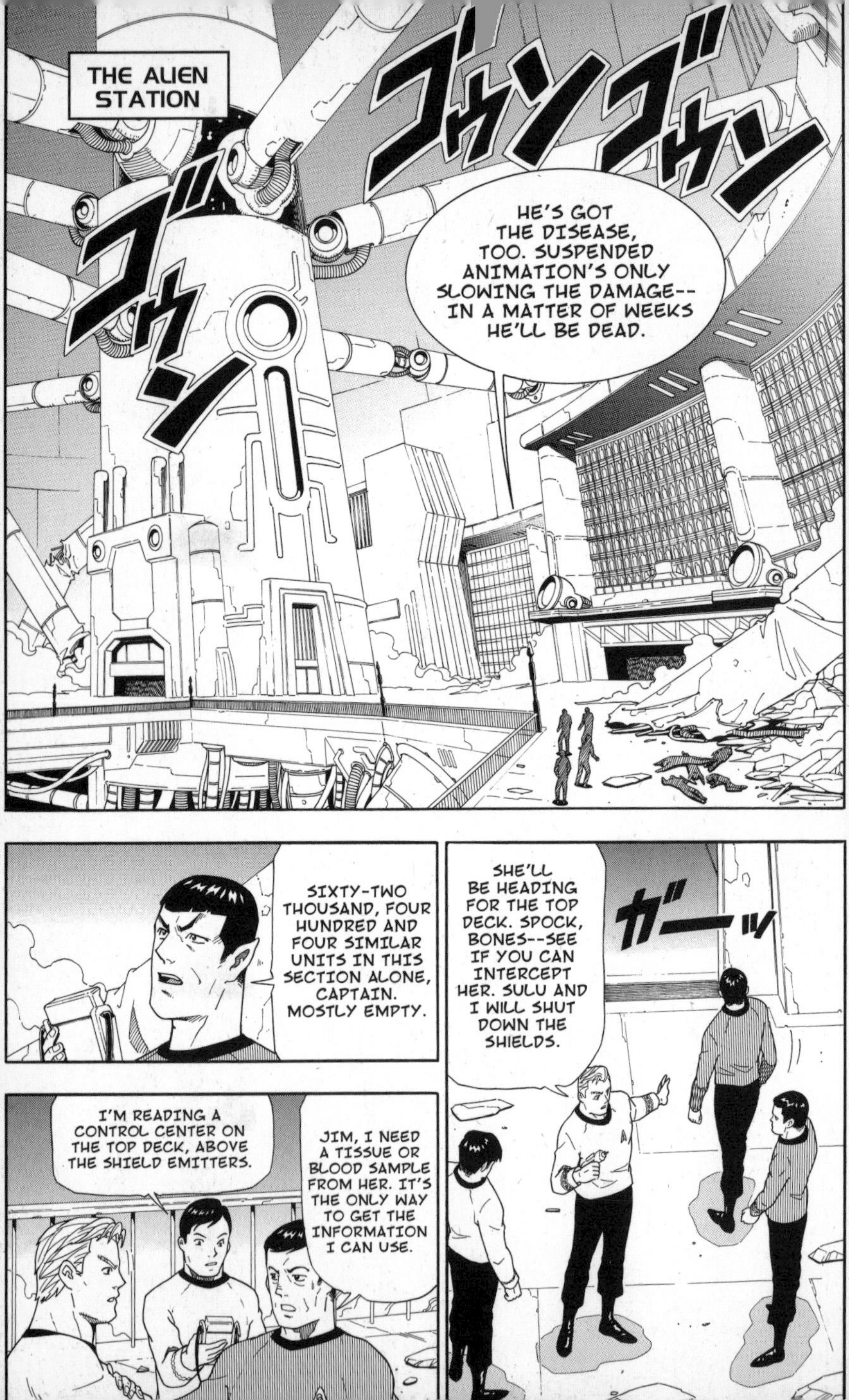
THE ALIEN STATION
ゴゥンゴゥン
ゴゥン
HE'S GOT THE DISEASE, TOO. SUSPENDED ANIMATION'S ONLY SLOWING THE DAMAGE-- IN A MATTER OF WEEKS HE'LL BE DEAD.
SIXTY-TWO THOUSAND, FOUR HUNDRED AND FOUR SIMILAR UNITS IN THIS SECTION ALONE, CAPTAIN. MOSTLY EMPTY.
I'M READING A CONTROL CENTER ON THE TOP DECK, ABOVE THE SHIELD EMITTERS.
JIM, I NEED A TISSUE OR BLOOD SAMPLE FROM HER. IT'S THE ONLY WAY TO GET THE INFORMATION I CAN USE.
SHE'LL BE HEADING FOR THE TOP DECK. SPOCK, BONES--SEE IF YOU CAN INTERCEPT HER. SULU AND I WILL SHUT DOWN THE SHIELDS.
ガーッ

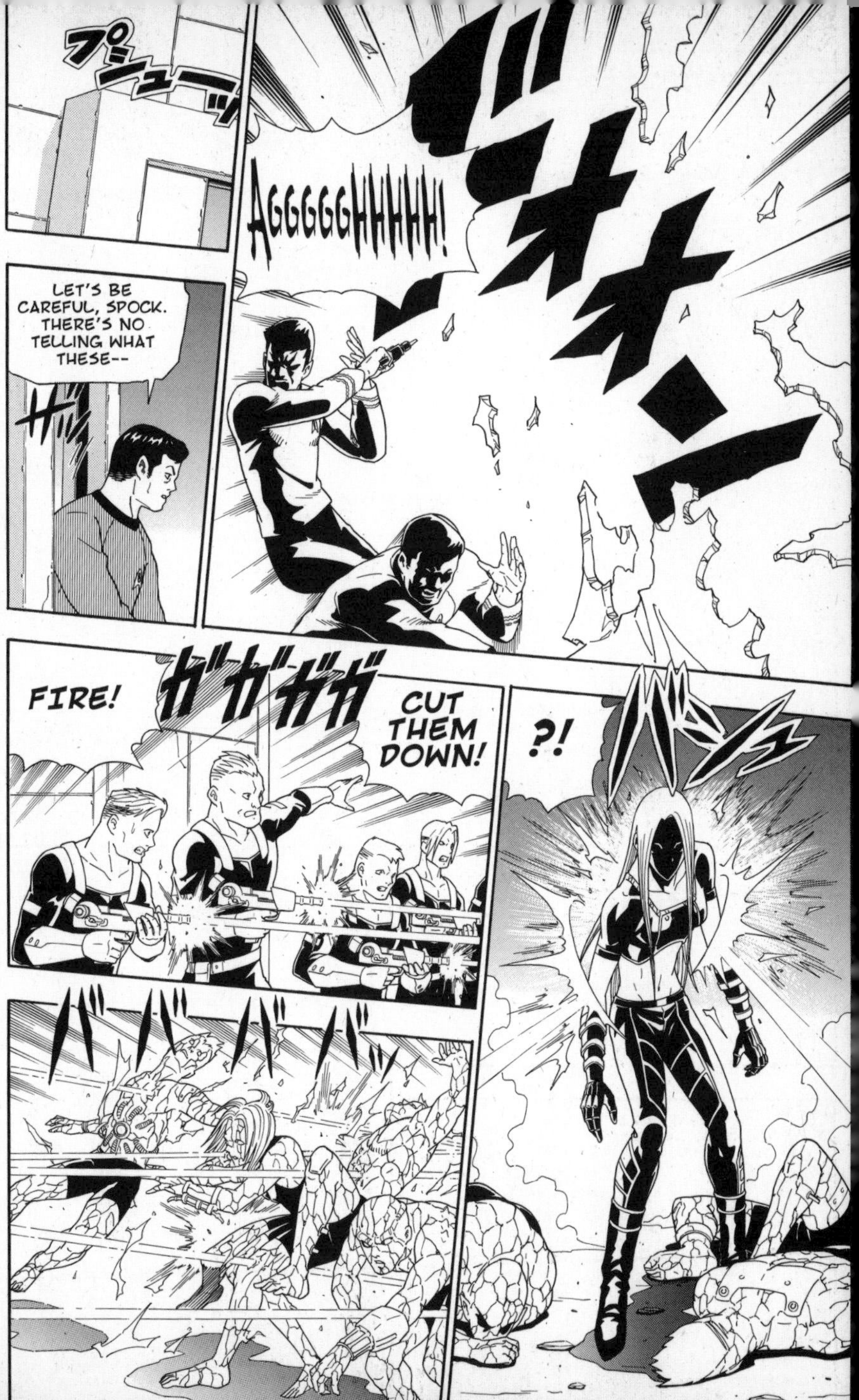

プシューッ
LET'S BE CAREFUL, SPOCK. THERE'S NO TELLING WHAT THESE--
ザッ
AGGGGGHHHHH!
FIRE!
ガガガガ
CUT THEM DOWN!
?!

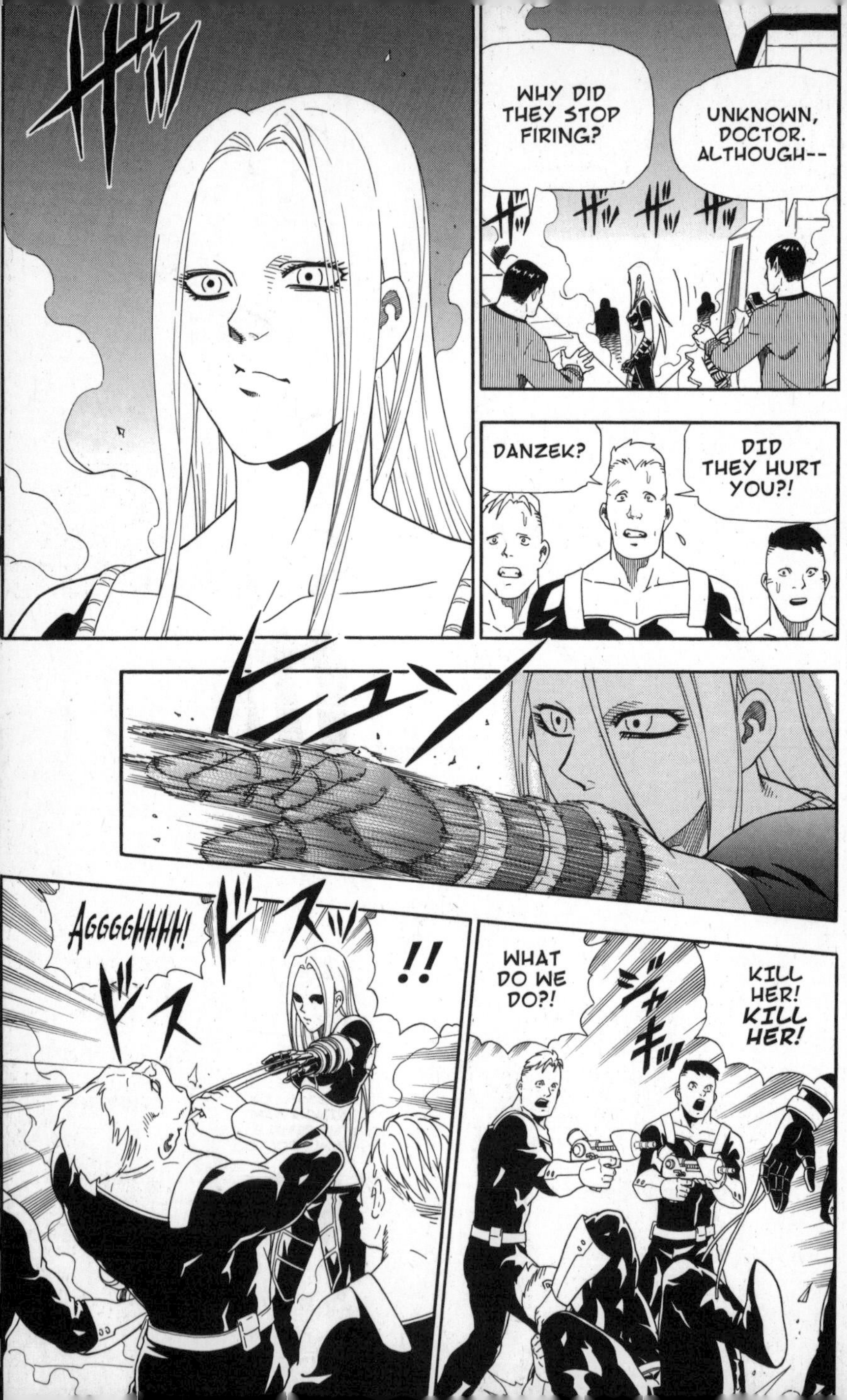
WHY DID THEY STOP FIRING?
UNKNOWN, DOCTOR. ALTHOUGH--
DANZEK?
DID THEY HURT YOU?!
ヒュン
AGGGGHHHH!
ドスッ
ドス
!!
WHAT DO WE DO?!
ジャキッ
KILL HER! KILL HER!

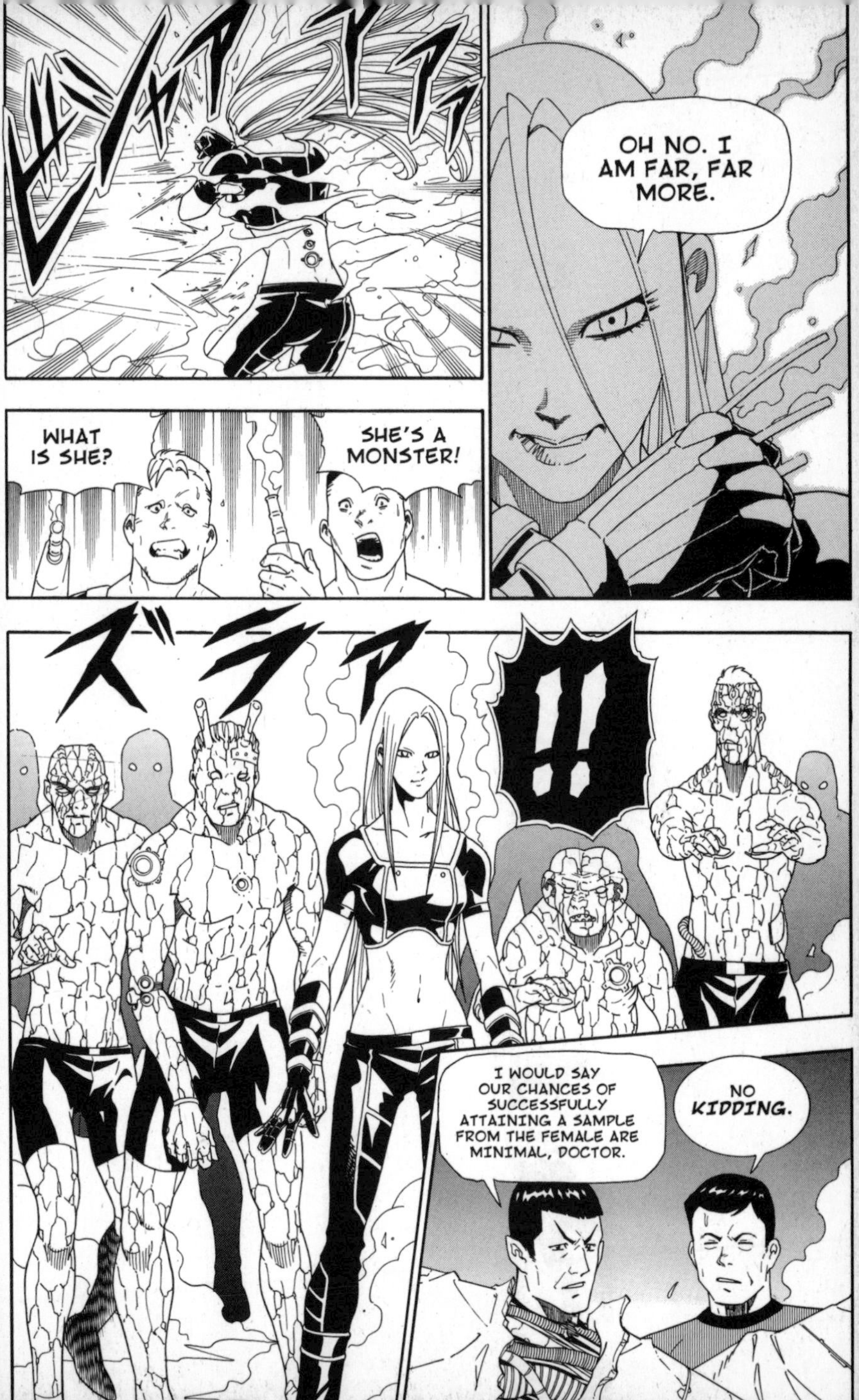
OH NO. I AM FAR, FAR MORE.
WHAT IS SHE?
SHE'S A MONSTER!
!!
I WOULD SAY OUR CHANCES OF SUCCESSFULLY ATTAINING A SAMPLE FROM THE FEMALE ARE MINIMAL, DOCTOR.
NO KIDDING.

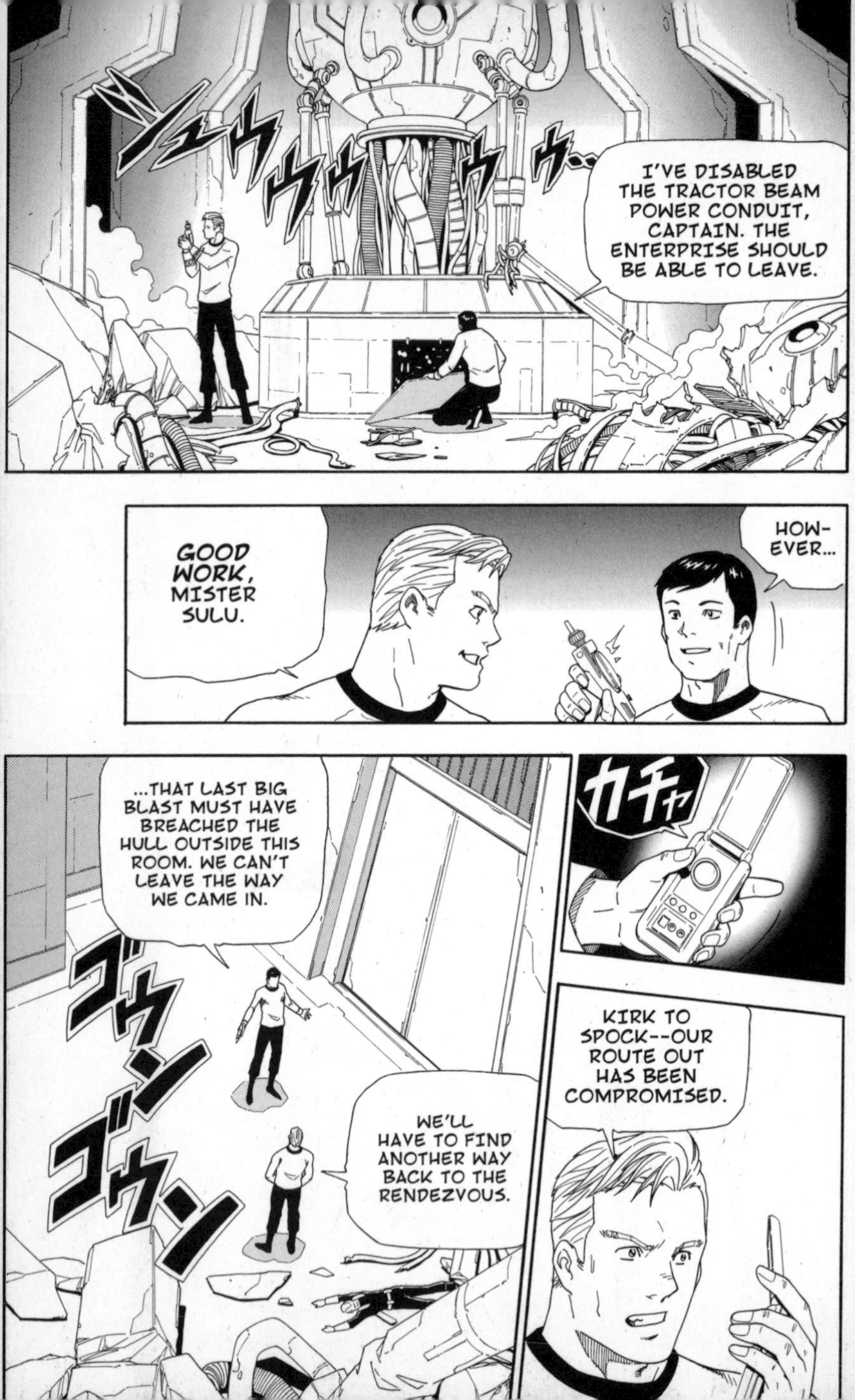
ジュウウウウウウ…
I'VE DISABLED THE TRACTOR BEAM POWER CONDUIT, CAPTAIN. THE ENTERPRISE SHOULD BE ABLE TO LEAVE.
GOOD WORK, MISTER SULU.
HOW-EVER...
...THAT LAST BIG BLAST MUST HAVE BREACHED THE HULL OUTSIDE THIS ROOM. WE CAN'T LEAVE THE WAY WE CAME IN.
ゴウン
ゴウン
WE'LL HAVE TO FIND ANOTHER WAY BACK TO THE RENDEZVOUS.
カチャ
KIRK TO SPOCK--OUR ROUTE OUT HAS BEEN COMPROMISED.

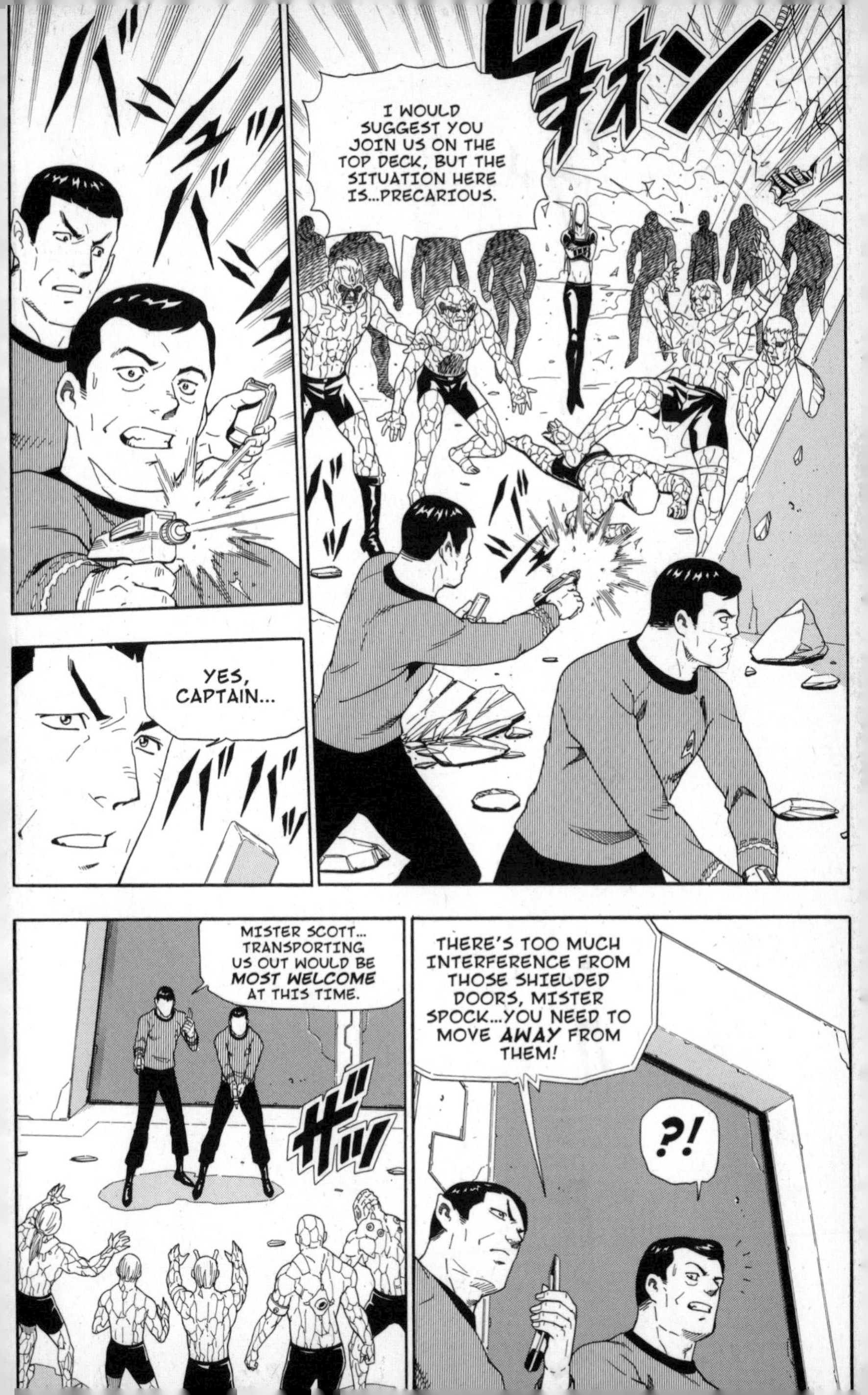

YES, CAPTAIN...
I WOULD SUGGEST YOU JOIN US ON THE TOP DECK, BUT THE SITUATION HERE IS...PRECARIOUS.
MISTER SCOTT... TRANSPORTING US OUT WOULD BE MOST WELCOME AT THIS TIME.
ザッ
THERE'S TOO MUCH INTERFERENCE FROM THOSE SHIELDED DOORS, MISTER SPOCK...YOU NEED TO MOVE AWAY FROM THEM!
?!

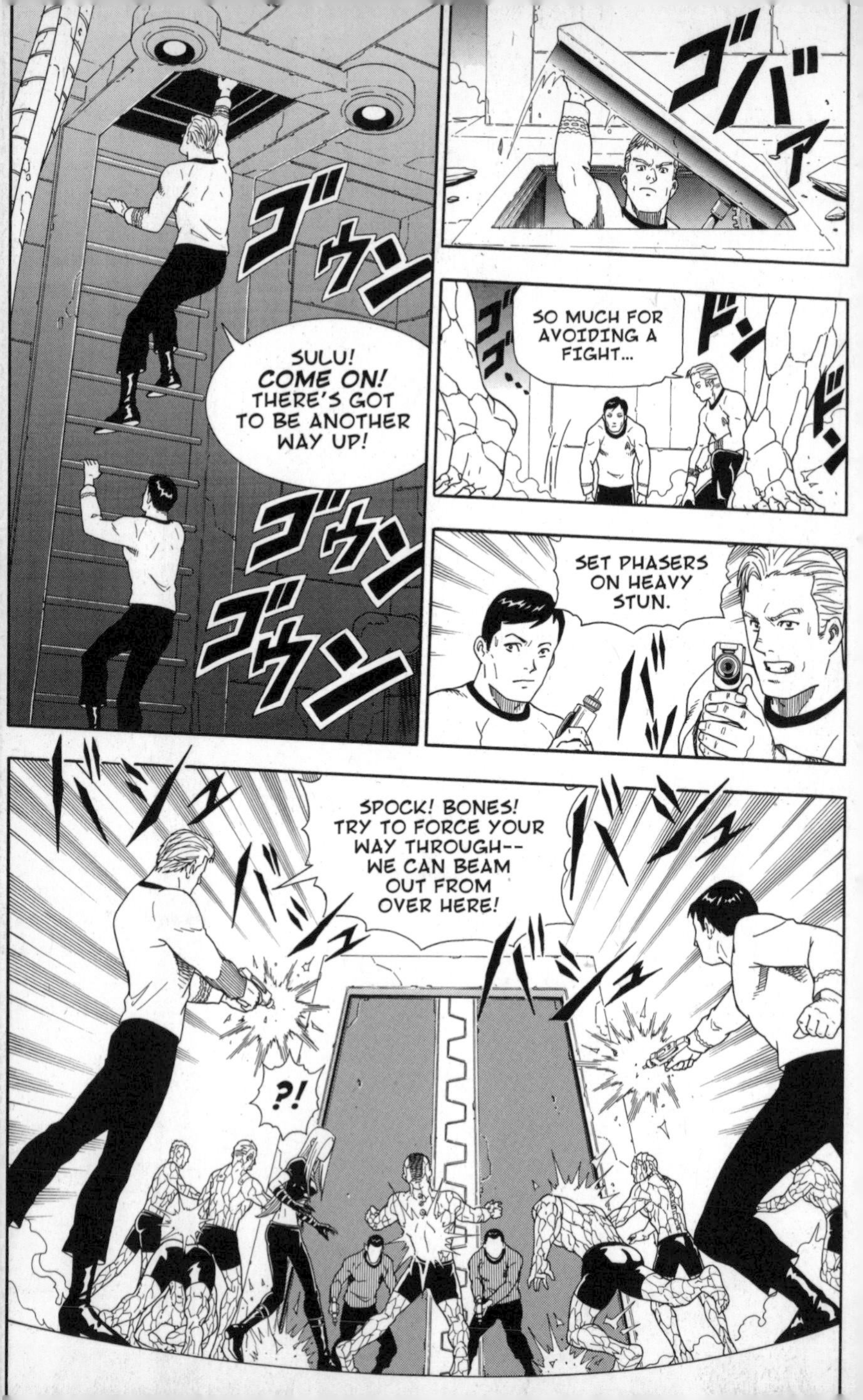

ゴウン
SULU! COME ON! THERE'S GOT TO BE ANOTHER WAY UP!
ゴウン
ゴウン
ゴバア
ゴゴ...
SO MUCH FOR AVOIDING A FIGHT...
ドン
ドン
SET PHASERS ON HEAVY STUN.
バ
バシュ
SPOCK! BONES! TRY TO FORCE YOUR WAY THROUGH-- WE CAN BEAM OUT FROM OVER HERE!
バシュ
バシュ
バシュ
?!

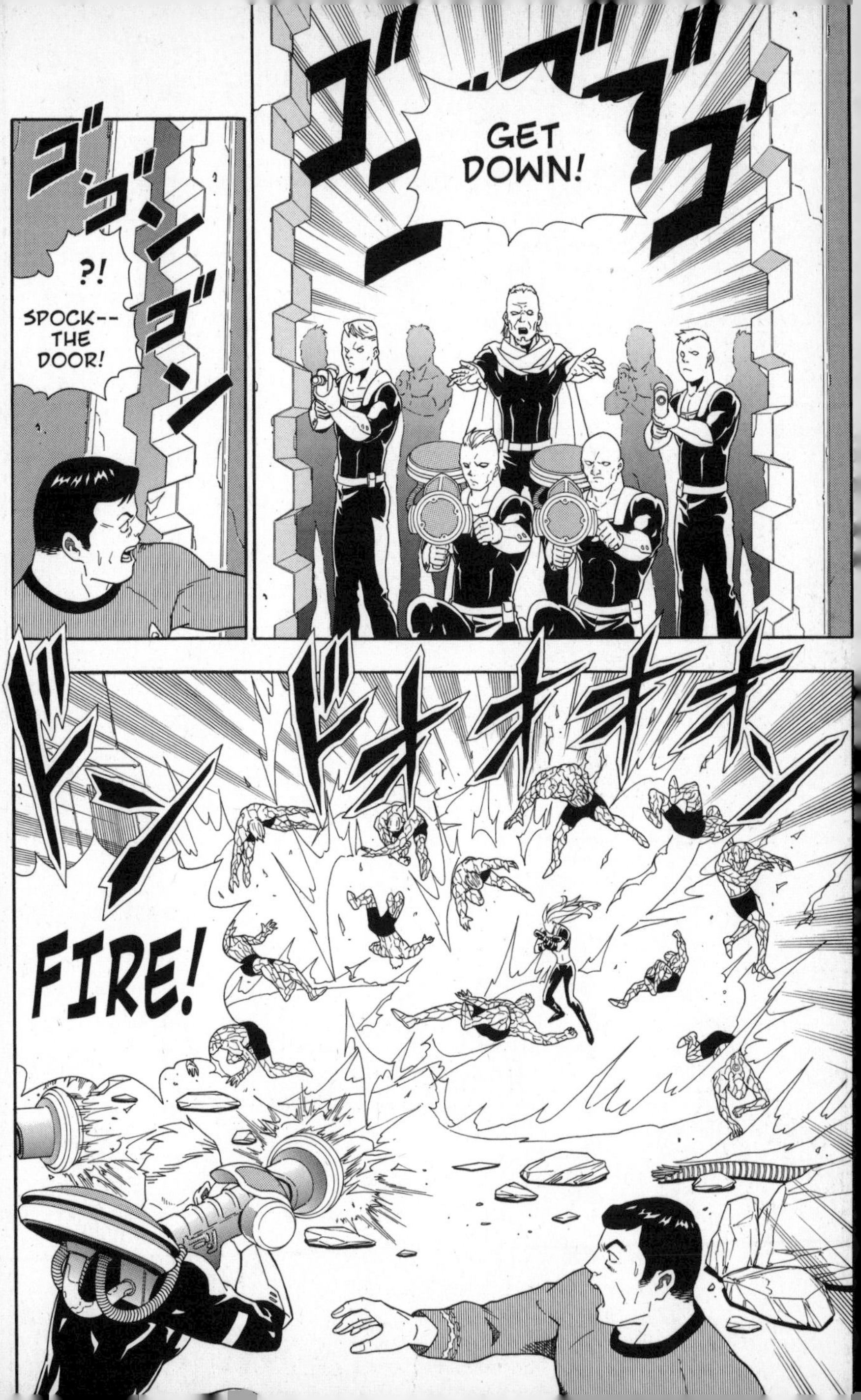
?!
SPOCK-- THE DOOR!
GET DOWN!
ドン
ドオオオン
FIRE!

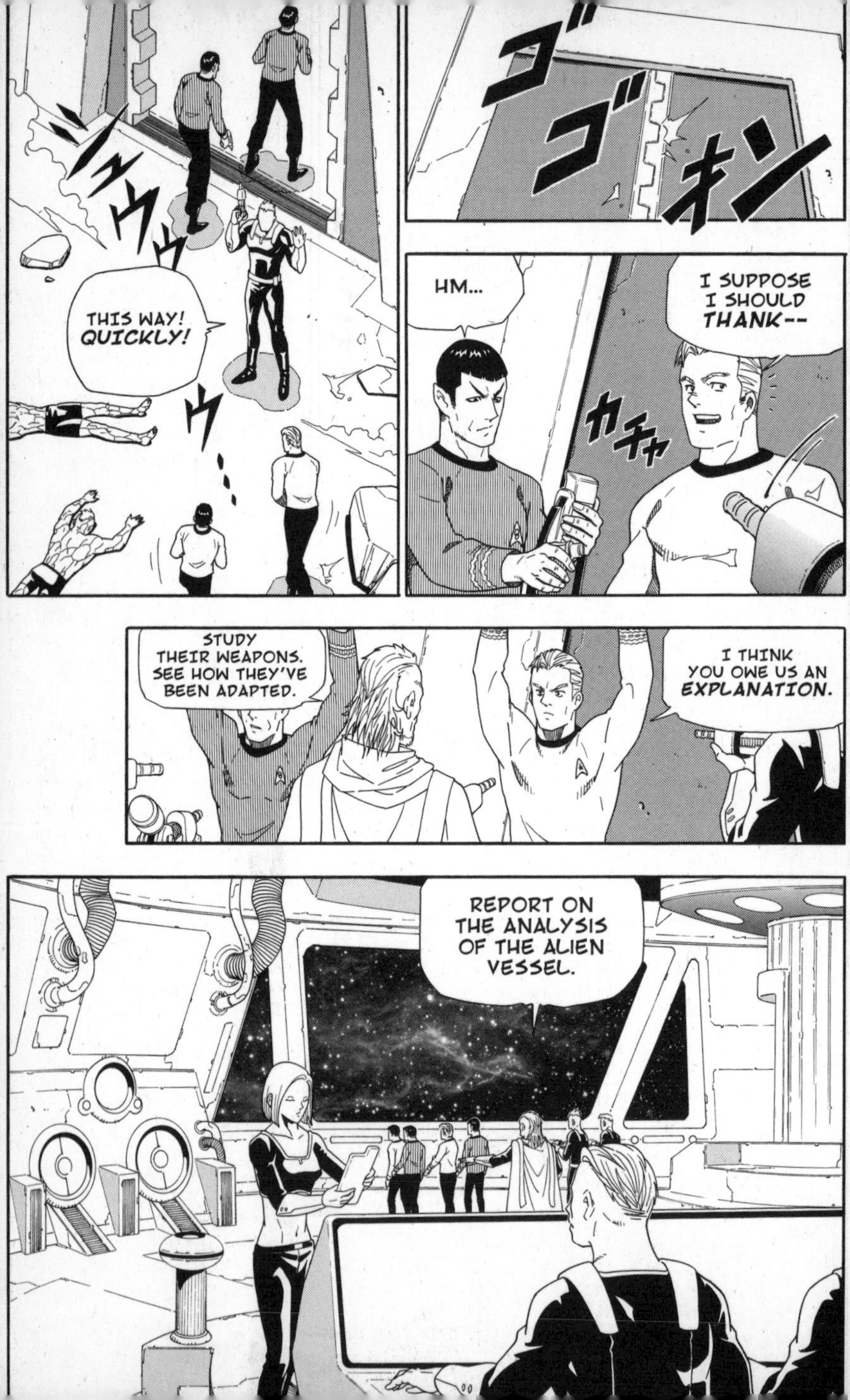

ジュウゥゥウ…
THIS WAY! **QUICKLY!**
ゴゴオン
HM...
I SUPPOSE I SHOULD ***THANK--***
カチャ
STUDY THEIR WEAPONS. SEE HOW THEY'VE BEEN ADAPTED.
I THINK YOU OWE US AN **EXPLANATION.**
REPORT ON THE ANALYSIS OF THE ALIEN VESSEL.

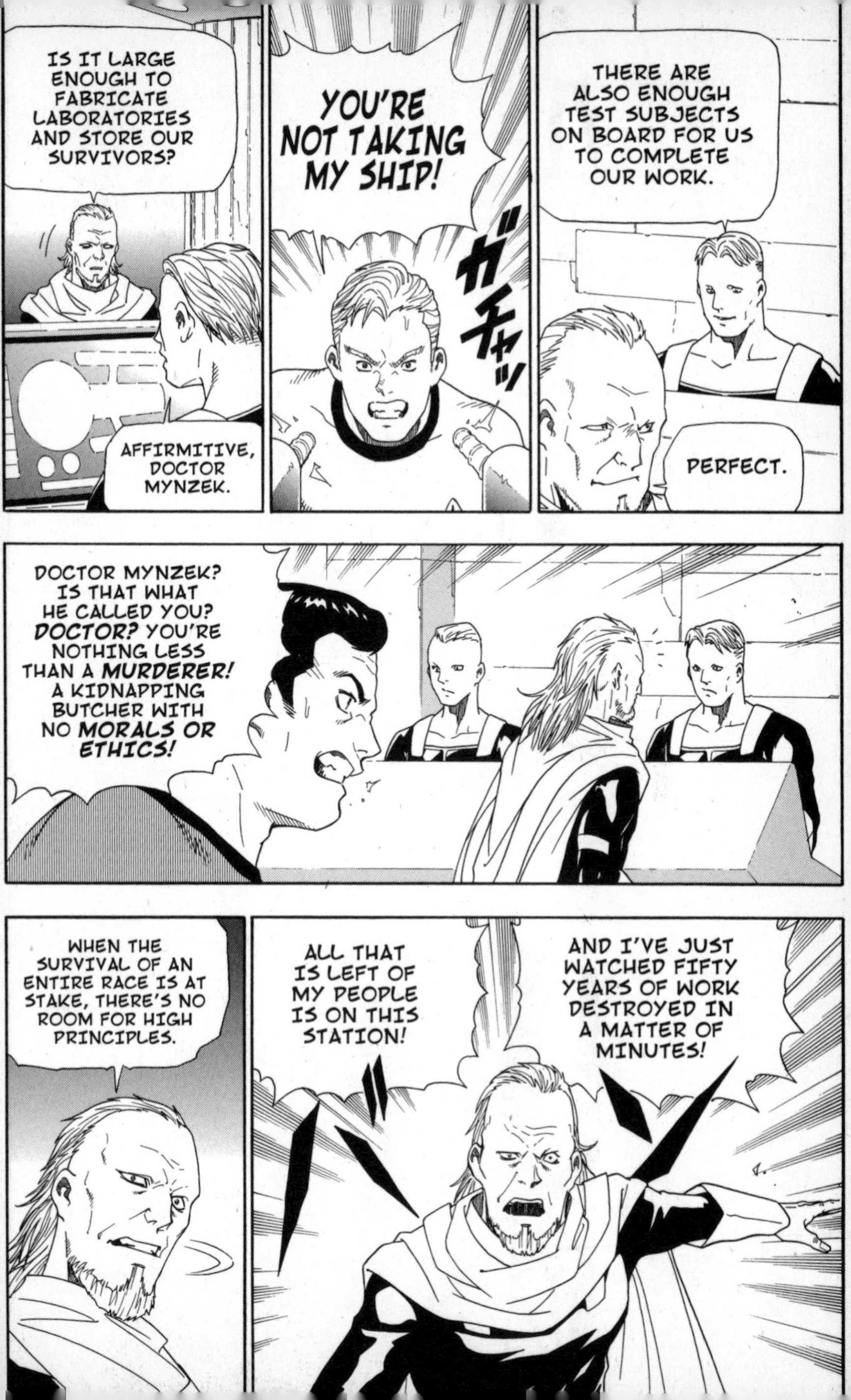
IS IT LARGE ENOUGH TO FABRICATE LABORATORIES AND STORE OUR SURVIVORS?
AFFIRMITIVE, DOCTOR MYNZEK.
YOU'RE NOT TAKING MY SHIP!
ガチャッ
THERE ARE ALSO ENOUGH TEST SUBJECTS ON BOARD FOR US TO COMPLETE OUR WORK.
PERFECT.
DOCTOR MYNZEK? IS THAT WHAT HE CALLED YOU? DOCTOR? YOU'RE NOTHING LESS THAN A MURDERER! A KIDNAPPING BUTCHER WITH NO MORALS OR ETHICS!
WHEN THE SURVIVAL OF AN ENTIRE RACE IS AT STAKE, THERE'S NO ROOM FOR HIGH PRINCIPLES.
ALL THAT IS LEFT OF MY PEOPLE IS ON THIS STATION!
AND I'VE JUST WATCHED FIFTY YEARS OF WORK DESTROYED IN A MATTER OF MINUTES!

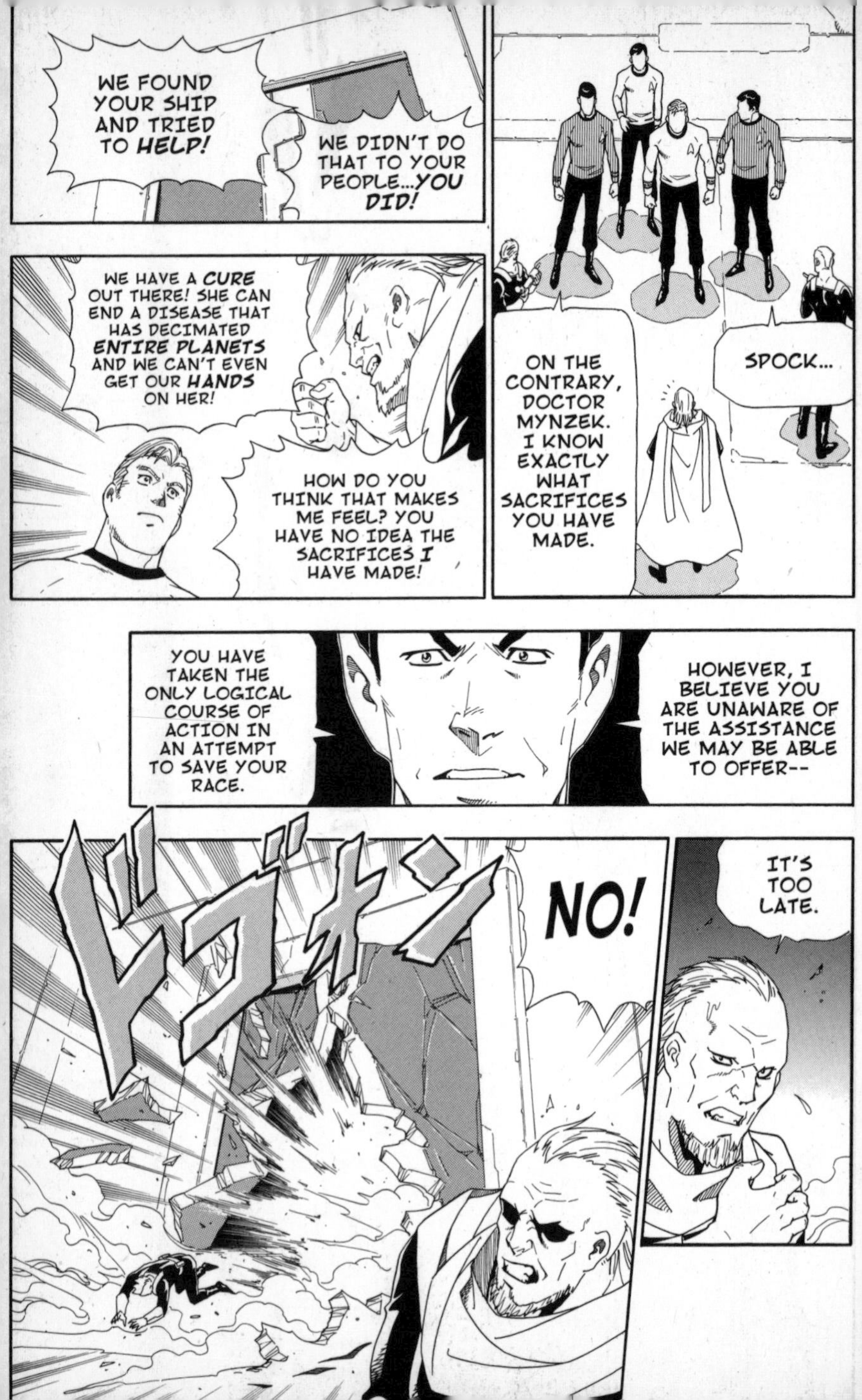
WE FOUND YOUR SHIP AND TRIED TO HELP!
WE DIDN'T DO THAT TO YOUR PEOPLE...YOU DID!
WE HAVE A CURE OUT THERE! SHE CAN END A DISEASE THAT HAS DECIMATED ENTIRE PLANETS AND WE CAN'T EVEN GET OUR HANDS ON HER!
HOW DO YOU THINK THAT MAKES ME FEEL? YOU HAVE NO IDEA THE SACRIFICES I HAVE MADE!
ON THE CONTRARY, DOCTOR MYNZEK. I KNOW EXACTLY WHAT SACRIFICES YOU HAVE MADE.
SPOCK...
YOU HAVE TAKEN THE ONLY LOGICAL COURSE OF ACTION IN AN ATTEMPT TO SAVE YOUR RACE.
HOWEVER, I BELIEVE YOU ARE UNAWARE OF THE ASSISTANCE WE MAY BE ABLE TO OFFER--
ドゴオン
NO!
IT'S TOO LATE.

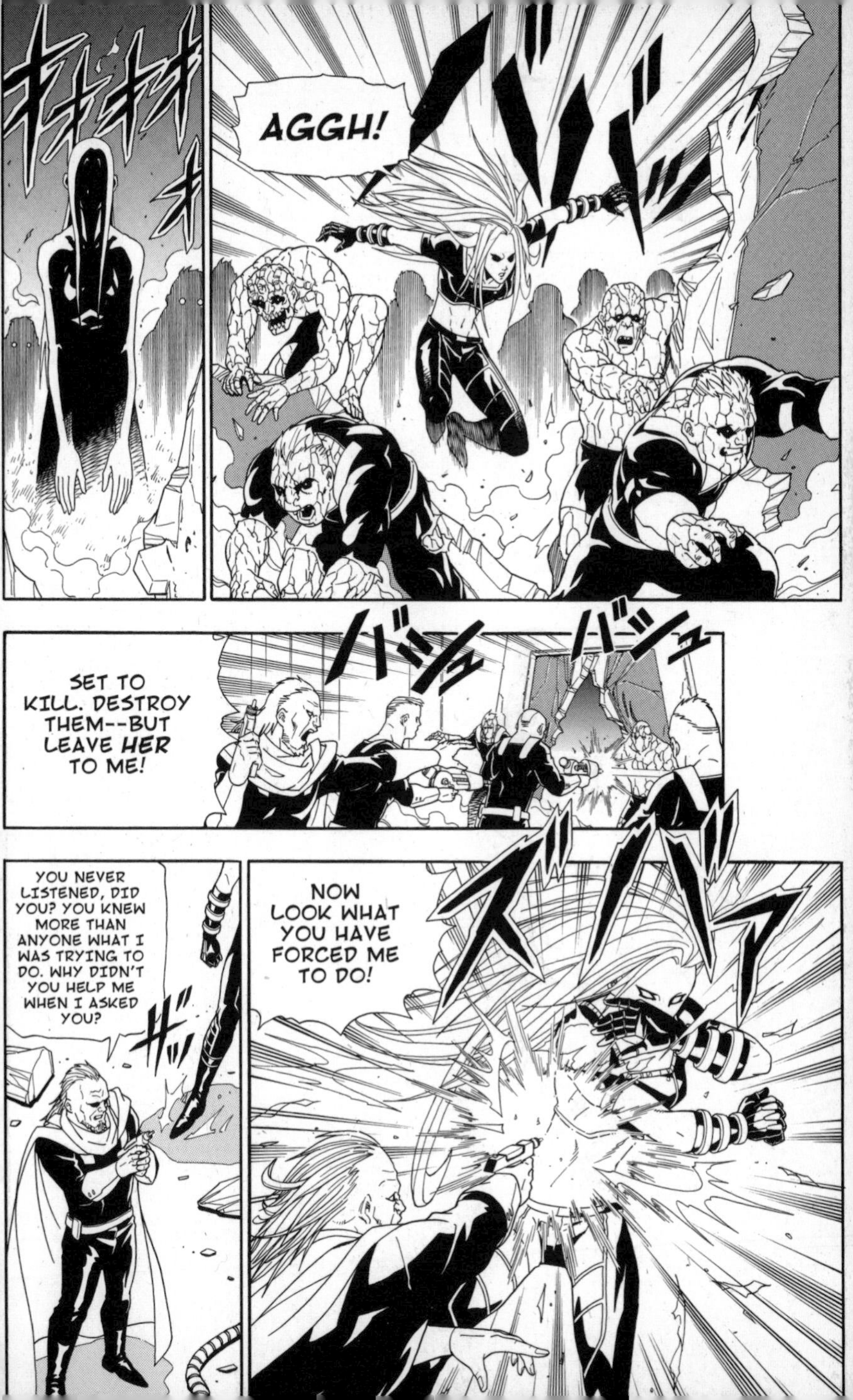
AGGH!
SET TO KILL. DESTROY THEM--BUT LEAVE HER TO ME!
YOU NEVER LISTENED, DID YOU? YOU KNEW MORE THAN ANYONE WHAT I WAS TRYING TO DO. WHY DIDN'T YOU HELP ME WHEN I ASKED YOU?
NOW LOOK WHAT YOU HAVE FORCED ME TO DO!

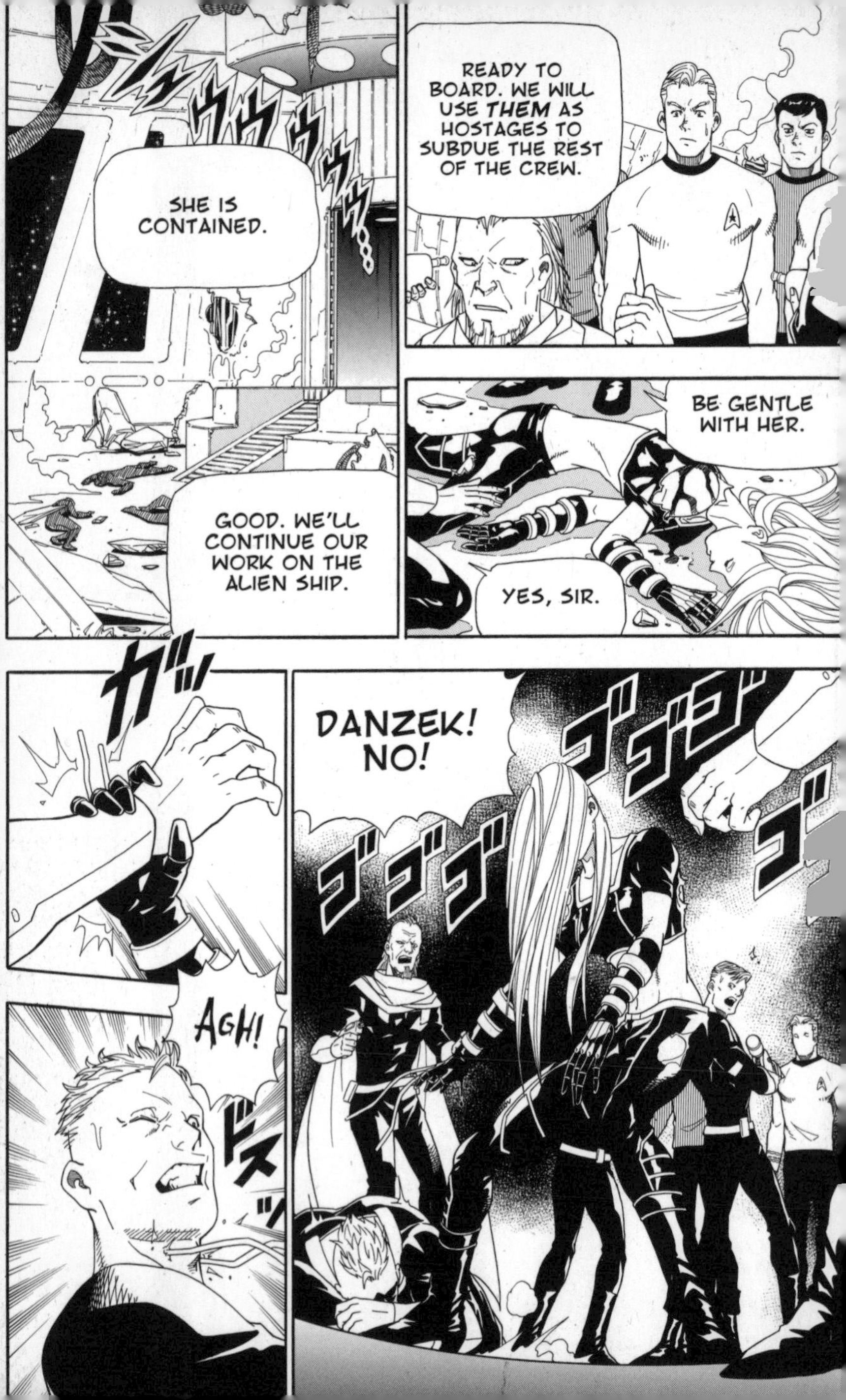
SHE IS CONTAINED.
GOOD. WE'LL CONTINUE OUR WORK ON THE ALIEN SHIP.
READY TO BOARD. WE WILL USE THEM AS HOSTAGES TO SUBDUE THE REST OF THE CREW.
BE GENTLE WITH HER.
YES, SIR.
AGH!
DANZEK! NO!

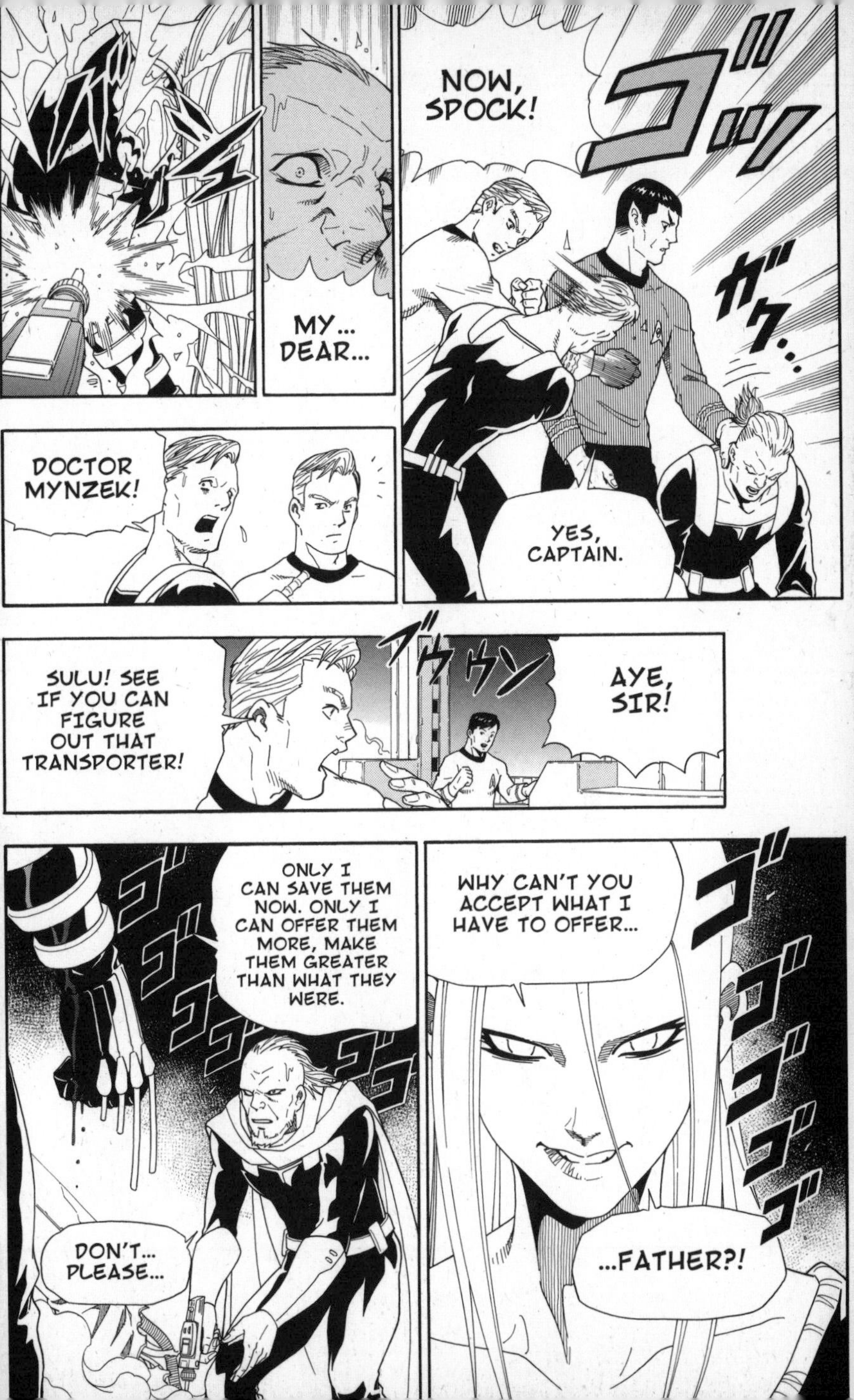
MY... DEAR...
DOCTOR MYNZEK!
NOW, SPOCK!
ゴッ
ガク…
YES, CAPTAIN.
SULU! SEE IF YOU CAN FIGURE OUT THAT TRANSPORTER!
ブゥン
AYE, SIR!
ONLY I CAN SAVE THEM NOW. ONLY I CAN OFFER THEM MORE, MAKE THEM GREATER THAN WHAT THEY WERE.
DON'T... PLEASE...
WHY CAN'T YOU ACCEPT WHAT I HAVE TO OFFER...
...FATHER?!

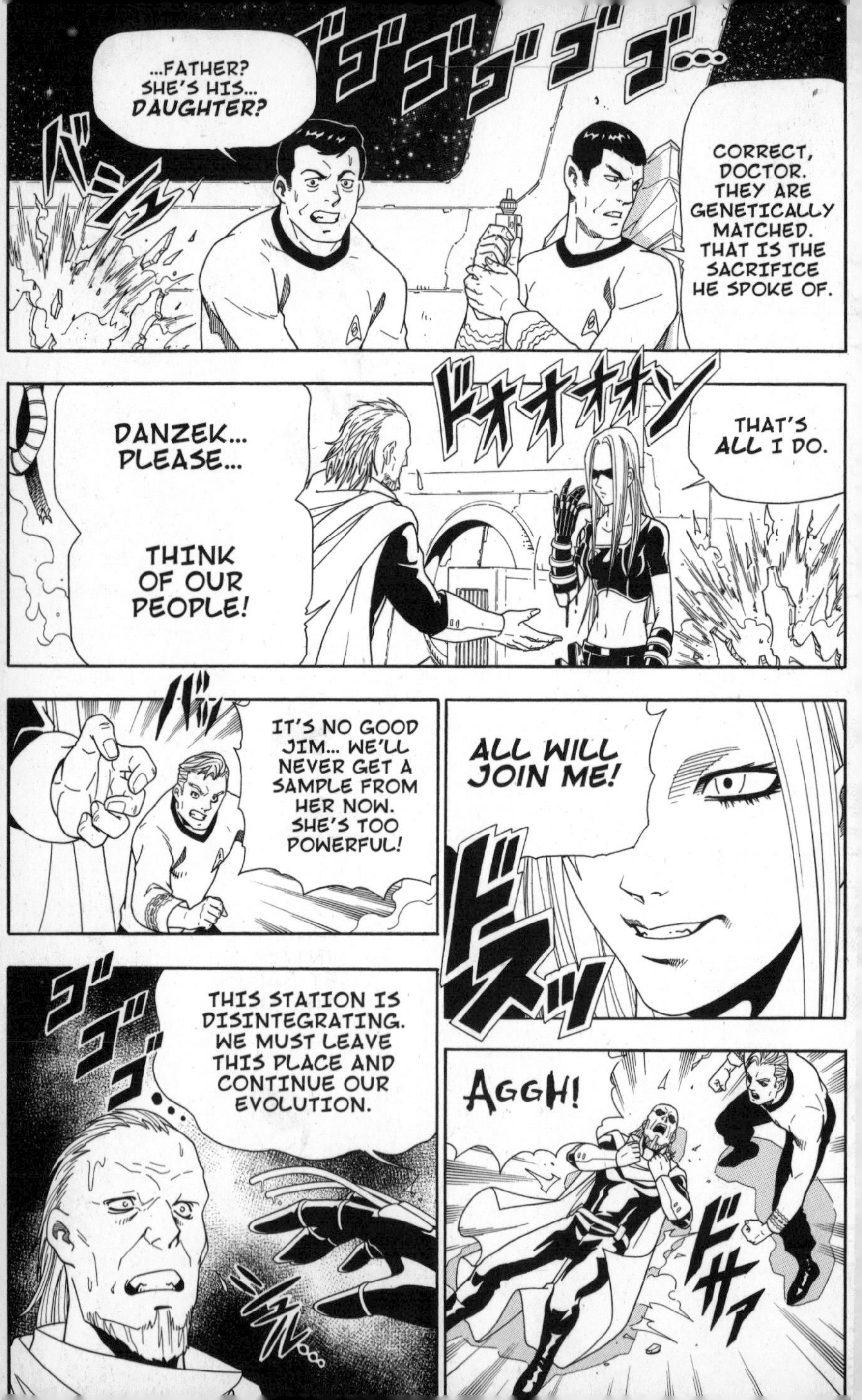
...FATHER? SHE'S HIS... DAUGHTER?
ゴゴゴゴゴゴ…
CORRECT, DOCTOR. THEY ARE GENETICALLY MATCHED. THAT IS THE SACRIFICE HE SPOKE OF.
DANZEK... PLEASE...
THINK OF OUR PEOPLE!
ドォオオオン
THAT'S ALL I DO.
バッ
IT'S NO GOOD JIM... WE'LL NEVER GET A SAMPLE FROM HER NOW. SHE'S TOO POWERFUL!
ALL WILL JOIN ME!
ドスッ
ゴゴゴ…
THIS STATION IS DISINTEGRATING. WE MUST LEAVE THIS PLACE AND CONTINUE OUR EVOLUTION.
AGGH!
ドサァ

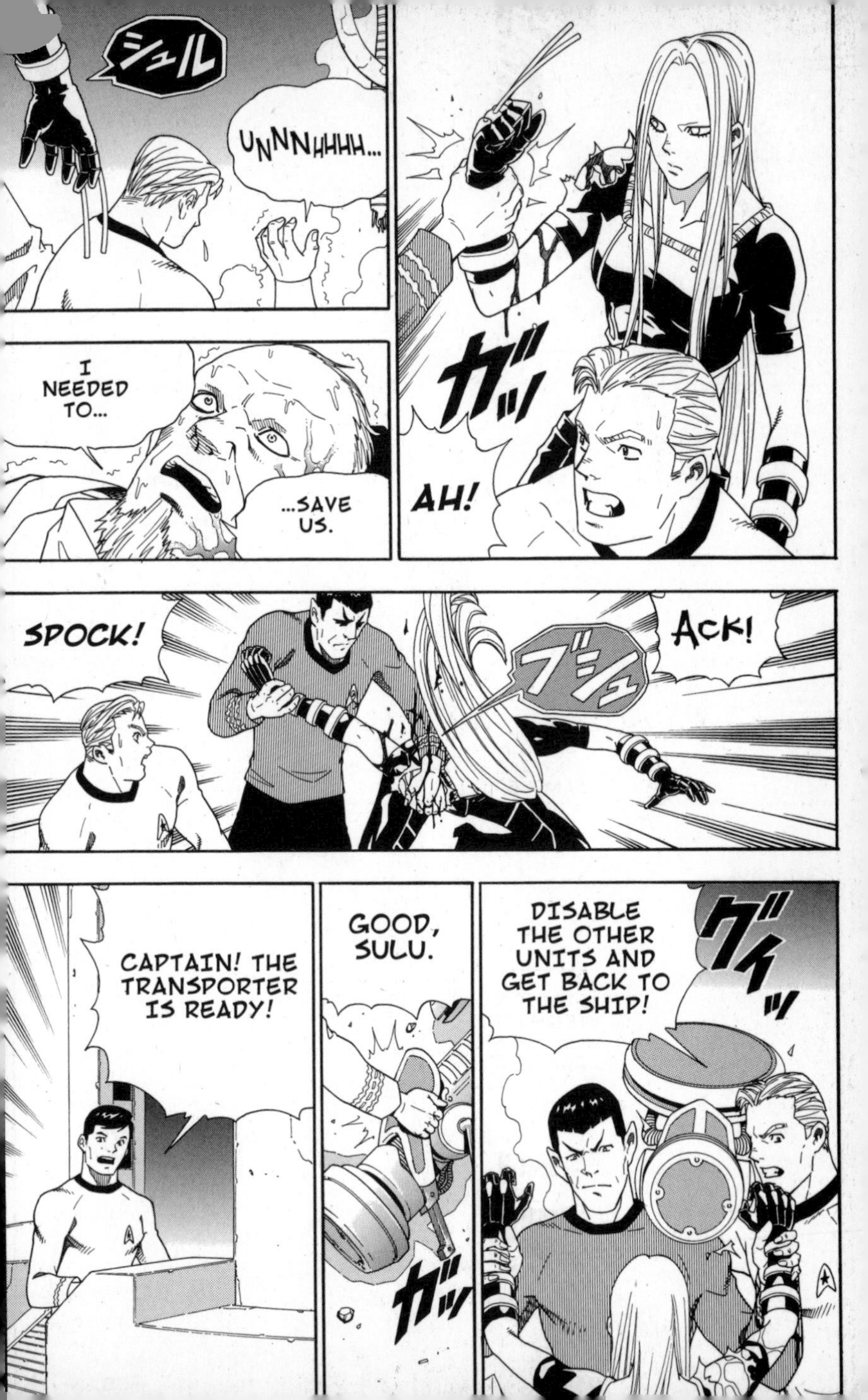
シュル
UNNNHHHH...
I NEEDED TO...
...SAVE US.
ガッ
AH!
SPOCK!
ブシュ
ACK!
CAPTAIN! THE TRANSPORTER IS READY!
GOOD, SULU.
ガッ
DISABLE THE OTHER UNITS AND GET BACK TO THE SHIP!
グイッ

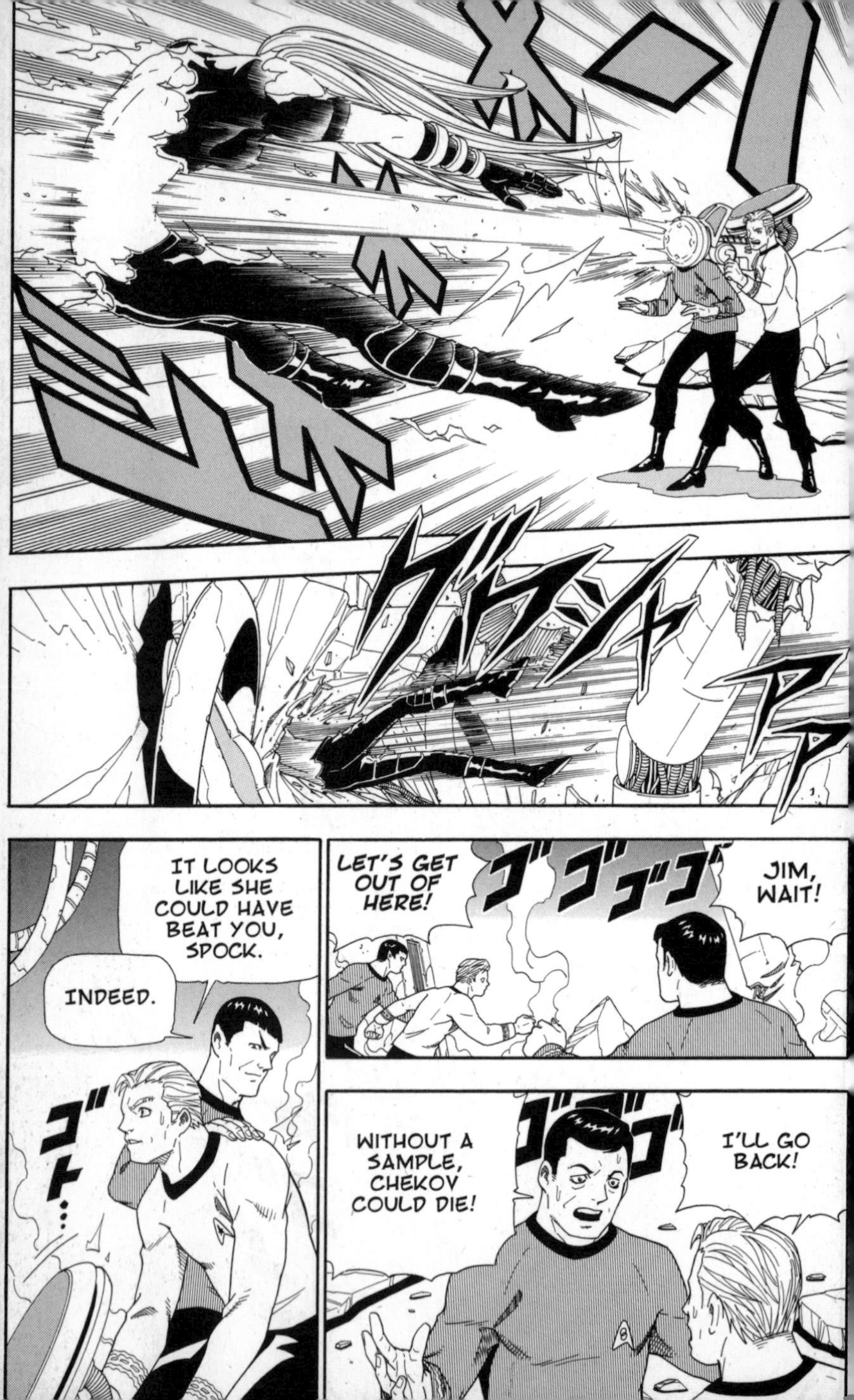
IT LOOKS LIKE SHE COULD HAVE BEAT YOU, SPOCK.
INDEED.
LET'S GET OUT OF HERE!
JIM, WAIT!
WITHOUT A SAMPLE, CHEKOV COULD DIE!
I'LL GO BACK!

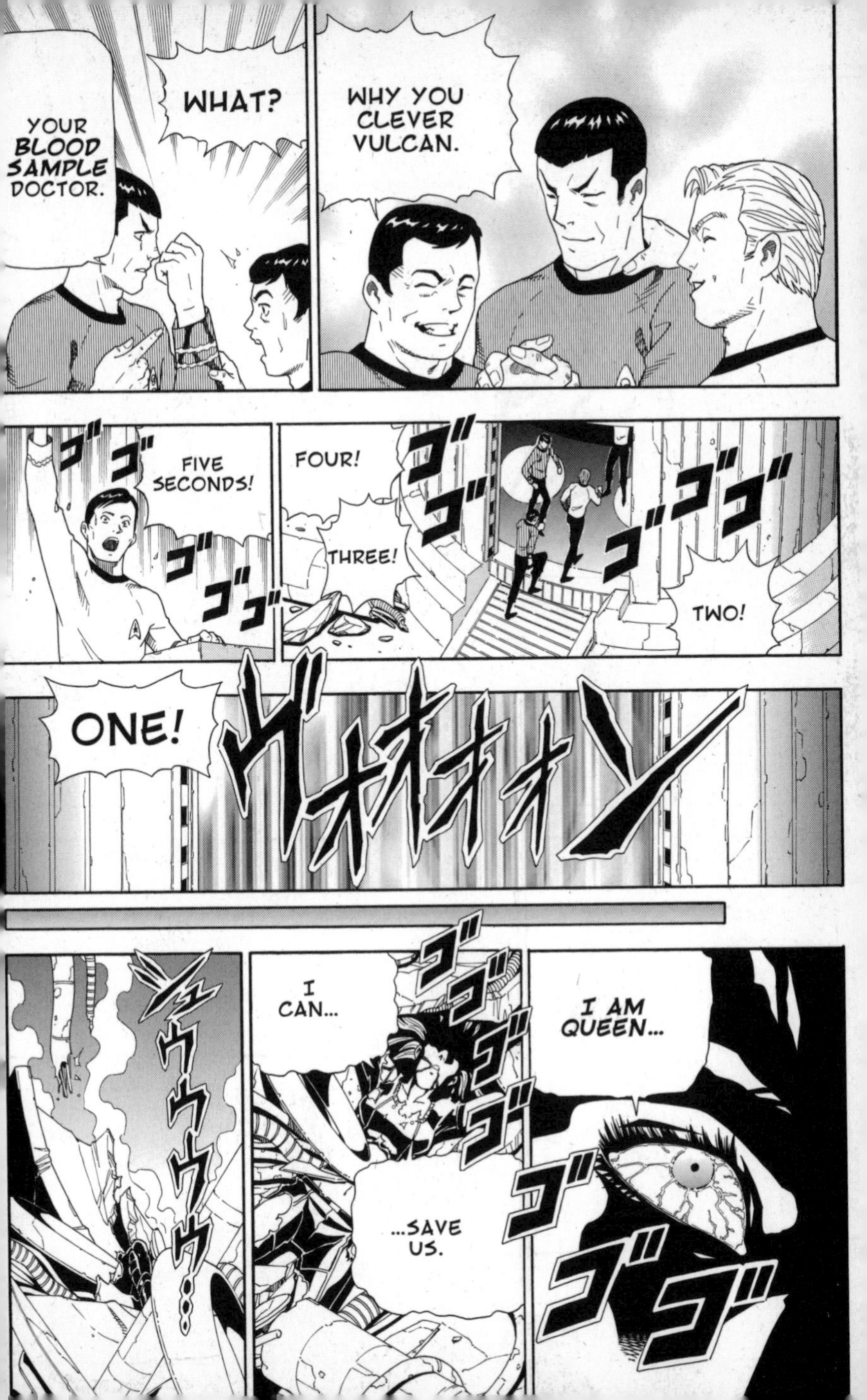
YOUR BLOOD SAMPLE DOCTOR.
WHAT?
WHY YOU CLEVER VULCAN.
ゴゴ
FIVE SECONDS!
ゴゴ
FOUR!
ゴゴ
THREE!
ゴゴゴゴ
TWO!
ONE!
ヴオオオオン
シュウウウウウ…
I CAN...
ゴゴゴゴ
...SAVE US.
I AM QUEEN...
ゴゴゴゴ

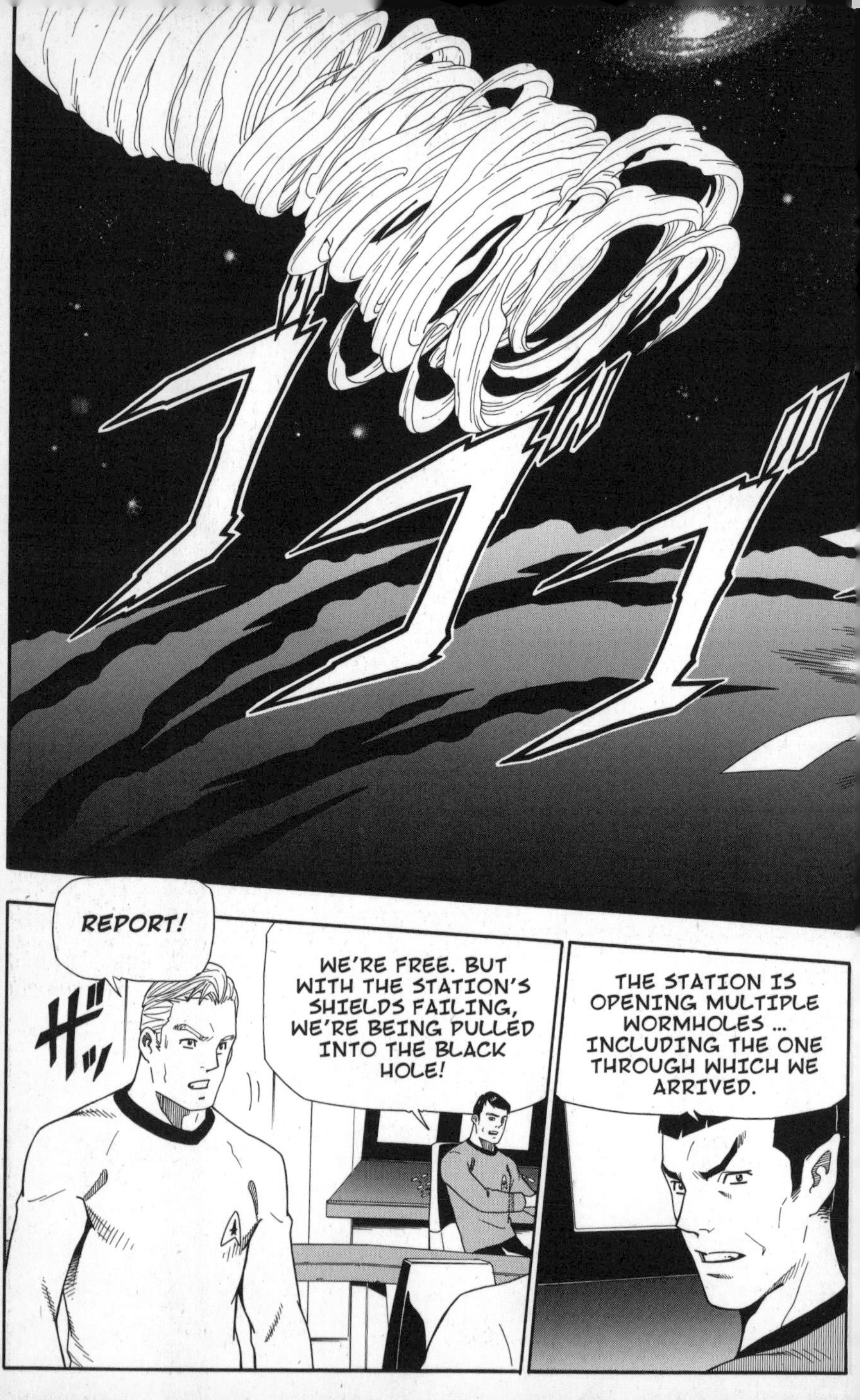
REPORT!
ザッ
WE'RE FREE. BUT WITH THE STATION'S SHIELDS FAILING, WE'RE BEING PULLED INTO THE BLACK HOLE!
THE STATION IS OPENING MULTIPLE WORMHOLES ... INCLUDING THE ONE THROUGH WHICH WE ARRIVED.

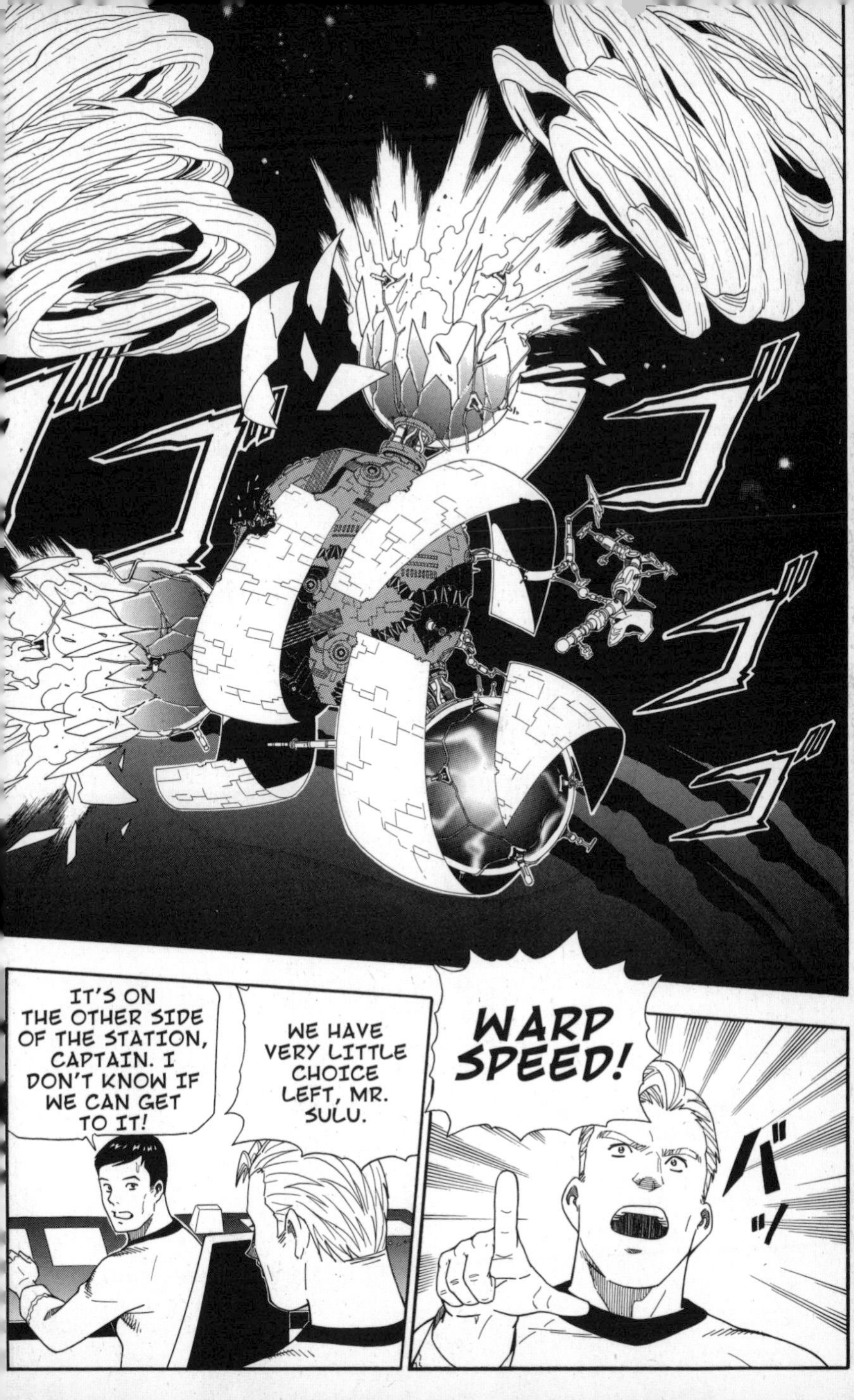
IT'S ON THE OTHER SIDE OF THE STATION, CAPTAIN. I DON'T KNOW IF WE CAN GET TO IT!
WE HAVE VERY LITTLE CHOICE LEFT, MR. SULU.
WARP SPEED!

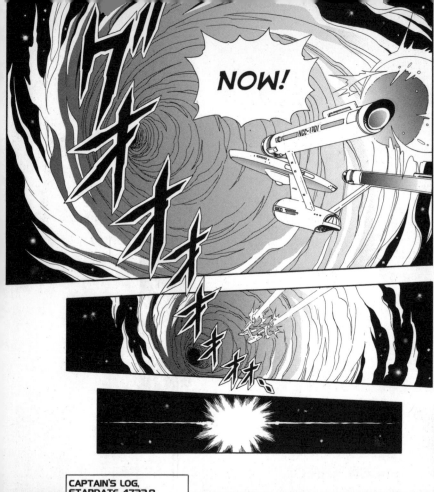

NOW!

CAPTAIN'S LOG, STARDATE 4722.8. THE ENTERPRISE ESCAPED ITS SPACE-TIME PRISON...AND CHEKOV IS ON HIS WAY TO RECOVERY.

HOWEVER, THE NATURE OF WHAT WE EXPERIENCED CONTINUES TO ELUDE US. I AM WORKING WITH MR. SPOCK AND DR. MCCOY TO COMPLETE OUR REPORT TO STARFLEET.

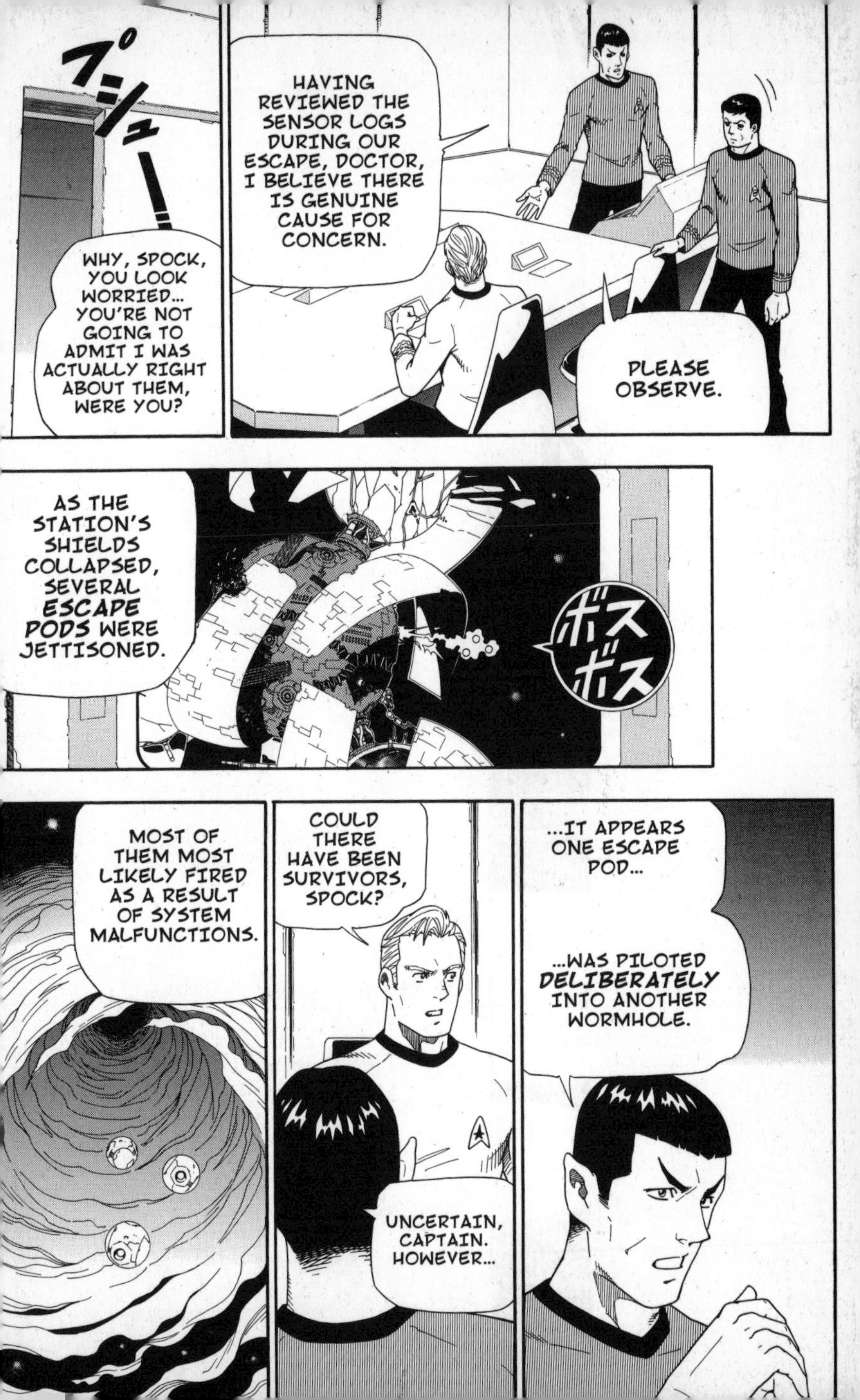

プシュー
WHY, SPOCK, YOU LOOK WORRIED... YOU'RE NOT GOING TO ADMIT I WAS ACTUALLY RIGHT ABOUT THEM, WERE YOU?
HAVING REVIEWED THE SENSOR LOGS DURING OUR ESCAPE, DOCTOR, I BELIEVE THERE IS GENUINE CAUSE FOR CONCERN.
PLEASE OBSERVE.
AS THE STATION'S SHIELDS COLLAPSED, SEVERAL **ESCAPE PODS** WERE JETTISONED.
ボスボス
MOST OF THEM MOST LIKELY FIRED AS A RESULT OF SYSTEM MALFUNCTIONS.
COULD THERE HAVE BEEN SURVIVORS, SPOCK?
UNCERTAIN, CAPTAIN. HOWEVER...
...IT APPEARS ONE ESCAPE POD...
...WAS PILOTED **DELIBERATELY** INTO ANOTHER WORMHOLE.

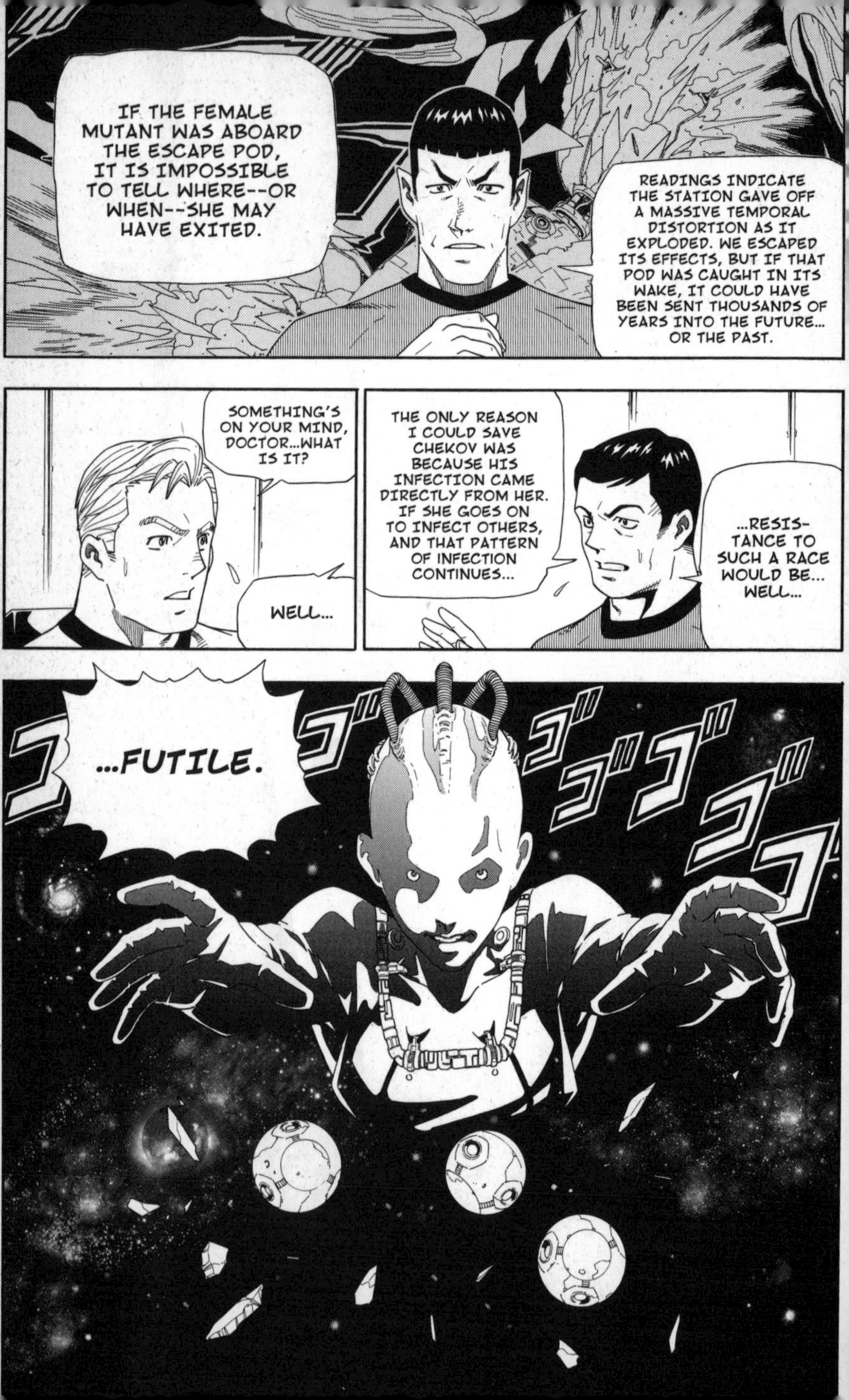
IF THE FEMALE MUTANT WAS ABOARD THE ESCAPE POD, IT IS IMPOSSIBLE TO TELL WHERE--OR WHEN--SHE MAY HAVE EXITED.
READINGS INDICATE THE STATION GAVE OFF A MASSIVE TEMPORAL DISTORTION AS IT EXPLODED. WE ESCAPED ITS EFFECTS, BUT IF THAT POD WAS CAUGHT IN ITS WAKE, IT COULD HAVE BEEN SENT THOUSANDS OF YEARS INTO THE FUTURE... OR THE PAST.
SOMETHING'S ON YOUR MIND, DOCTOR...WHAT IS IT?
WELL...
THE ONLY REASON I COULD SAVE CHEKOV WAS BECAUSE HIS INFECTION CAME DIRECTLY FROM HER. IF SHE GOES ON TO INFECT OTHERS, AND THAT PATTERN OF INFECTION CONTINUES...
...RESIS-TANCE TO SUCH A RACE WOULD BE... WELL...
...FUTILE.

UFP

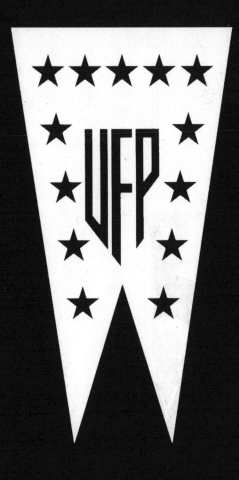

ANYTHING BUT ALONE

STORY BY JOSHUA ORTEGA
ART BY GREGORY GIOVANNI JOHNSON

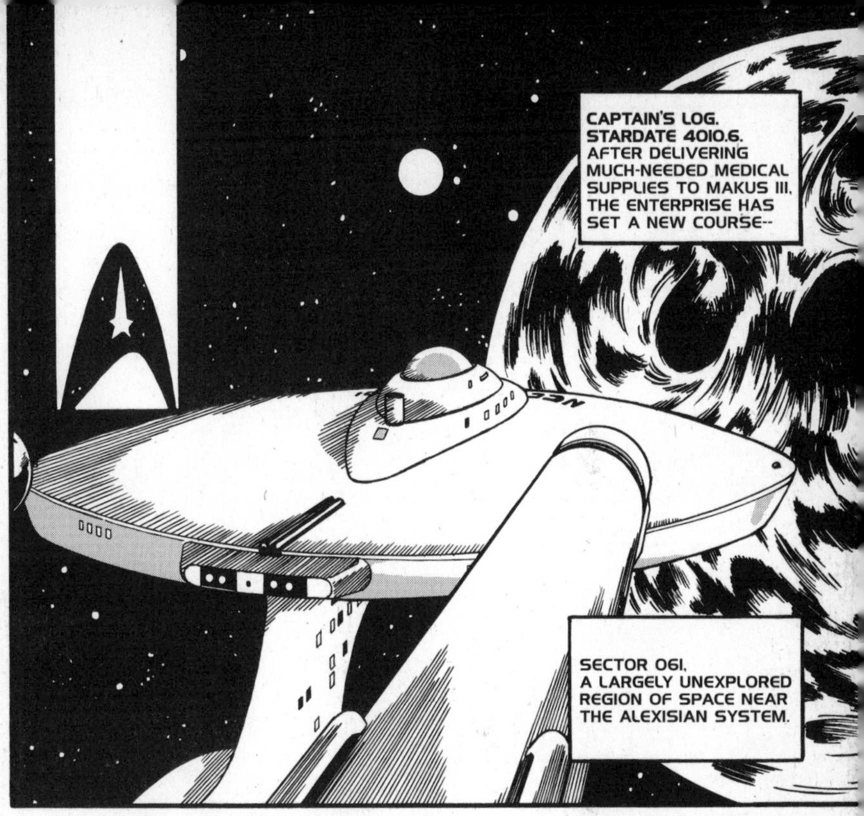
CAPTAIN'S LOG. STARDATE 4010.6. AFTER DELIVERING MUCH-NEEDED MEDICAL SUPPLIES TO MAKUS III, THE ENTERPRISE HAS SET A NEW COURSE--
SECTOR 061, A LARGELY UNEXPLORED REGION OF SPACE NEAR THE ALEXISIAN SYSTEM.
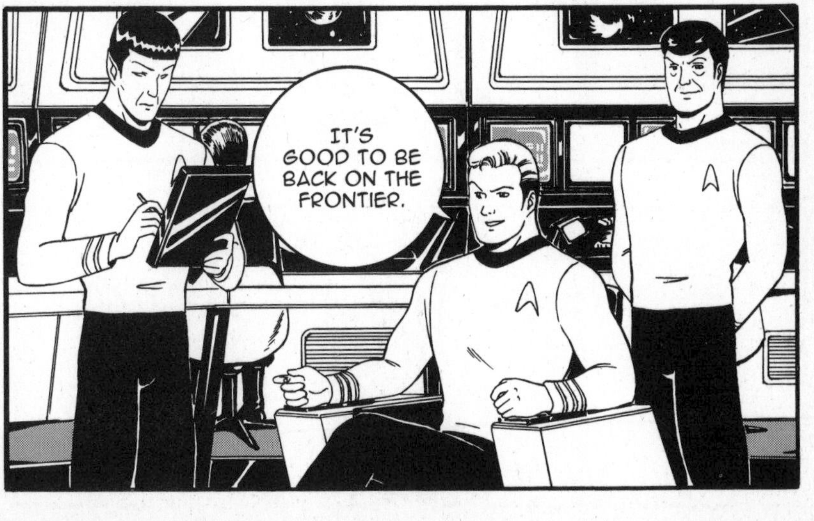
IT'S GOOD TO BE BACK ON THE FRONTIER.

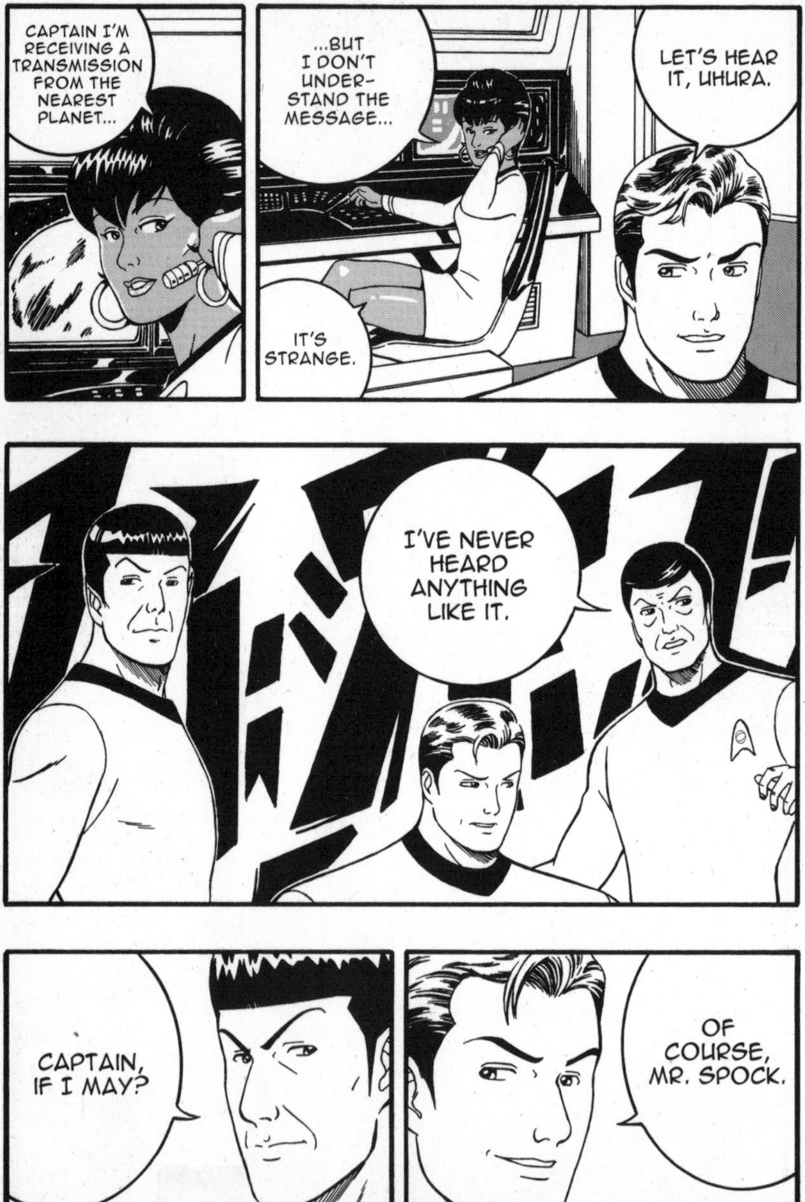
CAPTAIN I'M RECEIVING A TRANSMISSION FROM THE NEAREST PLANET...
...BUT I DON'T UNDER-STAND THE MESSAGE...
IT'S STRANGE.
LET'S HEAR IT, UHURA.
I'VE NEVER HEARD ANYTHING LIKE IT.
CAPTAIN, IF I MAY?
OF COURSE, MR. SPOCK.

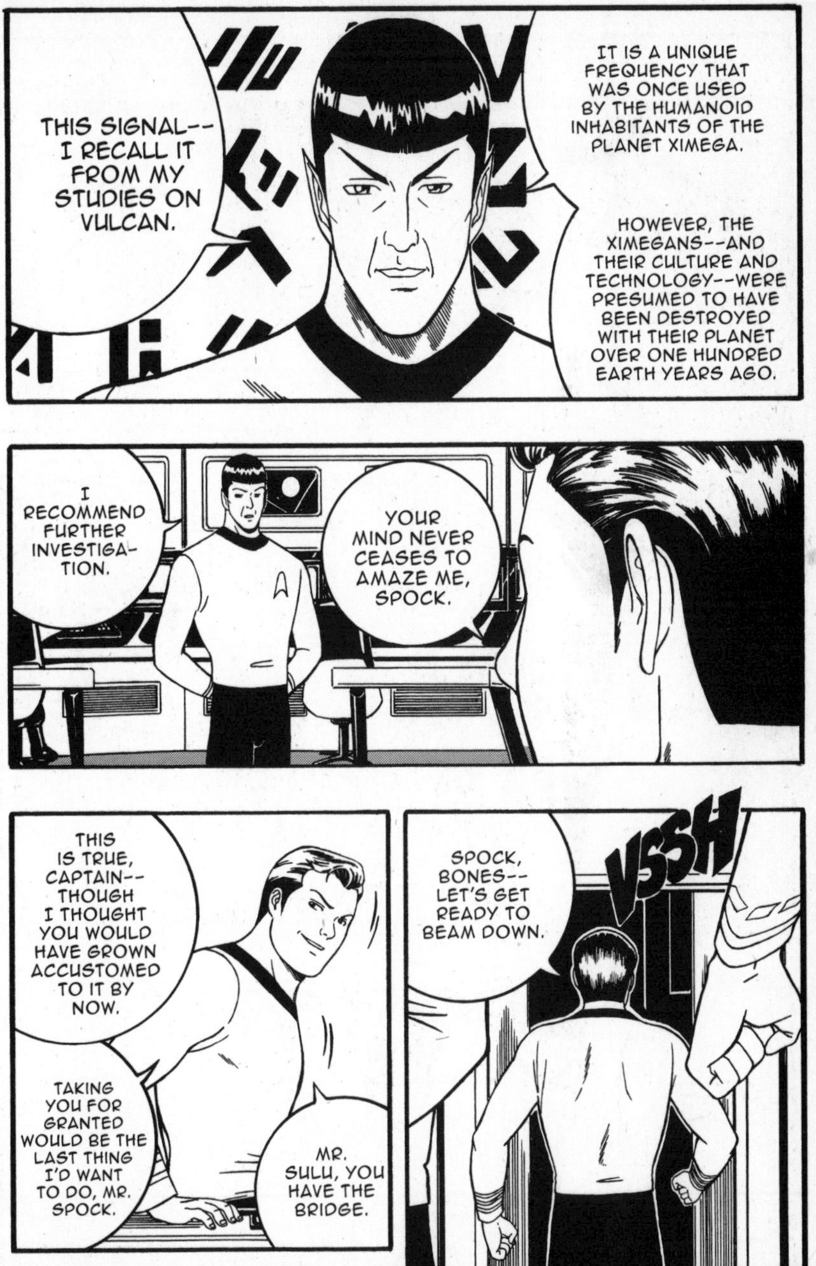
THIS SIGNAL-- I RECALL IT FROM MY STUDIES ON VULCAN.
IT IS A UNIQUE FREQUENCY THAT WAS ONCE USED BY THE HUMANOID INHABITANTS OF THE PLANET XIMEGA.
HOWEVER, THE XIMEGANS--AND THEIR CULTURE AND TECHNOLOGY--WERE PRESUMED TO HAVE BEEN DESTROYED WITH THEIR PLANET OVER ONE HUNDRED EARTH YEARS AGO.
I RECOMMEND FURTHER INVESTIGA-TION.
YOUR MIND NEVER CEASES TO AMAZE ME, SPOCK.
THIS IS TRUE, CAPTAIN-- THOUGH I THOUGHT YOU WOULD HAVE GROWN ACCUSTOMED TO IT BY NOW.
TAKING YOU FOR GRANTED WOULD BE THE LAST THING I'D WANT TO DO, MR. SPOCK.
MR. SULU, YOU HAVE THE BRIDGE.
SPOCK, BONES-- LET'S GET READY TO BEAM DOWN.
VSSH

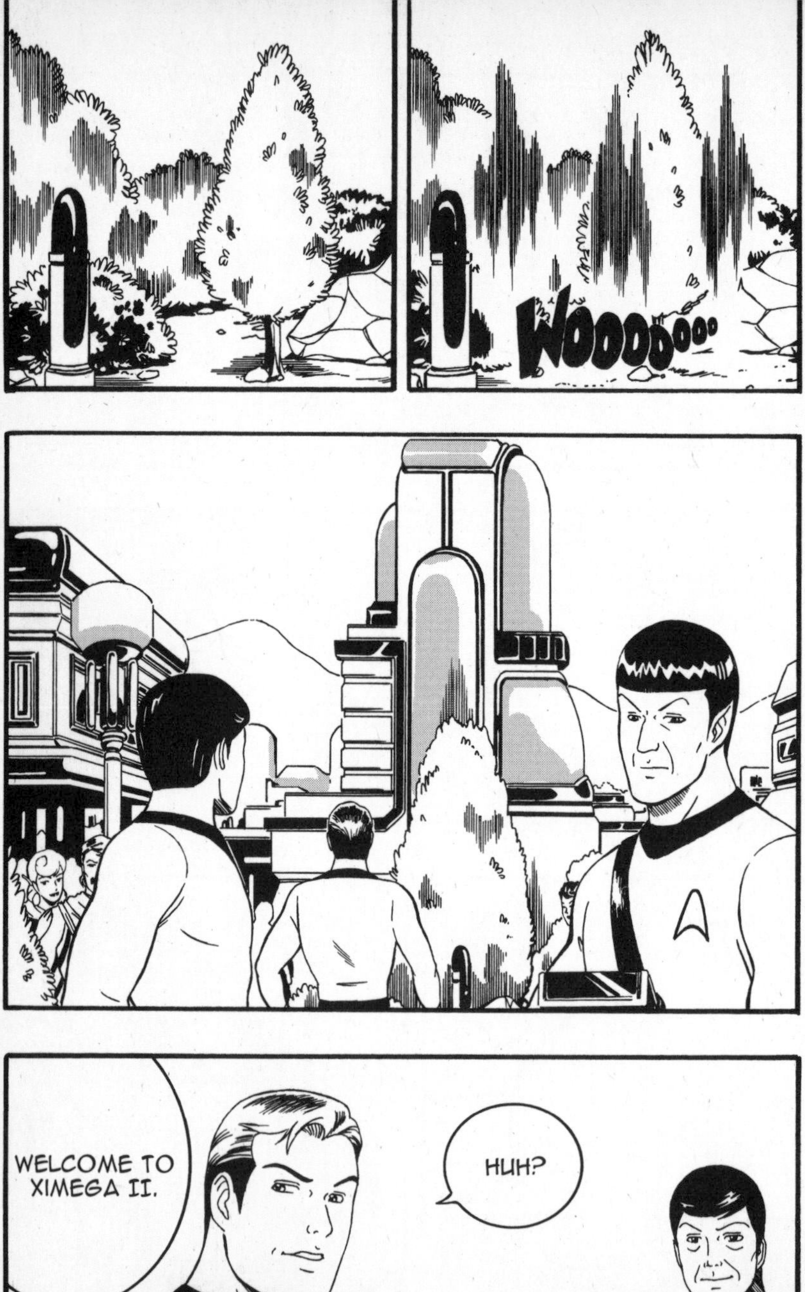
WOOOOooo
WELCOME TO XIMEGA II.
HUH?

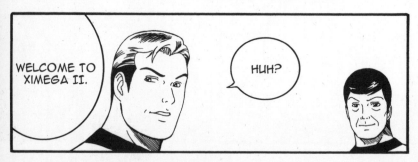

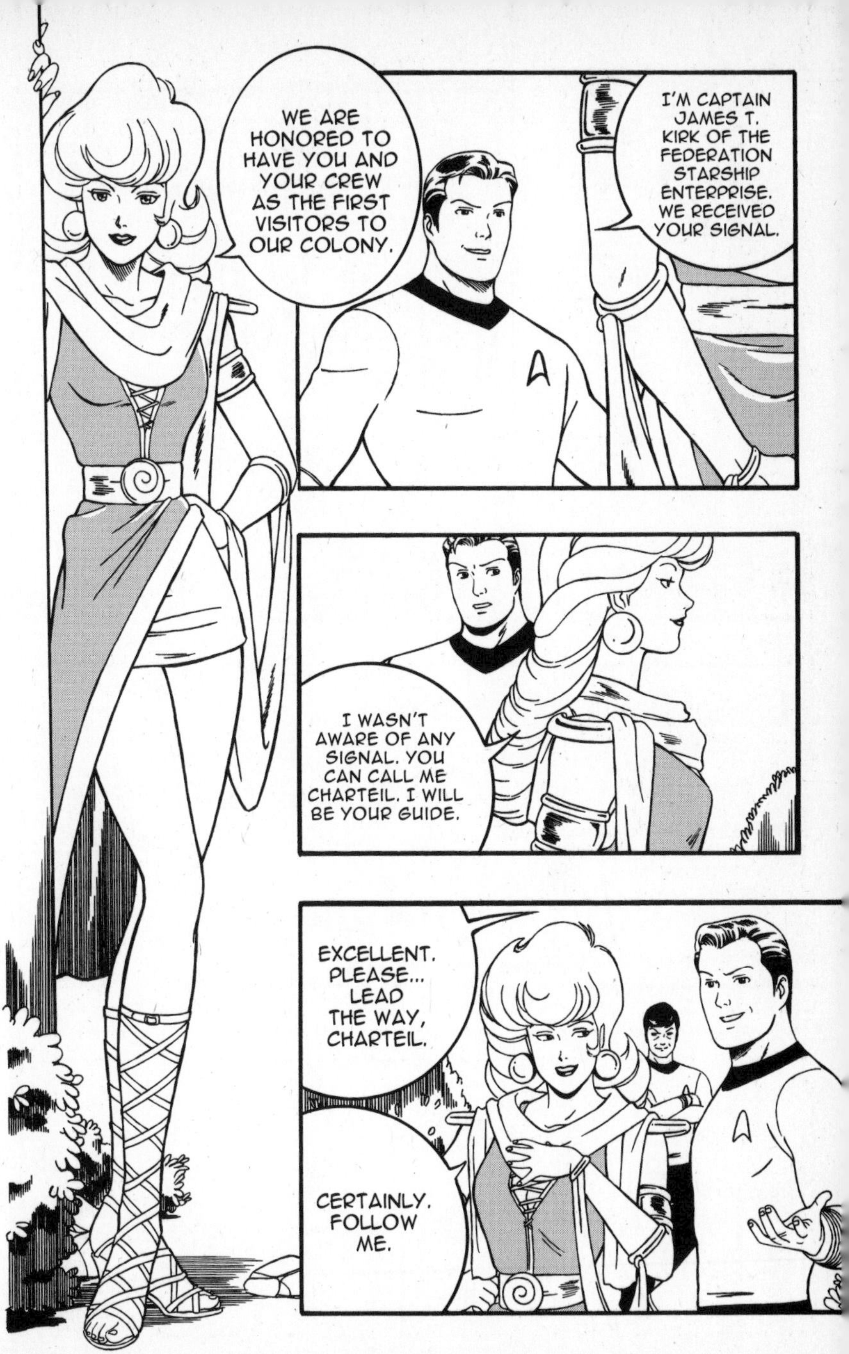
WE ARE HONORED TO HAVE YOU AND YOUR CREW AS THE FIRST VISITORS TO OUR COLONY.
I'M CAPTAIN JAMES T. KIRK OF THE FEDERATION STARSHIP ENTERPRISE. WE RECEIVED YOUR SIGNAL.
I WASN'T AWARE OF ANY SIGNAL. YOU CAN CALL ME CHARTEIL. I WILL BE YOUR GUIDE.
EXCELLENT. PLEASE... LEAD THE WAY, CHARTEIL.
CERTAINLY. FOLLOW ME.

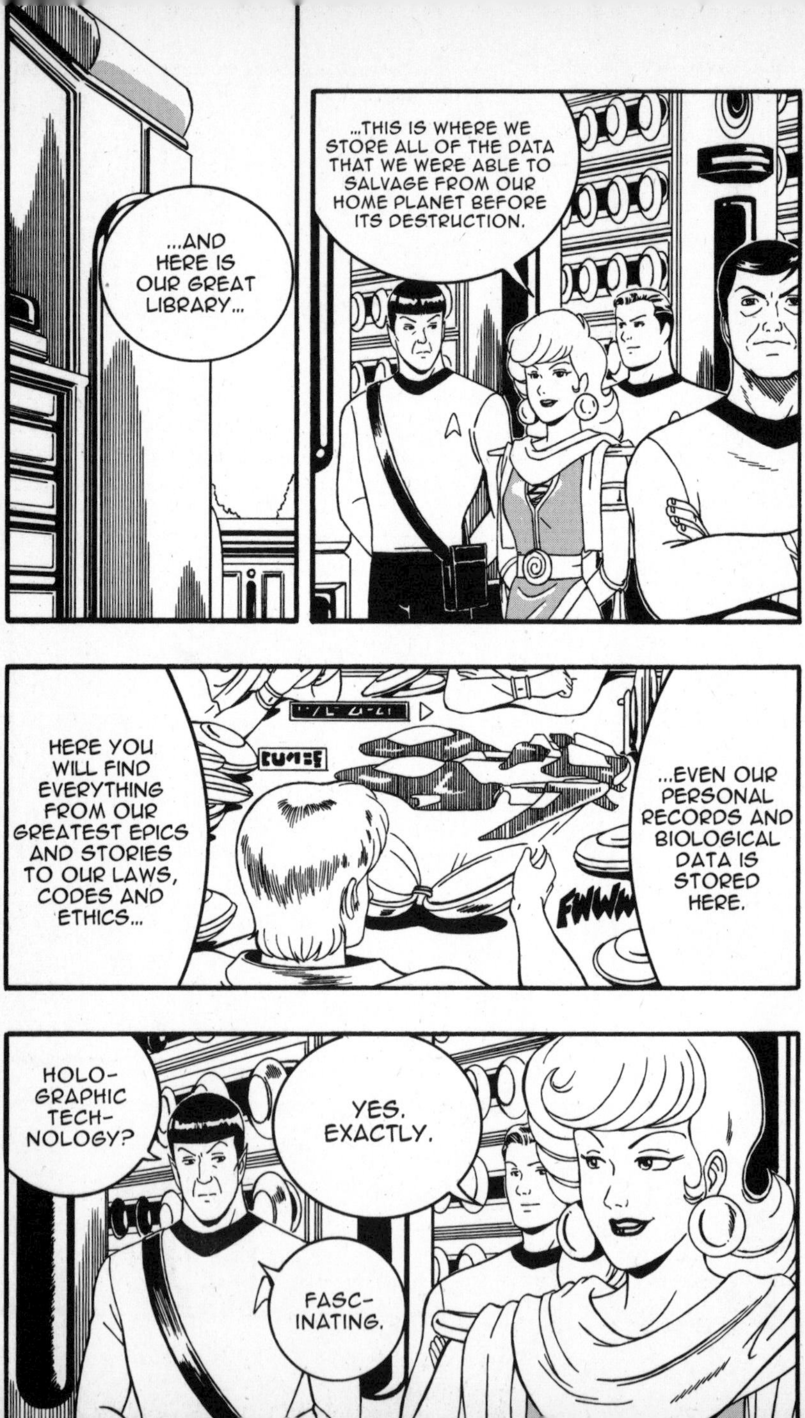
...AND HERE IS OUR GREAT LIBRARY...
...THIS IS WHERE WE STORE ALL OF THE DATA THAT WE WERE ABLE TO SALVAGE FROM OUR HOME PLANET BEFORE ITS DESTRUCTION.
HERE YOU WILL FIND EVERYTHING FROM OUR GREATEST EPICS AND STORIES TO OUR LAWS, CODES AND ETHICS...
...EVEN OUR PERSONAL RECORDS AND BIOLOGICAL DATA IS STORED HERE.
HOLO-GRAPHIC TECH-NOLOGY?
YES. EXACTLY.
FASC-INATING.

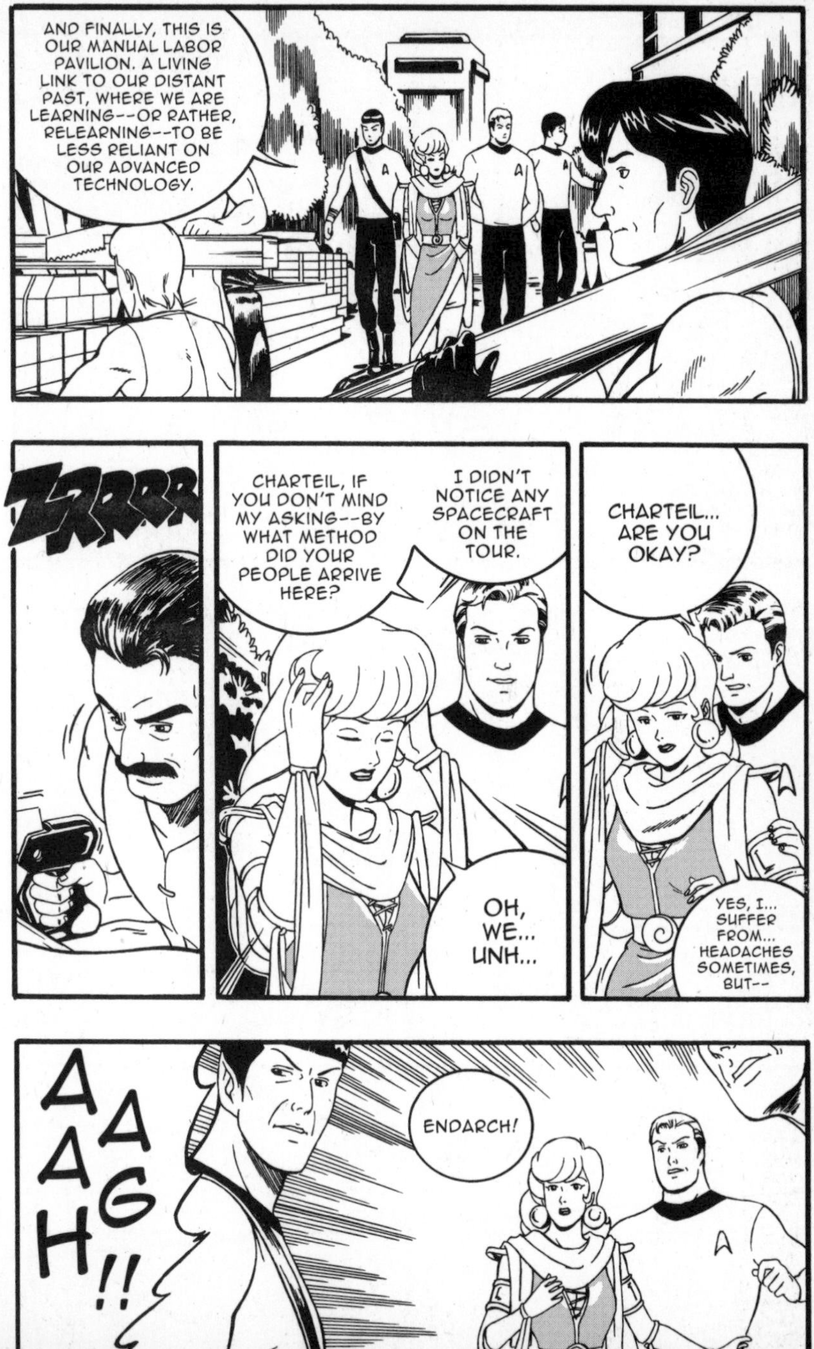

AND FINALLY, THIS IS OUR MANUAL LABOR PAVILION. A LIVING LINK TO OUR DISTANT PAST, WHERE WE ARE LEARNING--OR RATHER, RELEARNING--TO BE LESS RELIANT ON OUR ADVANCED TECHNOLOGY.
ZRRRR
CHARTEIL, IF YOU DON'T MIND MY ASKING--BY WHAT METHOD DID YOUR PEOPLE ARRIVE HERE?
I DIDN'T NOTICE ANY SPACECRAFT ON THE TOUR.
OH, WE... UNH...
CHARTEIL... ARE YOU OKAY?
YES, I... SUFFER FROM... HEADACHES SOMETIMES, BUT--
AAAGH!!
ENDARCH!

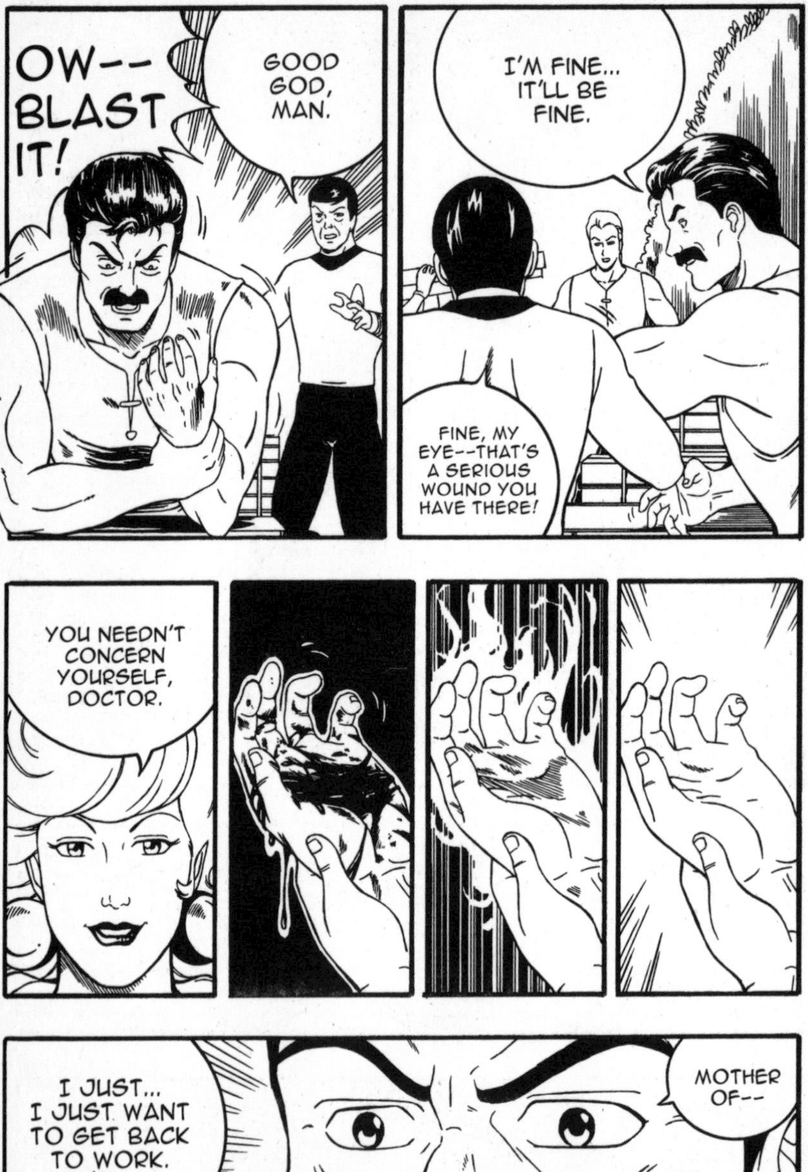
OW--
BLAST
IT!
GOOD
GOD,
MAN.
I'M FINE...
IT'LL BE
FINE.
FINE, MY
EYE--THAT'S
A SERIOUS
WOUND YOU
HAVE THERE!
YOU NEEDN'T
CONCERN
YOURSELF,
DOCTOR.
I JUST...
I JUST WANT
TO GET BACK
TO WORK.
MOTHER
OF--

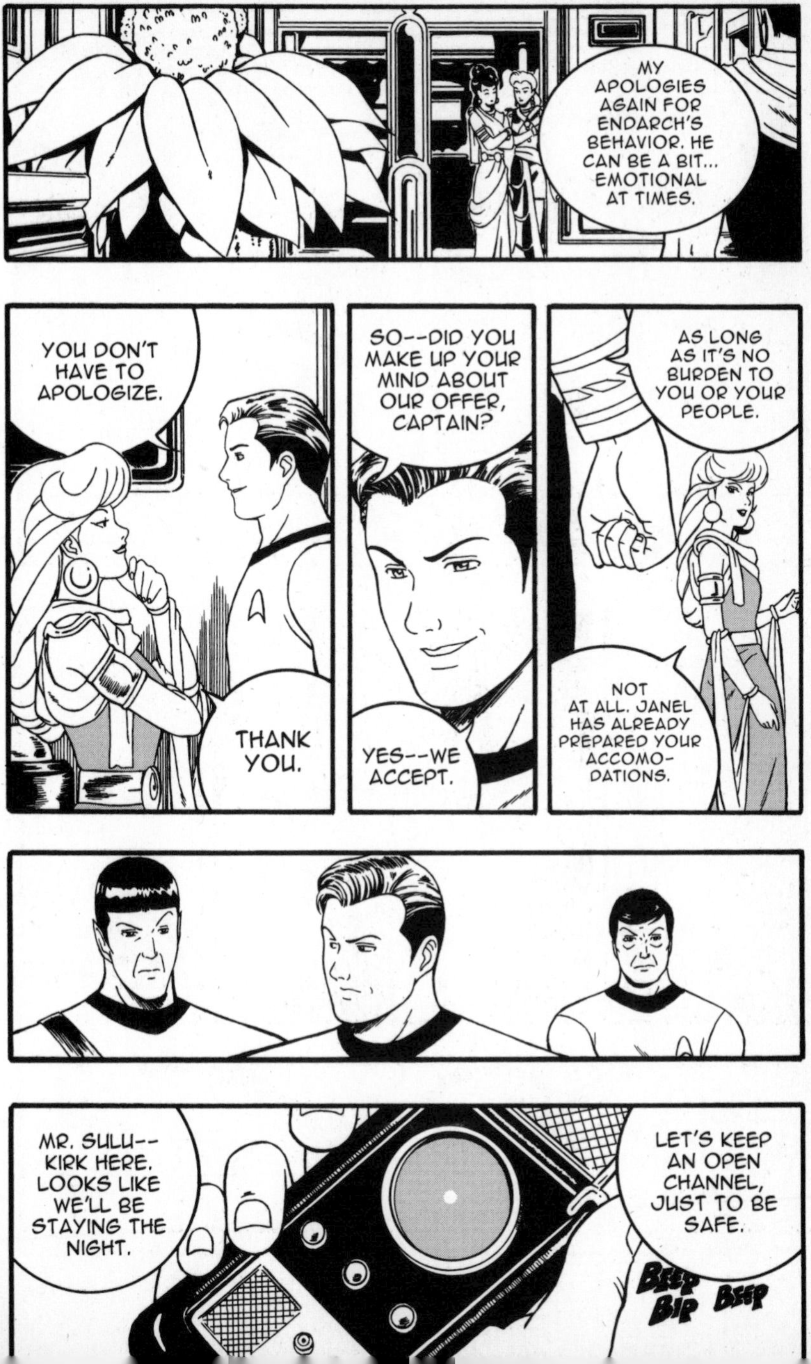
MY APOLOGIES AGAIN FOR ENDARCH'S BEHAVIOR. HE CAN BE A BIT... EMOTIONAL AT TIMES.
YOU DON'T HAVE TO APOLOGIZE.
THANK YOU.
SO--DID YOU MAKE UP YOUR MIND ABOUT OUR OFFER, CAPTAIN?
YES--WE ACCEPT.
AS LONG AS IT'S NO BURDEN TO YOU OR YOUR PEOPLE.
NOT AT ALL. JANEL HAS ALREADY PREPARED YOUR ACCOMO-DATIONS.
MR. SULU--KIRK HERE. LOOKS LIKE WE'LL BE STAYING THE NIGHT.
LET'S KEEP AN OPEN CHANNEL, JUST TO BE SAFE.
BEEP BIP BEEP

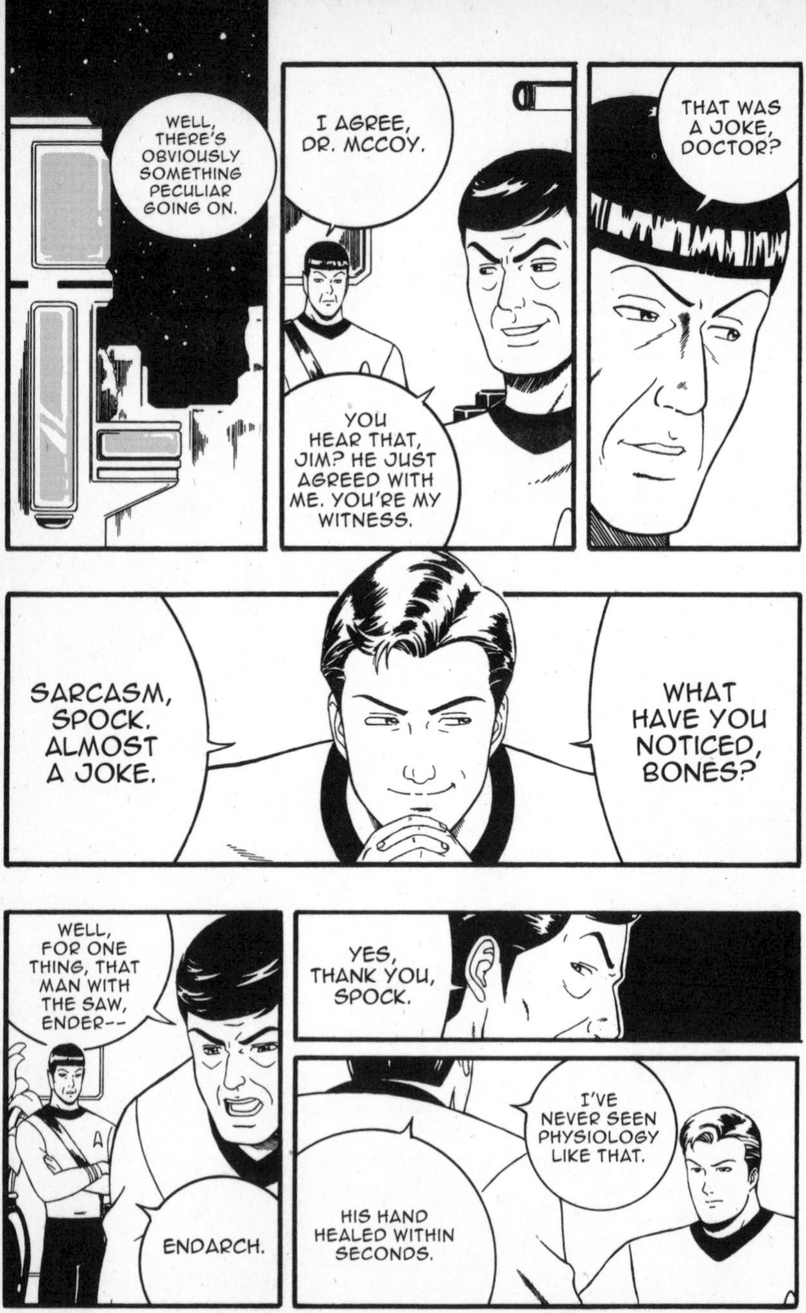
WELL, THERE'S OBVIOUSLY SOMETHING PECULIAR GOING ON.
I AGREE, DR. MCCOY.
YOU HEAR THAT, JIM? HE JUST AGREED WITH ME. YOU'RE MY WITNESS.
THAT WAS A JOKE, DOCTOR?
SARCASM, SPOCK. ALMOST A JOKE.
WHAT HAVE YOU NOTICED, BONES?
WELL, FOR ONE THING, THAT MAN WITH THE SAW, ENDER--
ENDARCH.
YES, THANK YOU, SPOCK.
I'VE NEVER SEEN PHYSIOLOGY LIKE THAT.
HIS HAND HEALED WITHIN SECONDS.

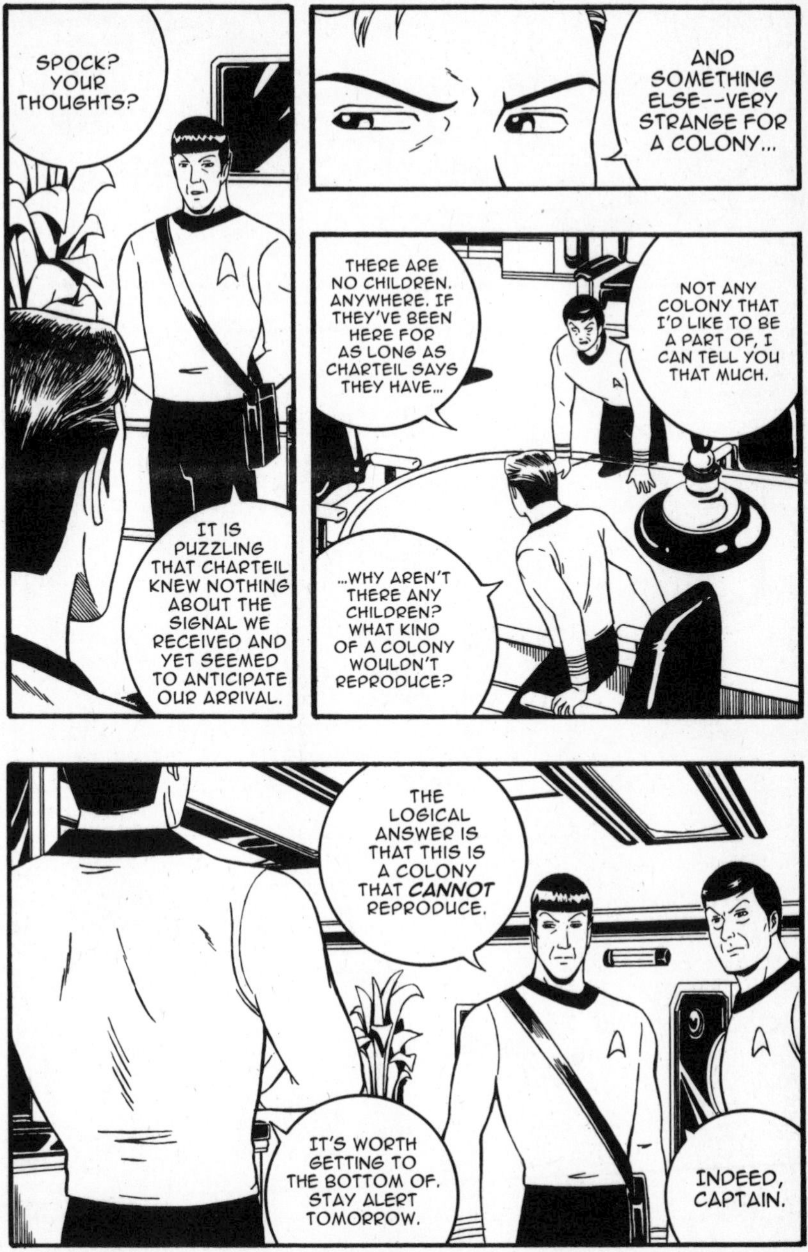
SPOCK? YOUR THOUGHTS?
IT IS PUZZLING THAT CHARTEIL KNEW NOTHING ABOUT THE SIGNAL WE RECEIVED AND YET SEEMED TO ANTICIPATE OUR ARRIVAL.
AND SOMETHING ELSE--VERY STRANGE FOR A COLONY...
THERE ARE NO CHILDREN. ANYWHERE. IF THEY'VE BEEN HERE FOR AS LONG AS CHARTEIL SAYS THEY HAVE...
...WHY AREN'T THERE ANY CHILDREN? WHAT KIND OF A COLONY WOULDN'T REPRODUCE?
NOT ANY COLONY THAT I'D LIKE TO BE A PART OF, I CAN TELL YOU THAT MUCH.
THE LOGICAL ANSWER IS THAT THIS IS A COLONY THAT *CANNOT* REPRODUCE.
IT'S WORTH GETTING TO THE BOTTOM OF. STAY ALERT TOMORROW.
INDEED, CAPTAIN.

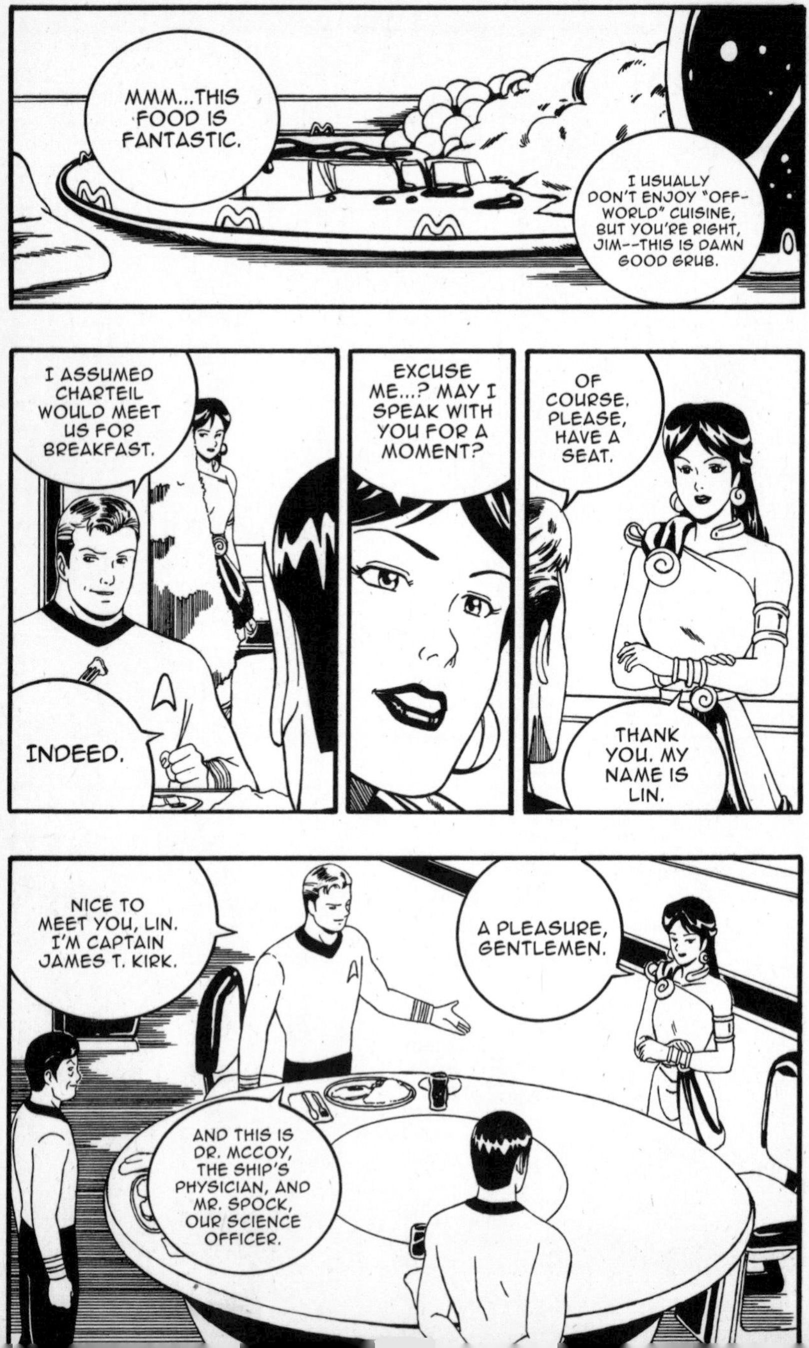
MMM...THIS FOOD IS FANTASTIC.
I USUALLY DON'T ENJOY "OFF-WORLD" CUISINE, BUT YOU'RE RIGHT, JIM--THIS IS DAMN GOOD GRUB.
I ASSUMED CHARTEIL WOULD MEET US FOR BREAKFAST.
INDEED.
EXCUSE ME...? MAY I SPEAK WITH YOU FOR A MOMENT?
OF COURSE. PLEASE, HAVE A SEAT.
THANK YOU. MY NAME IS LIN.
NICE TO MEET YOU, LIN. I'M CAPTAIN JAMES T. KIRK.
A PLEASURE, GENTLEMEN.
AND THIS IS DR. MCCOY, THE SHIP'S PHYSICIAN, AND MR. SPOCK, OUR SCIENCE OFFICER.

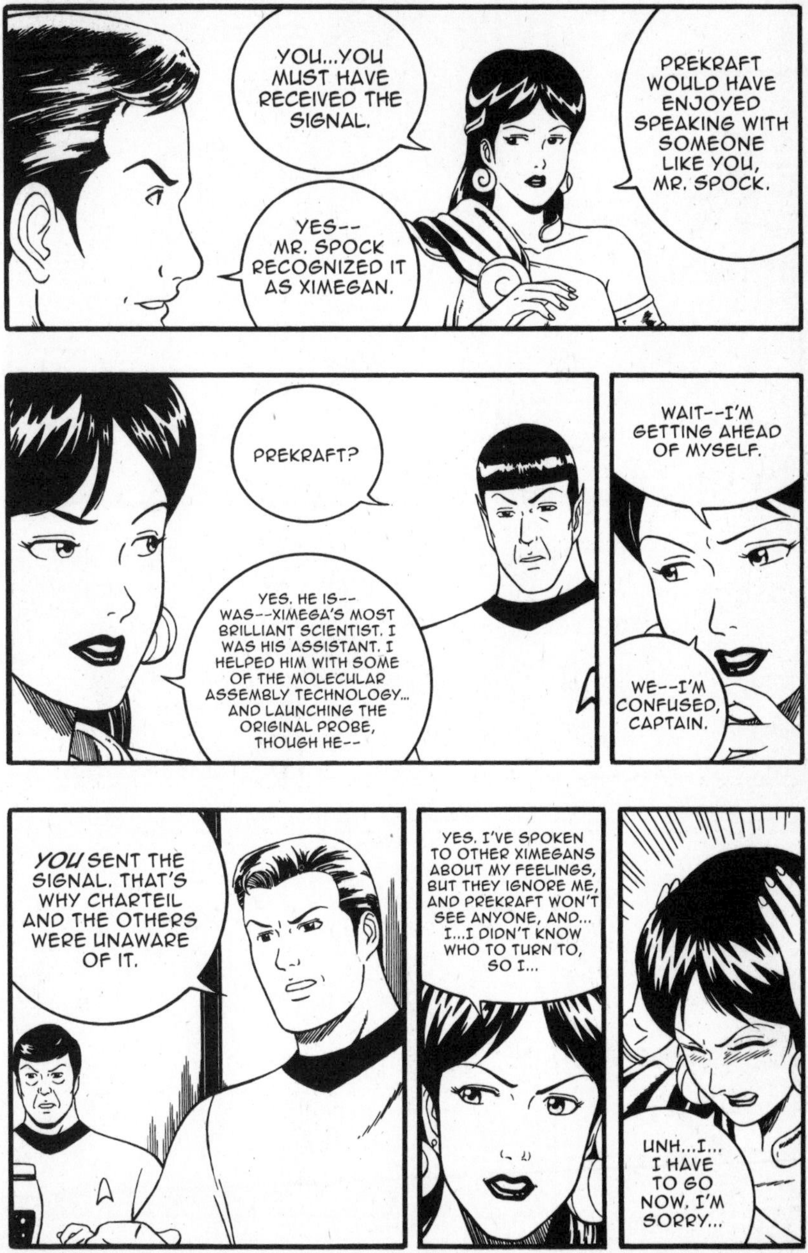
YOU...YOU MUST HAVE RECEIVED THE SIGNAL.
YES-- MR. SPOCK RECOGNIZED IT AS XIMEGAN.
PREKRAFT WOULD HAVE ENJOYED SPEAKING WITH SOMEONE LIKE YOU, MR. SPOCK.
PREKRAFT?
YES. HE IS-- WAS--XIMEGA'S MOST BRILLIANT SCIENTIST. I WAS HIS ASSISTANT. I HELPED HIM WITH SOME OF THE MOLECULAR ASSEMBLY TECHNOLOGY... AND LAUNCHING THE ORIGINAL PROBE, THOUGH HE--
WAIT--I'M GETTING AHEAD OF MYSELF.
WE--I'M CONFUSED, CAPTAIN.
YOU SENT THE SIGNAL. THAT'S WHY CHARTEIL AND THE OTHERS WERE UNAWARE OF IT.
YES. I'VE SPOKEN TO OTHER XIMEGANS ABOUT MY FEELINGS, BUT THEY IGNORE ME, AND PREKRAFT WON'T SEE ANYONE, AND... I...I DIDN'T KNOW WHO TO TURN TO, SO I...
UNH...I... I HAVE TO GO NOW. I'M SORRY...

DOES EVERYONE HERE SUFFER FROM MIGRAINES?

IT WOULD APPEAR SO, BONES.

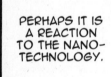

PERHAPS IT IS A REACTION TO THE NANO-TECHNOLOGY.

EXPLAIN, SPOCK.

I BELIEVE I UNDERSTAND AT LEAST PART OF WHAT'S GOING ON HERE.

LIN MENTIONED MOLECULAR ASSEMBLERS AND THE "ORIGINAL PROBE." I BELIEVE SHE WAS REFERRING TO A HYPOTHETICAL FORM OF NANOTECHNOLOGY THAT IS REMARKABLY SIMILAR TO ONE FIRST POSITED BY AN EARTH PHYSICIST, DR. JOHN VON NEUMANN, IN THE MID-20TH CENTURY.

VON NEUMANN THEORIZED THAT AN INTERSTELLAR DEVICE SUCH AS A PROBE COULD BE EQUIPPED WITH SELF-REPLICATING MOLECULAR ASSEMBLERS, OR NANOMACHINES.

BY REARRANGING MATTER AT AN ATOMIC LEVEL, THESE MICROSCOPIC MACHINES COULD THEORETICALLY BUILD A CITY, CREATE FOOD, LIVESTOCK-- OR EVEN SENTIENT LIFE-- SIMPLY BY MANIPULATING THE SURROUNDING ENVIRONMENT.

HORSEFEATHERS, SPOCK. CLONING IS ONE THING, BUT YOU CAN'T JUST CREATE *PEOPLE* FROM THIN AIR--THAT'S IMPOSSIBLE.

I BEG TO DIFFER, DOCTOR. WERE ONE TO DEVELOP A TECHNOLOGY CAPABLE OF STORING CONSCIOUSNESS AS ELECTRONIC DATA, IT IS THEORETICALLY POSSIBLE TO COMBINE IT WITH NANO-SCALE ENGINES TO GENERATE AN ENTIRE COLONY OF HUMAN BEINGS.

THAT'S PURE SCIENCE FICTION. NO ONE HAS THAT KIND OF TECHNOLOGY.

IT IS, AS I SAID, THEORETICAL.

BUT HISTORY HAS SHOWN THAT WHAT WAS ONCE REGARDED AS FICTION OFTEN BECOMES REALITY.

SPOCK, DO YOU REALLY THINK THAT'S WHAT'S GOING ON HERE?

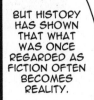

WHY ENDARCH'S WOUND HEALED SO FAST? WHY THERE'S NO SIGN OF A SPACE-CRAFT...?

I AM ONLY SAYING THAT IT IS POSSIBLE, CAPTAIN. MAYBE THIS SCIENTIST-- PREKRAFT-- COULD PROVIDE US WITH THE ANSWERS WE SEEK.

AGREED. LET'S FINISH UP OUR MEAL AND--

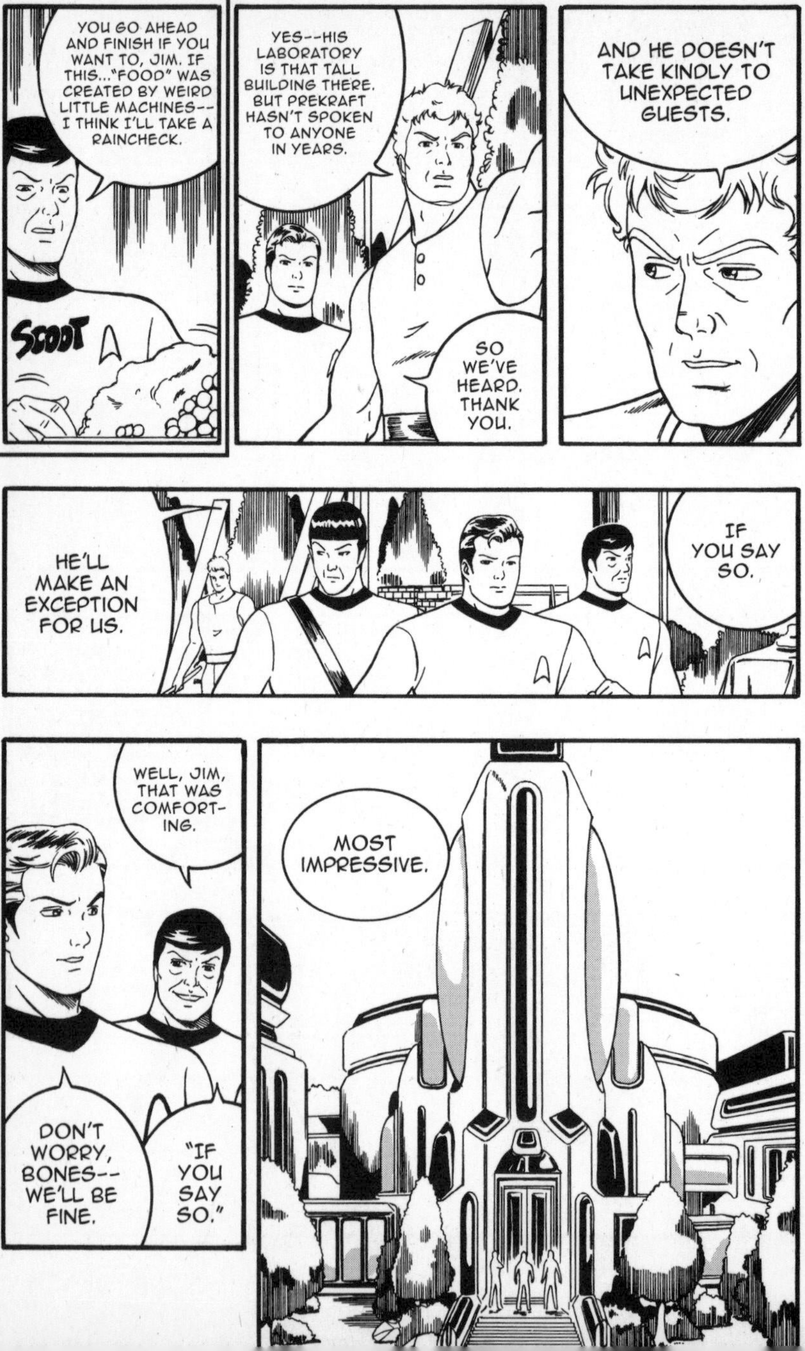
YOU GO AHEAD AND FINISH IF YOU WANT TO, JIM. IF THIS..."FOOD" WAS CREATED BY WEIRD LITTLE MACHINES-- I THINK I'LL TAKE A RAINCHECK.
SCOOT
YES--HIS LABORATORY IS THAT TALL BUILDING THERE. BUT PREKRAFT HASN'T SPOKEN TO ANYONE IN YEARS.
SO WE'VE HEARD. THANK YOU.
AND HE DOESN'T TAKE KINDLY TO UNEXPECTED GUESTS.
HE'LL MAKE AN EXCEPTION FOR US.
IF YOU SAY SO.
WELL, JIM, THAT WAS COMFORT-ING.
DON'T WORRY, BONES-- WE'LL BE FINE.
"IF YOU SAY SO."
MOST IMPRESSIVE.

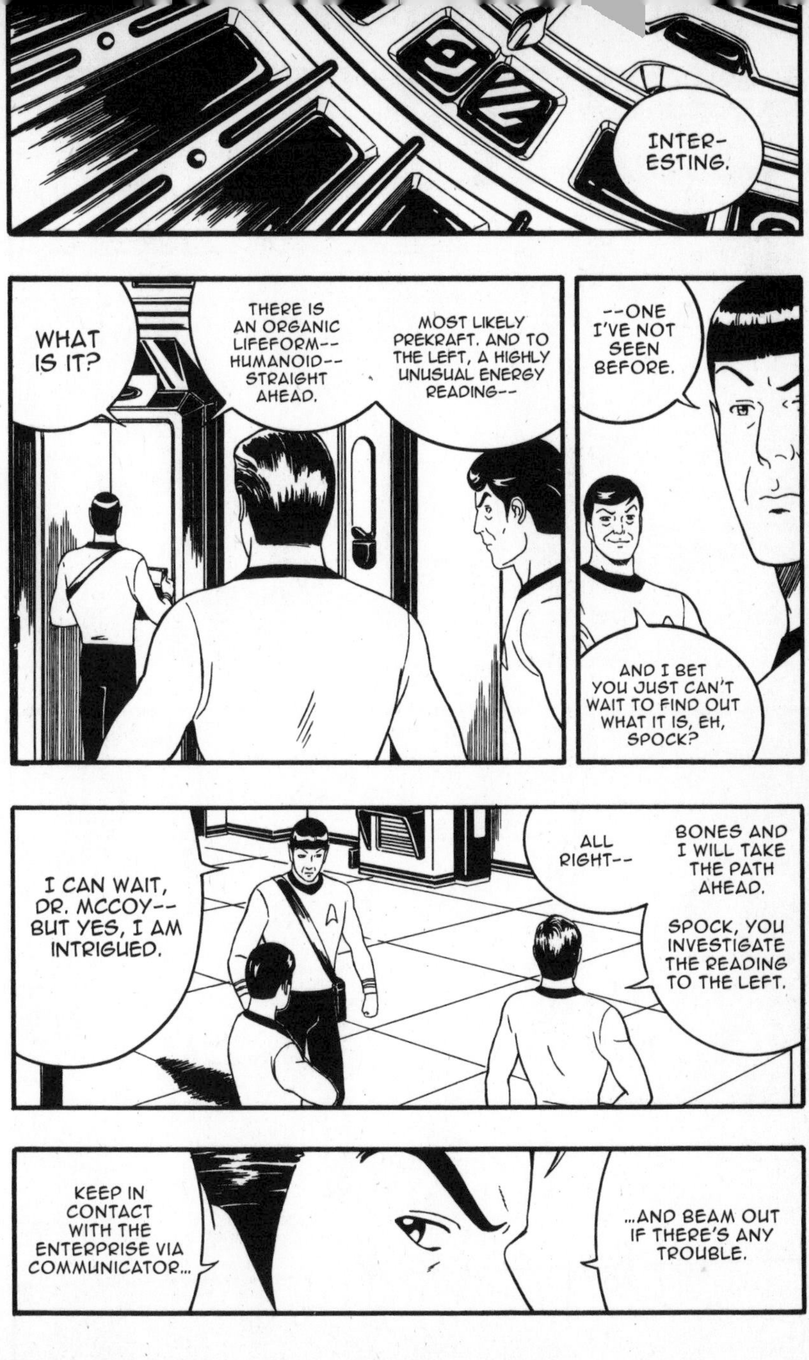
INTER-
ESTING.
WHAT IS IT?
THERE IS AN ORGANIC LIFEFORM-- HUMANOID-- STRAIGHT AHEAD.
MOST LIKELY PREKRAFT. AND TO THE LEFT, A HIGHLY UNUSUAL ENERGY READING--
--ONE I'VE NOT SEEN BEFORE.
AND I BET YOU JUST CAN'T WAIT TO FIND OUT WHAT IT IS, EH, SPOCK?
I CAN WAIT, DR. MCCOY-- BUT YES, I AM INTRIGUED.
ALL RIGHT--
BONES AND I WILL TAKE THE PATH AHEAD.
SPOCK, YOU INVESTIGATE THE READING TO THE LEFT.
KEEP IN CONTACT WITH THE ENTERPRISE VIA COMMUNICATOR...
...AND BEAM OUT IF THERE'S ANY TROUBLE.

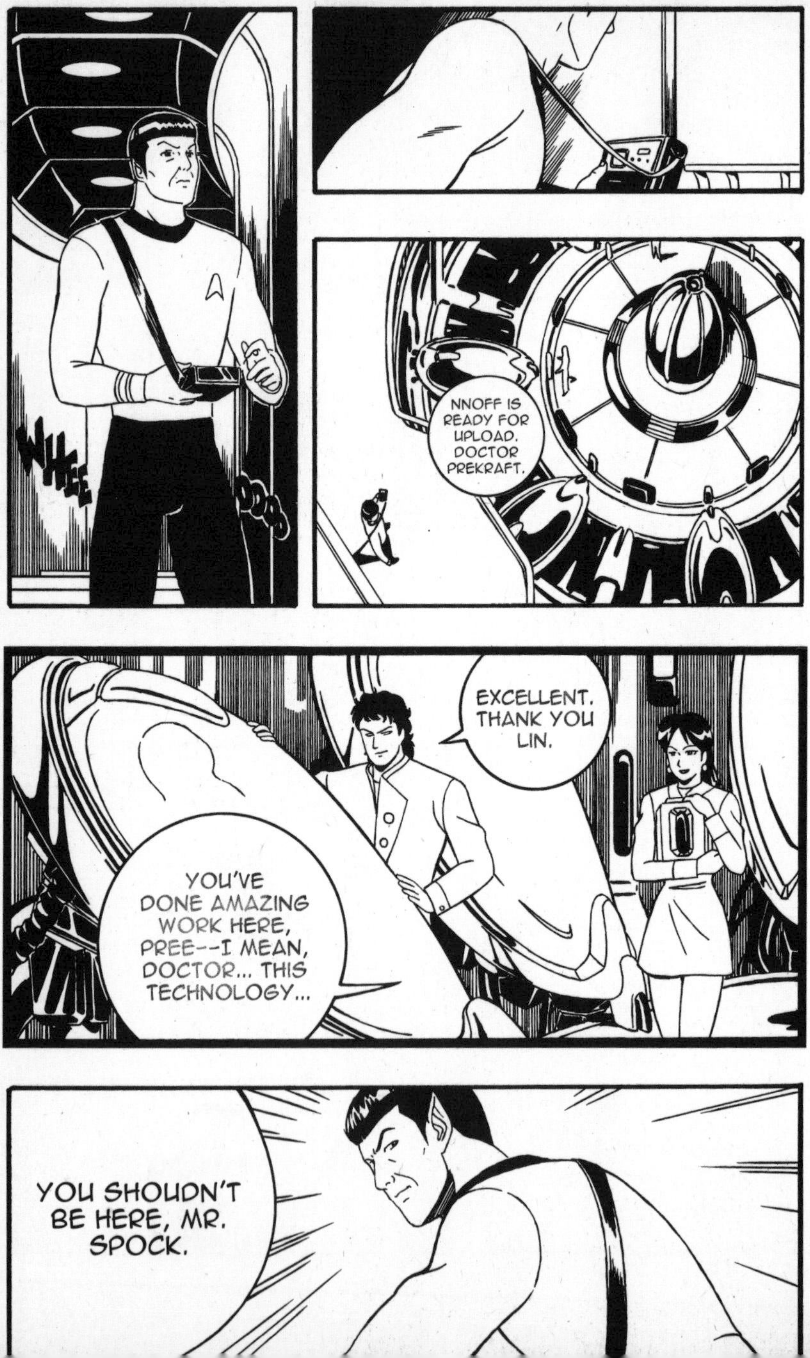
WHEE
OOSS
NNOFF IS READY FOR UPLOAD. DOCTOR PREKRAFT.
EXCELLENT. THANK YOU LIN.
YOU'VE DONE AMAZING WORK HERE, PREE--I MEAN, DOCTOR... THIS TECHNOLOGY...
YOU SHOUDN'T BE HERE, MR. SPOCK.

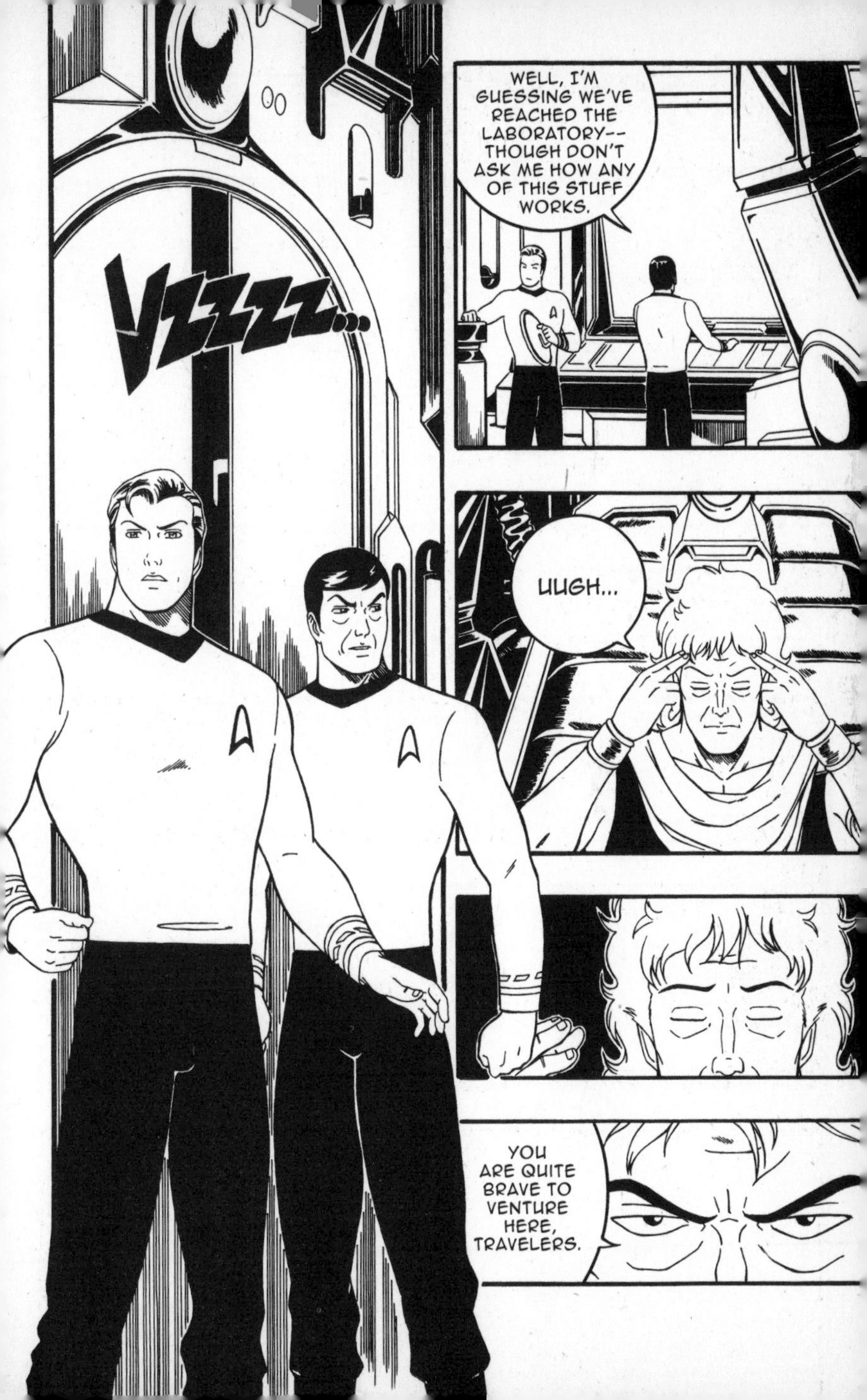
VZZZZ...
WELL, I'M GUESSING WE'VE REACHED THE LABORATORY-- THOUGH DON'T ASK ME HOW ANY OF THIS STUFF WORKS.
UUGH...
YOU ARE QUITE BRAVE TO VENTURE HERE, TRAVELERS.

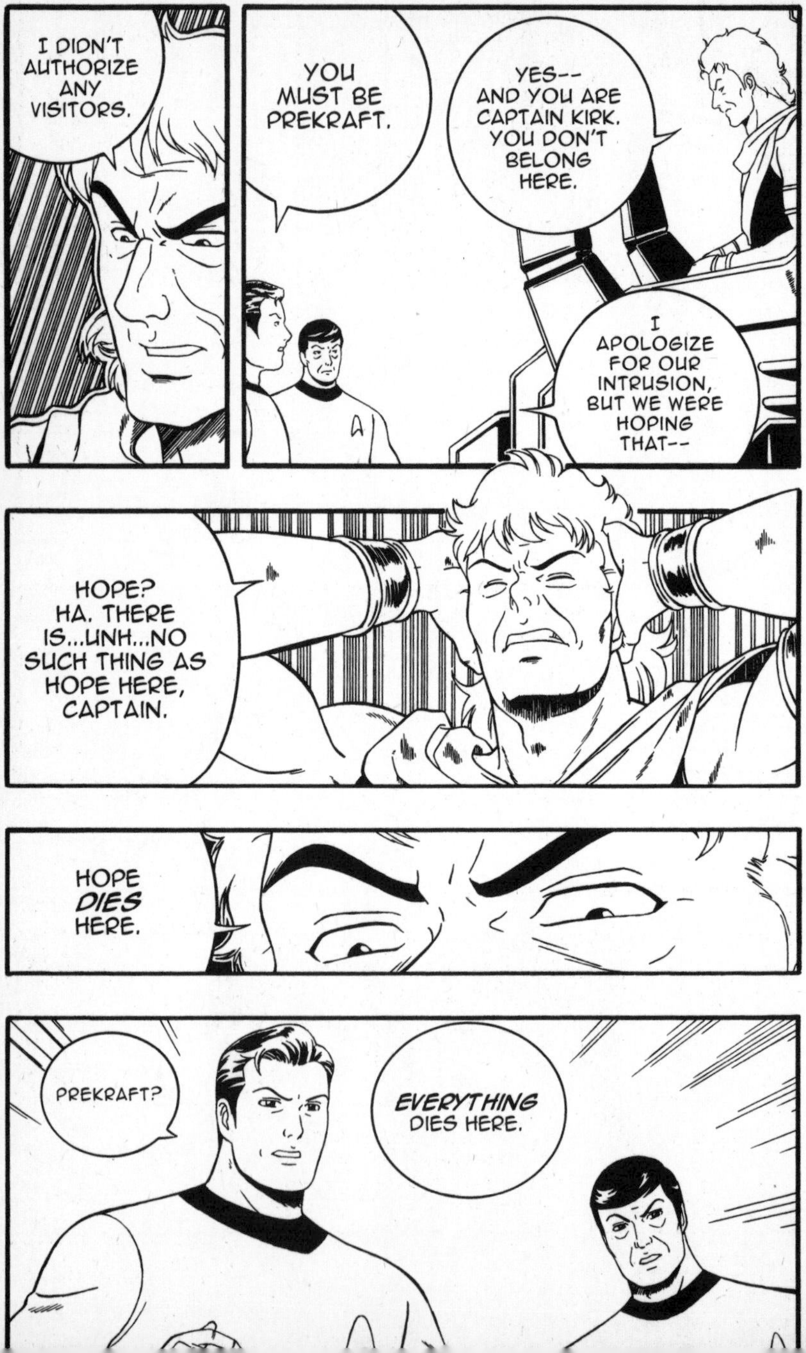
I DIDN'T AUTHORIZE ANY VISITORS.
YOU MUST BE PREKRAFT.
YES-- AND YOU ARE CAPTAIN KIRK. YOU DON'T BELONG HERE.
I APOLOGIZE FOR OUR INTRUSION, BUT WE WERE HOPING THAT--
HOPE? HA. THERE IS...UNH...NO SUCH THING AS HOPE HERE, CAPTAIN.
HOPE *DIES* HERE.
PREKRAFT?
EVERYTHING DIES HERE.

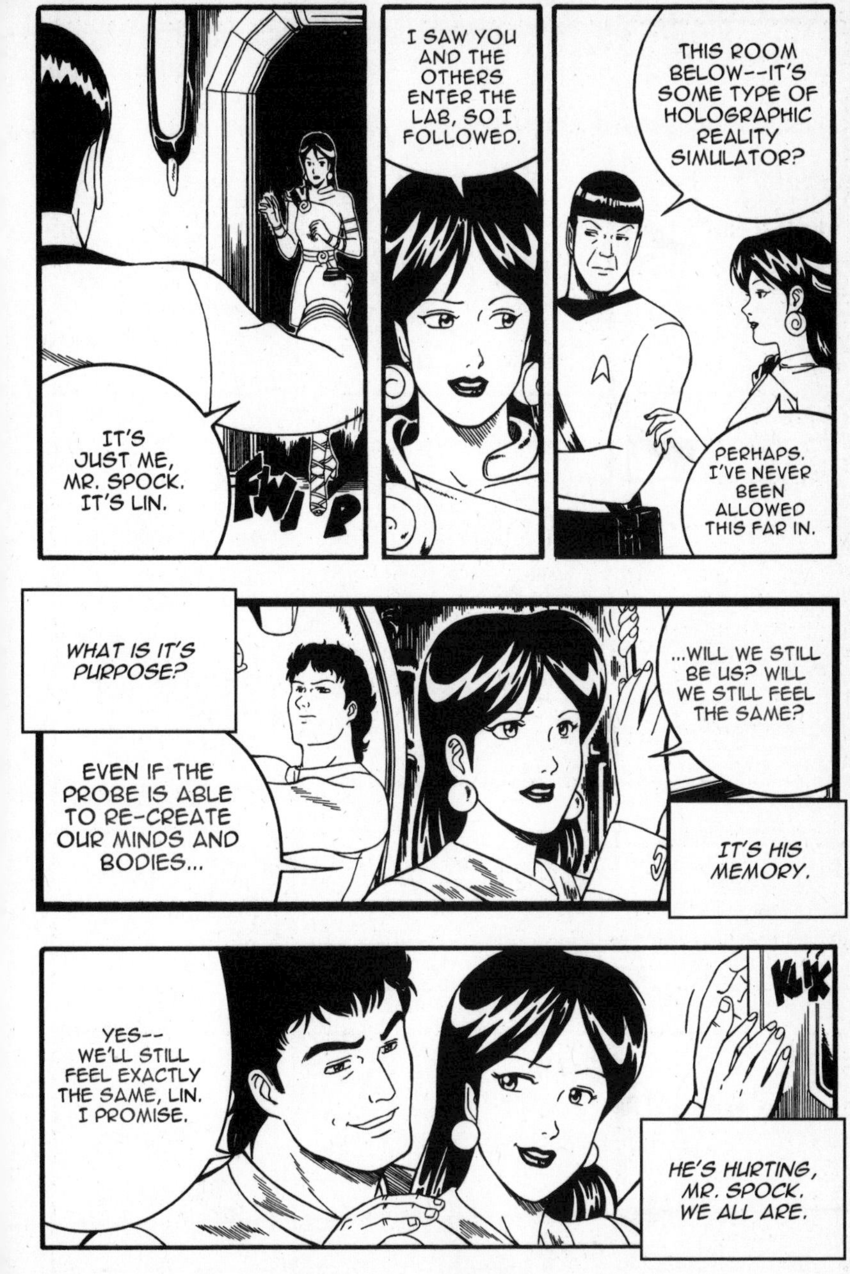
IT'S JUST ME, MR. SPOCK. IT'S LIN.
FWIP
I SAW YOU AND THE OTHERS ENTER THE LAB, SO I FOLLOWED.
THIS ROOM BELOW--IT'S SOME TYPE OF HOLOGRAPHIC REALITY SIMULATOR?
PERHAPS. I'VE NEVER BEEN ALLOWED THIS FAR IN.
WHAT IS IT'S PURPOSE?
EVEN IF THE PROBE IS ABLE TO RE-CREATE OUR MINDS AND BODIES...
...WILL WE STILL BE US? WILL WE STILL FEEL THE SAME?
IT'S HIS MEMORY.
YES-- WE'LL STILL FEEL EXACTLY THE SAME, LIN. I PROMISE.
KLIK
HE'S HURTING, MR. SPOCK. WE ALL ARE.

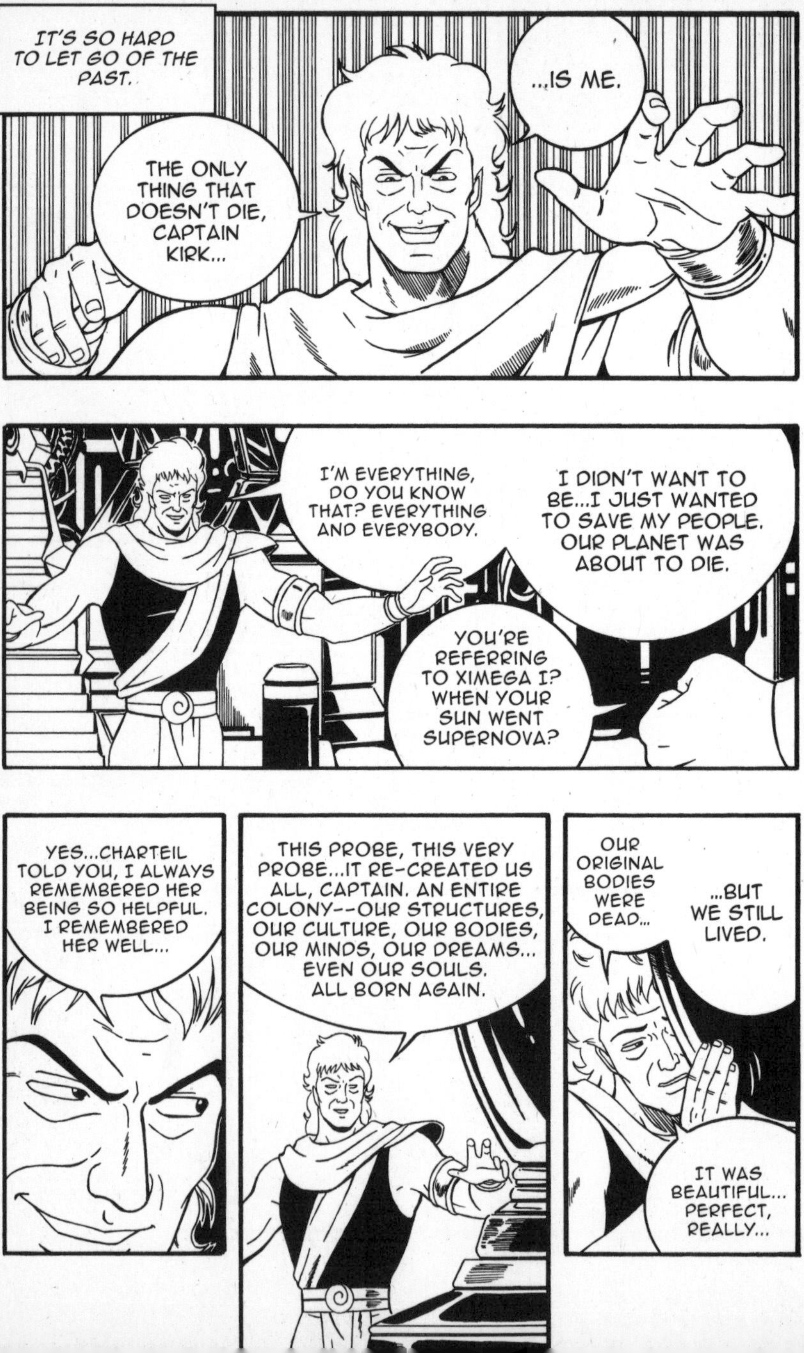
IT'S SO HARD TO LET GO OF THE PAST.
THE ONLY THING THAT DOESN'T DIE, CAPTAIN KIRK...
...IS ME.
I'M EVERYTHING, DO YOU KNOW THAT? EVERYTHING AND EVERYBODY.
I DIDN'T WANT TO BE...I JUST WANTED TO SAVE MY PEOPLE. OUR PLANET WAS ABOUT TO DIE.
YOU'RE REFERRING TO XIMEGA I? WHEN YOUR SUN WENT SUPERNOVA?
YES...CHARTEIL TOLD YOU, I ALWAYS REMEMBERED HER BEING SO HELPFUL. I REMEMBERED HER WELL...
THIS PROBE, THIS VERY PROBE...IT RE-CREATED US ALL, CAPTAIN. AN ENTIRE COLONY--OUR STRUCTURES, OUR CULTURE, OUR BODIES, OUR MINDS, OUR DREAMS... EVEN OUR SOULS. ALL BORN AGAIN.
OUR ORIGINAL BODIES WERE DEAD...
...BUT WE STILL LIVED.
IT WAS BEAUTIFUL... PERFECT, REALLY...

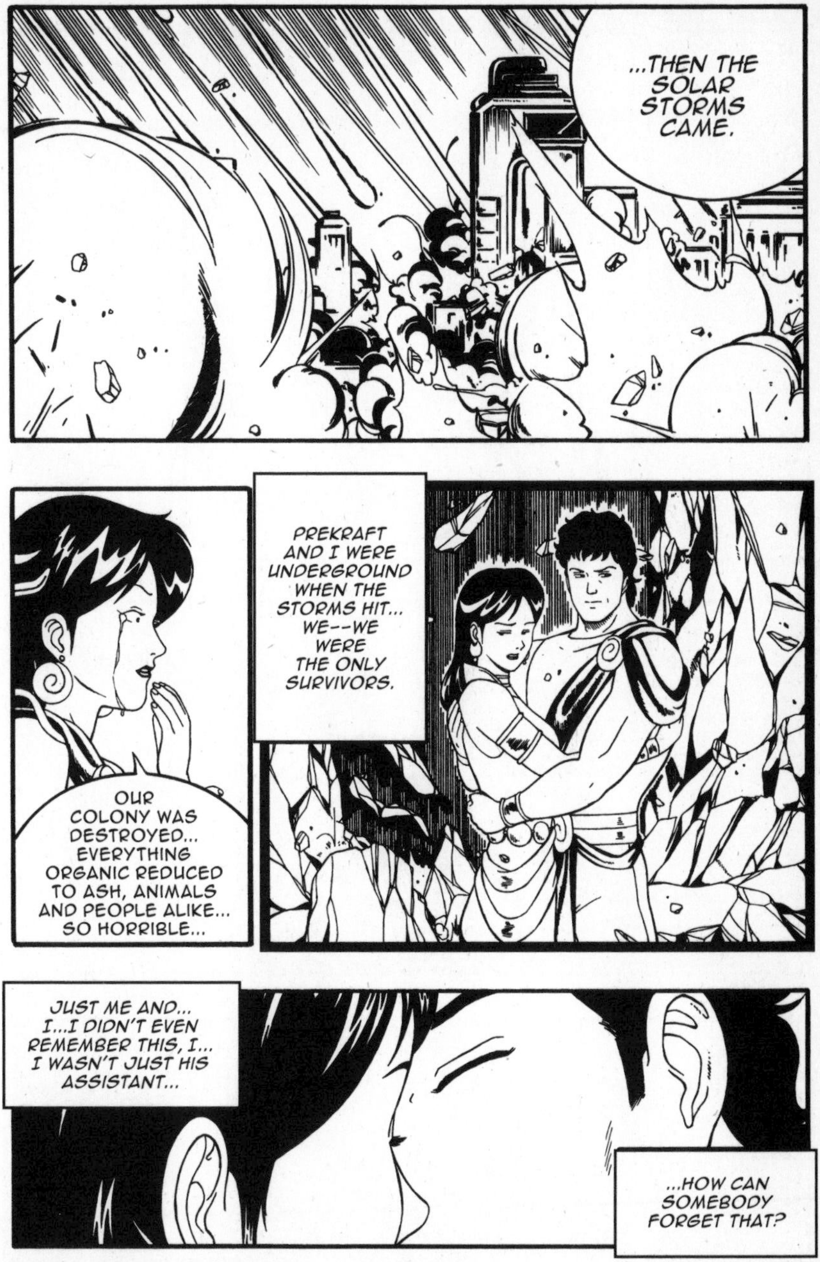
...THEN THE SOLAR STORMS CAME.
PREKRAFT AND I WERE UNDERGROUND WHEN THE STORMS HIT... WE--WE WERE THE ONLY SURVIVORS.
OUR COLONY WAS DESTROYED... EVERYTHING ORGANIC REDUCED TO ASH, ANIMALS AND PEOPLE ALIKE... SO HORRIBLE...
JUST ME AND... I...I DIDN'T EVEN REMEMBER THIS, I... I WASN'T JUST HIS ASSISTANT...
...HOW CAN SOMEBODY FORGET THAT?

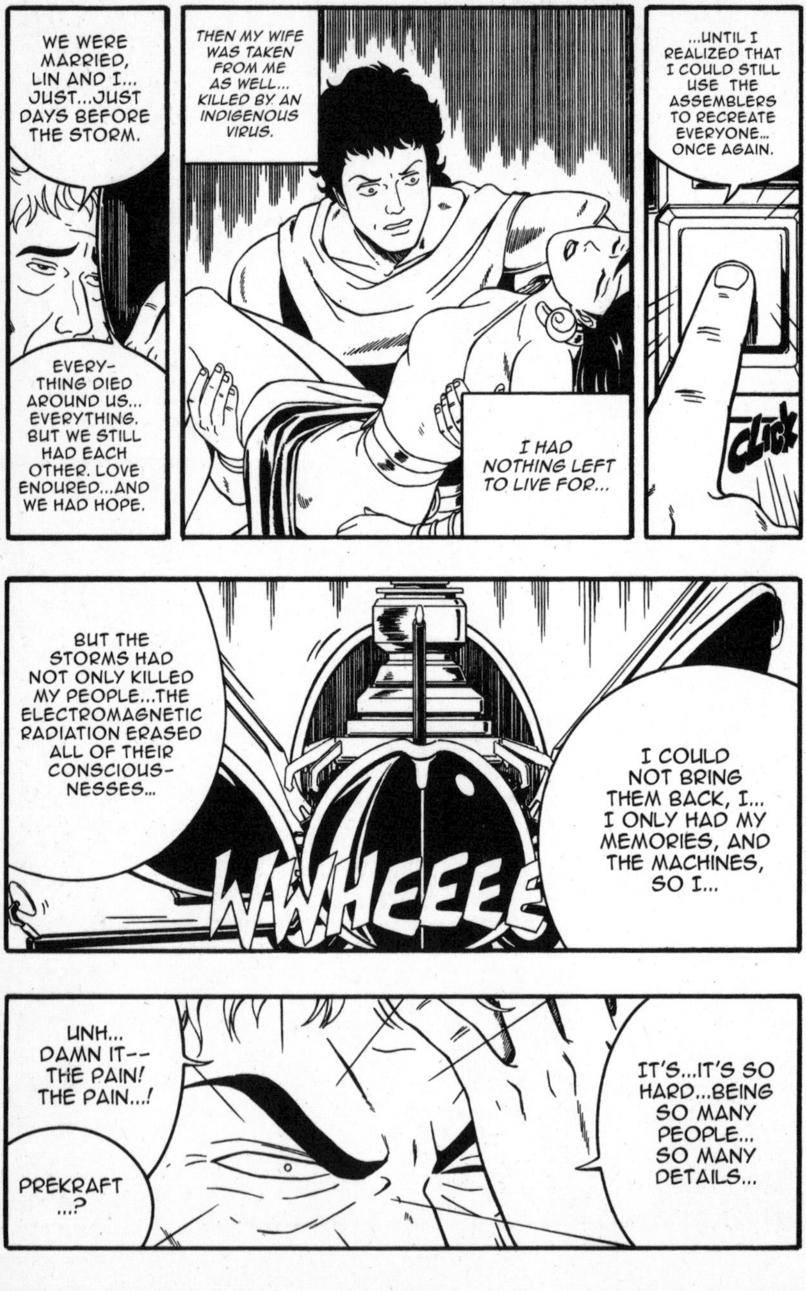
WE WERE MARRIED, LIN AND I... JUST...JUST DAYS BEFORE THE STORM.
EVERY-THING DIED AROUND US... EVERYTHING. BUT WE STILL HAD EACH OTHER. LOVE ENDURED...AND WE HAD HOPE.
THEN MY WIFE WAS TAKEN FROM ME AS WELL... KILLED BY AN INDIGENOUS VIRUS.
I HAD NOTHING LEFT TO LIVE FOR...
...UNTIL I REALIZED THAT I COULD STILL USE THE ASSEMBLERS TO RECREATE EVERYONE... ONCE AGAIN.
CLICK
BUT THE STORMS HAD NOT ONLY KILLED MY PEOPLE...THE ELECTROMAGNETIC RADIATION ERASED ALL OF THEIR CONSCIOUS-NESSES...
WWHEEEE
I COULD NOT BRING THEM BACK, I... I ONLY HAD MY MEMORIES, AND THE MACHINES, SO I...
UNH... DAMN IT-- THE PAIN! THE PAIN...!
PREKRAFT ...?
IT'S...IT'S SO HARD...BEING SO MANY PEOPLE... SO MANY DETAILS...

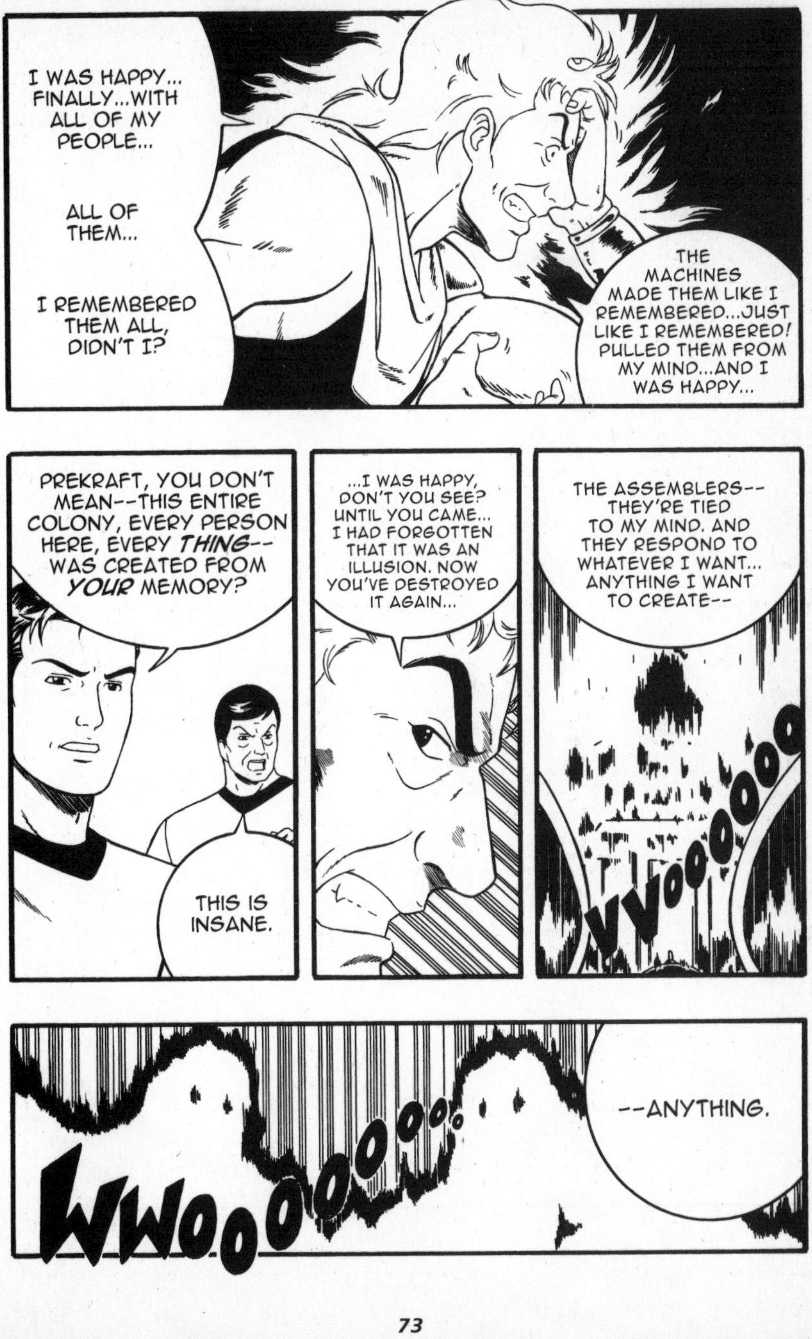
I WAS HAPPY... FINALLY...WITH ALL OF MY PEOPLE...
ALL OF THEM...
I REMEMBERED THEM ALL, DIDN'T I?
THE MACHINES MADE THEM LIKE I REMEMBERED...JUST LIKE I REMEMBERED! PULLED THEM FROM MY MIND...AND I WAS HAPPY...
PREKRAFT, YOU DON'T MEAN--THIS ENTIRE COLONY, EVERY PERSON HERE, EVERY *THING*--WAS CREATED FROM *YOUR* MEMORY?
THIS IS INSANE.
...I WAS HAPPY, DON'T YOU SEE? UNTIL YOU CAME... I HAD FORGOTTEN THAT IT WAS AN ILLUSION. NOW YOU'VE DESTROYED IT AGAIN...
THE ASSEMBLERS--THEY'RE TIED TO MY MIND. AND THEY RESPOND TO WHATEVER I WANT... ANYTHING I WANT TO CREATE--
VVOOOOOOO
WWOOOOOOOOO
--ANYTHING.

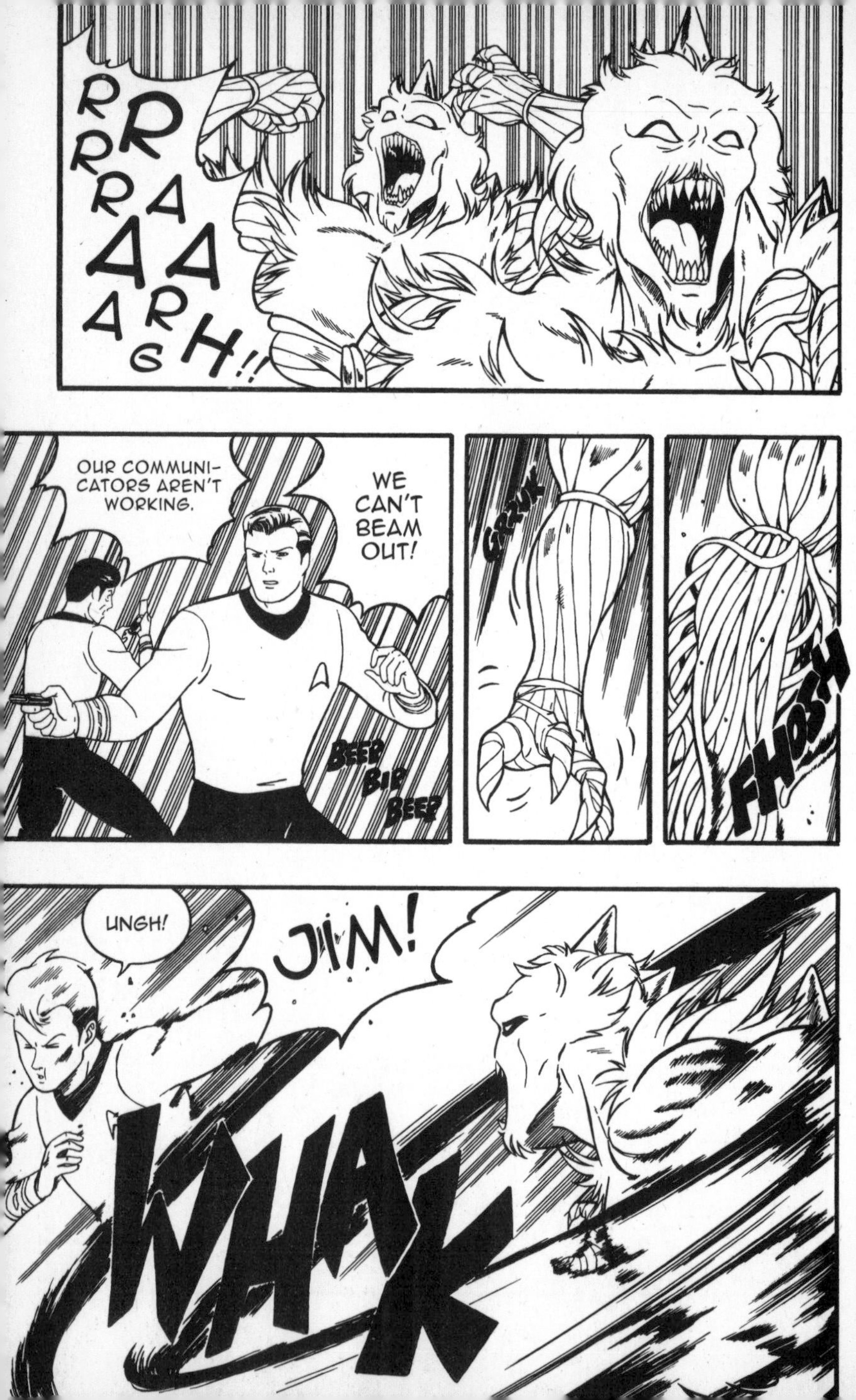
RRRRAAAARGH!!
OUR COMMUNI-CATORS AREN'T WORKING.
WE CAN'T BEAM OUT!
BEEP BIP BEEP
GRRUK
FHOSH
UNGH!
JIM!
WHAK

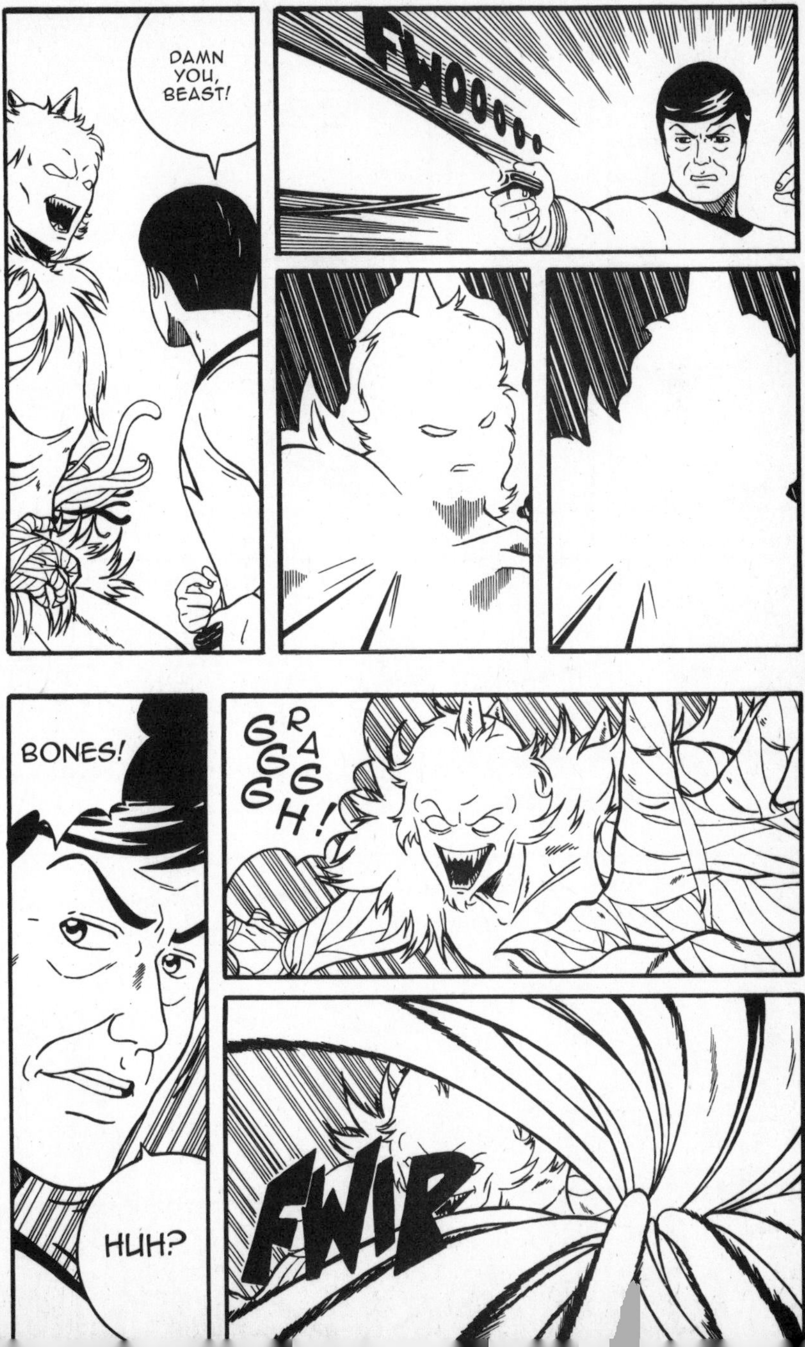
DAMN YOU, BEAST!
FWOOOOO
BONES!
GRAGGGGH!
HUH?
FWIP

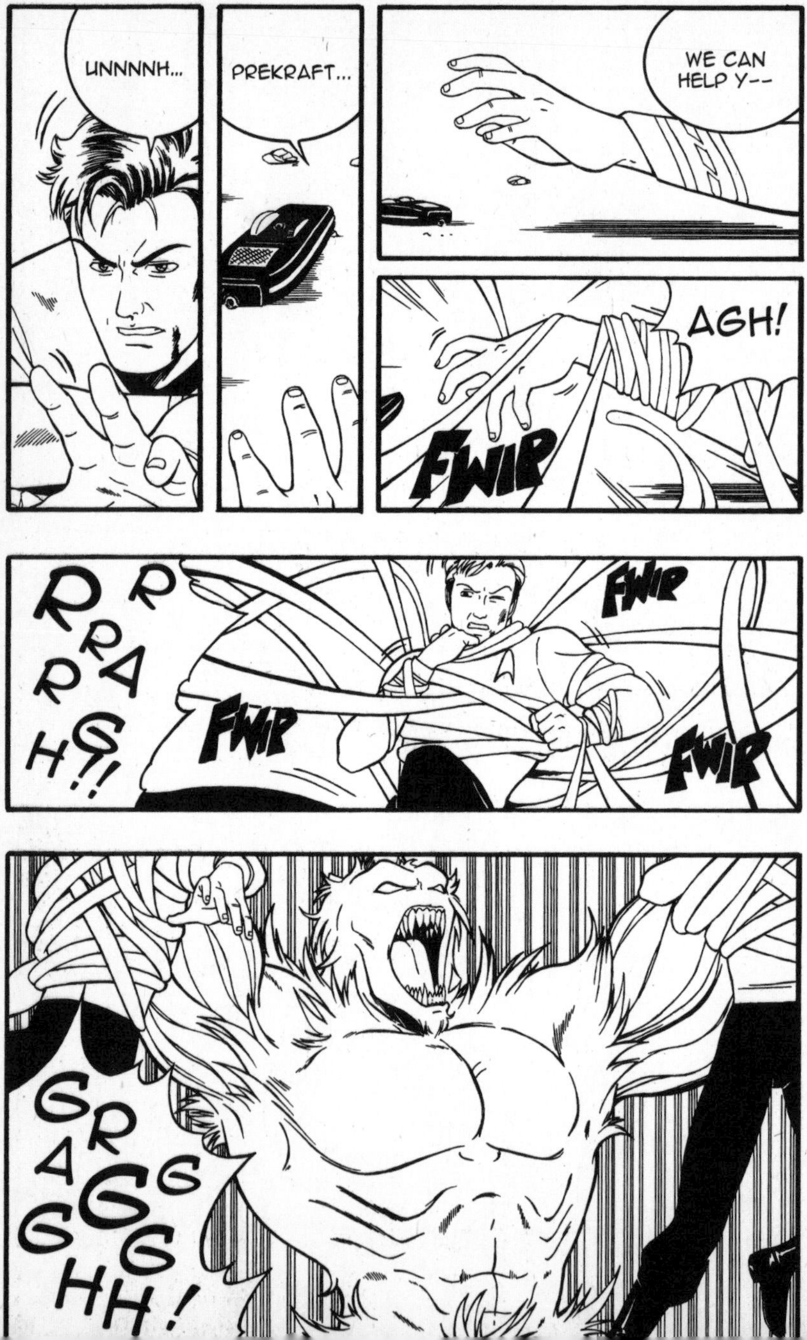
UNNNNH...
PREKRAFT...
WE CAN HELP Y--
AGH!
FWIP
RRRASH?!!
FWIP
FWIP
FWIP
GRAGGGGHH!

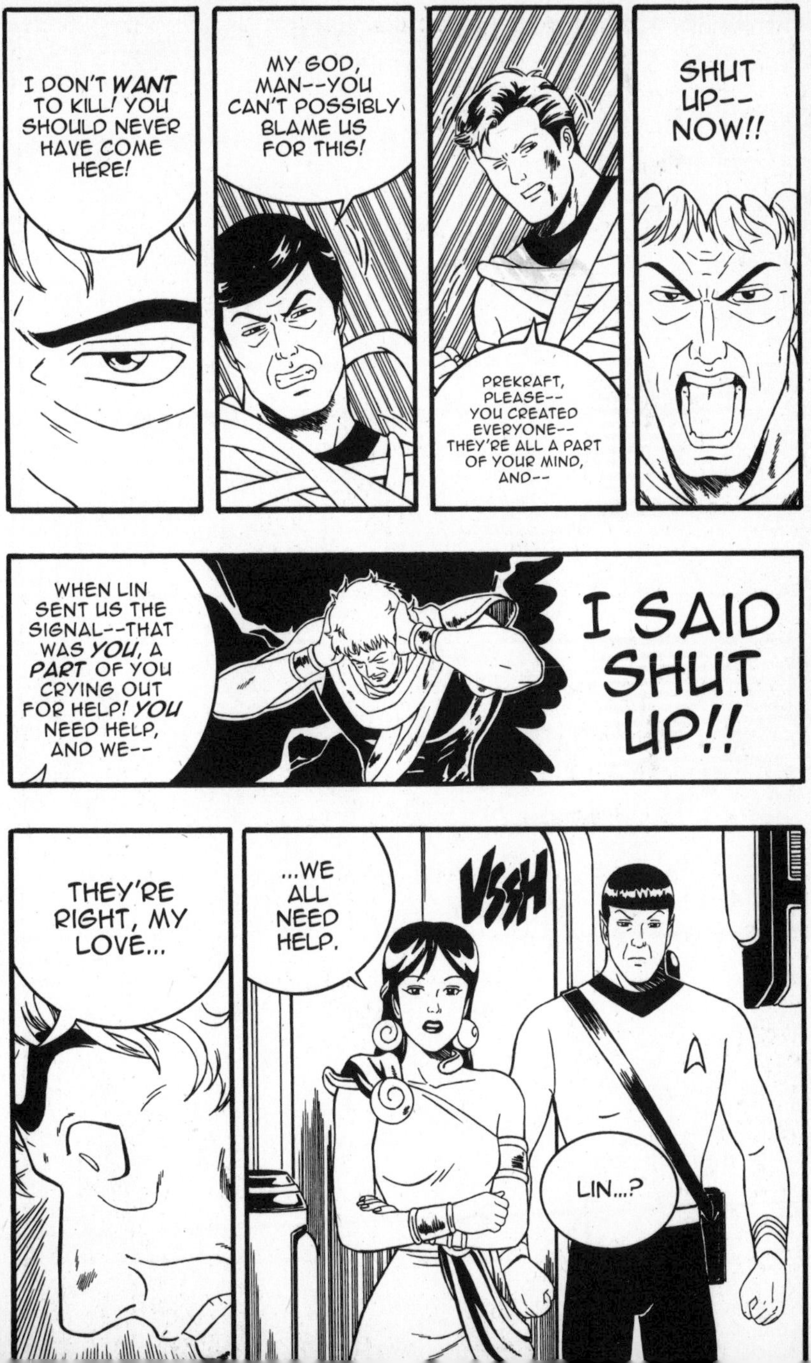
I DON'T *WANT* TO KILL! YOU SHOULD NEVER HAVE COME HERE!
MY GOD, MAN--YOU CAN'T POSSIBLY BLAME US FOR THIS!
PREKRAFT, PLEASE-- YOU CREATED EVERYONE-- THEY'RE ALL A PART OF YOUR MIND, AND--
SHUT UP-- NOW!!
WHEN LIN SENT US THE SIGNAL--THAT WAS *YOU*, A *PART* OF YOU CRYING OUT FOR HELP! *YOU* NEED HELP, AND WE--
I SAID SHUT UP!!
THEY'RE RIGHT, MY LOVE...
...WE ALL NEED HELP.
VSSH
LIN...?

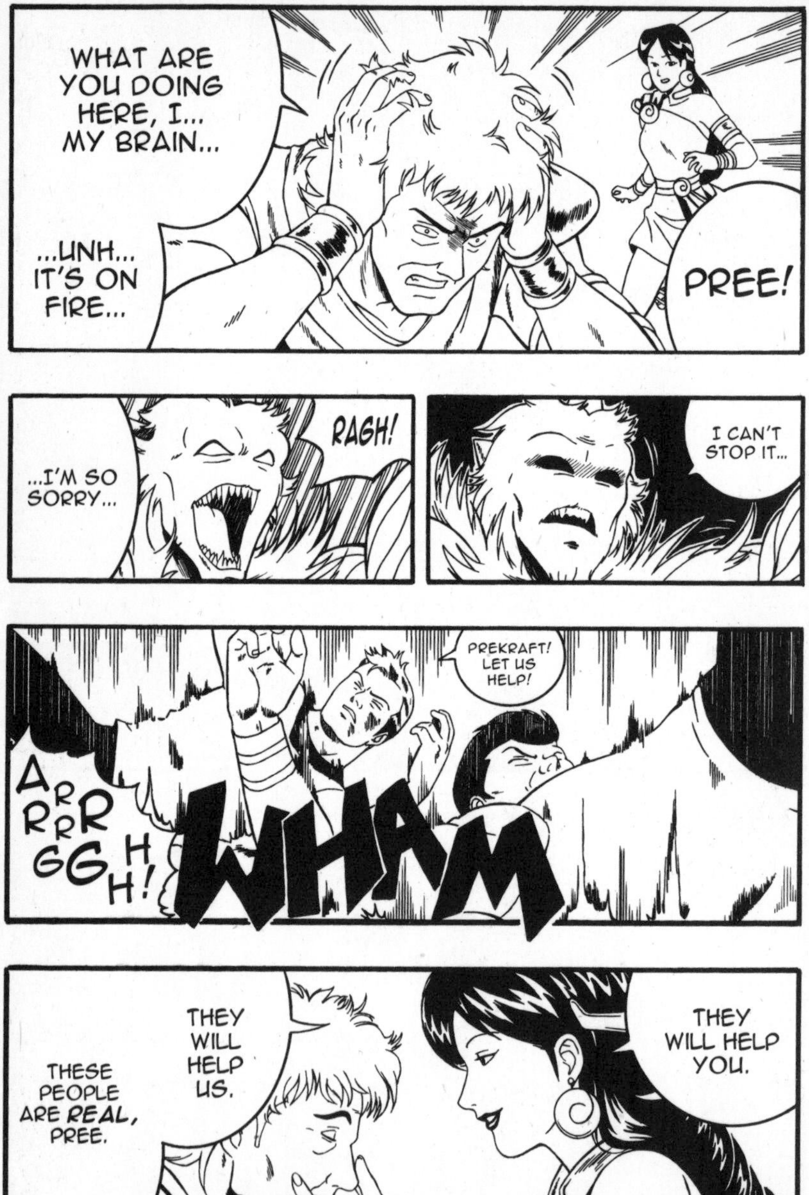
WHAT ARE YOU DOING HERE, I... MY BRAIN...
...UNH... IT'S ON FIRE...
PREE!
...I'M SO SORRY...
RAGH!
I CAN'T STOP IT...
PREKRAFT! LET US HELP!
ARRRRGGHH!
WHAM
THESE PEOPLE ARE REAL, PREE.
THEY WILL HELP US.
THEY WILL HELP YOU.

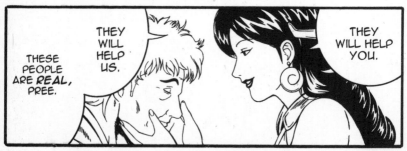

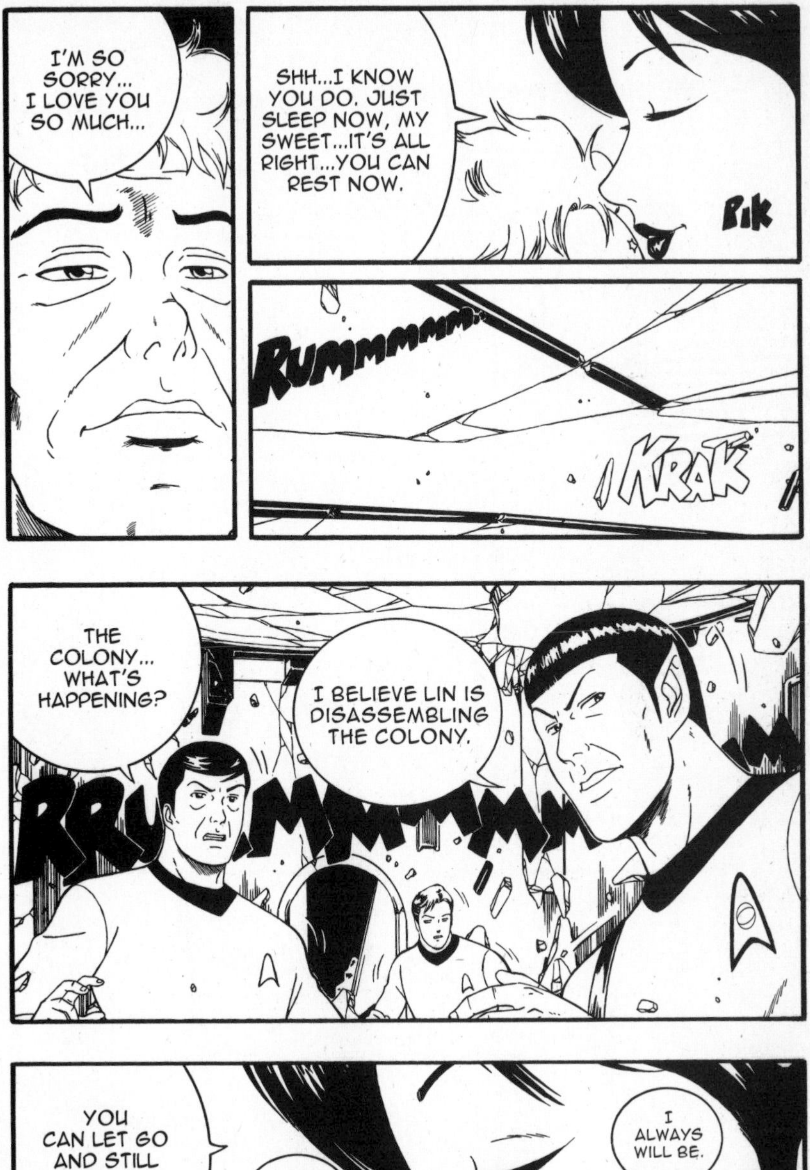
I'M SO SORRY... I LOVE YOU SO MUCH...
SHH...I KNOW YOU DO. JUST SLEEP NOW, MY SWEET...IT'S ALL RIGHT...YOU CAN REST NOW.
PIK
RUMMMMM
KRAK
THE COLONY... WHAT'S HAPPENING?
I BELIEVE LIN IS DISASSEMBLING THE COLONY.
RRUMMMMM
YOU CAN LET GO AND STILL REMEMBER ME.
I AM WITH YOU.
I ALWAYS WILL BE.

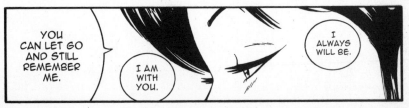

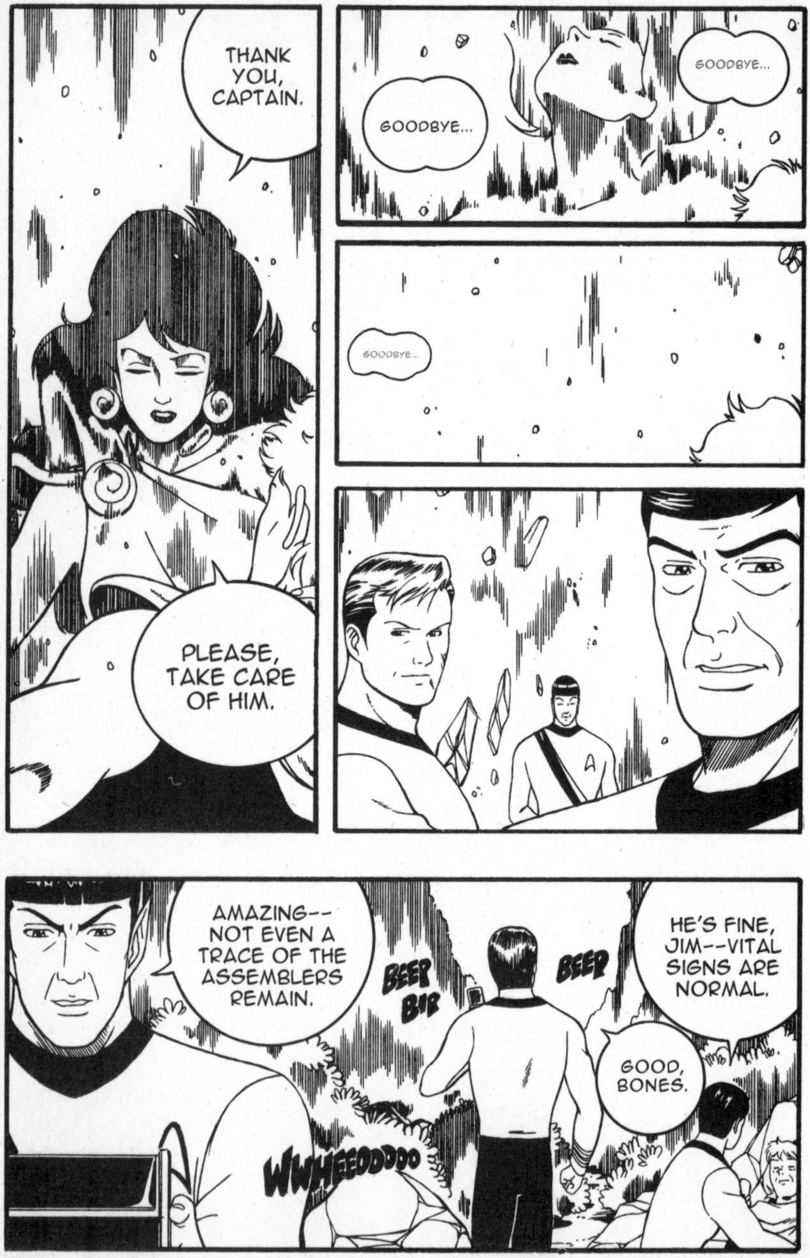
THANK YOU, CAPTAIN.
PLEASE, TAKE CARE OF HIM.
GOODBYE...
GOODBYE...
GOODBYE...
AMAZING-- NOT EVEN A TRACE OF THE ASSEMBLERS REMAIN.
BEEP
BIB
BEEP
HE'S FINE, JIM--VITAL SIGNS ARE NORMAL.
GOOD, BONES.
WWHEEDDDDO

SCOTTY--KIRK HERE. BEAM US UP...PLUS ONE.

WWOOOOOO

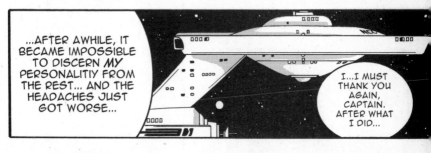

...AFTER AWHILE, IT BECAME IMPOSSIBLE TO DISCERN *MY* PERSONALITIY FROM THE REST... AND THE HEADACHES JUST GOT WORSE...

I...I MUST THANK YOU AGAIN, CAPTAIN. AFTER WHAT I DID...

IT'S THE PAST, PREKRAFT-- DON'T DWELL ON IT.

YOU'RE RIGHT-- AND THAT'S EXACTLY WHAT LIN WOULD HAVE TOLD ME. I WILL ALWAYS CHERISH HER MEMORY, CAPTAIN KIRK...AND THIS CHANCE AT A NEW BEGINNING.

I'M SURE YOU WILL.

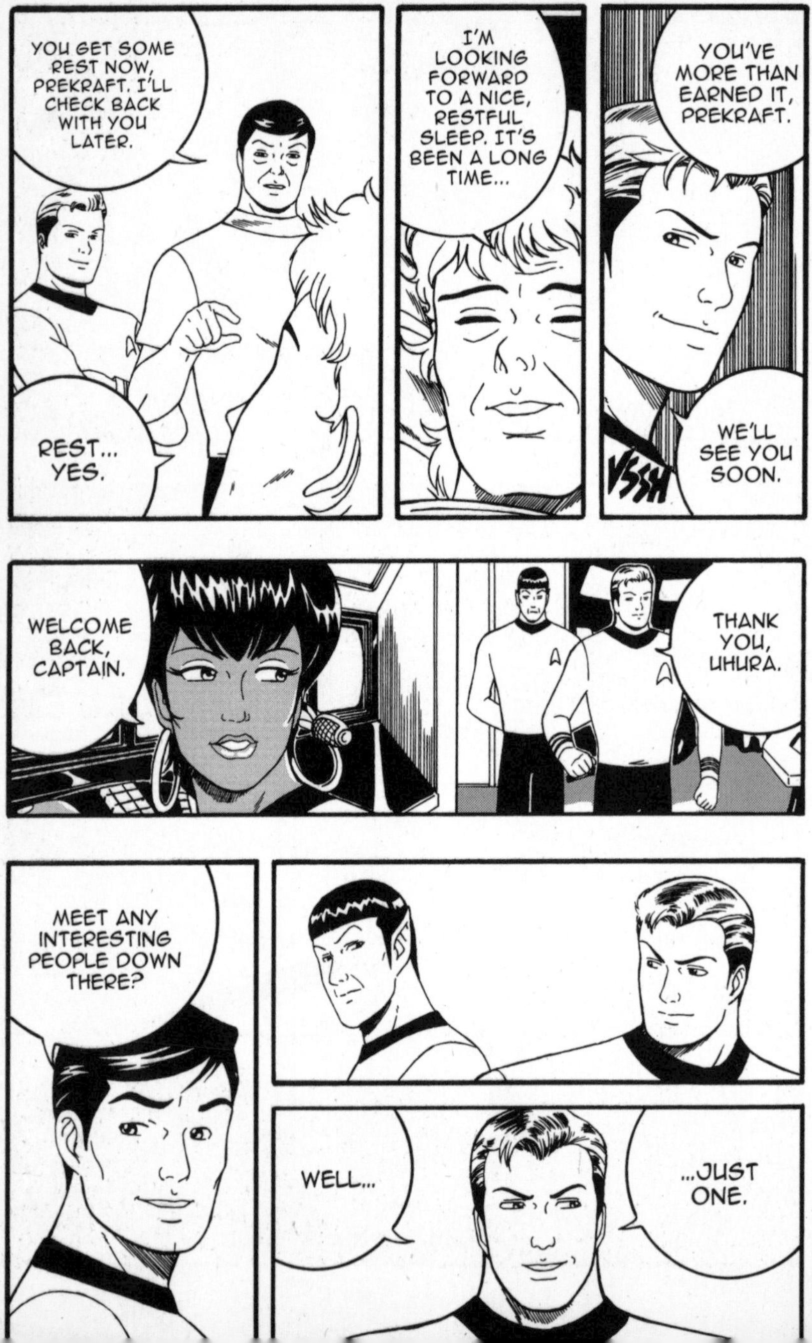
YOU GET SOME REST NOW, PREKRAFT. I'LL CHECK BACK WITH YOU LATER.
REST... YES.
I'M LOOKING FORWARD TO A NICE, RESTFUL SLEEP. IT'S BEEN A LONG TIME...
YOU'VE MORE THAN EARNED IT, PREKRAFT.
VSSH
WE'LL SEE YOU SOON.
WELCOME BACK, CAPTAIN.
THANK YOU, UHURA.
MEET ANY INTERESTING PEOPLE DOWN THERE?
WELL...
...JUST ONE.

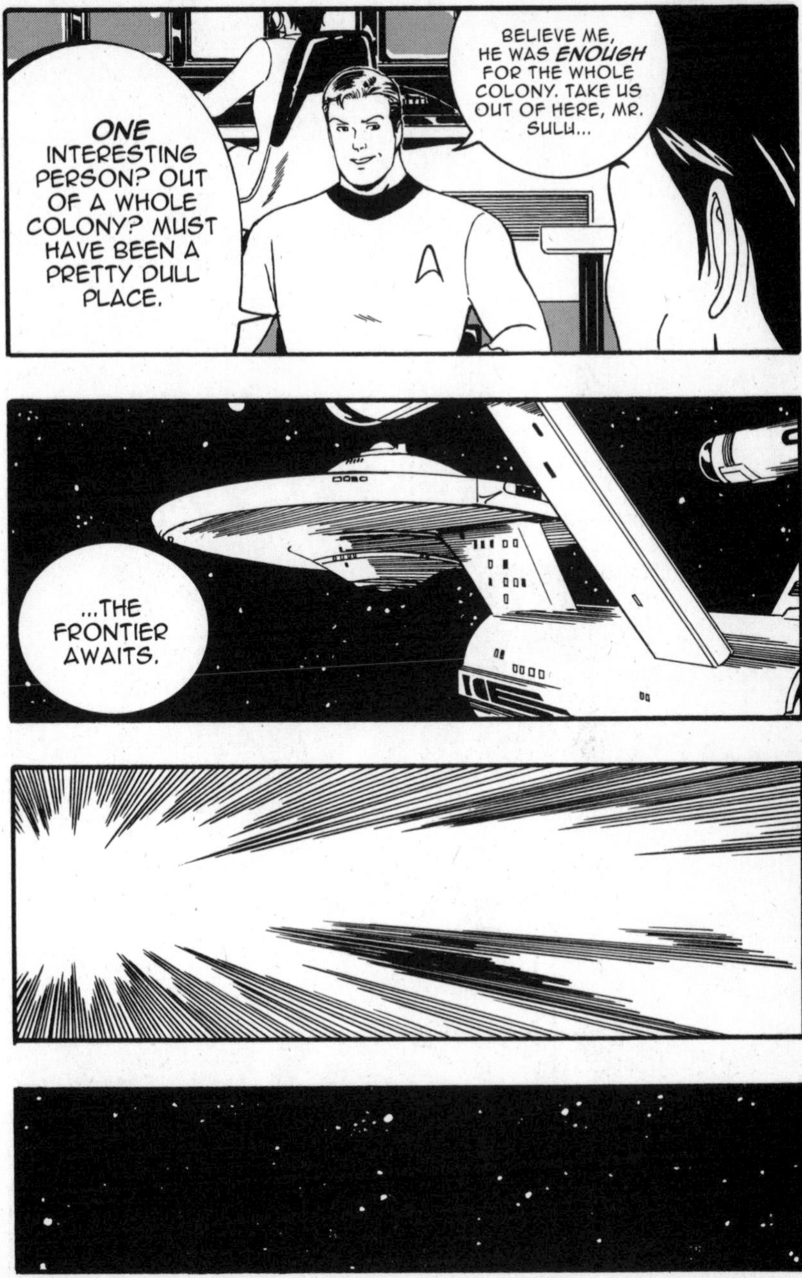
ONE INTERESTING PERSON? OUT OF A WHOLE COLONY? MUST HAVE BEEN A PRETTY DULL PLACE.
BELIEVE ME, HE WAS ENOUGH FOR THE WHOLE COLONY. TAKE US OUT OF HERE, MR. SULU...
...THE FRONTIER AWAITS.

'TIL DEATH

STORY BY MIKE W. BARR
ART BY JEONG MO YANG

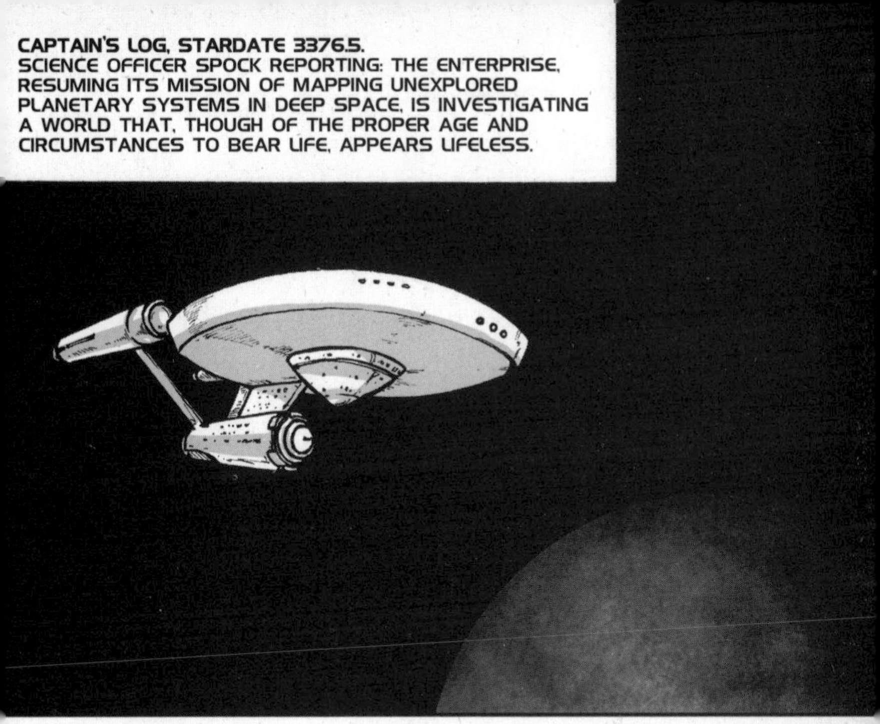
CAPTAIN'S LOG, STARDATE 3376.5.
SCIENCE OFFICER SPOCK REPORTING: THE ENTERPRISE, RESUMING ITS MISSION OF MAPPING UNEXPLORED PLANETARY SYSTEMS IN DEEP SPACE, IS INVESTIGATING A WORLD THAT, THOUGH OF THE PROPER AGE AND CIRCUMSTANCES TO BEAR LIFE, APPEARS LIFELESS.

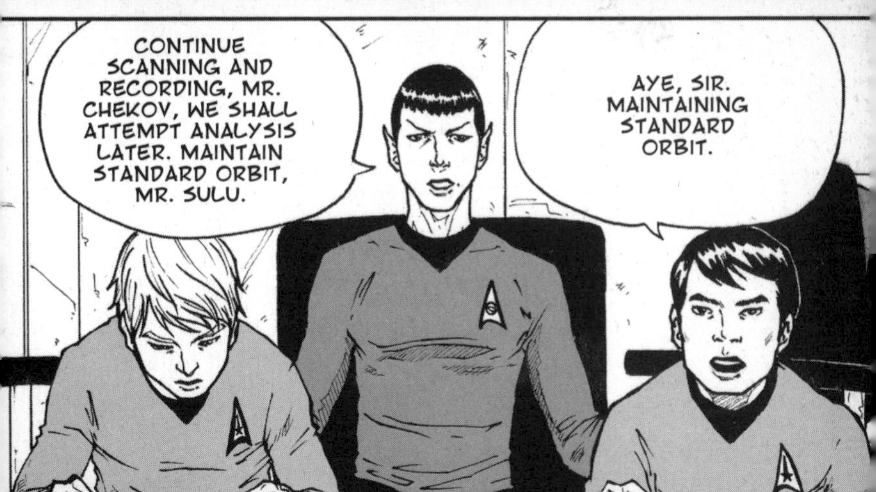
CONTINUE SCANNING AND RECORDING, MR. CHEKOV, WE SHALL ATTEMPT ANALYSIS LATER. MAINTAIN STANDARD ORBIT, MR. SULU.
AYE, SIR. MAINTAINING STANDARD ORBIT.

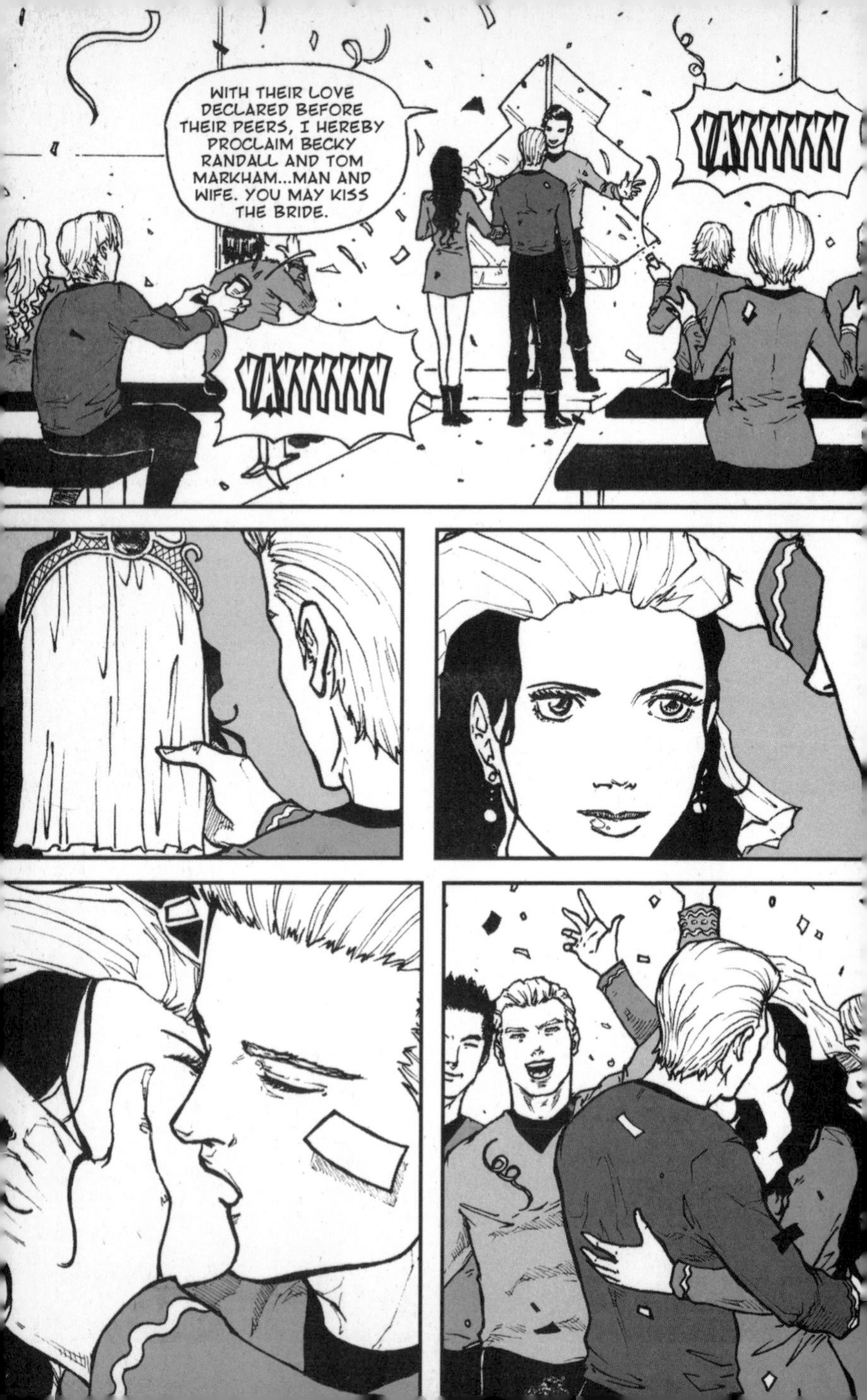
WITH THEIR LOVE DECLARED BEFORE THEIR PEERS, I HEREBY PROCLAIM BECKY RANDALL AND TOM MARKHAM...MAN AND WIFE. YOU MAY KISS THE BRIDE.
YAYYYYYY
YAYYYYYY

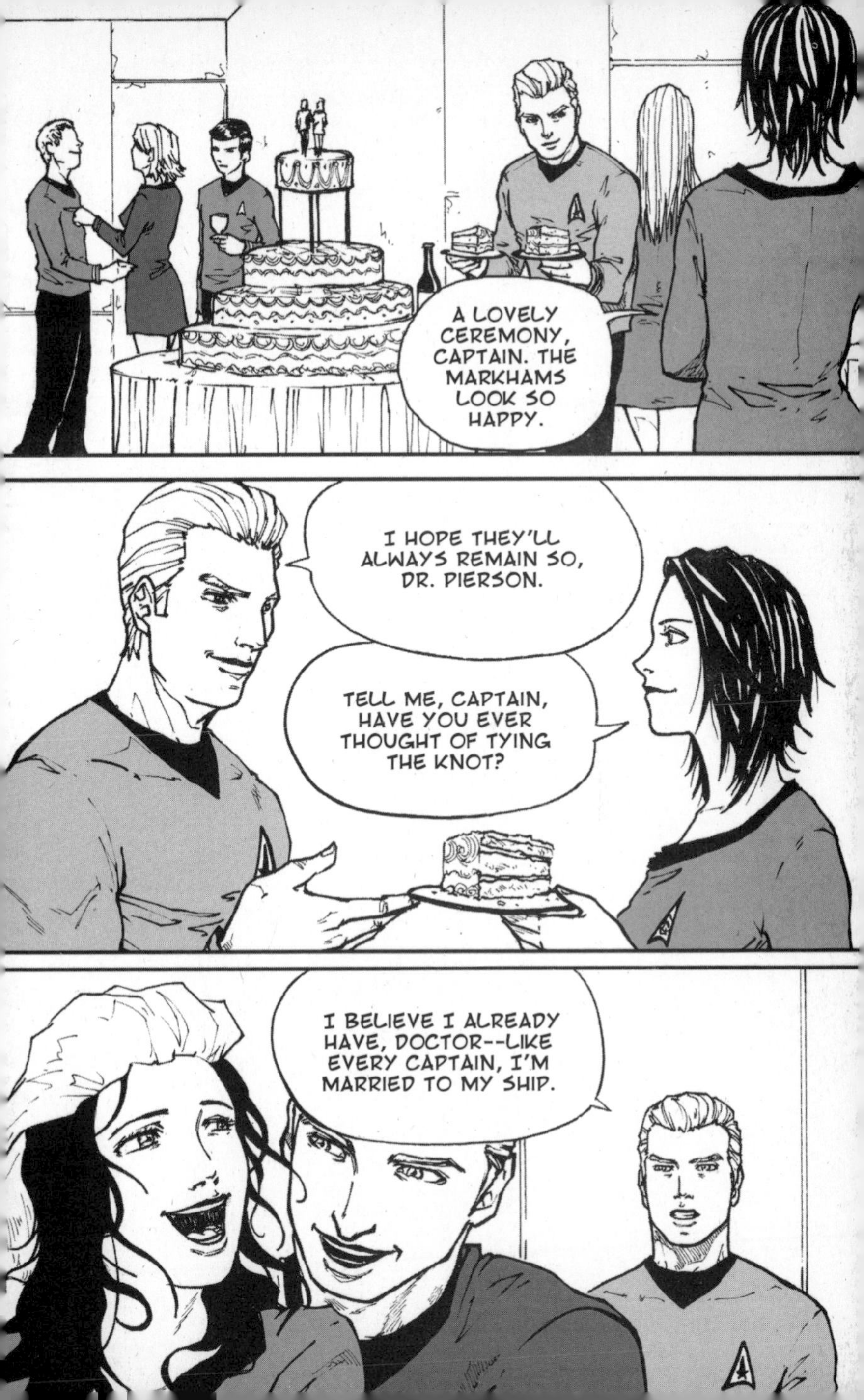
A LOVELY CEREMONY, CAPTAIN. THE MARKHAMS LOOK SO HAPPY.
I HOPE THEY'LL ALWAYS REMAIN SO, DR. PIERSON.
TELL ME, CAPTAIN, HAVE YOU EVER THOUGHT OF TYING THE KNOT?
I BELIEVE I ALREADY HAVE, DOCTOR--LIKE EVERY CAPTAIN, I'M MARRIED TO MY SHIP.

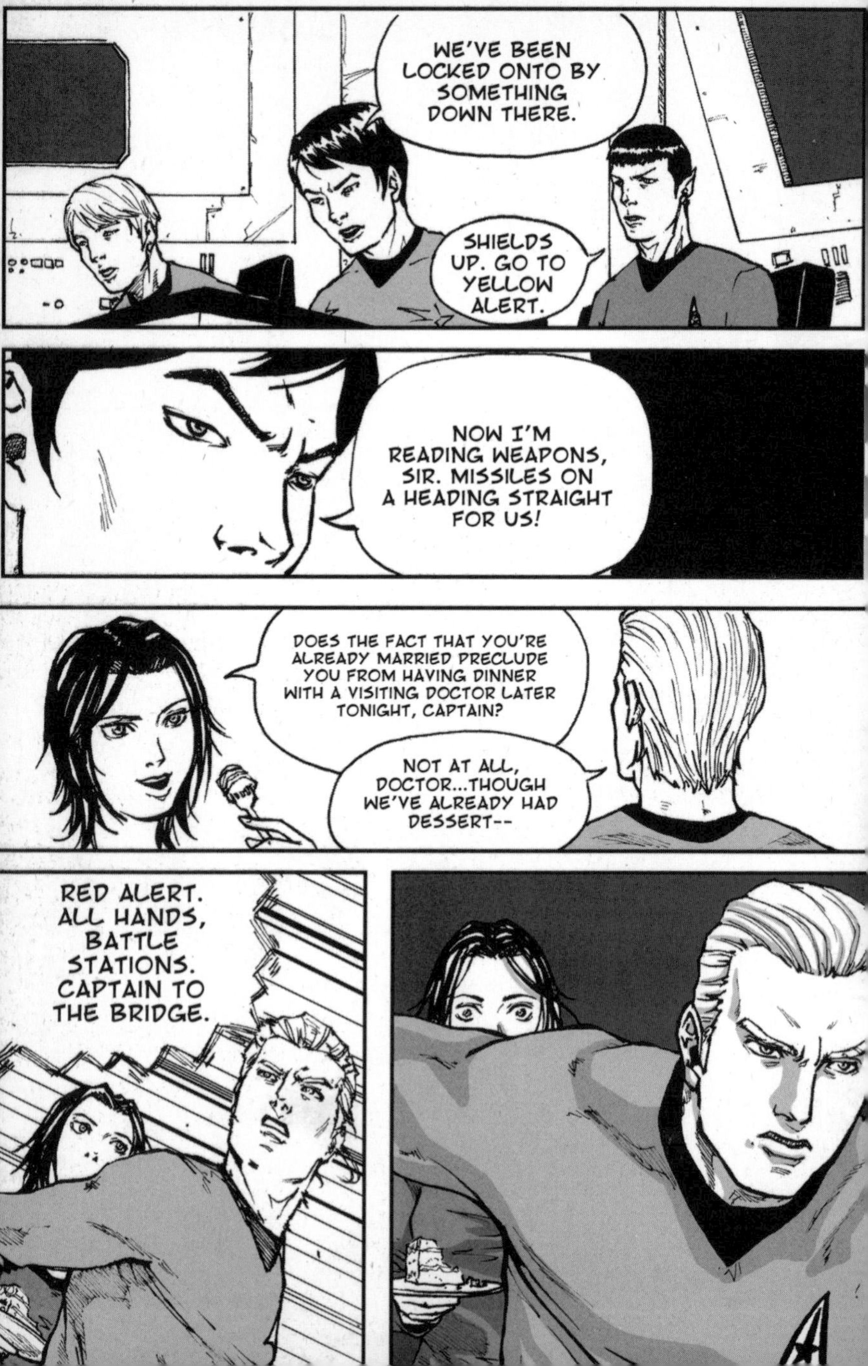
WE'VE BEEN LOCKED ONTO BY SOMETHING DOWN THERE.
SHIELDS UP. GO TO YELLOW ALERT.
NOW I'M READING WEAPONS, SIR. MISSILES ON A HEADING STRAIGHT FOR US!
DOES THE FACT THAT YOU'RE ALREADY MARRIED PRECLUDE YOU FROM HAVING DINNER WITH A VISITING DOCTOR LATER TONIGHT, CAPTAIN?
NOT AT ALL, DOCTOR...THOUGH WE'VE ALREADY HAD DESSERT--
RED ALERT. ALL HANDS, BATTLE STATIONS. CAPTAIN TO THE BRIDGE.

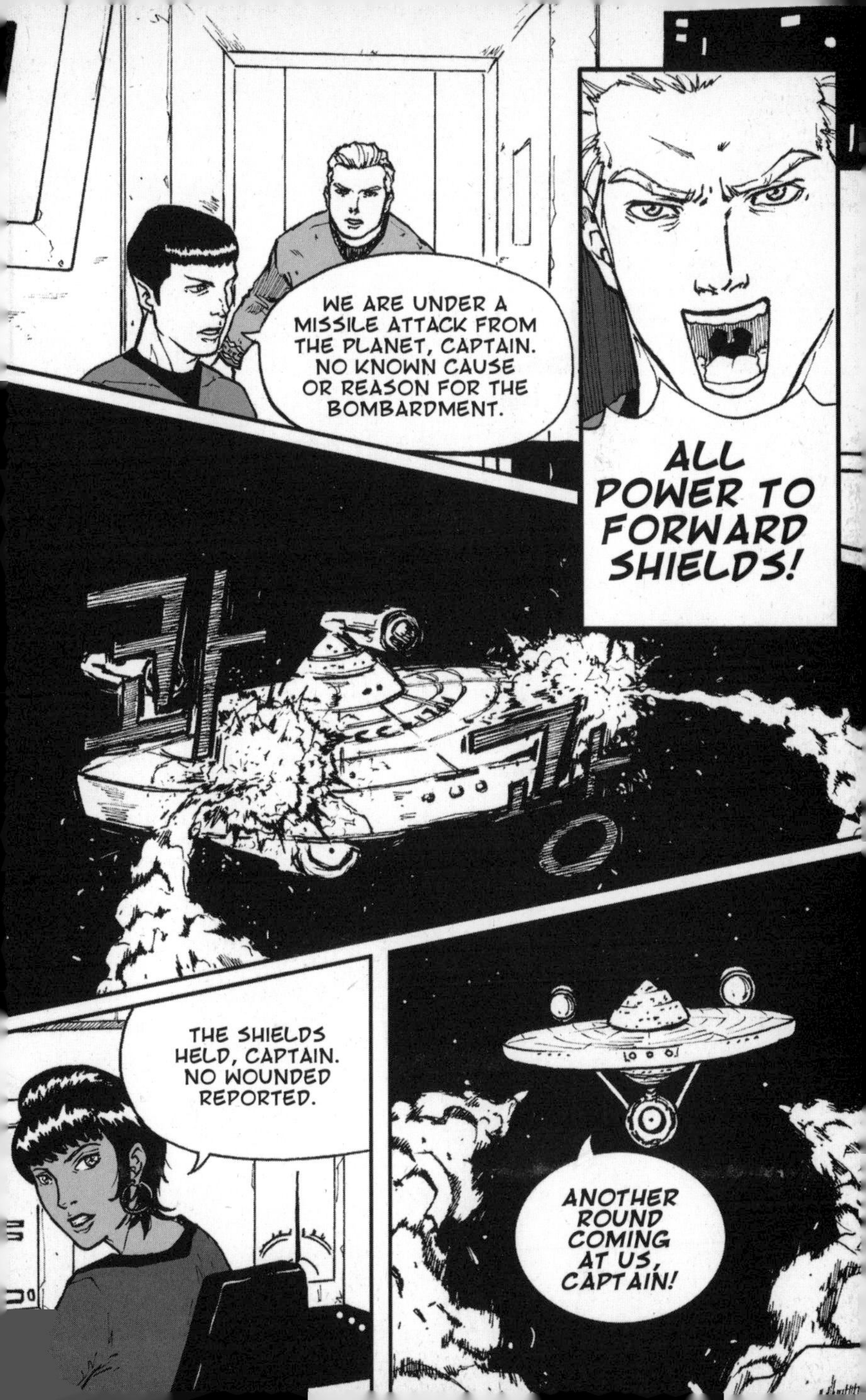
WE ARE UNDER A MISSILE ATTACK FROM THE PLANET, CAPTAIN. NO KNOWN CAUSE OR REASON FOR THE BOMBARDMENT.
ALL POWER TO FORWARD SHIELDS!
THE SHIELDS HELD, CAPTAIN. NO WOUNDED REPORTED.
ANOTHER ROUND COMING AT US, CAPTAIN!

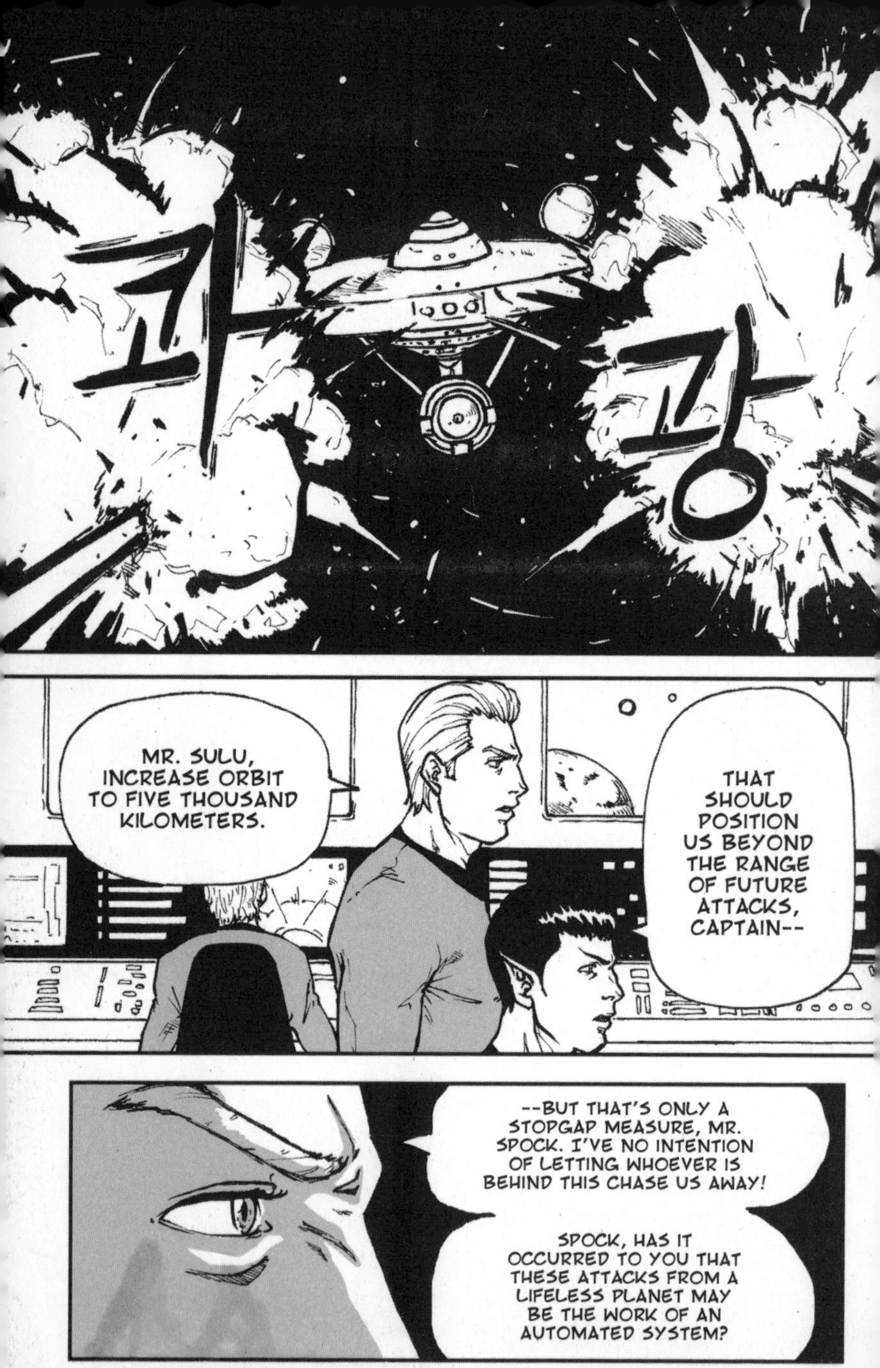
콰광
MR. SULU, INCREASE ORBIT TO FIVE THOUSAND KILOMETERS.
THAT SHOULD POSITION US BEYOND THE RANGE OF FUTURE ATTACKS, CAPTAIN--
--BUT THAT'S ONLY A STOPGAP MEASURE, MR. SPOCK. I'VE NO INTENTION OF LETTING WHOEVER IS BEHIND THIS CHASE US AWAY!
SPOCK, HAS IT OCCURRED TO YOU THAT THESE ATTACKS FROM A LIFELESS PLANET MAY BE THE WORK OF AN AUTOMATED SYSTEM?

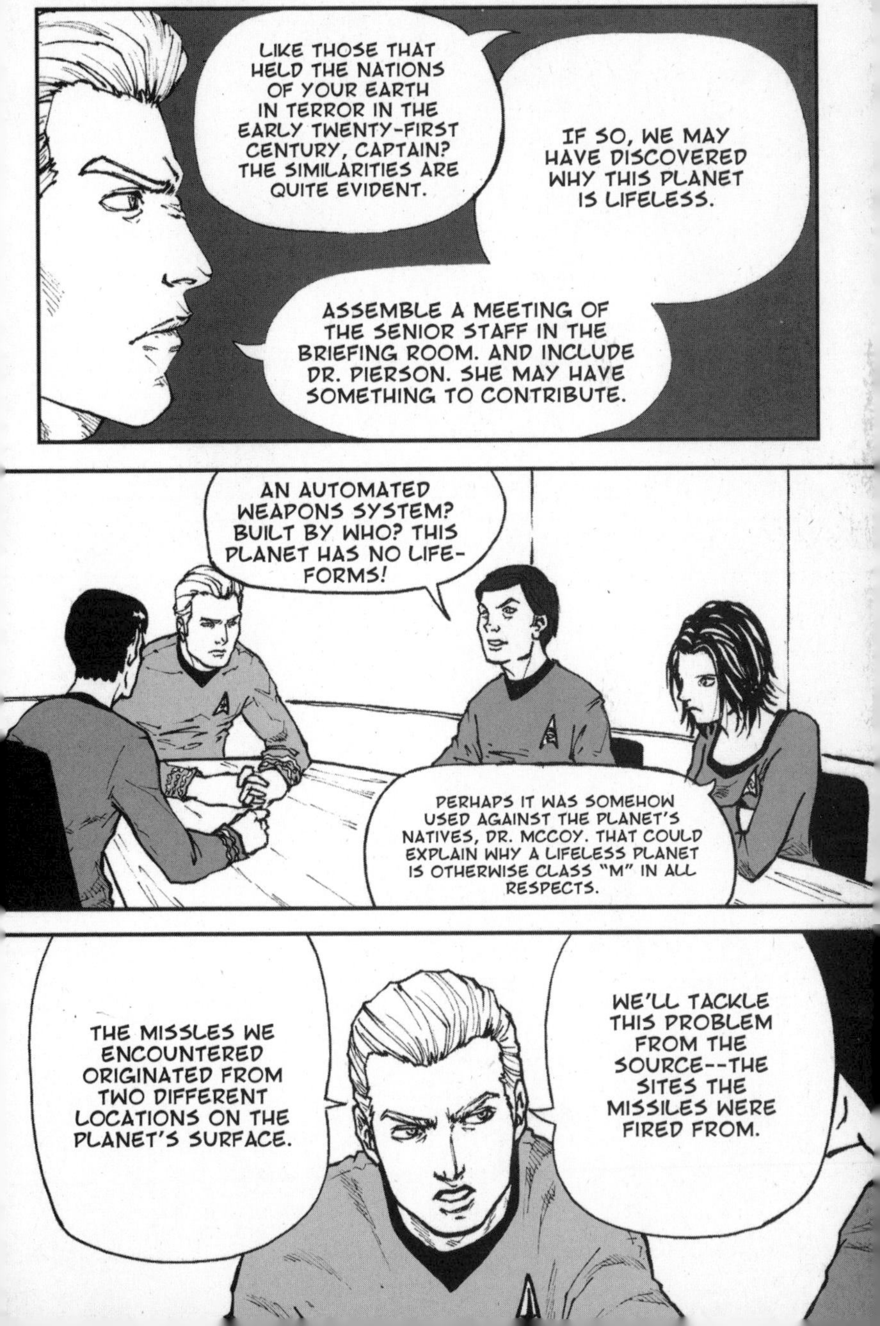
LIKE THOSE THAT HELD THE NATIONS OF YOUR EARTH IN TERROR IN THE EARLY TWENTY-FIRST CENTURY, CAPTAIN? THE SIMILARITIES ARE QUITE EVIDENT.
IF SO, WE MAY HAVE DISCOVERED WHY THIS PLANET IS LIFELESS.
ASSEMBLE A MEETING OF THE SENIOR STAFF IN THE BRIEFING ROOM. AND INCLUDE DR. PIERSON. SHE MAY HAVE SOMETHING TO CONTRIBUTE.
AN AUTOMATED WEAPONS SYSTEM? BUILT BY WHO? THIS PLANET HAS NO LIFE-FORMS!
PERHAPS IT WAS SOMEHOW USED AGAINST THE PLANET'S NATIVES, DR. MCCOY. THAT COULD EXPLAIN WHY A LIFELESS PLANET IS OTHERWISE CLASS "M" IN ALL RESPECTS.
THE MISSLES WE ENCOUNTERED ORIGINATED FROM TWO DIFFERENT LOCATIONS ON THE PLANET'S SURFACE.
WE'LL TACKLE THIS PROBLEM FROM THE SOURCE--THE SITES THE MISSILES WERE FIRED FROM.

I'LL COMMAND ONE LANDING PARTY...

...SPOCK, YOU'LL TAKE THE OTHER.

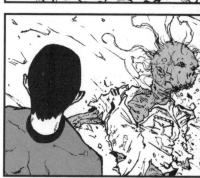

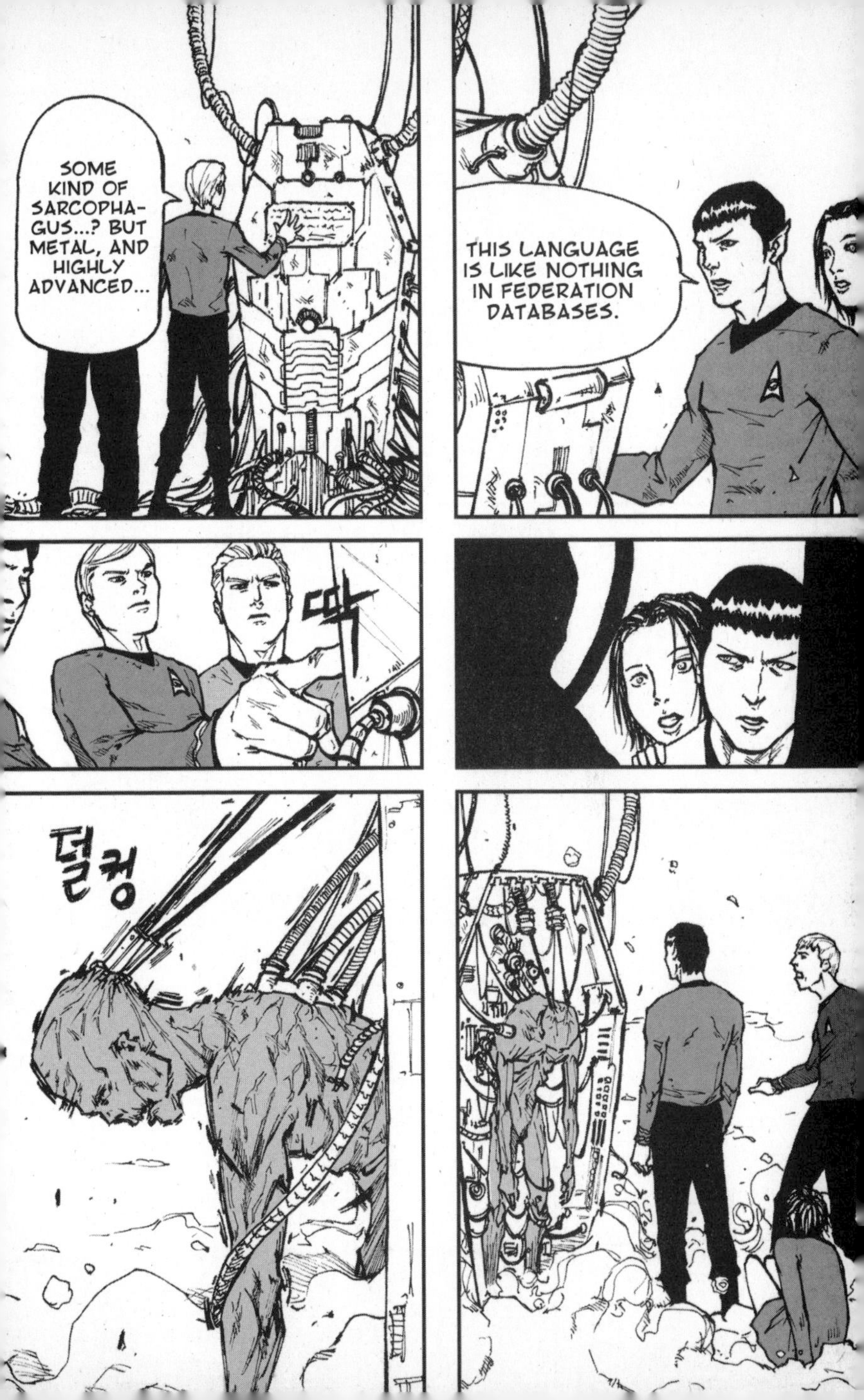
SOME KIND OF SARCOPHAGUS...? BUT METAL, AND HIGHLY ADVANCED...
THIS LANGUAGE IS LIKE NOTHING IN FEDERATION DATABASES.
덜컹

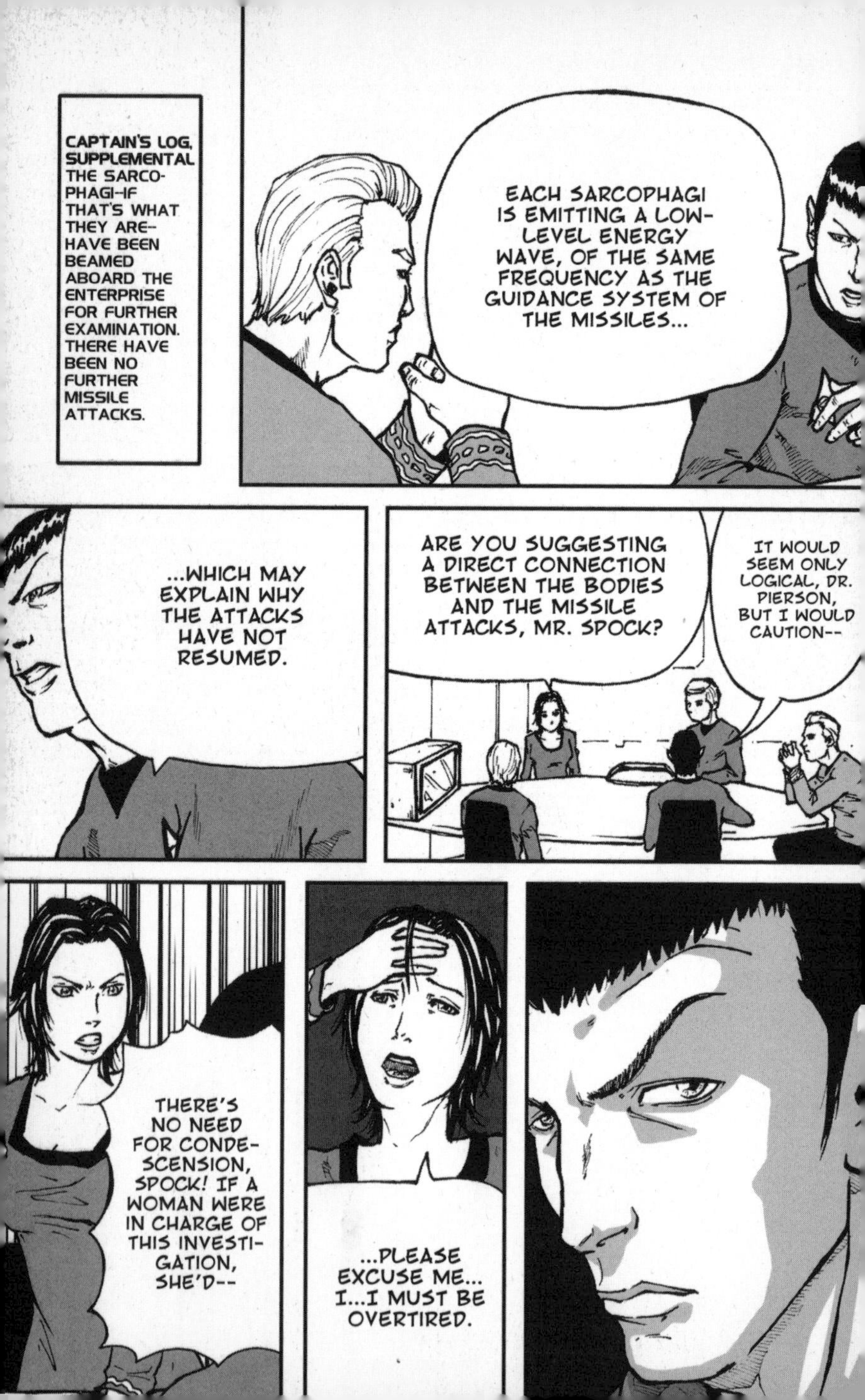
CAPTAIN'S LOG, SUPPLEMENTAL THE SARCOPHAGI--IF THAT'S WHAT THEY ARE--HAVE BEEN BEAMED ABOARD THE ENTERPRISE FOR FURTHER EXAMINATION. THERE HAVE BEEN NO FURTHER MISSILE ATTACKS.
EACH SARCOPHAGI IS EMITTING A LOW-LEVEL ENERGY WAVE, OF THE SAME FREQUENCY AS THE GUIDANCE SYSTEM OF THE MISSILES...
...WHICH MAY EXPLAIN WHY THE ATTACKS HAVE NOT RESUMED.
ARE YOU SUGGESTING A DIRECT CONNECTION BETWEEN THE BODIES AND THE MISSILE ATTACKS, MR. SPOCK?
IT WOULD SEEM ONLY LOGICAL, DR. PIERSON, BUT I WOULD CAUTION--
THERE'S NO NEED FOR CONDESCENSION, SPOCK! IF A WOMAN WERE IN CHARGE OF THIS INVESTIGATION, SHE'D--
...PLEASE EXCUSE ME... I...I MUST BE OVERTIRED.

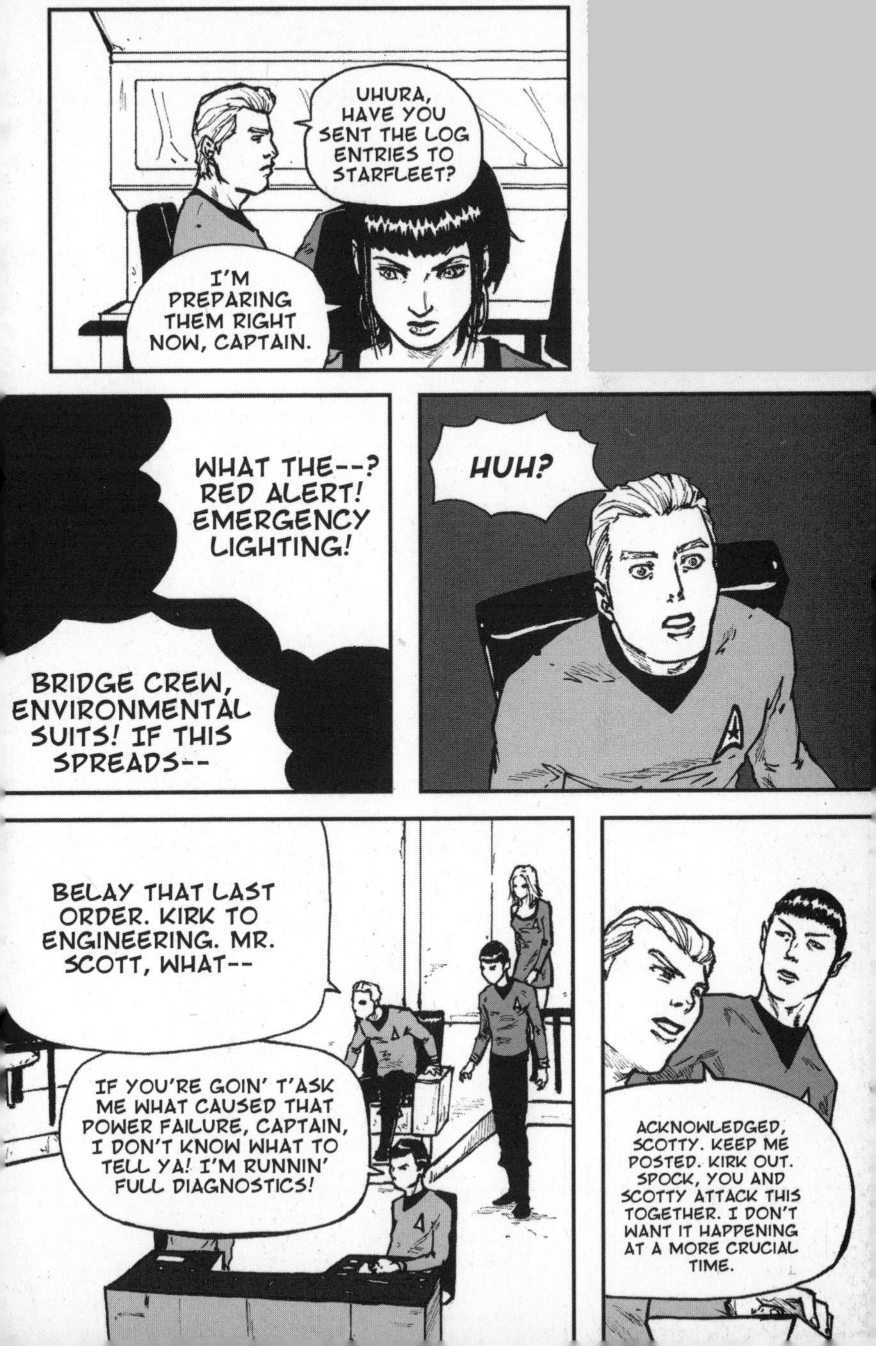
UHURA, HAVE YOU SENT THE LOG ENTRIES TO STARFLEET?
I'M PREPARING THEM RIGHT NOW, CAPTAIN.
WHAT THE--? RED ALERT! EMERGENCY LIGHTING!
BRIDGE CREW, ENVIRONMENTAL SUITS! IF THIS SPREADS--
HUH?
BELAY THAT LAST ORDER. KIRK TO ENGINEERING. MR. SCOTT, WHAT--
IF YOU'RE GOIN' T'ASK ME WHAT CAUSED THAT POWER FAILURE, CAPTAIN, I DON'T KNOW WHAT TO TELL YA! I'M RUNNIN' FULL DIAGNOSTICS!
ACKNOWLEDGED, SCOTTY. KEEP ME POSTED. KIRK OUT. SPOCK, YOU AND SCOTTY ATTACK THIS TOGETHER. I DON'T WANT IT HAPPENING AT A MORE CRUCIAL TIME.

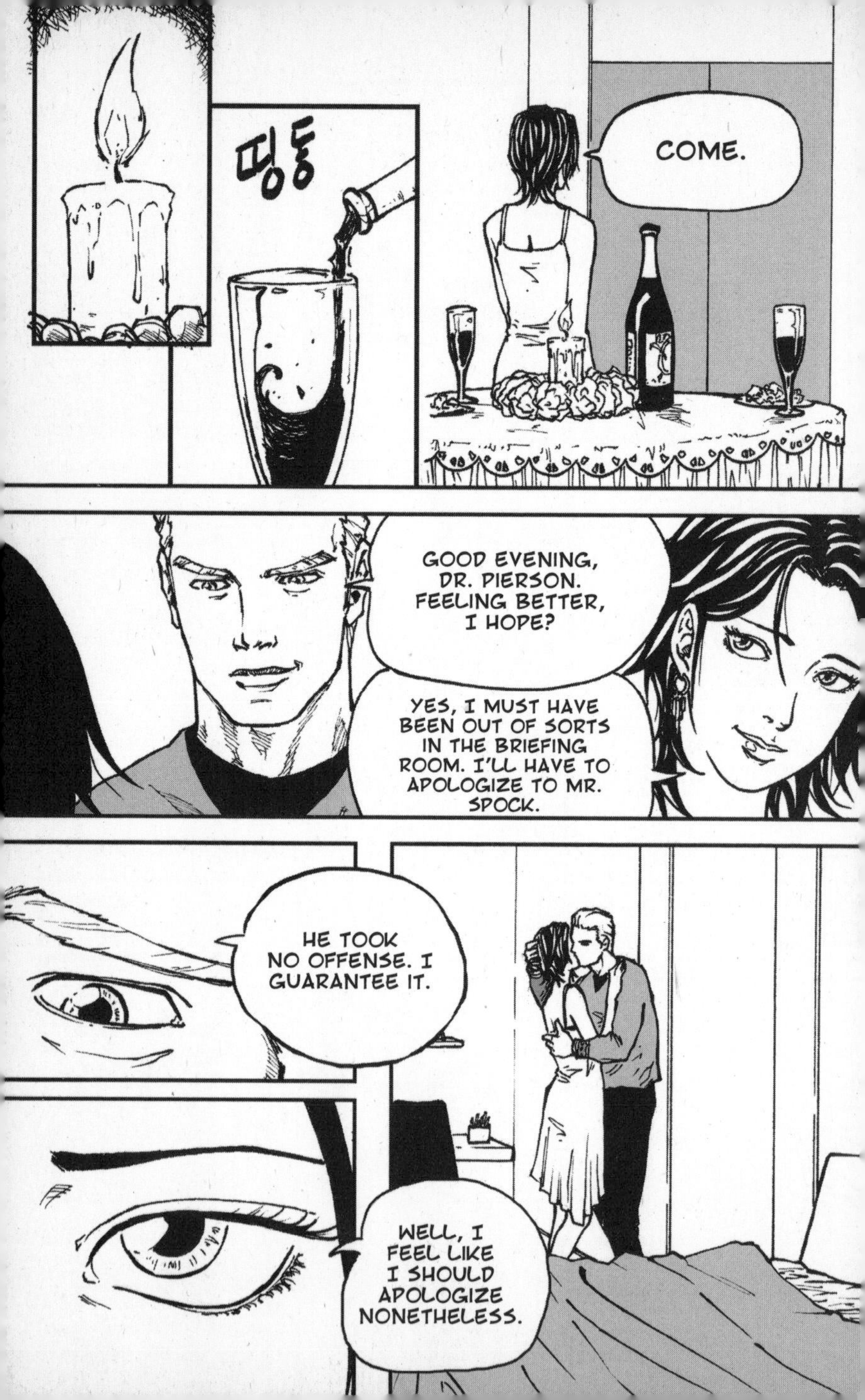

띵동
COME.
GOOD EVENING, DR. PIERSON. FEELING BETTER, I HOPE?
YES, I MUST HAVE BEEN OUT OF SORTS IN THE BRIEFING ROOM. I'LL HAVE TO APOLOGIZE TO MR. SPOCK.
HE TOOK NO OFFENSE. I GUARANTEE IT.
WELL, I FEEL LIKE I SHOULD APOLOGIZE NONETHELESS.

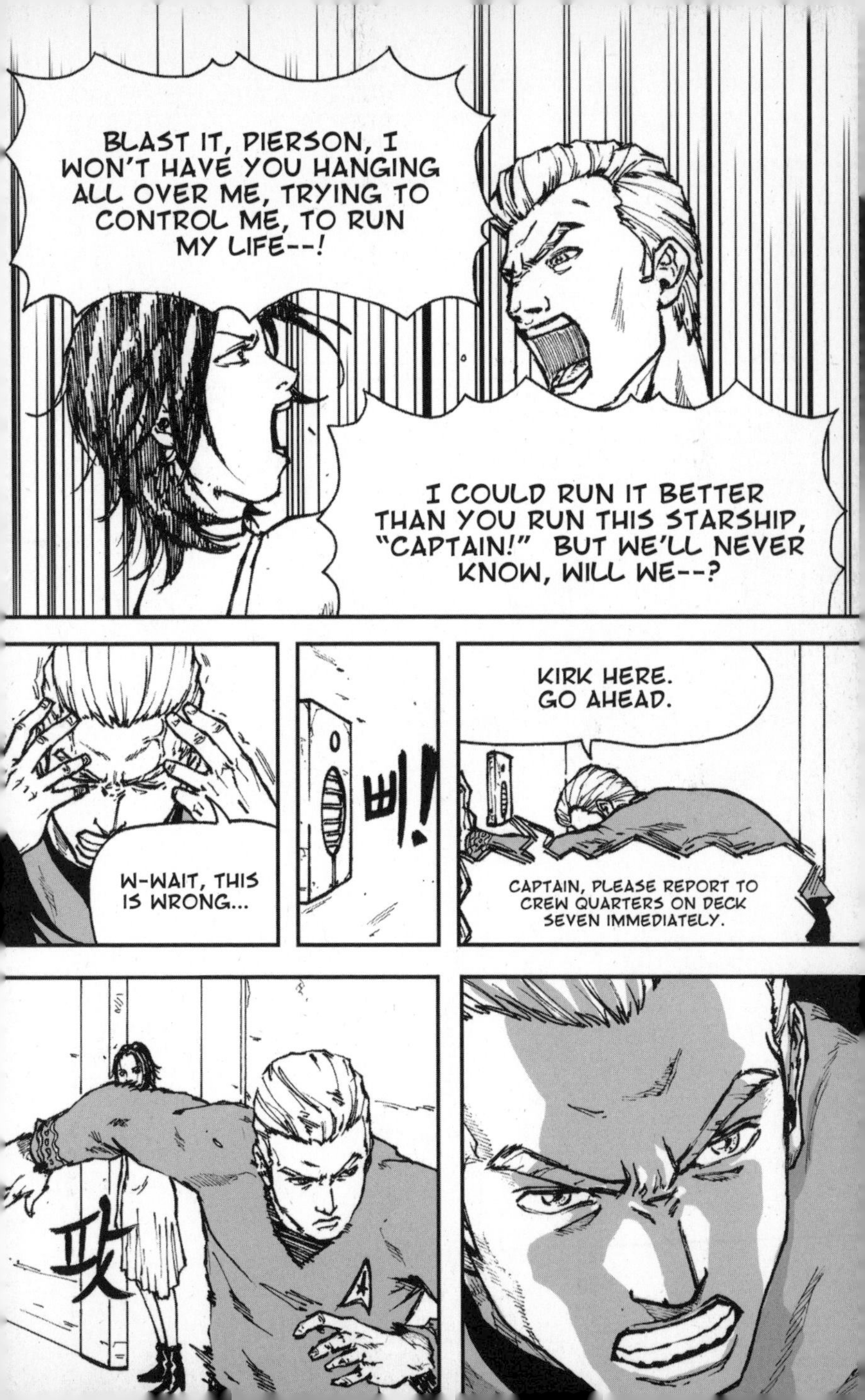
BLAST IT, PIERSON, I WON'T HAVE YOU HANGING ALL OVER ME, TRYING TO CONTROL ME, TO RUN MY LIFE--!
I COULD RUN IT BETTER THAN YOU RUN THIS STARSHIP, "CAPTAIN!" BUT WE'LL NEVER KNOW, WILL WE--?
W-WAIT, THIS IS WRONG...
삐!
KIRK HERE. GO AHEAD.
CAPTAIN, PLEASE REPORT TO CREW QUARTERS ON DECK SEVEN IMMEDIATELY.
팟

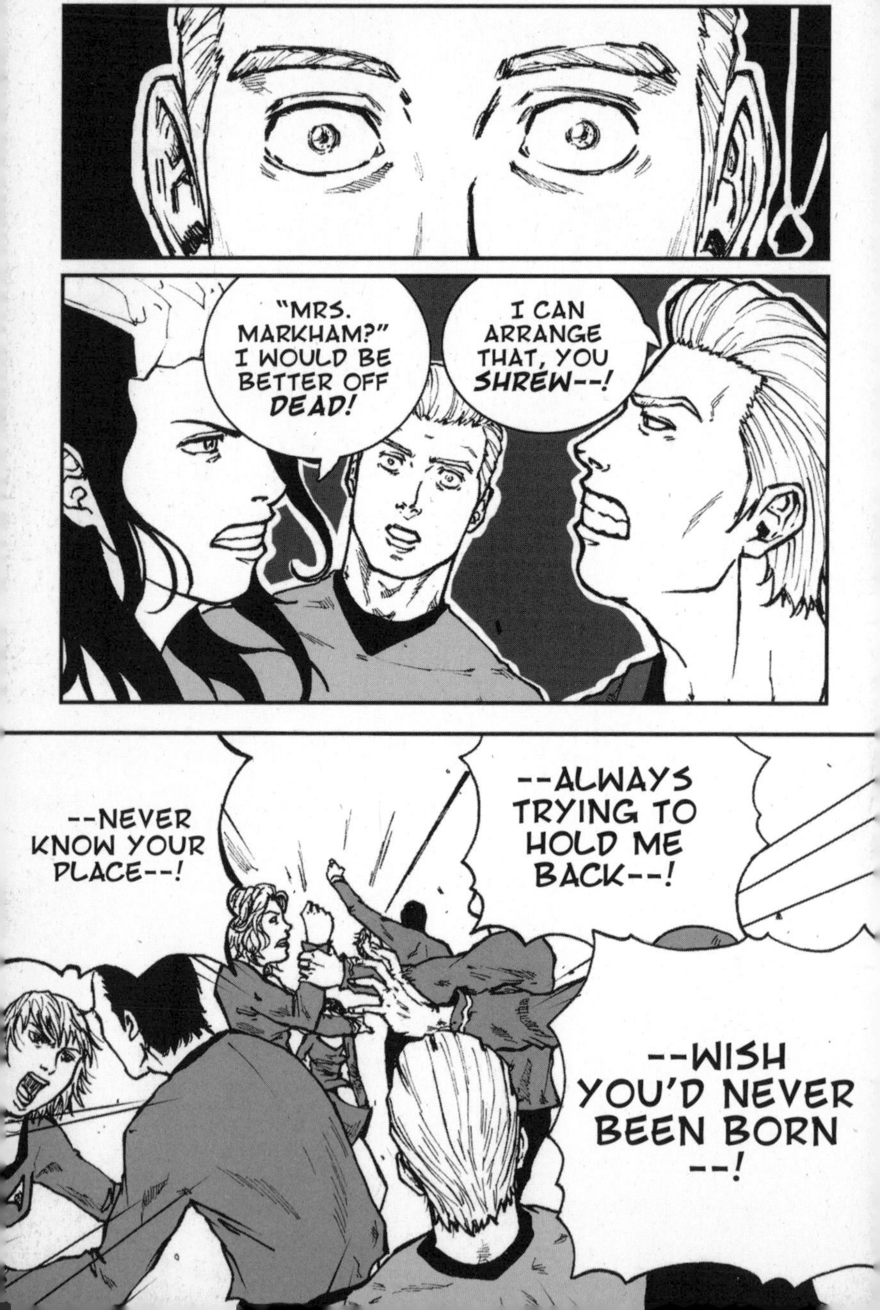
"MRS. MARKHAM?" I WOULD BE BETTER OFF DEAD!
I CAN ARRANGE THAT, YOU SHREW--!
--NEVER KNOW YOUR PLACE--!
--ALWAYS TRYING TO HOLD ME BACK--!
--WISH YOU'D NEVER BEEN BORN --!

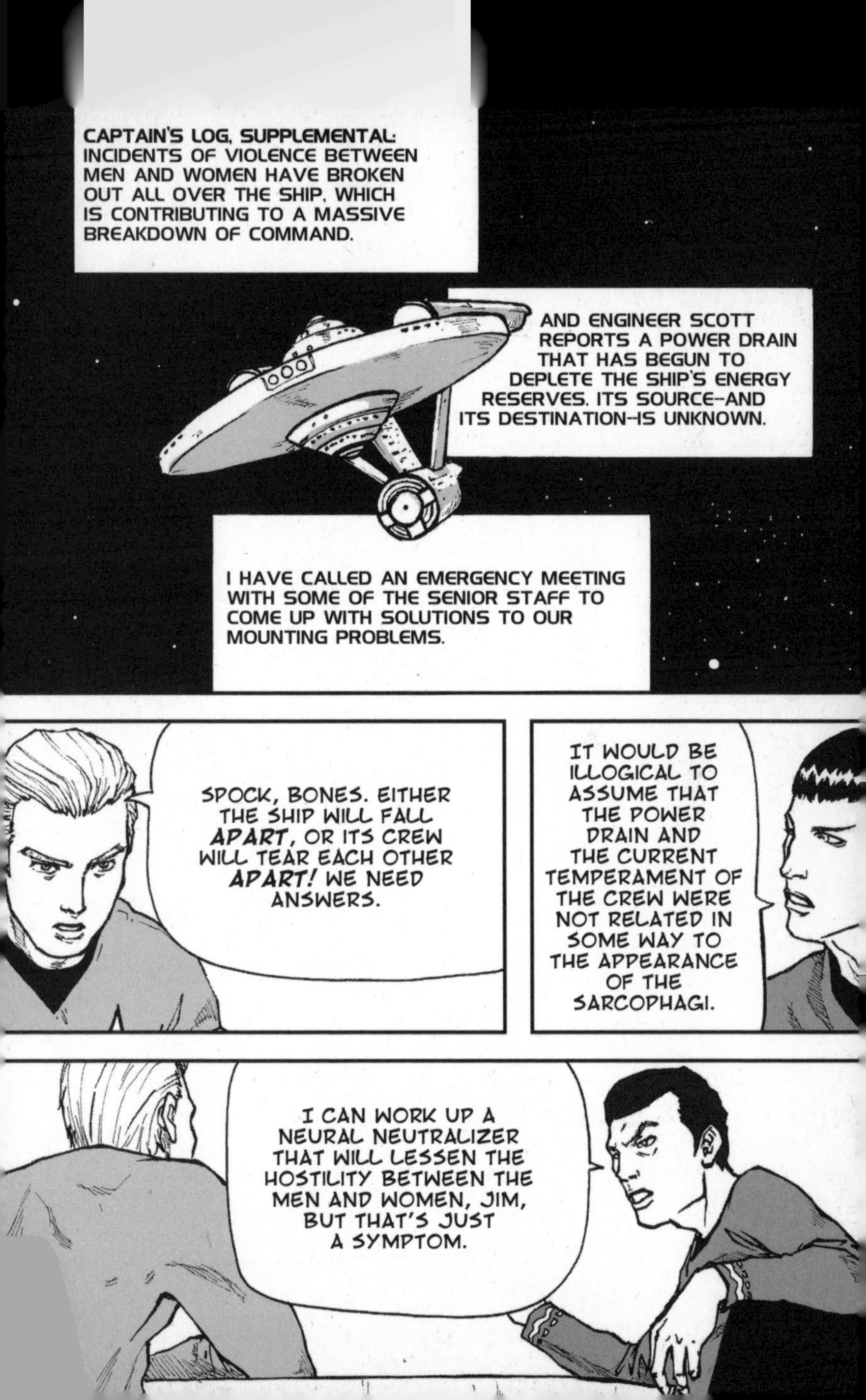

CAPTAIN'S LOG, SUPPLEMENTAL: INCIDENTS OF VIOLENCE BETWEEN MEN AND WOMEN HAVE BROKEN OUT ALL OVER THE SHIP, WHICH IS CONTRIBUTING TO A MASSIVE BREAKDOWN OF COMMAND.
AND ENGINEER SCOTT REPORTS A POWER DRAIN THAT HAS BEGUN TO DEPLETE THE SHIP'S ENERGY RESERVES. ITS SOURCE--AND ITS DESTINATION--IS UNKNOWN.
I HAVE CALLED AN EMERGENCY MEETING WITH SOME OF THE SENIOR STAFF TO COME UP WITH SOLUTIONS TO OUR MOUNTING PROBLEMS.
SPOCK, BONES. EITHER THE SHIP WILL FALL *APART*, OR ITS CREW WILL TEAR EACH OTHER *APART!* WE NEED ANSWERS.
IT WOULD BE ILLOGICAL TO ASSUME THAT THE POWER DRAIN AND THE CURRENT TEMPERAMENT OF THE CREW WERE NOT RELATED IN SOME WAY TO THE APPEARANCE OF THE SARCOPHAGI.
I CAN WORK UP A NEURAL NEUTRALIZER THAT WILL LESSEN THE HOSTILITY BETWEEN THE MEN AND WOMEN, JIM, BUT THAT'S JUST A SYMPTOM.

YOU'VE NO IDEA WHAT'S CAUSING IT? NO IDEA HOW TO COMBAT IT? RESIST IT?

NONE. BUT WE'D NEED TO FIND OUT QUICK. THAT NEUTRALIZER MIGHT NOT WORK FOR VERY LONG.

UNDERSTOOD. SCOTTY SAYS WE DON'T HAVE ENOUGH POWER TO BEAM THOSE SCARCOPHAGI BACK DOWN TO THE PLANET...SO WE'LL HAVE TO DO WHAT WE CAN HERE.

CAPTAIN, I WOULD REGRET THE WANTON DESTRUCTION OF TWO SUCH ARTIFACTS FROM AN UNKNOWN PEOPLE.

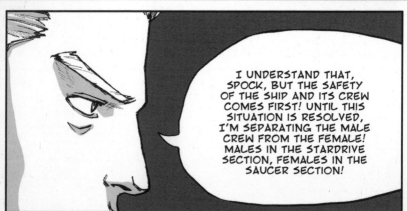

I UNDERSTAND THAT, SPOCK, BUT THE SAFETY OF THE SHIP AND ITS CREW COMES FIRST! UNTIL THIS SITUATION IS RESOLVED, I'M SEPARATING THE MALE CREW FROM THE FEMALE! MALES IN THE STARDRIVE SECTION, FEMALES IN THE SAUCER SECTION!

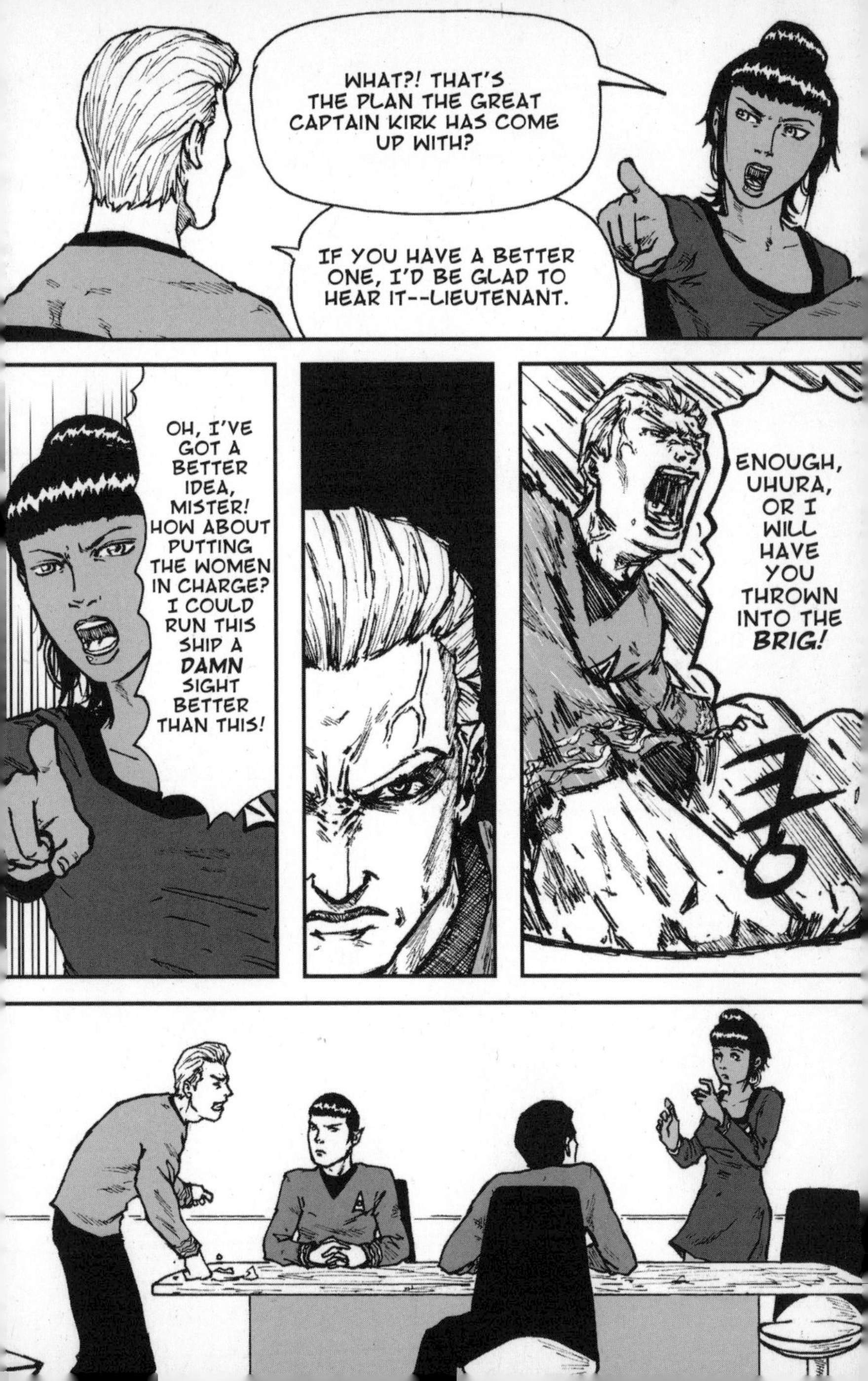
WHAT?! THAT'S THE PLAN THE GREAT CAPTAIN KIRK HAS COME UP WITH?
IF YOU HAVE A BETTER ONE, I'D BE GLAD TO HEAR IT--LIEUTENANT.
OH, I'VE GOT A BETTER IDEA, MISTER! HOW ABOUT PUTTING THE WOMEN IN CHARGE? I COULD RUN THIS SHIP A **DAMN** SIGHT BETTER THAN THIS!
ENOUGH, UHURA, OR I WILL HAVE YOU THROWN INTO THE ***BRIG!***

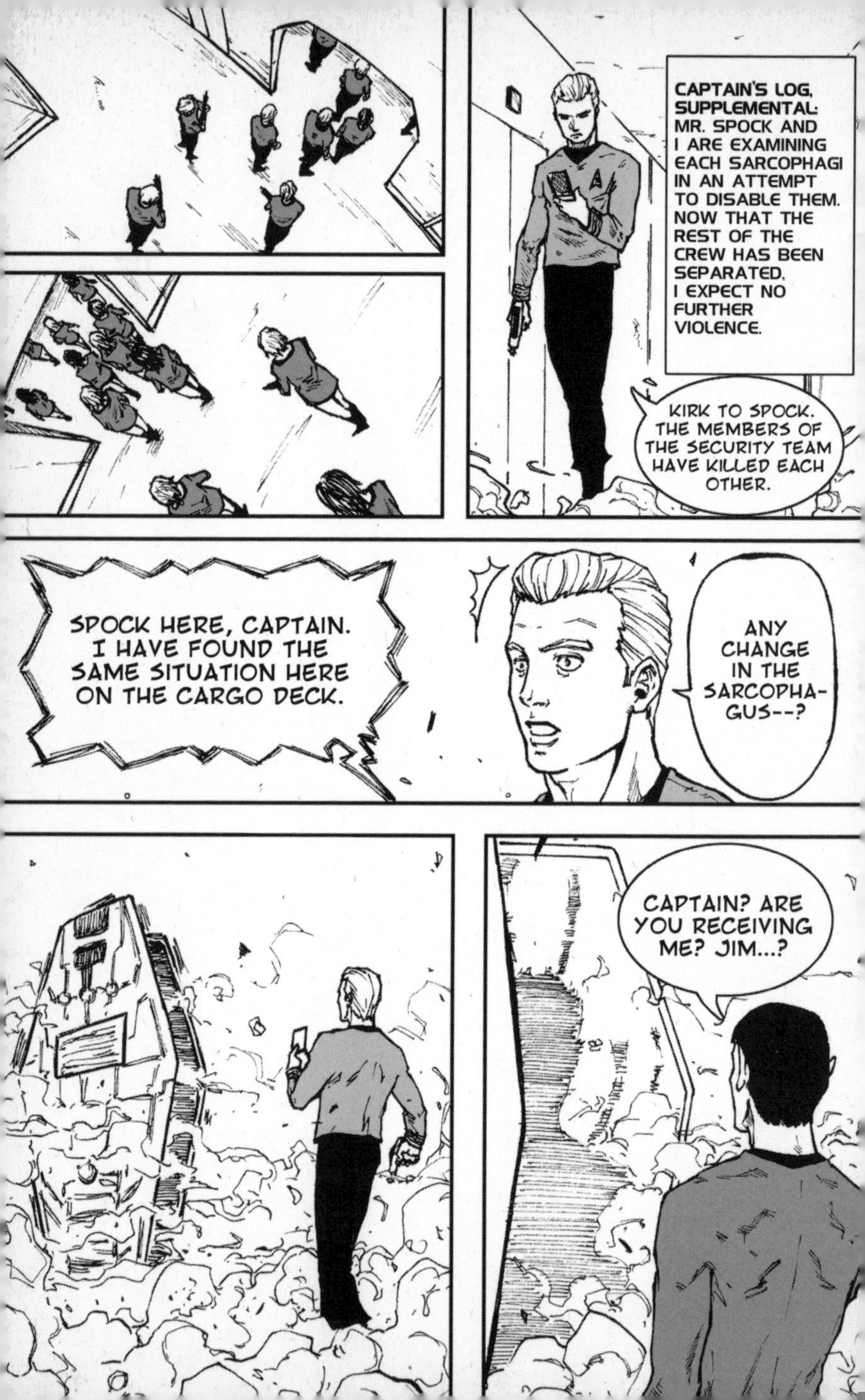
CAPTAIN'S LOG, SUPPLEMENTAL: MR. SPOCK AND I ARE EXAMINING EACH SARCOPHAGI IN AN ATTEMPT TO DISABLE THEM. NOW THAT THE REST OF THE CREW HAS BEEN SEPARATED, I EXPECT NO FURTHER VIOLENCE.
KIRK TO SPOCK. THE MEMBERS OF THE SECURITY TEAM HAVE KILLED EACH OTHER.
SPOCK HERE, CAPTAIN. I HAVE FOUND THE SAME SITUATION HERE ON THE CARGO DECK.
ANY CHANGE IN THE SARCOPHA-GUS--?
CAPTAIN? ARE YOU RECEIVING ME? JIM...?

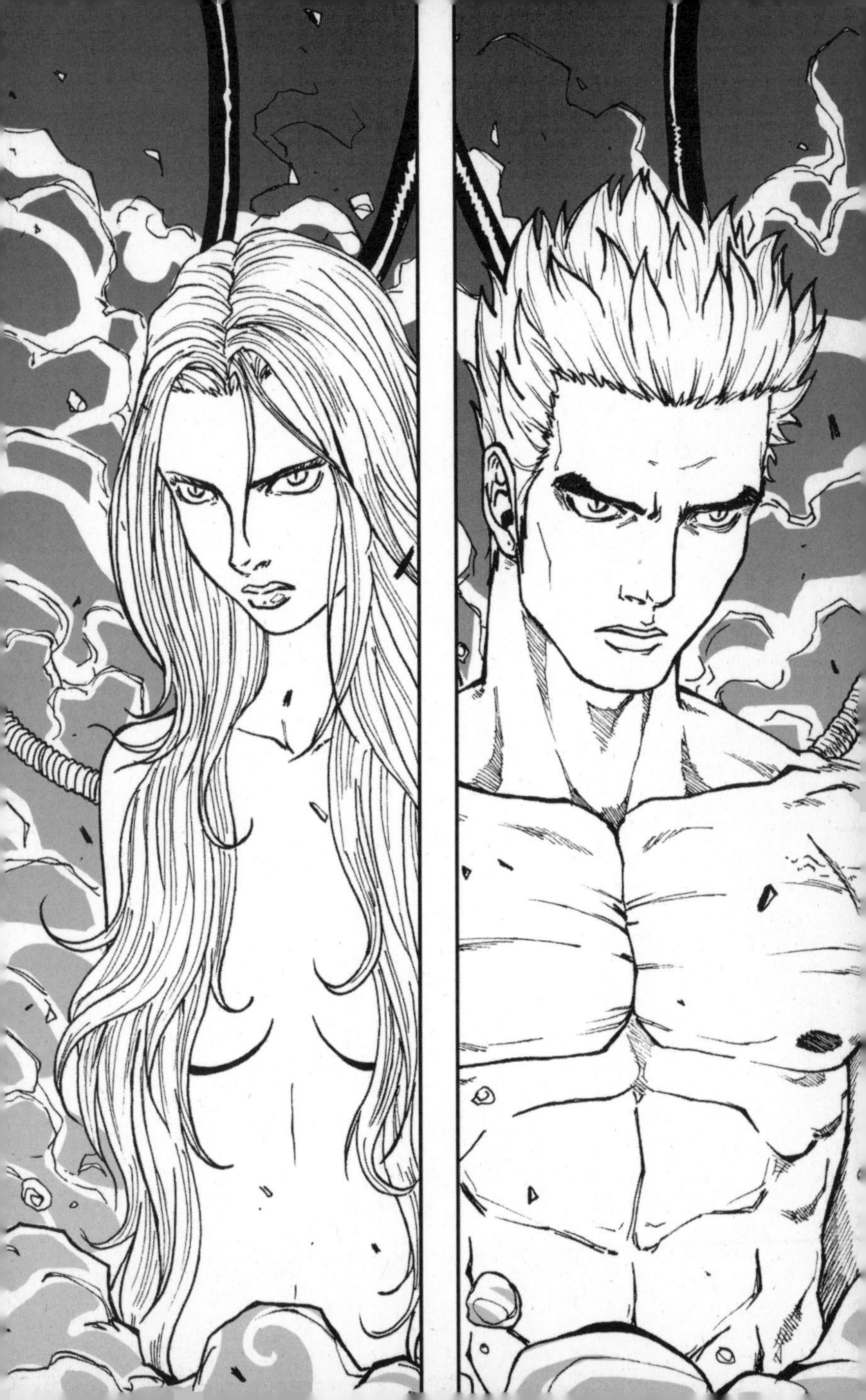

JIM, IT'S MCCOY. WHERE ARE YOU?

I CAN'T RAISE SPOCK. HAVE YOU HEARD FROM HIM?

...B-BONES?

JIM? ARE YOU ALL RIGHT?

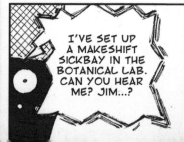

I'VE SET UP A MAKESHIFT SICKBAY IN THE BOTANICAL LAB. CAN YOU HEAR ME? JIM...?

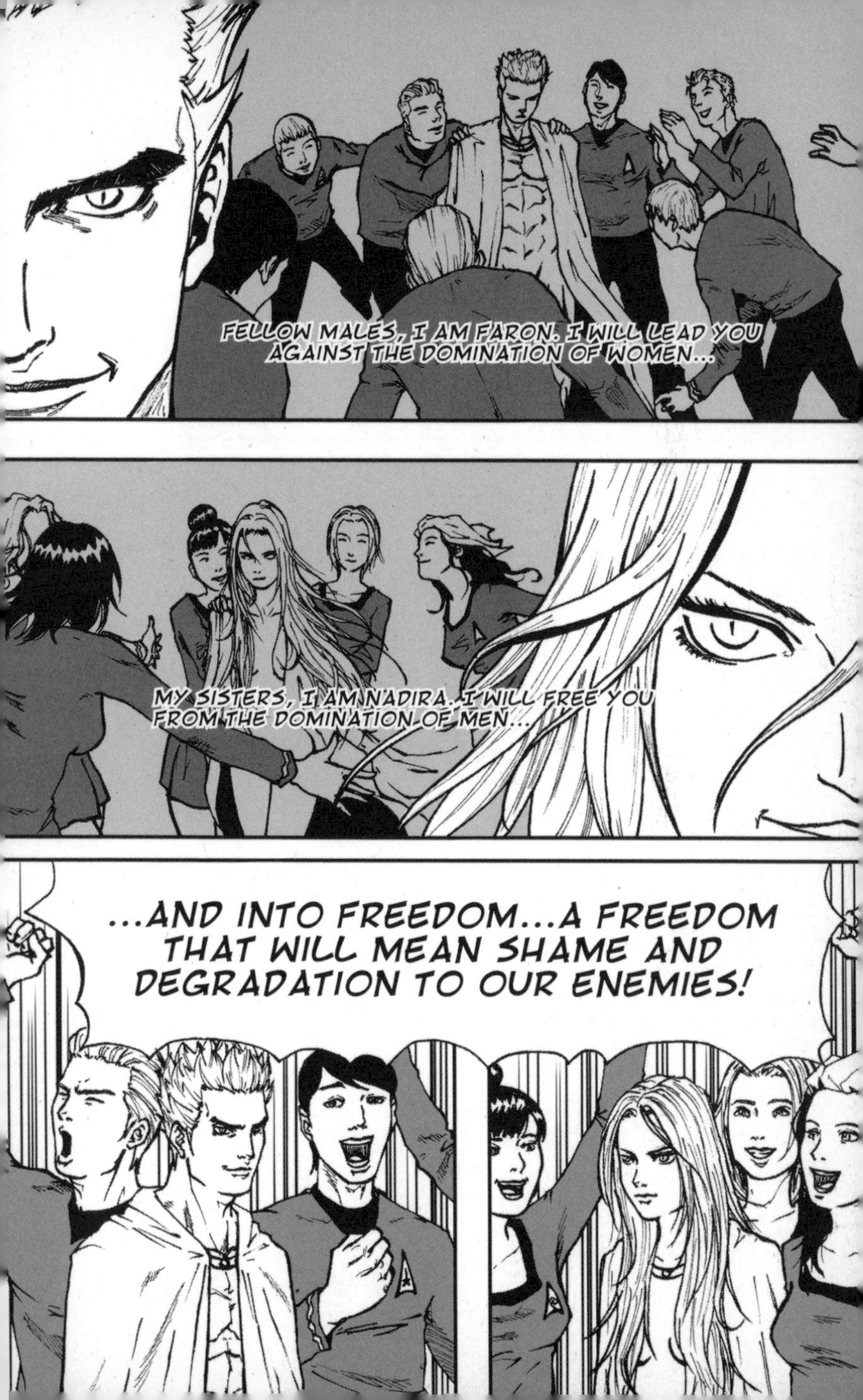
FELLOW MALES, I AM FARON. I WILL LEAD YOU AGAINST THE DOMINATION OF WOMEN...
MY SISTERS, I AM NADIRA. I WILL FREE YOU FROM THE DOMINATION OF MEN...
...AND INTO FREEDOM...A FREEDOM THAT WILL MEAN SHAME AND DEGRADATION TO OUR ENEMIES!

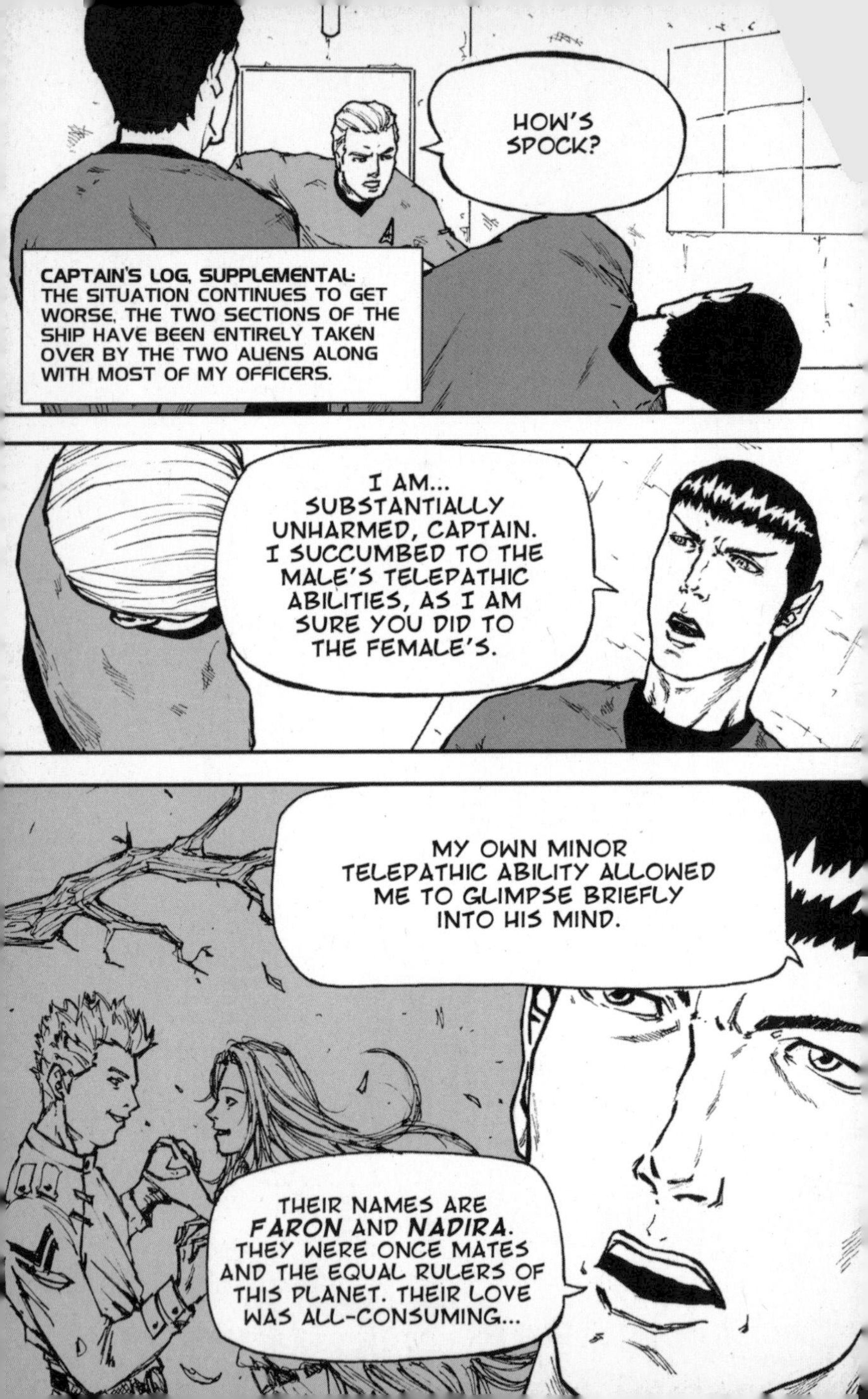
HOW'S SPOCK?
CAPTAIN'S LOG, SUPPLEMENTAL: THE SITUATION CONTINUES TO GET WORSE. THE TWO SECTIONS OF THE SHIP HAVE BEEN ENTIRELY TAKEN OVER BY THE TWO ALIENS ALONG WITH MOST OF MY OFFICERS.
I AM... SUBSTANTIALLY UNHARMED, CAPTAIN. I SUCCUMBED TO THE MALE'S TELEPATHIC ABILITIES, AS I AM SURE YOU DID TO THE FEMALE'S.
MY OWN MINOR TELEPATHIC ABILITY ALLOWED ME TO GLIMPSE BRIEFLY INTO HIS MIND.
THEIR NAMES ARE ***FARON*** AND ***NADIRA***. THEY WERE ONCE MATES AND THE EQUAL RULERS OF THIS PLANET. THEIR LOVE WAS ALL-CONSUMING...

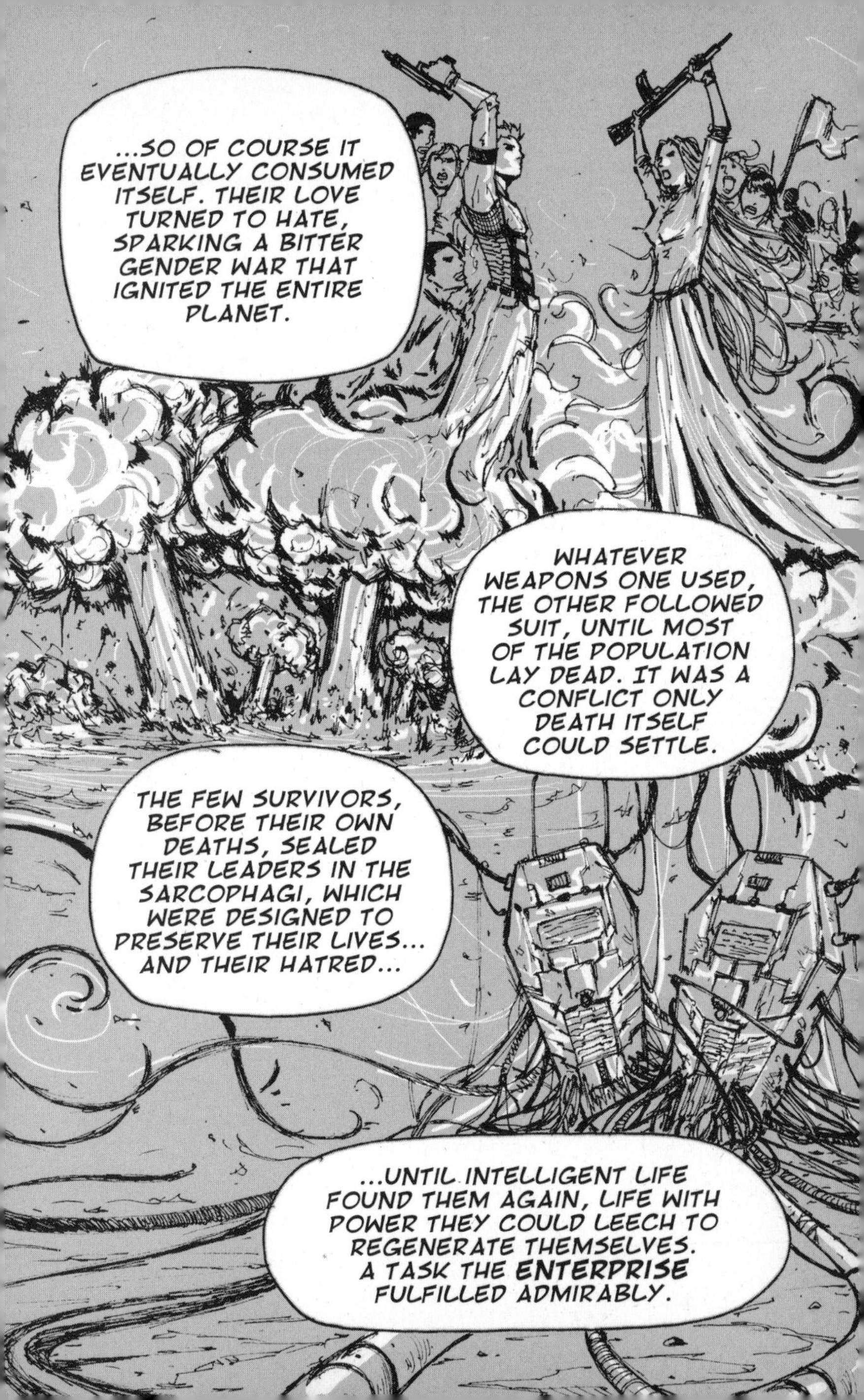
...SO OF COURSE IT EVENTUALLY CONSUMED ITSELF. THEIR LOVE TURNED TO HATE, SPARKING A BITTER GENDER WAR THAT IGNITED THE ENTIRE PLANET.
WHATEVER WEAPONS ONE USED, THE OTHER FOLLOWED SUIT, UNTIL MOST OF THE POPULATION LAY DEAD. IT WAS A CONFLICT ONLY DEATH ITSELF COULD SETTLE.
THE FEW SURVIVORS, BEFORE THEIR OWN DEATHS, SEALED THEIR LEADERS IN THE SARCOPHAGI, WHICH WERE DESIGNED TO PRESERVE THEIR LIVES... AND THEIR HATRED...
...UNTIL INTELLIGENT LIFE FOUND THEM AGAIN, LIFE WITH POWER THEY COULD LEECH TO REGENERATE THEMSELVES. A TASK THE ENTERPRISE FULFILLED ADMIRABLY.

I'M A DOCTOR, NOT AN ELECTRICIAN--BUT THOSE COFFINS WE FOUND THEM IN ACTUALLY CONTAIN RESTORATIVE CIRCUITRY, DESIGNED TO REGENERATE THEIR BODIES.

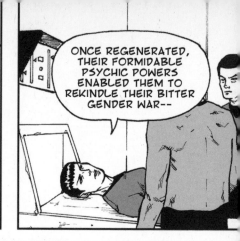

ONCE REGENERATED, THEIR FORMIDABLE PSYCHIC POWERS ENABLED THEM TO REKINDLE THEIR BITTER GENDER WAR--

--USING MY CREW AS THEIR SOLDIERS. MCCOY, IS IT POSSIBLE TO INCAPACITATE THE ENTIRE CREW?

IF WE CAN GET TO THE AUXILIARY CONTROL CENTER IN THE SAUCER SECTION, I COULD FLOOD THE SHIP WITH THE INTRUDER CONTROL GAS. AS FOR US...

...THIS NEURAL NEUTRALIZER WILL LET US WITHSTAND THE EFFECTS OF FARON'S PSYCHIC WHAMMY--FOR A SHORT TIME, ANYWAY. I'VE GOT A SHOT FOR EACH OF US.

I WILL REQUIRE NONE, DOCTOR. NOW THAT I AM AWARE OF THEM, FARON'S PSYCHIC POWERS PRESENT NO CHALLENGE TO ME.

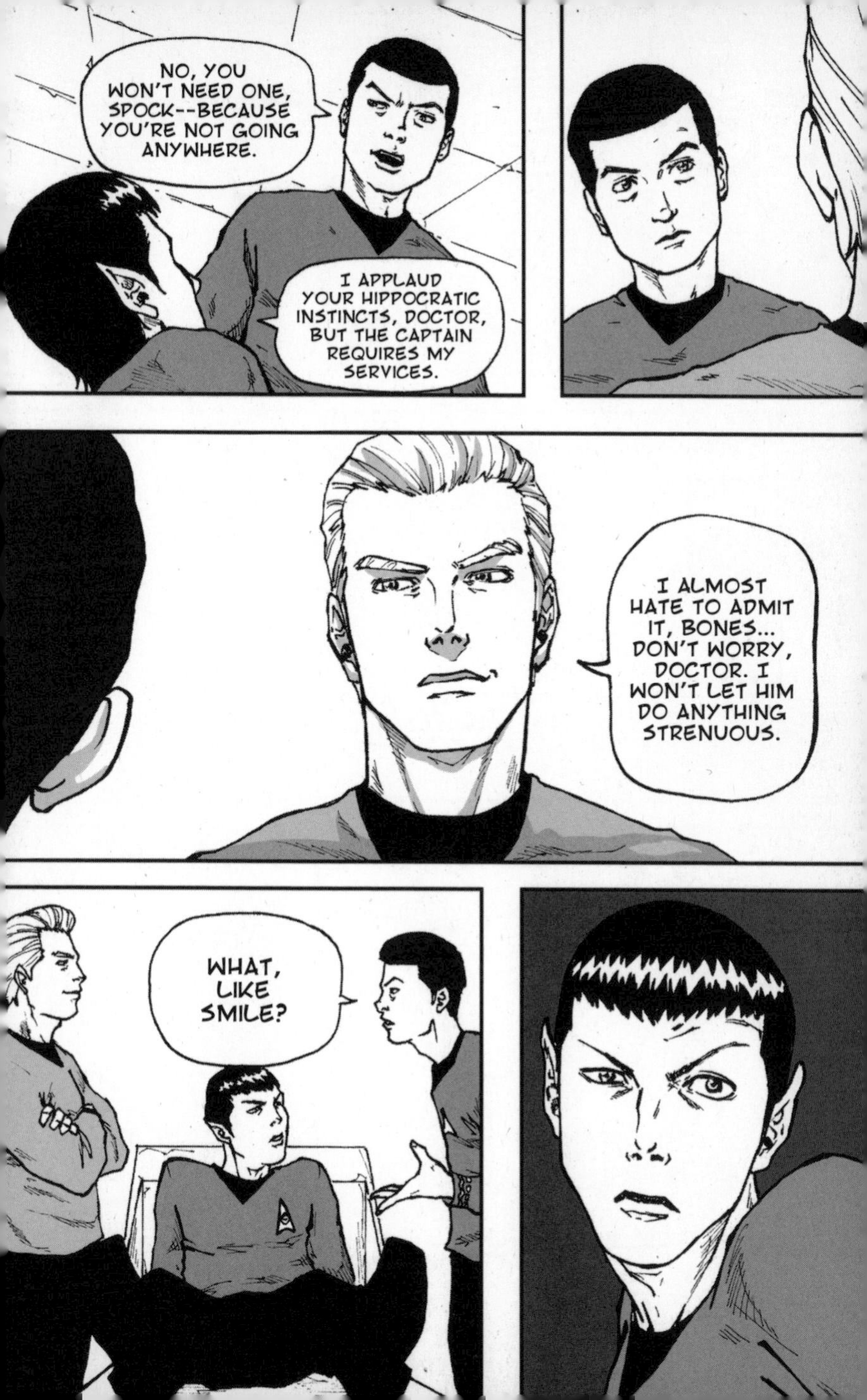
NO, YOU WON'T NEED ONE, SPOCK--BECAUSE YOU'RE NOT GOING ANYWHERE.
I APPLAUD YOUR HIPPOCRATIC INSTINCTS, DOCTOR, BUT THE CAPTAIN REQUIRES MY SERVICES.
I ALMOST HATE TO ADMIT IT, BONES... DON'T WORRY, DOCTOR. I WON'T LET HIM DO ANYTHING STRENUOUS.
WHAT, LIKE SMILE?

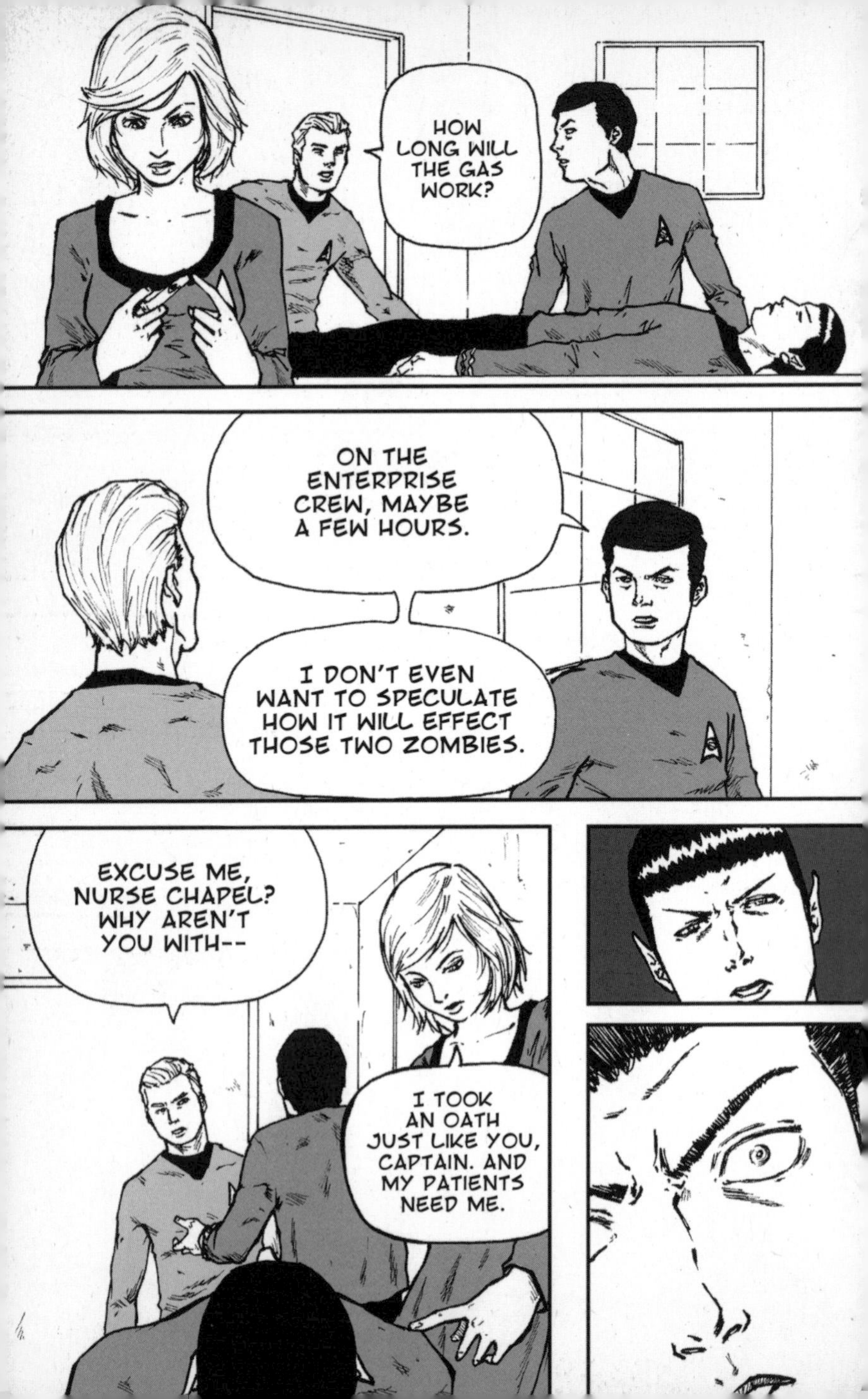
HOW LONG WILL THE GAS WORK?
ON THE ENTERPRISE CREW, MAYBE A FEW HOURS.
I DON'T EVEN WANT TO SPECULATE HOW IT WILL EFFECT THOSE TWO ZOMBIES.
EXCUSE ME, NURSE CHAPEL? WHY AREN'T YOU WITH--
I TOOK AN OATH JUST LIKE YOU, CAPTAIN. AND MY PATIENTS NEED ME.

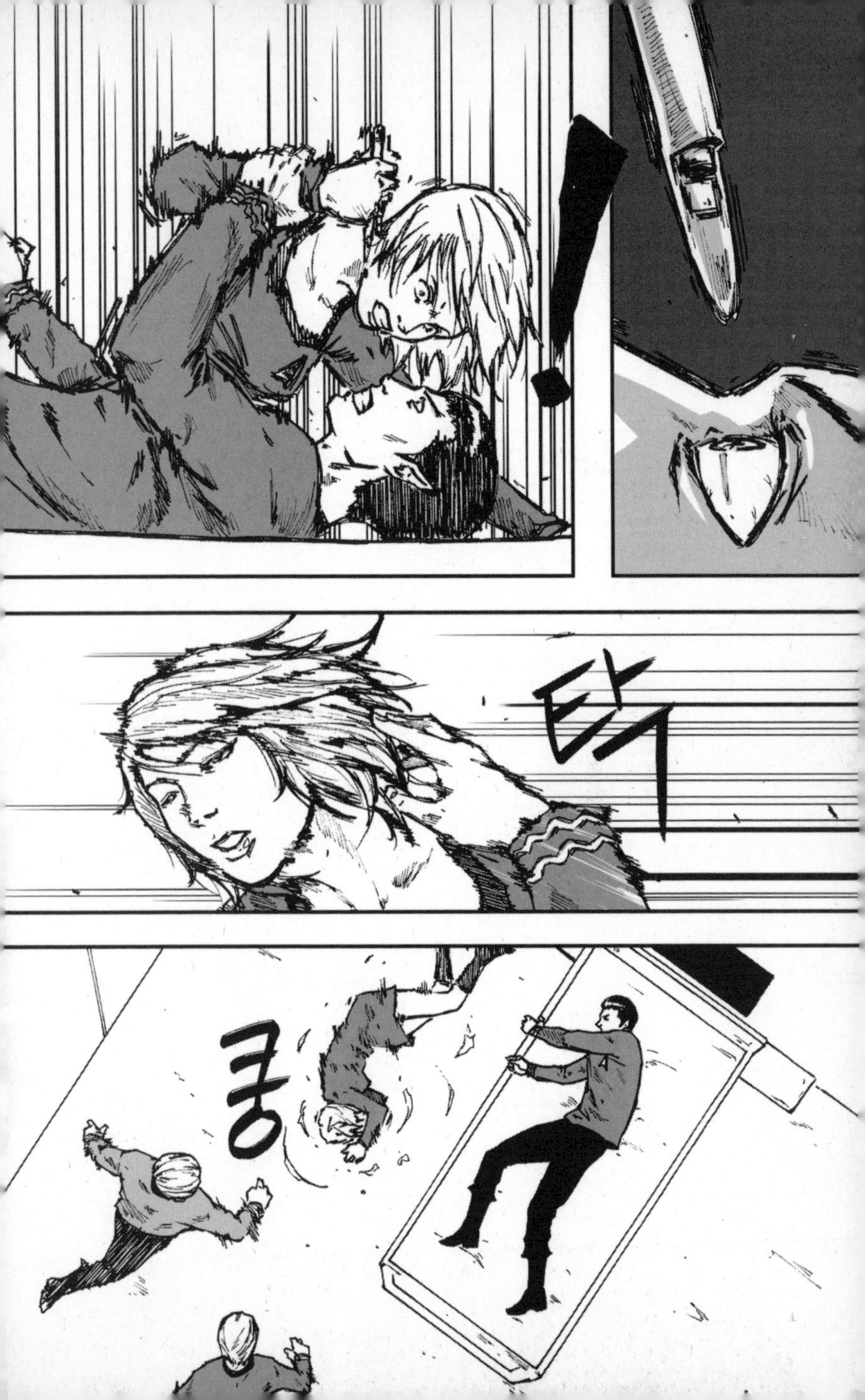
탁
쿵

GAS! TYPICAL MALE TREACHERY! SISTER UHURA! CLOSE THE VENTS AND SEND A TEAM TO IT'S SOURCE.

YES, SISTER NADIRA!

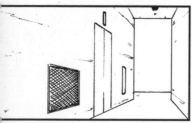

THEY WERE ABLE TO OVERRIDE OUR SECURITY CODES, WHICH PROBABLY MEANS THAT THEY KNOW WE'RE--

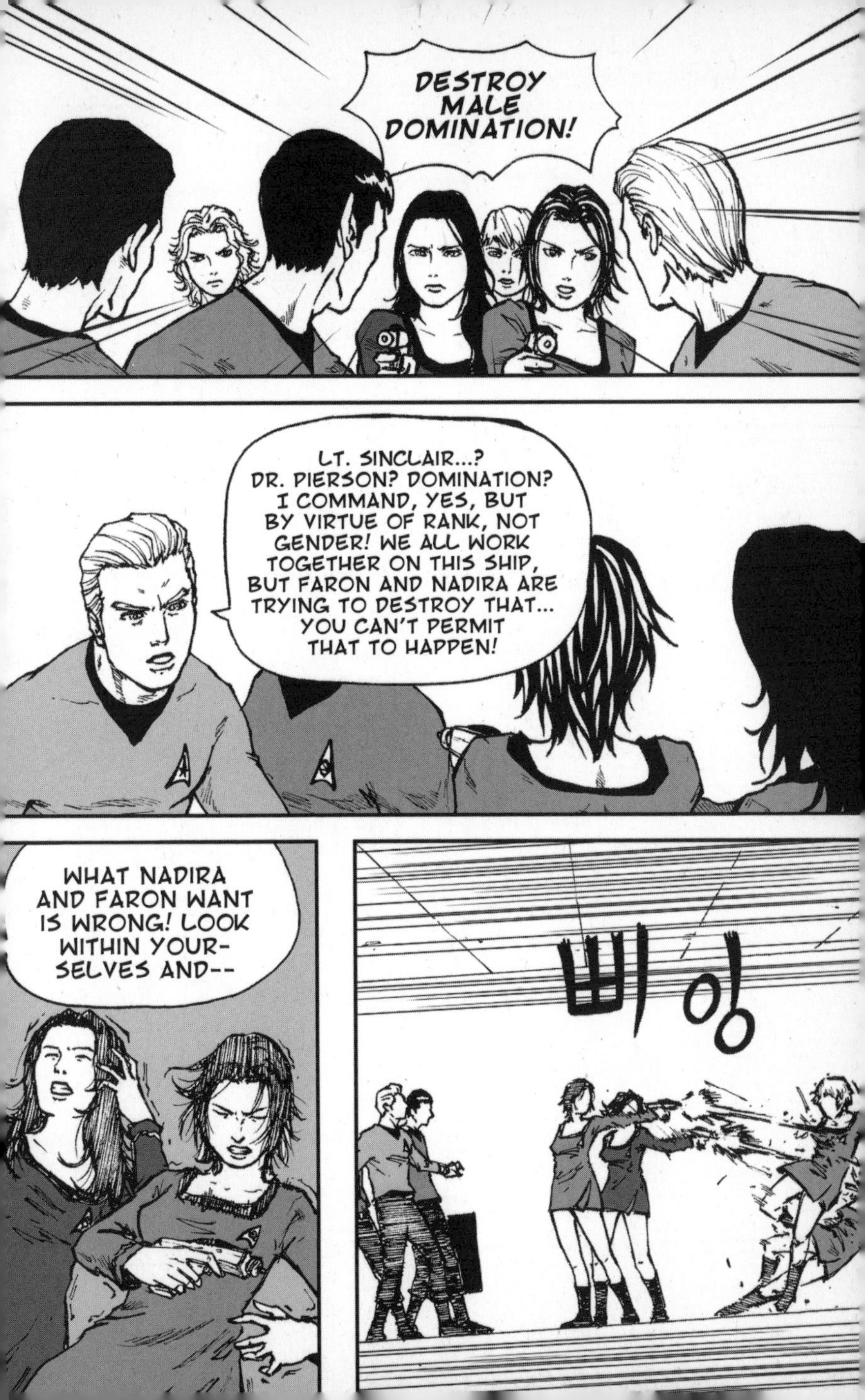
DESTROY MALE DOMINATION!
LT. SINCLAIR...? DR. PIERSON? DOMINATION? I COMMAND, YES, BUT BY VIRTUE OF RANK, NOT GENDER! WE ALL WORK TOGETHER ON THIS SHIP, BUT FARON AND NADIRA ARE TRYING TO DESTROY THAT... YOU CAN'T PERMIT THAT TO HAPPEN!
WHAT NADIRA AND FARON WANT IS WRONG! LOOK WITHIN YOUR-SELVES AND--
삐잉

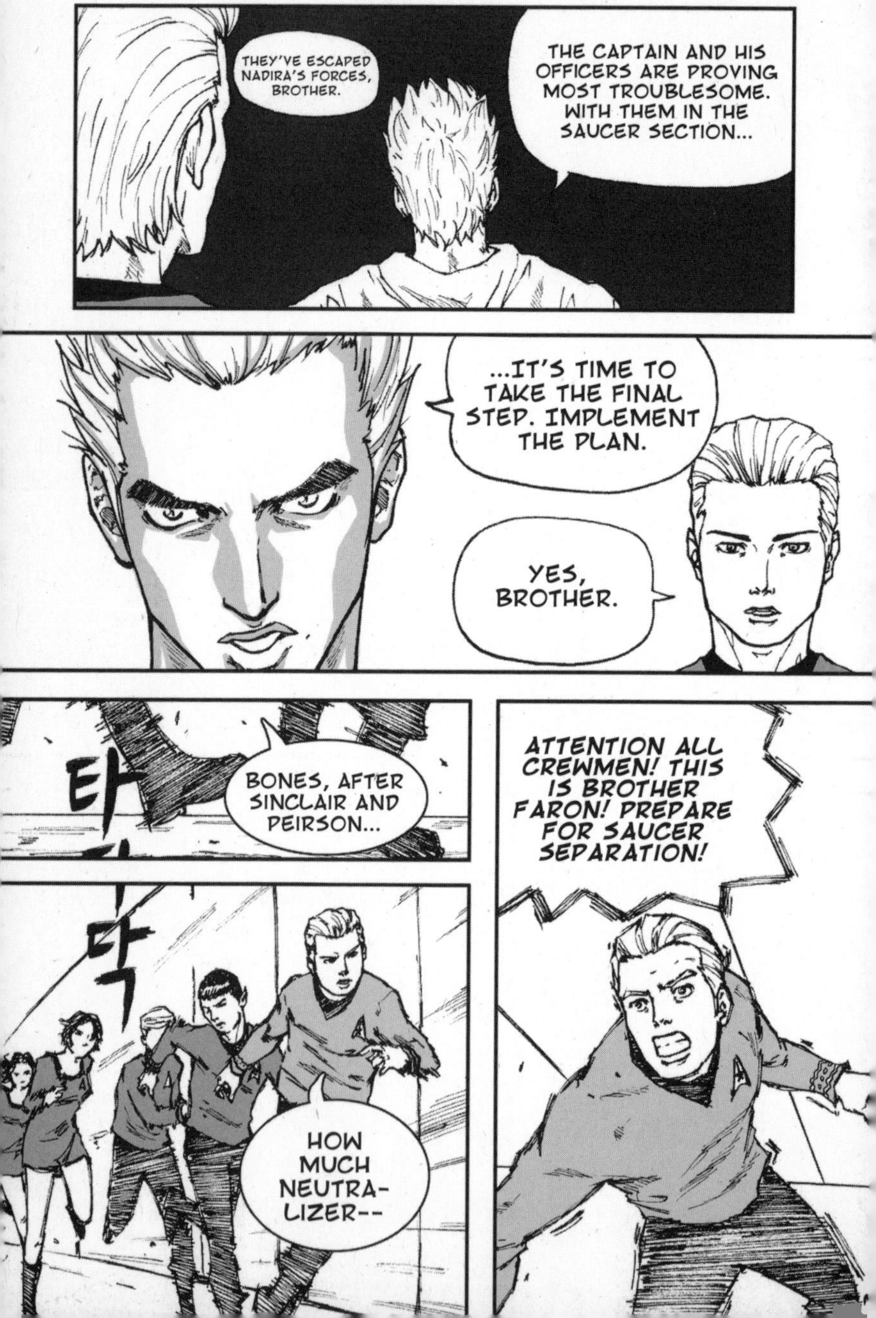
THEY'VE ESCAPED NADIRA'S FORCES, BROTHER.
THE CAPTAIN AND HIS OFFICERS ARE PROVING MOST TROUBLESOME. WITH THEM IN THE SAUCER SECTION...
...IT'S TIME TO TAKE THE FINAL STEP. IMPLEMENT THE PLAN.
YES, BROTHER.
타닥
BONES, AFTER SINCLAIR AND PEIRSON...
HOW MUCH NEUTRA-LIZER--
ATTENTION ALL CREWMEN! THIS IS BROTHER FARON! PREPARE FOR SAUCER SEPARATION!

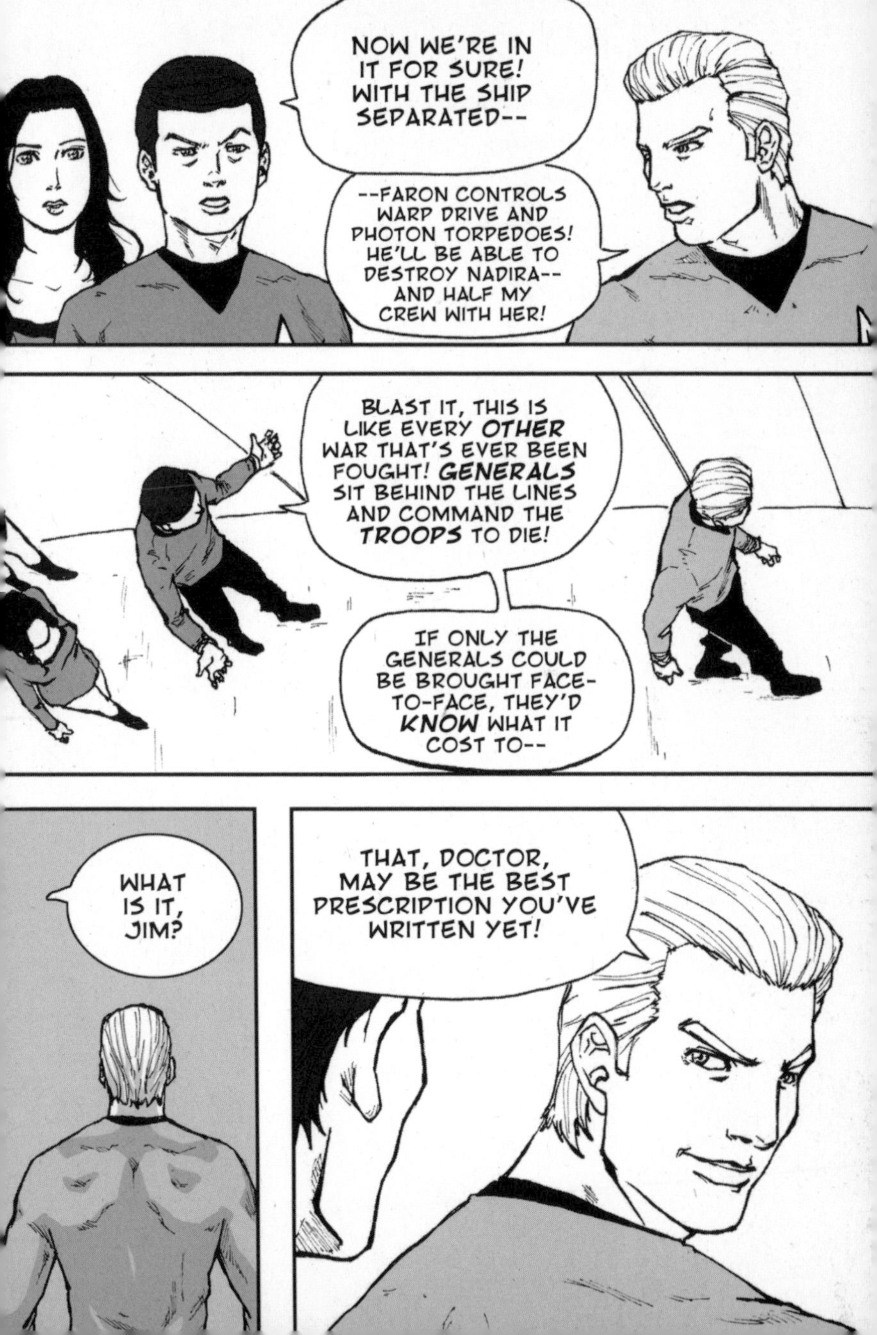
NOW WE'RE IN IT FOR SURE! WITH THE SHIP SEPARATED--
--FARON CONTROLS WARP DRIVE AND PHOTON TORPEDOES! HE'LL BE ABLE TO DESTROY NADIRA-- AND HALF MY CREW WITH HER!
BLAST IT, THIS IS LIKE EVERY *OTHER* WAR THAT'S EVER BEEN FOUGHT! *GENERALS* SIT BEHIND THE LINES AND COMMAND THE *TROOPS* TO DIE!
IF ONLY THE GENERALS COULD BE BROUGHT FACE-TO-FACE, THEY'D *KNOW* WHAT IT COST TO--
WHAT IS IT, JIM?
THAT, DOCTOR, MAY BE THE BEST PRESCRIPTION YOU'VE WRITTEN YET!

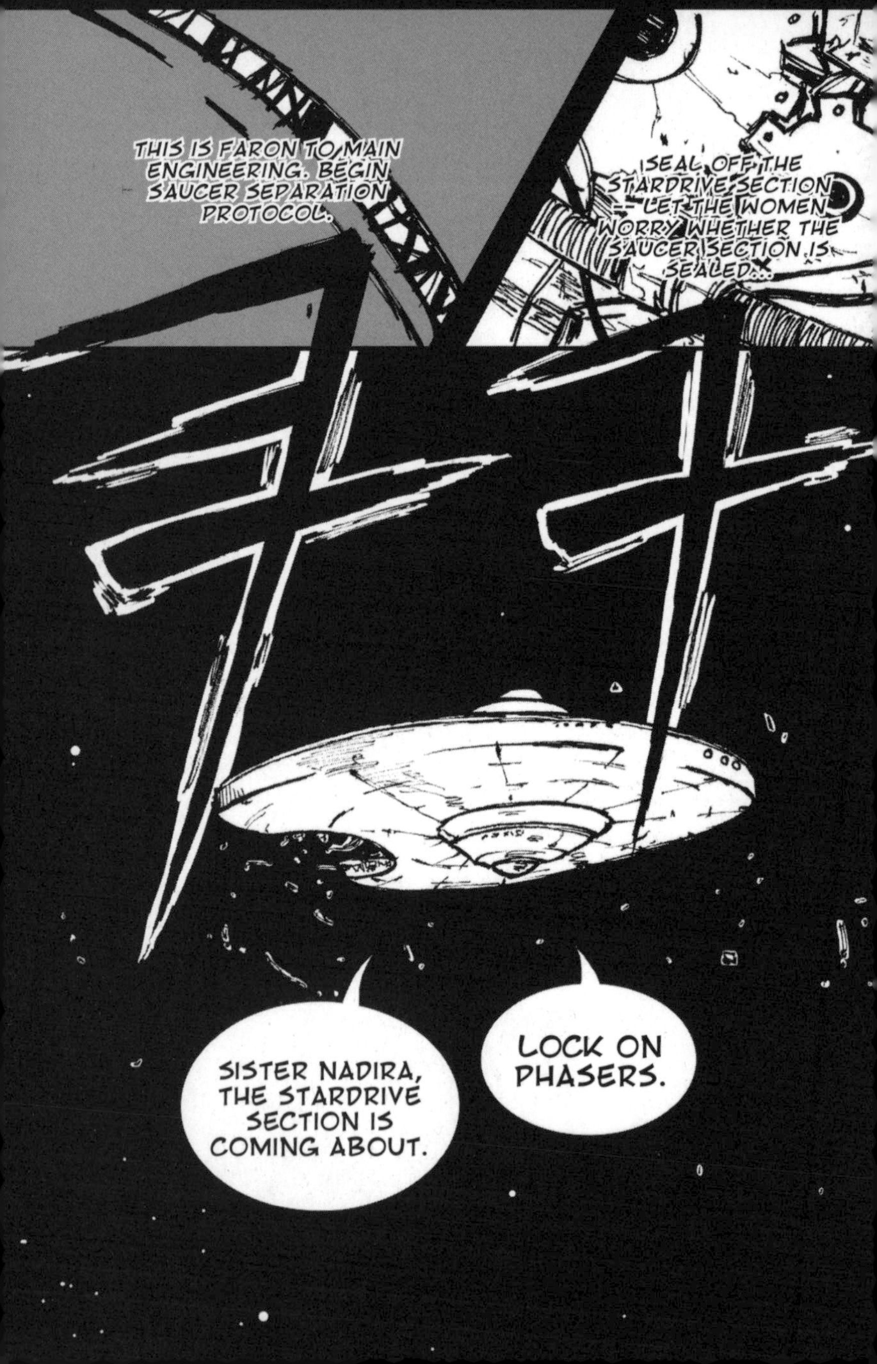
THIS IS FARON TO MAIN ENGINEERING. BEGIN SAUCER SEPARATION PROTOCOL.
SEAL OFF THE STARDRIVE SECTION -- LET THE WOMEN WORRY WHETHER THE SAUCER SECTION IS SEALED...
SISTER NADIRA, THE STARDRIVE SECTION IS COMING ABOUT.
LOCK ON PHASERS.

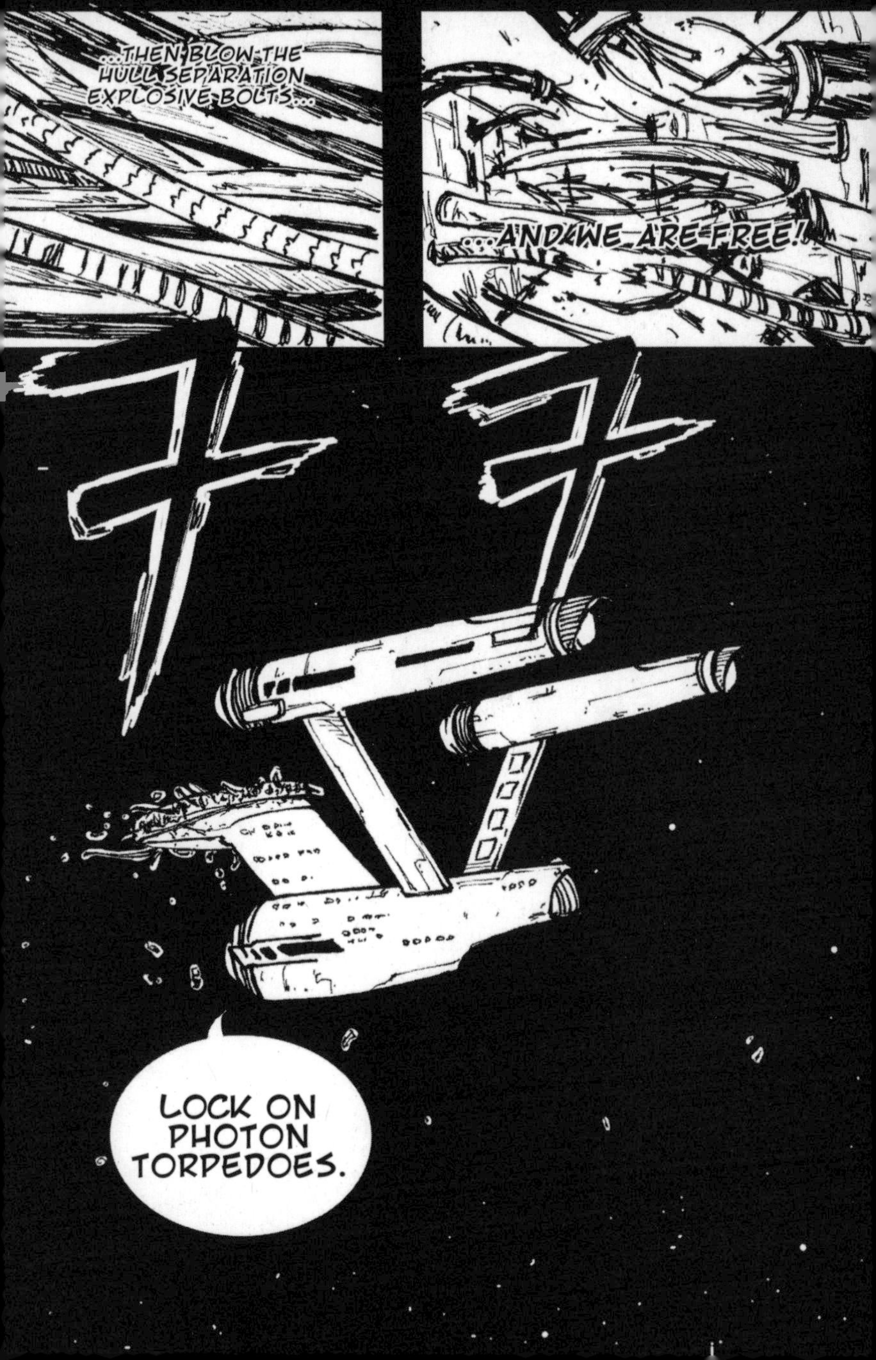
...THEN BLOW THE HULL SEPARATION EXPLOSIVE BOLTS...
...AND WE ARE FREE!
LOCK ON PHOTON TORPEDOES.

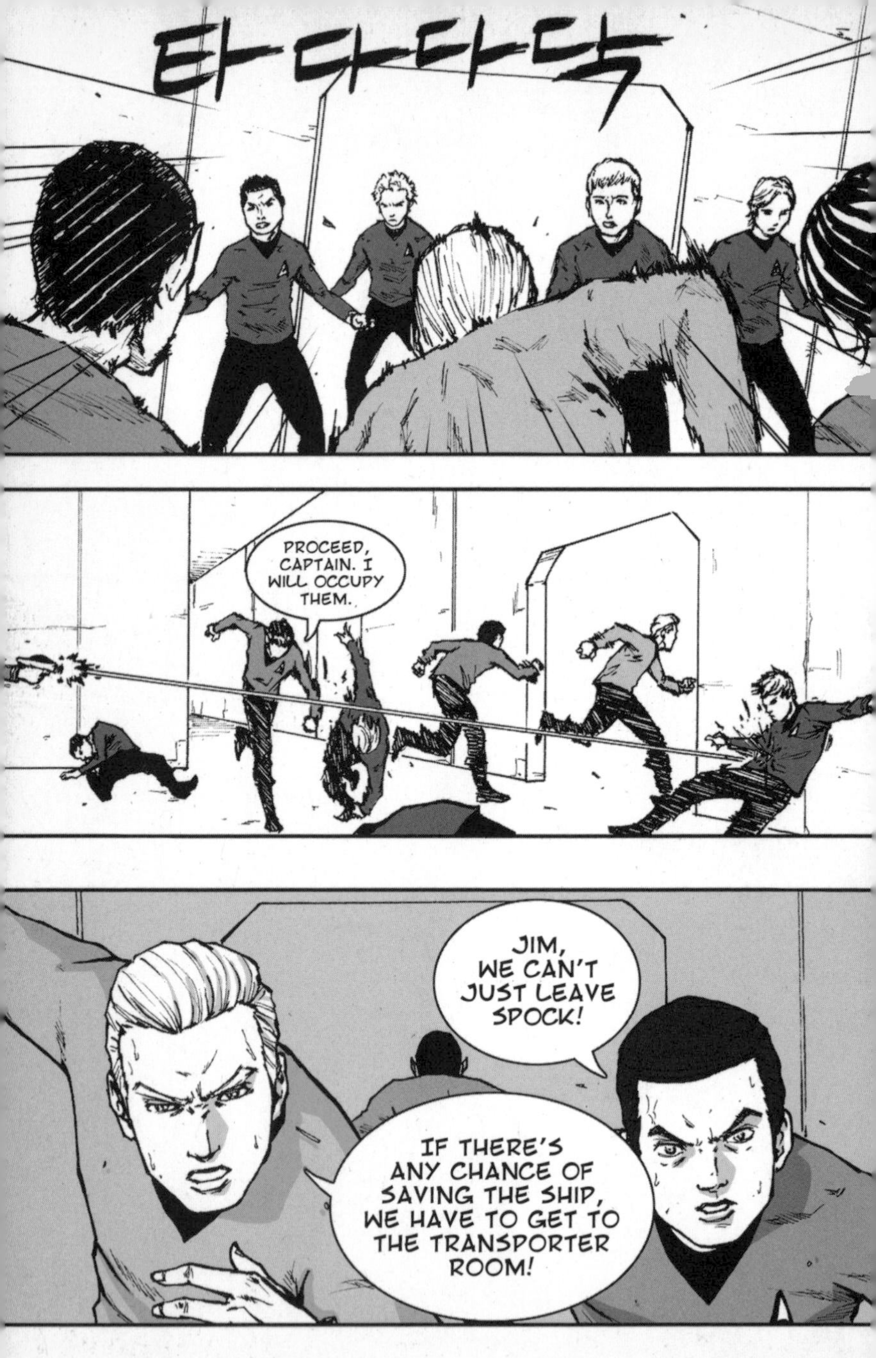
타다다닥
PROCEED, CAPTAIN. I WILL OCCUPY THEM.
JIM, WE CAN'T JUST LEAVE SPOCK!
IF THERE'S ANY CHANCE OF SAVING THE SHIP, WE HAVE TO GET TO THE TRANSPORTER ROOM!

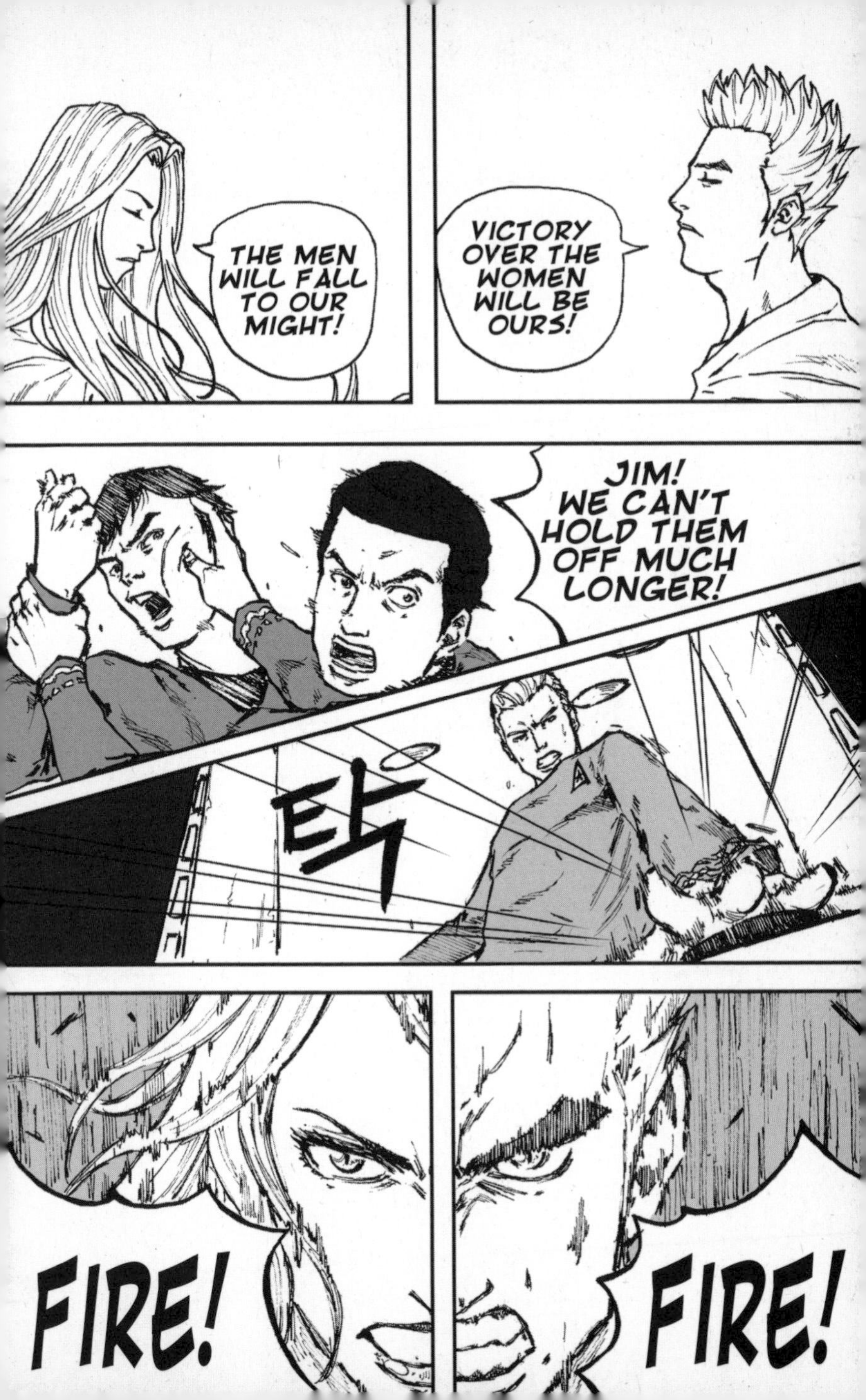
THE MEN WILL FALL TO OUR MIGHT!
VICTORY OVER THE WOMEN WILL BE OURS!
JIM! WE CAN'T HOLD THEM OFF MUCH LONGER!
FIRE!
FIRE!

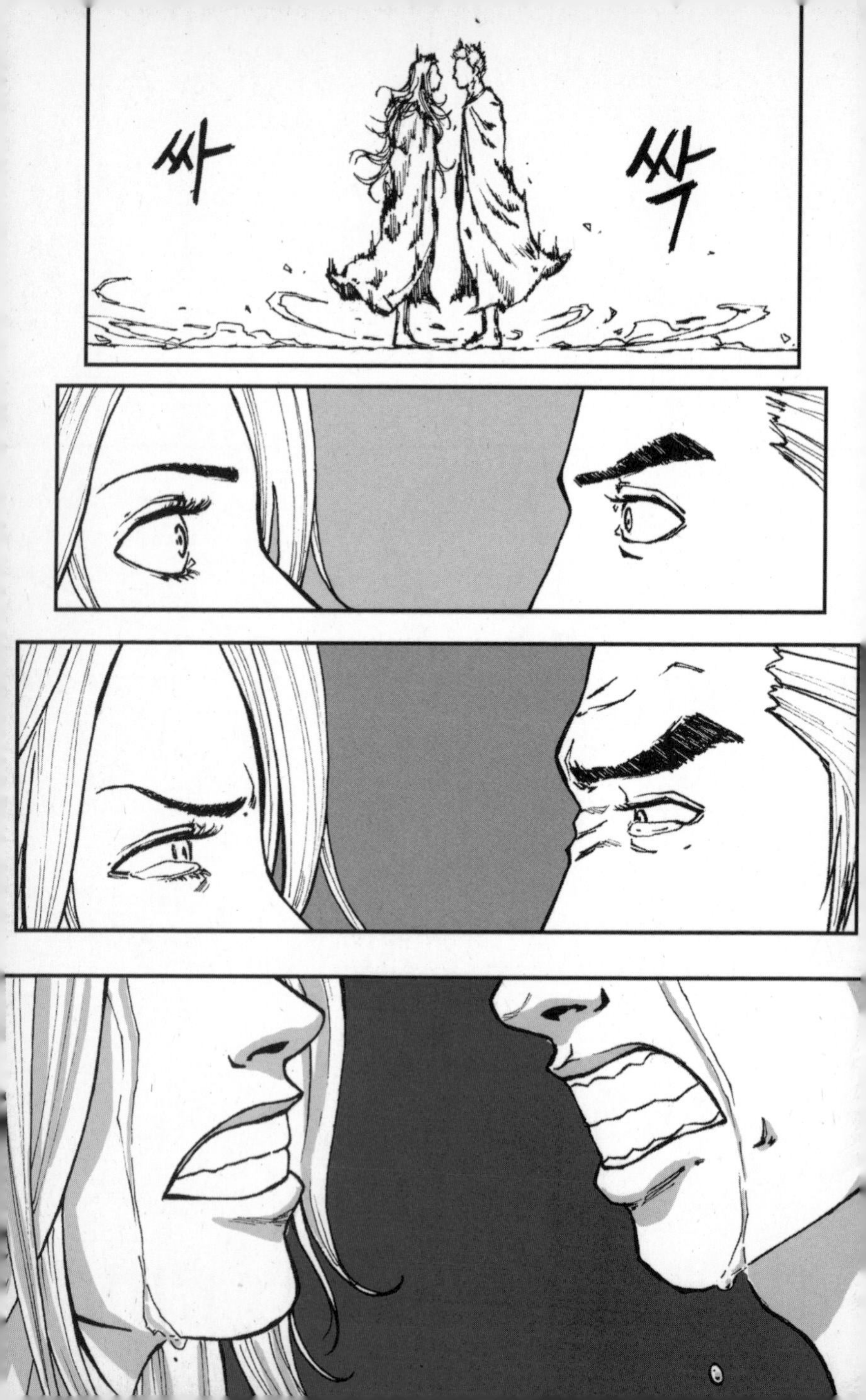
싹
싸

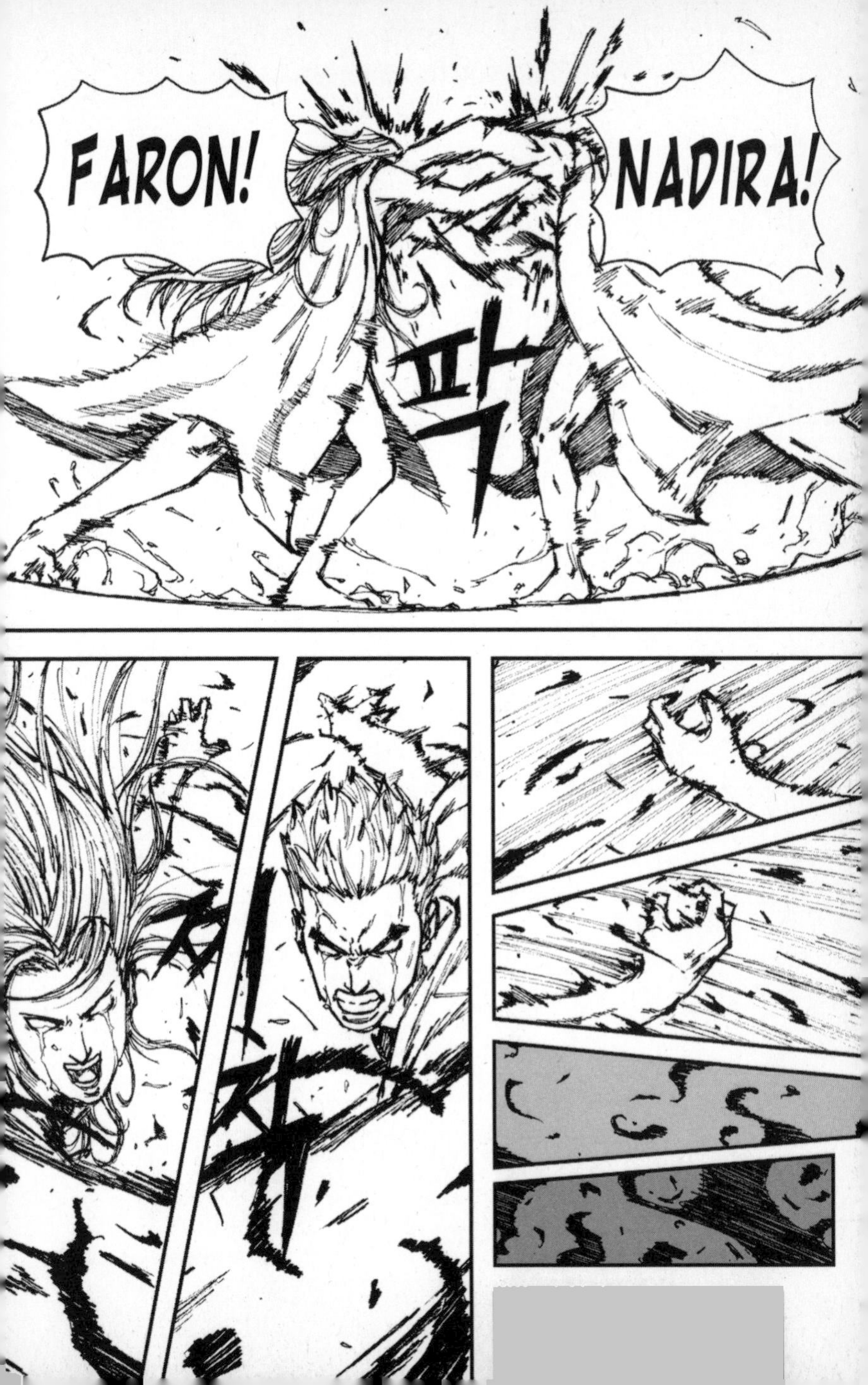
FARON!
NADIRA!
팍

[redacted]

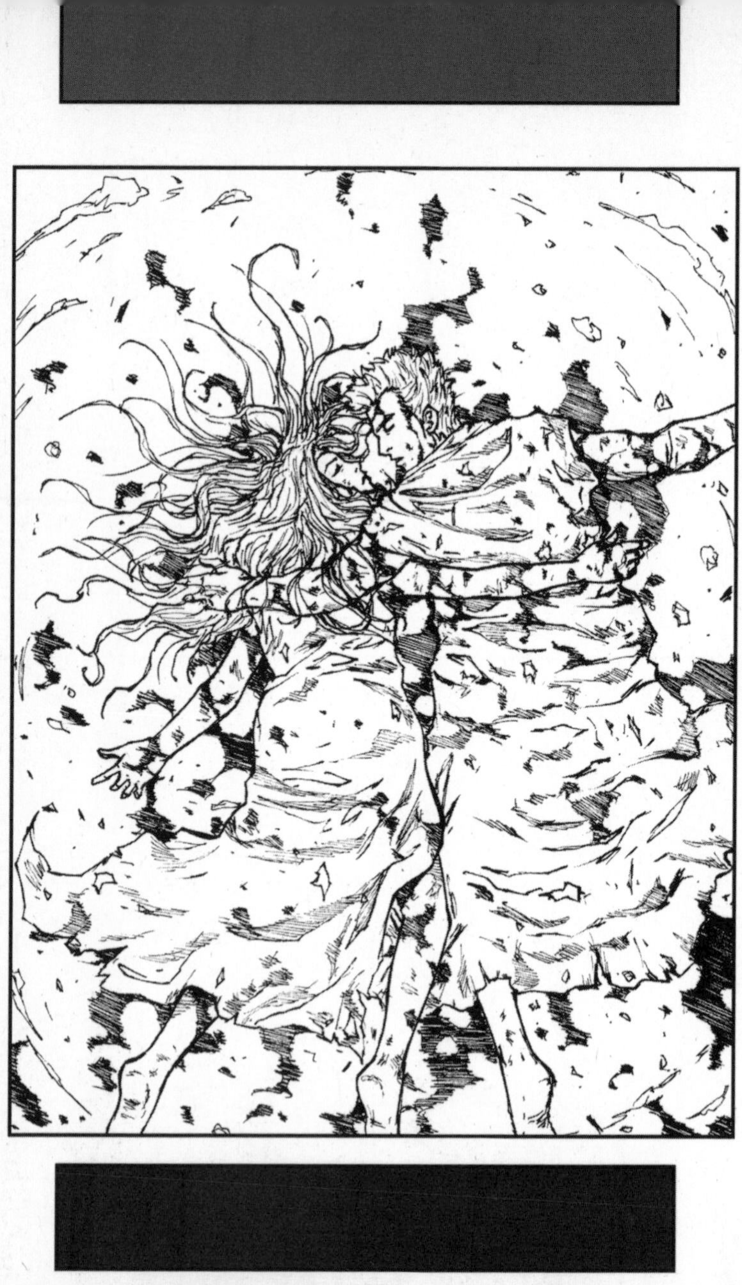

[redacted]

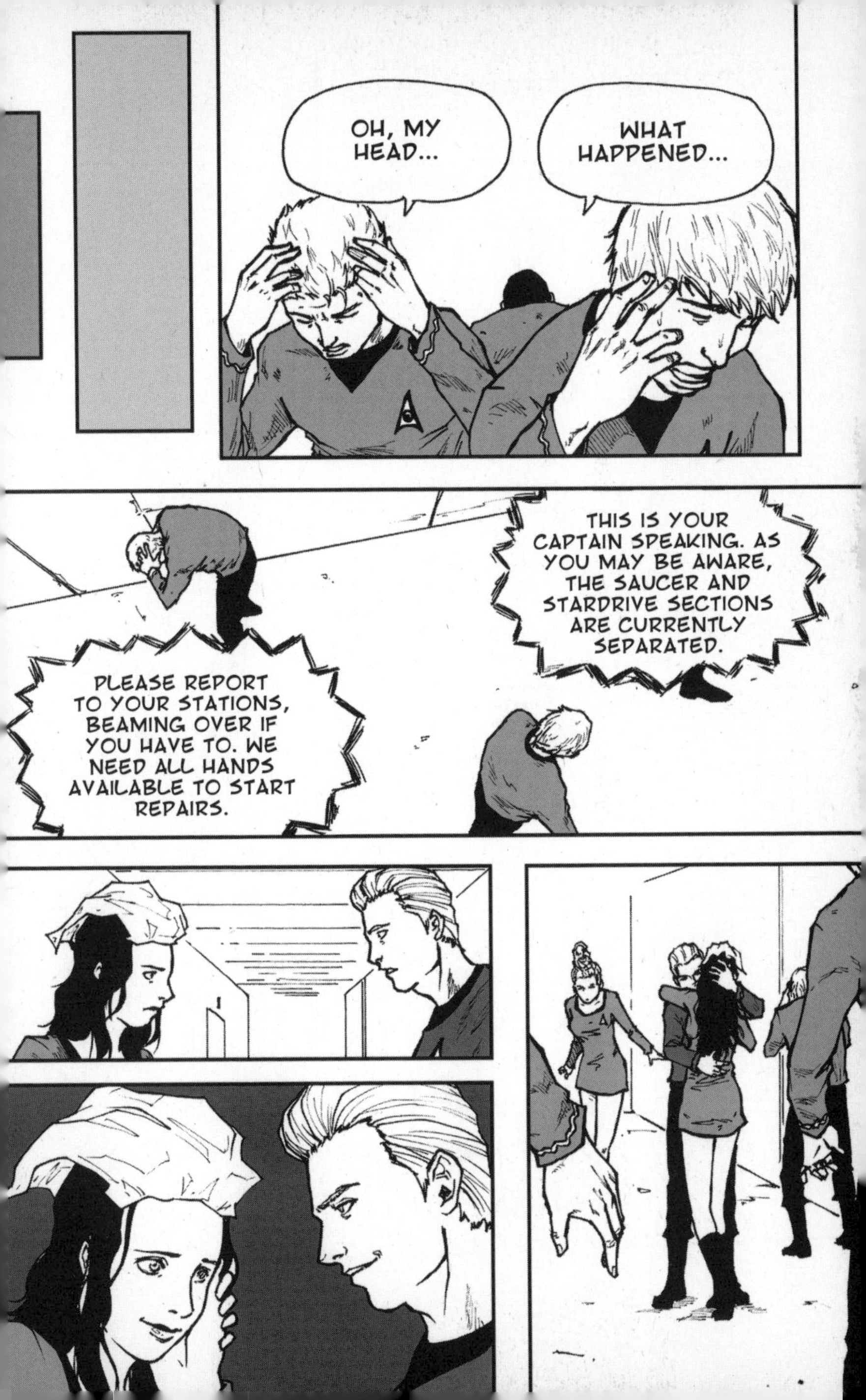
OH, MY HEAD...
WHAT HAPPENED...
THIS IS YOUR CAPTAIN SPEAKING. AS YOU MAY BE AWARE, THE SAUCER AND STARDRIVE SECTIONS ARE CURRENTLY SEPARATED.
PLEASE REPORT TO YOUR STATIONS, BEAMING OVER IF YOU HAVE TO. WE NEED ALL HANDS AVAILABLE TO START REPAIRS.

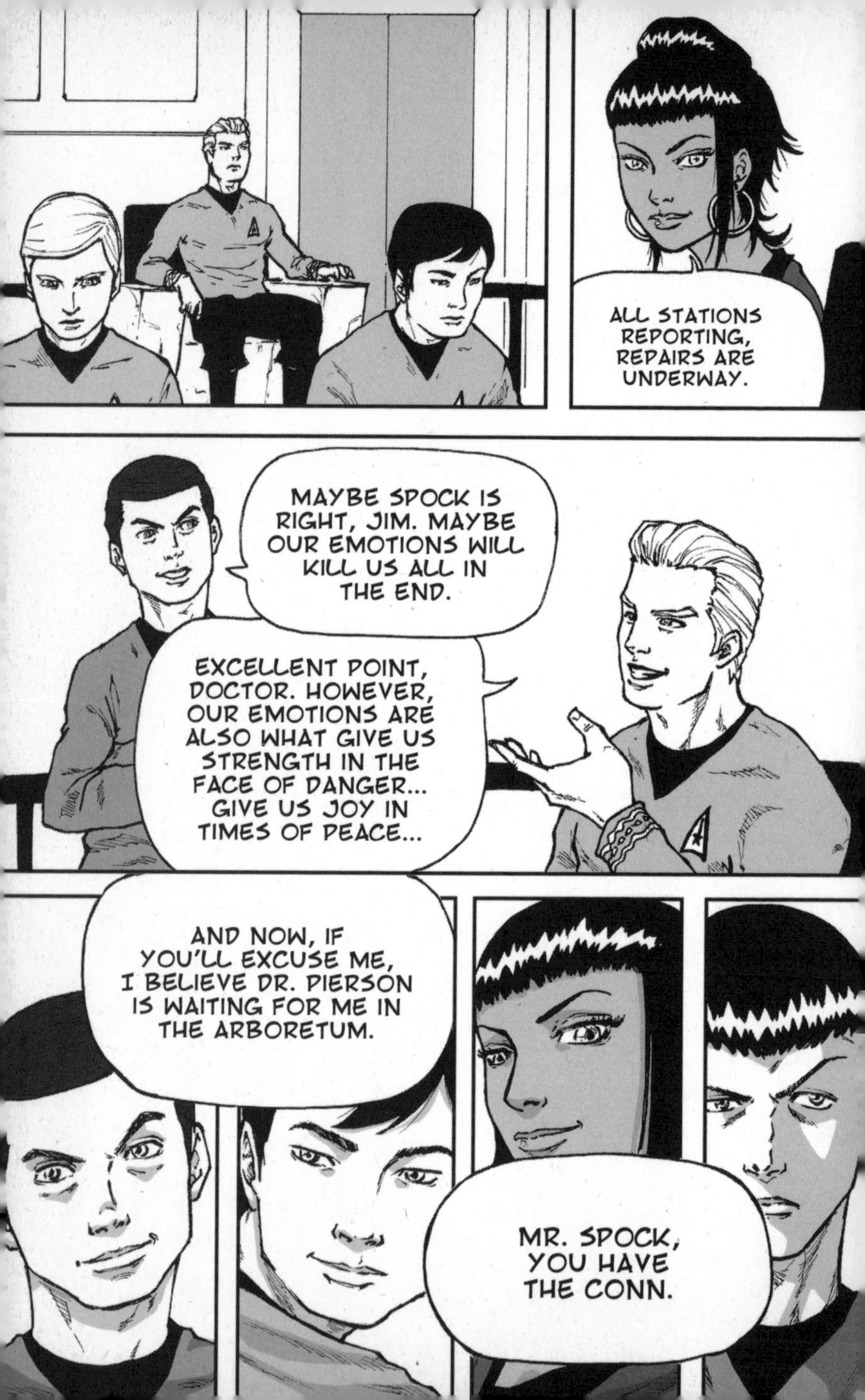
ALL STATIONS REPORTING, REPAIRS ARE UNDERWAY.
MAYBE SPOCK IS RIGHT, JIM. MAYBE OUR EMOTIONS WILL KILL US ALL IN THE END.
EXCELLENT POINT, DOCTOR. HOWEVER, OUR EMOTIONS ARE ALSO WHAT GIVE US STRENGTH IN THE FACE OF DANGER... GIVE US JOY IN TIMES OF PEACE...
AND NOW, IF YOU'LL EXCUSE ME, I BELIEVE DR. PIERSON IS WAITING FOR ME IN THE ARBORETUM.
MR. SPOCK, YOU HAVE THE CONN.

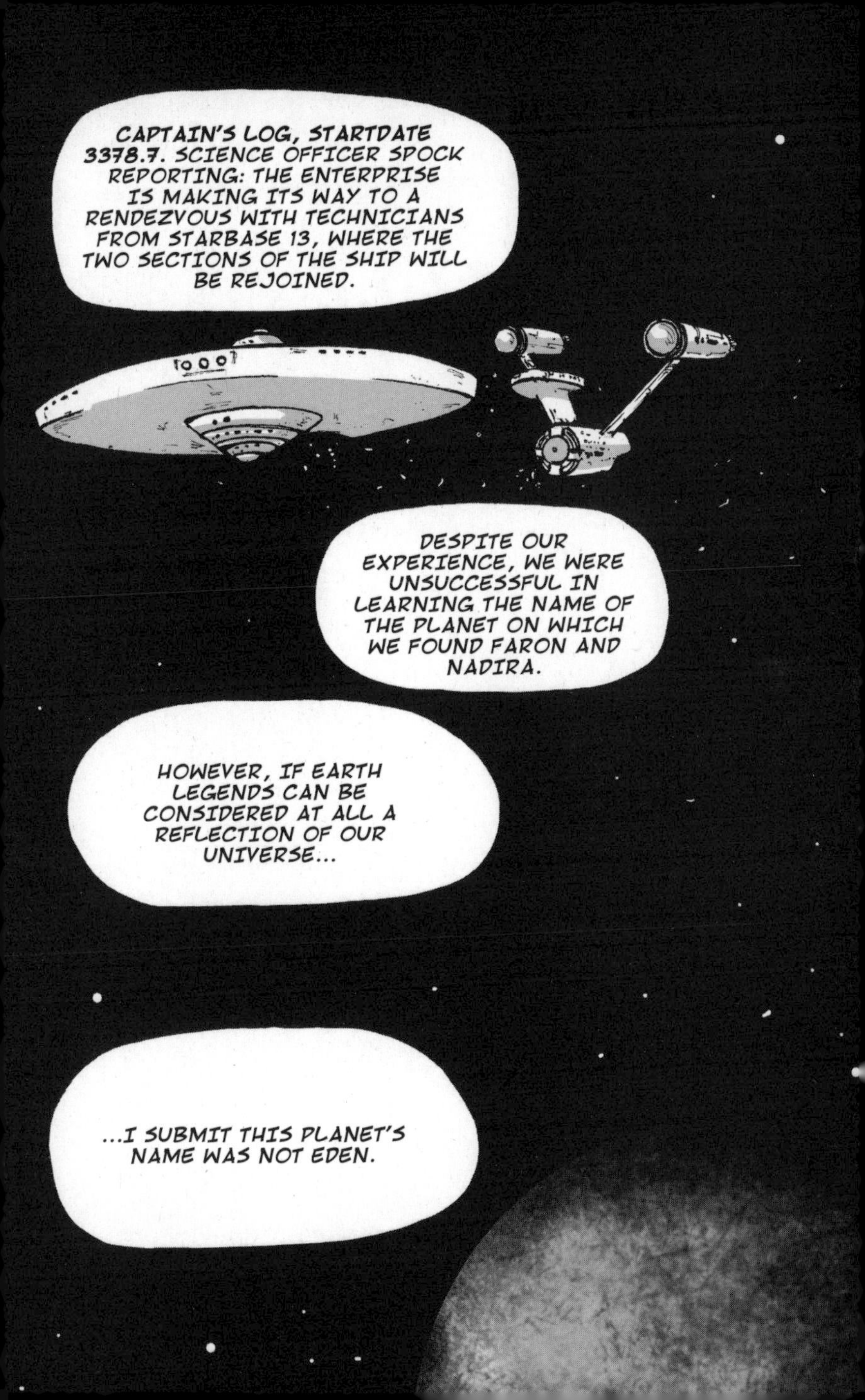
CAPTAIN'S LOG, STARTDATE 3378.7. SCIENCE OFFICER SPOCK REPORTING: THE ENTERPRISE IS MAKING ITS WAY TO A RENDEZVOUS WITH TECHNICIANS FROM STARBASE 13, WHERE THE TWO SECTIONS OF THE SHIP WILL BE REJOINED.
DESPITE OUR EXPERIENCE, WE WERE UNSUCCESSFUL IN LEARNING THE NAME OF THE PLANET ON WHICH WE FOUND FARON AND NADIRA.
HOWEVER, IF EARTH LEGENDS CAN BE CONSIDERED AT ALL A REFLECTION OF OUR UNIVERSE...
...I SUBMIT THIS PLANET'S NAME WAS NOT EDEN.

OBAN

STORY BY JIM ALEXANDER
ART BY MICHAEL SHELFER

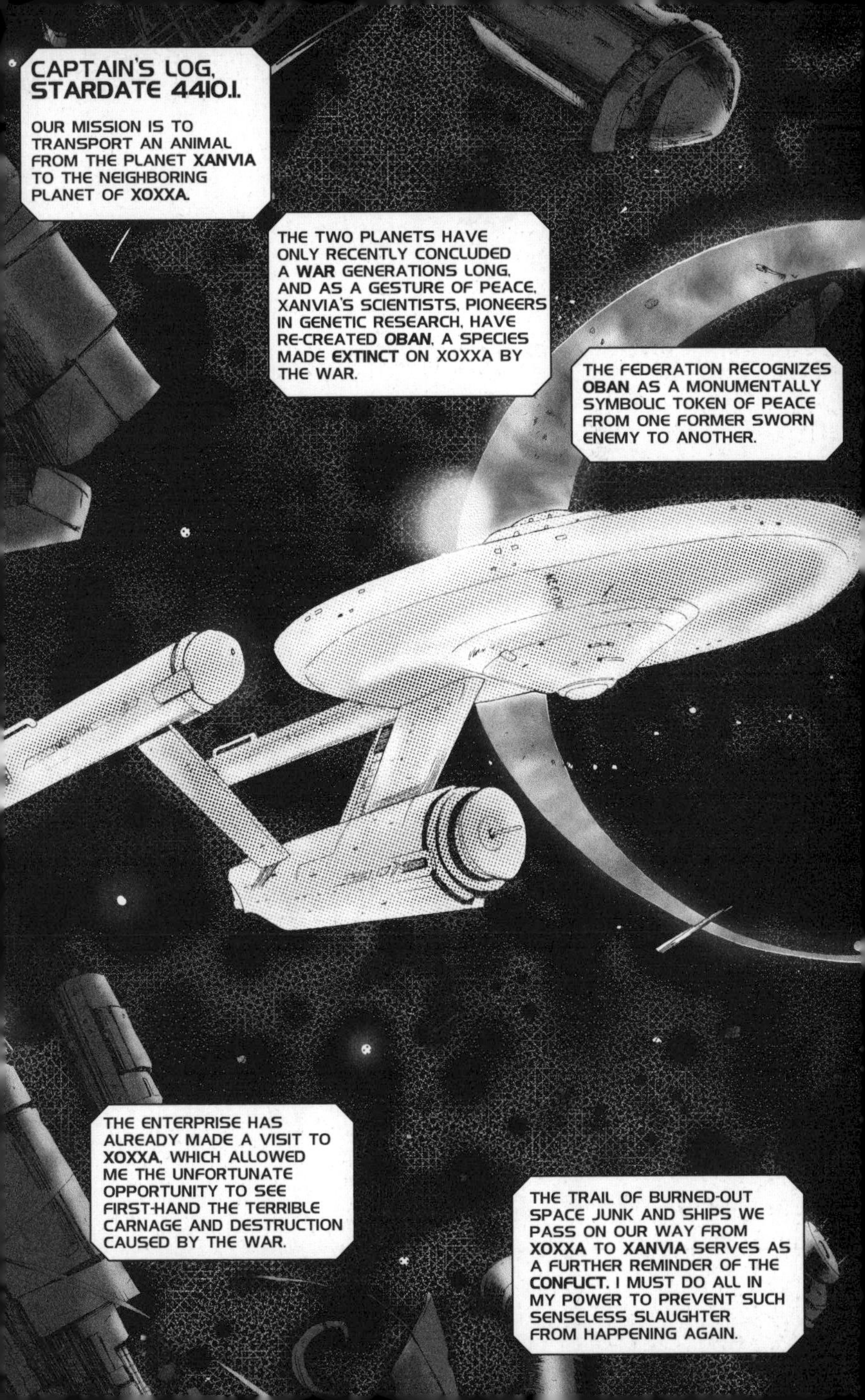
CAPTAIN'S LOG, STARDATE 4410.1.
OUR MISSION IS TO TRANSPORT AN ANIMAL FROM THE PLANET XANVIA TO THE NEIGHBORING PLANET OF XOXXA.
THE TWO PLANETS HAVE ONLY RECENTLY CONCLUDED A WAR GENERATIONS LONG, AND AS A GESTURE OF PEACE, XANVIA'S SCIENTISTS, PIONEERS IN GENETIC RESEARCH, HAVE RE-CREATED OBAN, A SPECIES MADE EXTINCT ON XOXXA BY THE WAR.
THE FEDERATION RECOGNIZES OBAN AS A MONUMENTALLY SYMBOLIC TOKEN OF PEACE FROM ONE FORMER SWORN ENEMY TO ANOTHER.
THE ENTERPRISE HAS ALREADY MADE A VISIT TO XOXXA, WHICH ALLOWED ME THE UNFORTUNATE OPPORTUNITY TO SEE FIRST-HAND THE TERRIBLE CARNAGE AND DESTRUCTION CAUSED BY THE WAR.
THE TRAIL OF BURNED-OUT SPACE JUNK AND SHIPS WE PASS ON OUR WAY FROM XOXXA TO XANVIA SERVES AS A FURTHER REMINDER OF THE CONFLICT. I MUST DO ALL IN MY POWER TO PREVENT SUCH SENSELESS SLAUGHTER FROM HAPPENING AGAIN.

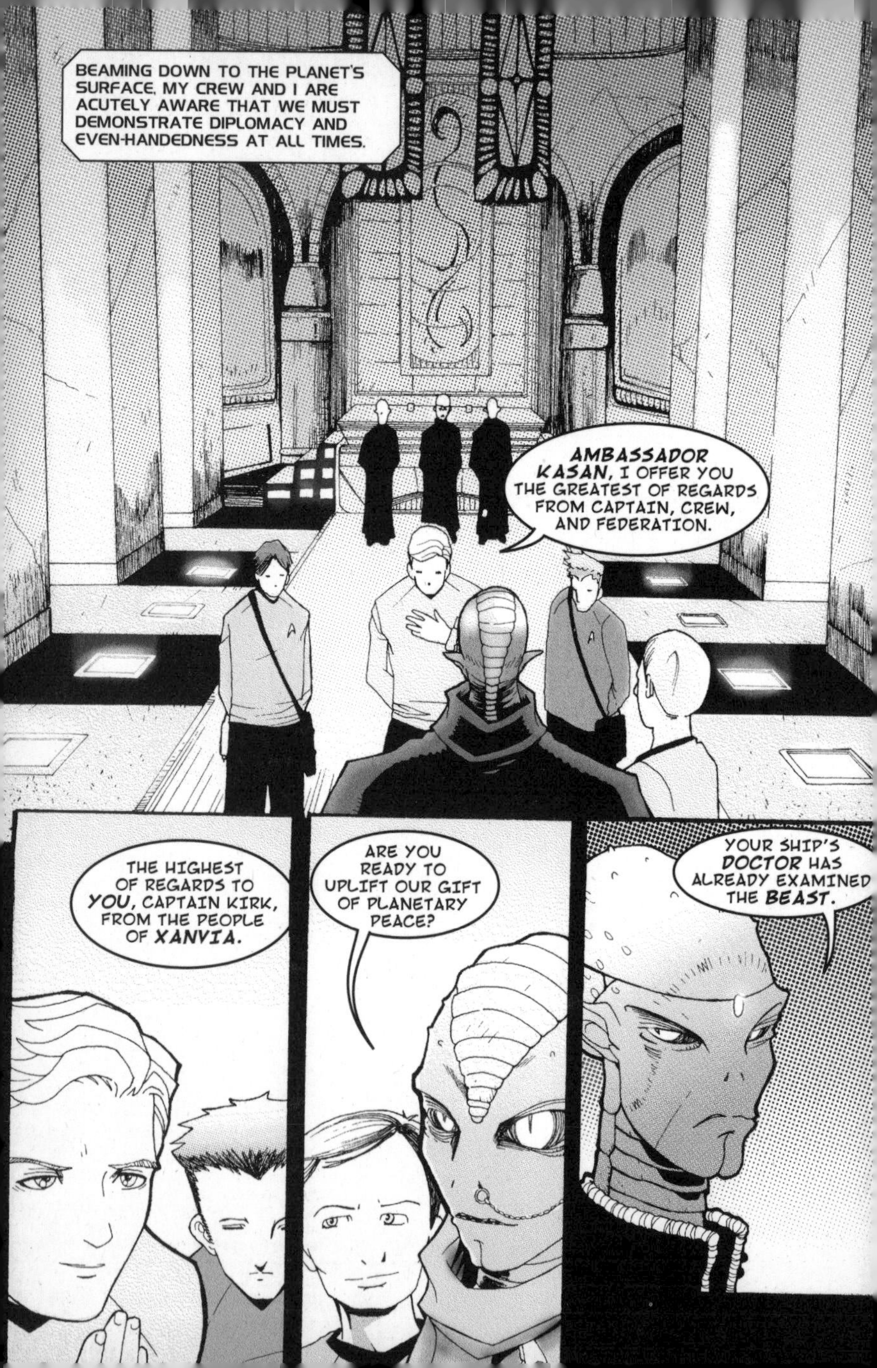
BEAMING DOWN TO THE PLANET'S SURFACE, MY CREW AND I ARE ACUTELY AWARE THAT WE MUST DEMONSTRATE DIPLOMACY AND EVEN-HANDEDNESS AT ALL TIMES.
AMBASSADOR KASAN, I OFFER YOU THE GREATEST OF REGARDS FROM CAPTAIN, CREW, AND FEDERATION.
THE HIGHEST OF REGARDS TO YOU, CAPTAIN KIRK, FROM THE PEOPLE OF XANVIA.
ARE YOU READY TO UPLIFT OUR GIFT OF PLANETARY PEACE?
YOUR SHIP'S DOCTOR HAS ALREADY EXAMINED THE BEAST.

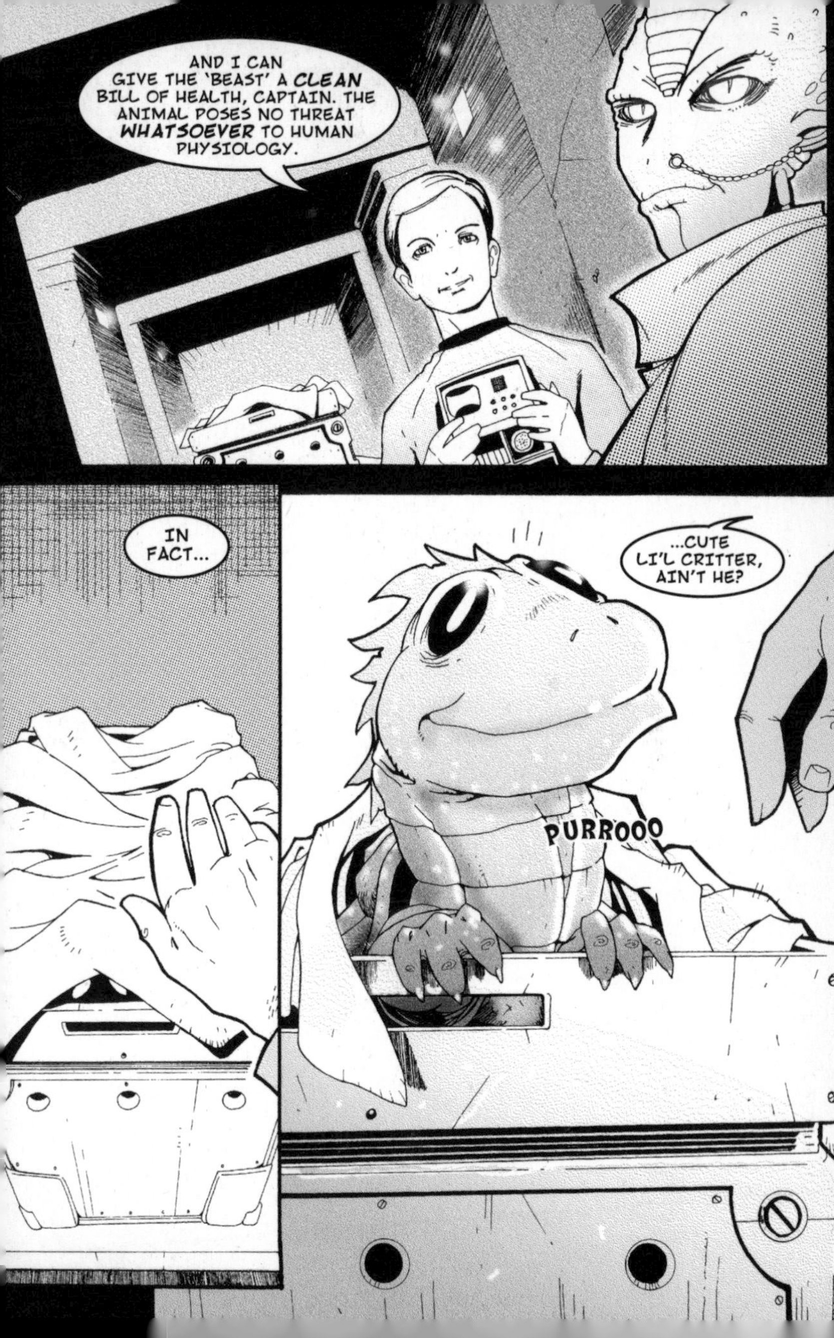
AND I CAN GIVE THE 'BEAST' A CLEAN BILL OF HEALTH, CAPTAIN. THE ANIMAL POSES NO THREAT WHATSOEVER TO HUMAN PHYSIOLOGY.
IN FACT...
...CUTE LI'L CRITTER, AIN'T HE?
PURROOO

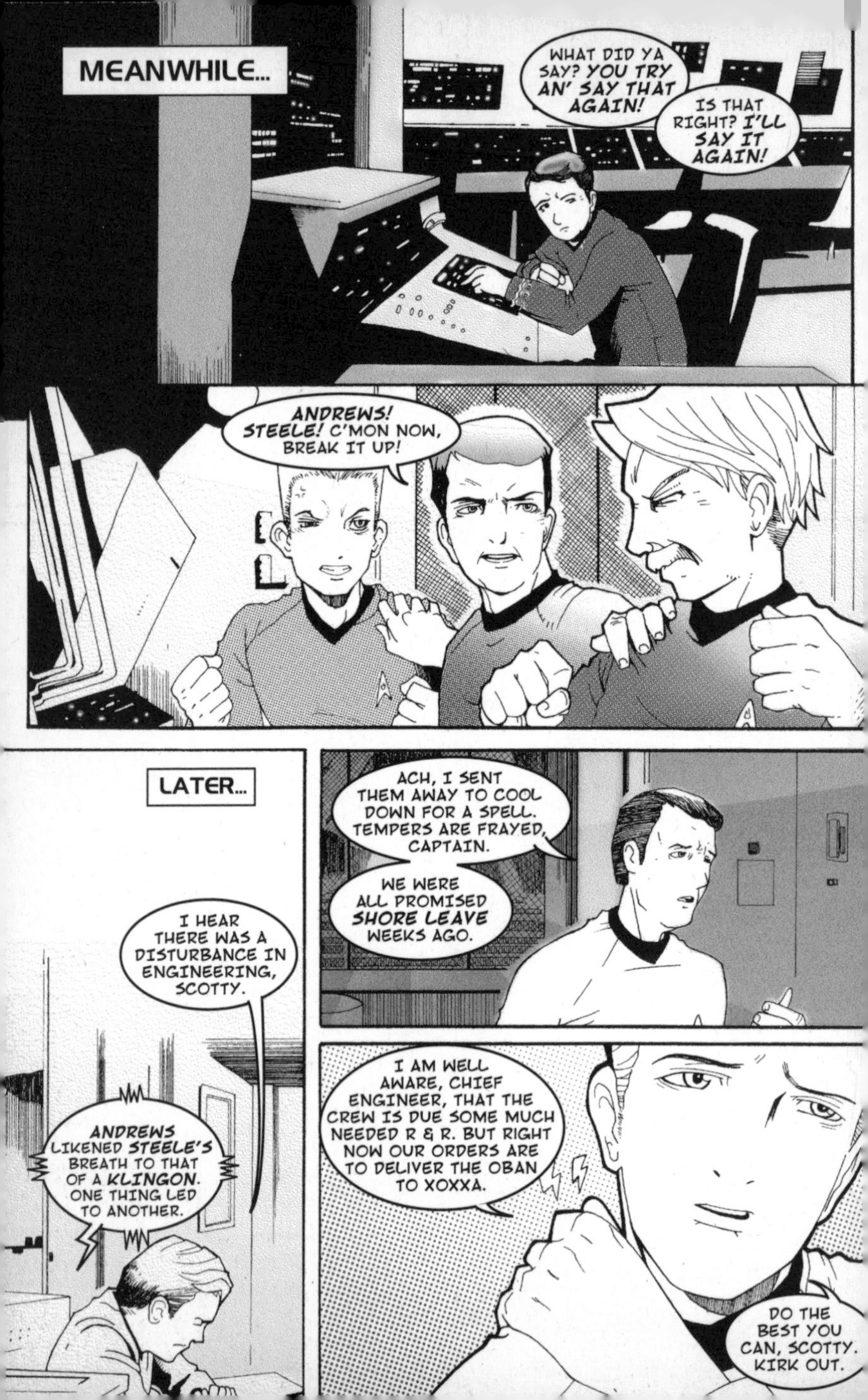
MEANWHILE...
WHAT DID YA SAY? YOU TRY AN' SAY THAT AGAIN!
IS THAT RIGHT? I'LL SAY IT AGAIN!
ANDREWS! STEELE! C'MON NOW, BREAK IT UP!
LATER...
I HEAR THERE WAS A DISTURBANCE IN ENGINEERING, SCOTTY.
ANDREWS LIKENED STEELE'S BREATH TO THAT OF A KLINGON. ONE THING LED TO ANOTHER.
ACH, I SENT THEM AWAY TO COOL DOWN FOR A SPELL. TEMPERS ARE FRAYED, CAPTAIN.
WE WERE ALL PROMISED SHORE LEAVE WEEKS AGO.
I AM WELL AWARE, CHIEF ENGINEER, THAT THE CREW IS DUE SOME MUCH NEEDED R & R. BUT RIGHT NOW OUR ORDERS ARE TO DELIVER THE OBAN TO XOXXA.
DO THE BEST YOU CAN, SCOTTY. KIRK OUT.

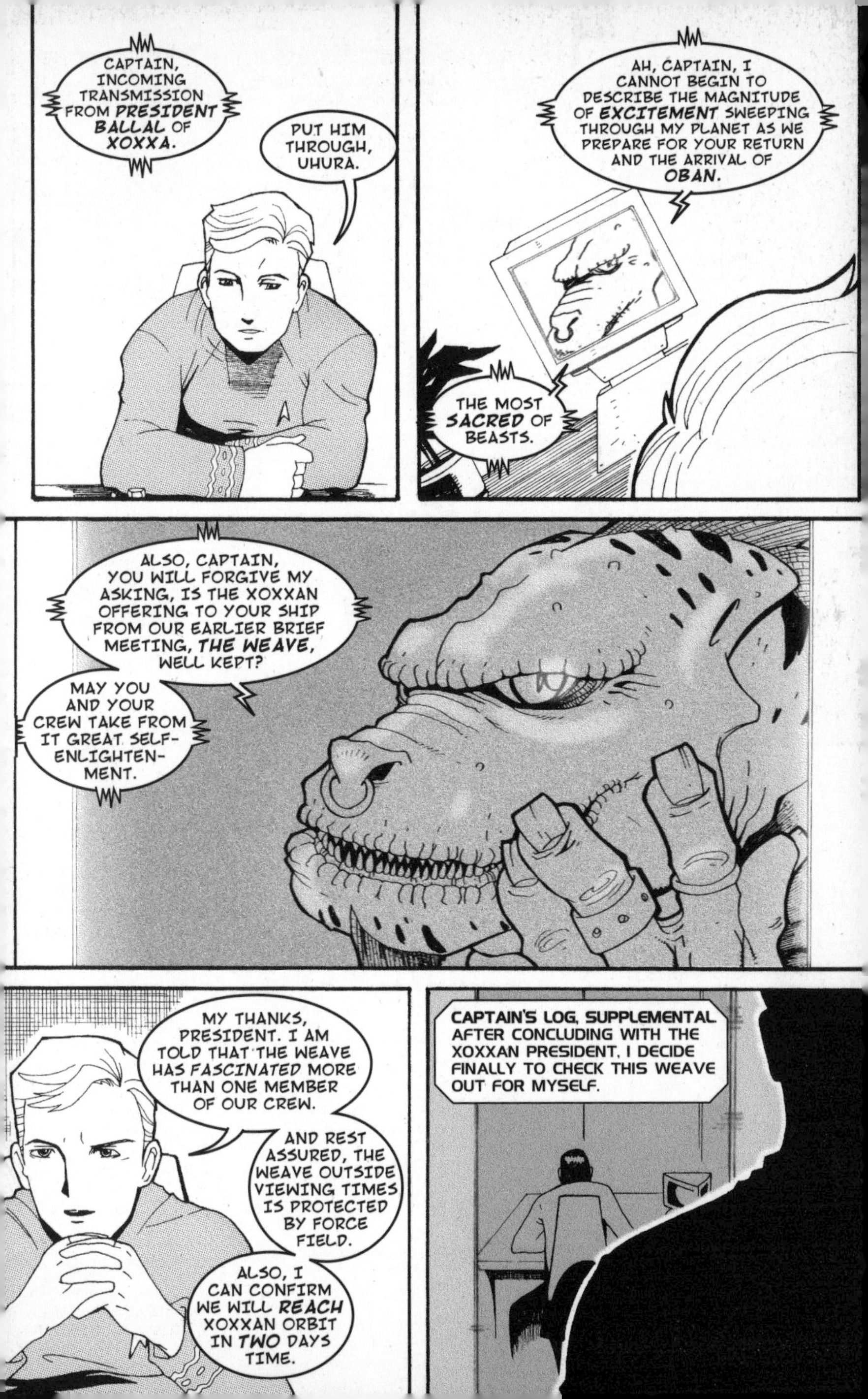
CAPTAIN, INCOMING TRANSMISSION FROM PRESIDENT BALLAL OF XOXXA.
PUT HIM THROUGH, UHURA.
AH, CAPTAIN, I CANNOT BEGIN TO DESCRIBE THE MAGNITUDE OF EXCITEMENT SWEEPING THROUGH MY PLANET AS WE PREPARE FOR YOUR RETURN AND THE ARRIVAL OF OBAN.
THE MOST SACRED OF BEASTS.
ALSO, CAPTAIN, YOU WILL FORGIVE MY ASKING, IS THE XOXXAN OFFERING TO YOUR SHIP FROM OUR EARLIER BRIEF MEETING, THE WEAVE, WELL KEPT?
MAY YOU AND YOUR CREW TAKE FROM IT GREAT SELF-ENLIGHTENMENT.
MY THANKS, PRESIDENT. I AM TOLD THAT THE WEAVE HAS FASCINATED MORE THAN ONE MEMBER OF OUR CREW.
AND REST ASSURED, THE WEAVE OUTSIDE VIEWING TIMES IS PROTECTED BY FORCE FIELD.
ALSO, I CAN CONFIRM WE WILL REACH XOXXAN ORBIT IN TWO DAYS TIME.
CAPTAIN'S LOG, SUPPLEMENTAL
AFTER CONCLUDING WITH THE XOXXAN PRESIDENT, I DECIDE FINALLY TO CHECK THIS WEAVE OUT FOR MYSELF.

FASCINATING. THE WEAVE IS A SCREEN THAT CONTAINS EMPATHICALLY REACTIVE *MICROSCOPIC CREATURES*, WHICH HAVE THE ABILITY TO CHANGE COLOR AND SHAPE.

THEY FORM IMAGES AND PATTERNS THAT REFLECT THE *EMOTIONS* OF THE PERSON LOOKING DIRECTLY AT IT.

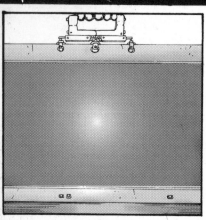

NOT MUCH OF A *PATTERN* EMERGING THERE, MR. SPOCK.

OF COURSE, CAPTAIN. I HAVE NO STRONG EMOTIONS FOR THE WEAVE TO REFLECT. PERHAPS IF YOU WOULD LIKE TO TRY.

HMPH.

THE TINY CREATURES READ BASIC SUBLIMINAL EFFECTS *DIRECT* FROM THE BRAIN.

JIM, FROM WHAT I CAN SEE, YOU ARE SORELY TROUBLED.

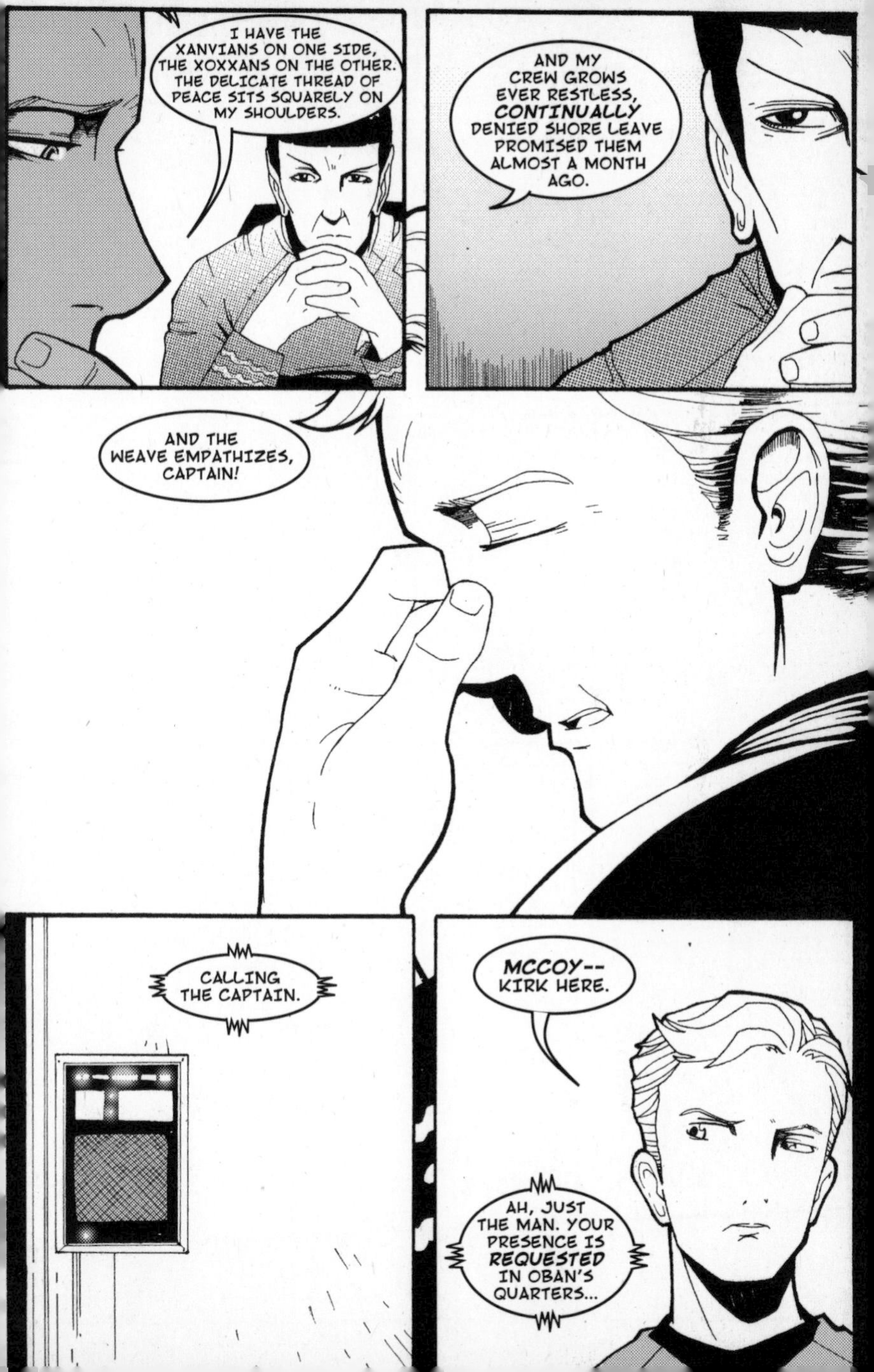
I HAVE THE XANVIANS ON ONE SIDE, THE XOXXANS ON THE OTHER. THE DELICATE THREAD OF PEACE SITS SQUARELY ON MY SHOULDERS.
AND MY CREW GROWS EVER RESTLESS, CONTINUALLY DENIED SHORE LEAVE PROMISED THEM ALMOST A MONTH AGO.
AND THE WEAVE EMPATHIZES, CAPTAIN!
CALLING THE CAPTAIN.
MCCOY-- KIRK HERE.
AH, JUST THE MAN. YOUR PRESENCE IS REQUESTED IN OBAN'S QUARTERS...

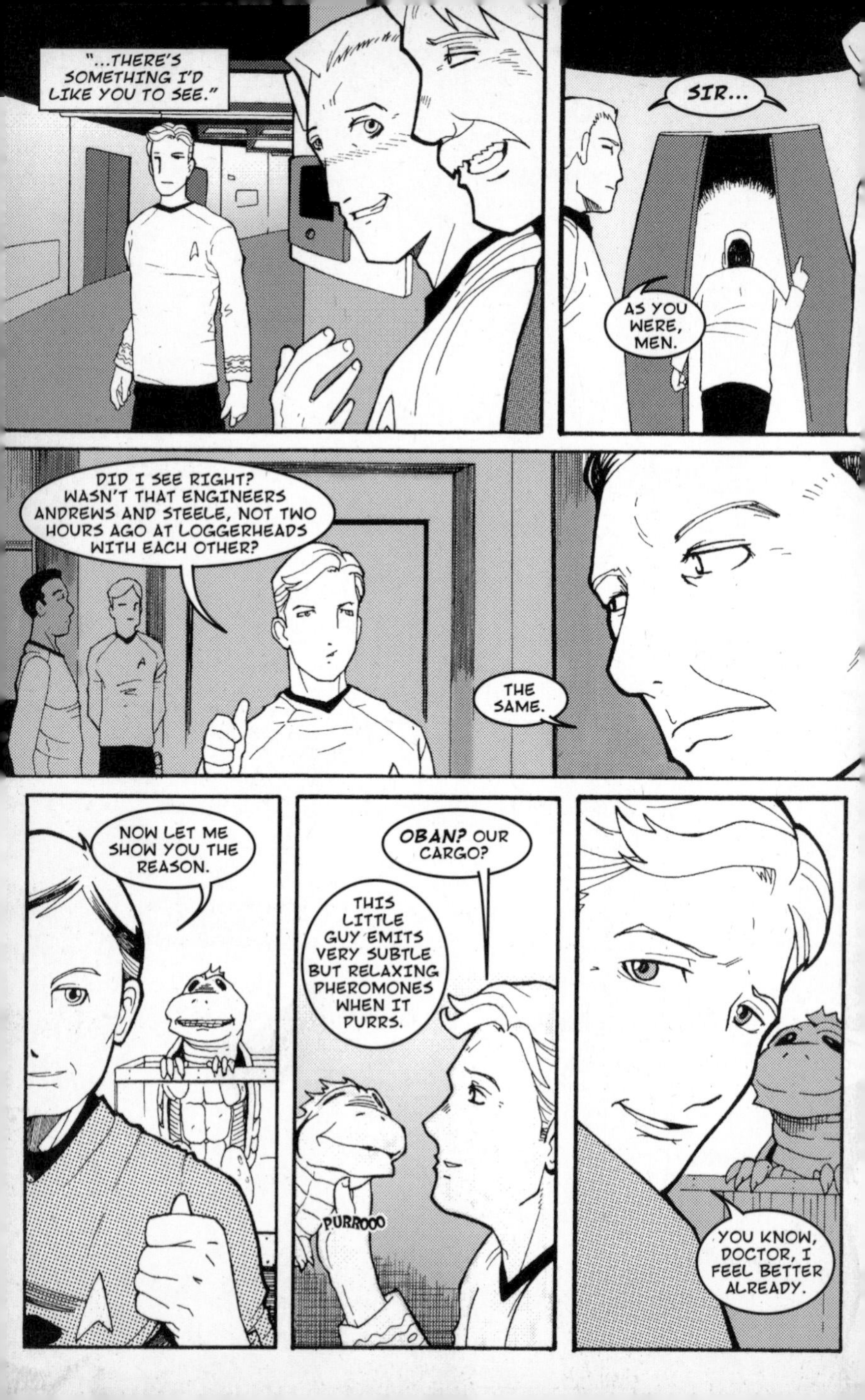
"...THERE'S SOMETHING I'D LIKE YOU TO SEE."
SIR...
AS YOU WERE, MEN.
DID I SEE RIGHT? WASN'T THAT ENGINEERS ANDREWS AND STEELE, NOT TWO HOURS AGO AT LOGGERHEADS WITH EACH OTHER?
THE SAME.
NOW LET ME SHOW YOU THE REASON.
OBAN? OUR CARGO?
THIS LITTLE GUY EMITS VERY SUBTLE BUT RELAXING PHEROMONES WHEN IT PURRS.
PURROOO
YOU KNOW, DOCTOR, I FEEL BETTER ALREADY.

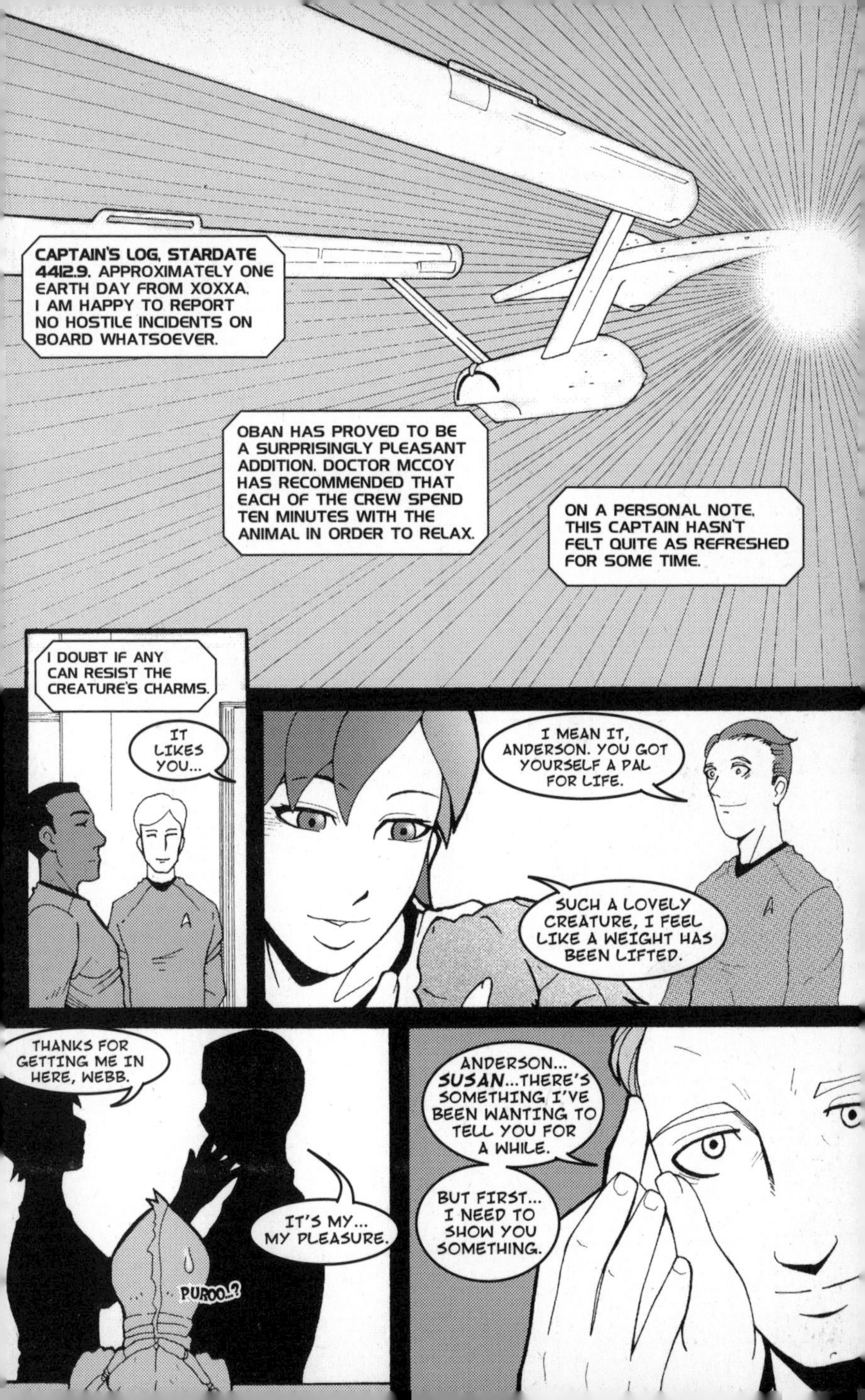
CAPTAIN'S LOG, STARDATE 4412.9. APPROXIMATELY ONE EARTH DAY FROM XOXXA, I AM HAPPY TO REPORT NO HOSTILE INCIDENTS ON BOARD WHATSOEVER.
OBAN HAS PROVED TO BE A SURPRISINGLY PLEASANT ADDITION. DOCTOR MCCOY HAS RECOMMENDED THAT EACH OF THE CREW SPEND TEN MINUTES WITH THE ANIMAL IN ORDER TO RELAX.
ON A PERSONAL NOTE, THIS CAPTAIN HASN'T FELT QUITE AS REFRESHED FOR SOME TIME.
I DOUBT IF ANY CAN RESIST THE CREATURE'S CHARMS.
IT LIKES YOU...
I MEAN IT, ANDERSON. YOU GOT YOURSELF A PAL FOR LIFE.
SUCH A LOVELY CREATURE, I FEEL LIKE A WEIGHT HAS BEEN LIFTED.
THANKS FOR GETTING ME IN HERE, WEBB.
IT'S MY... MY PLEASURE.
PUROO..?
ANDERSON... *SUSAN*...THERE'S SOMETHING I'VE BEEN WANTING TO TELL YOU FOR A WHILE.
BUT FIRST... I NEED TO SHOW YOU SOMETHING.

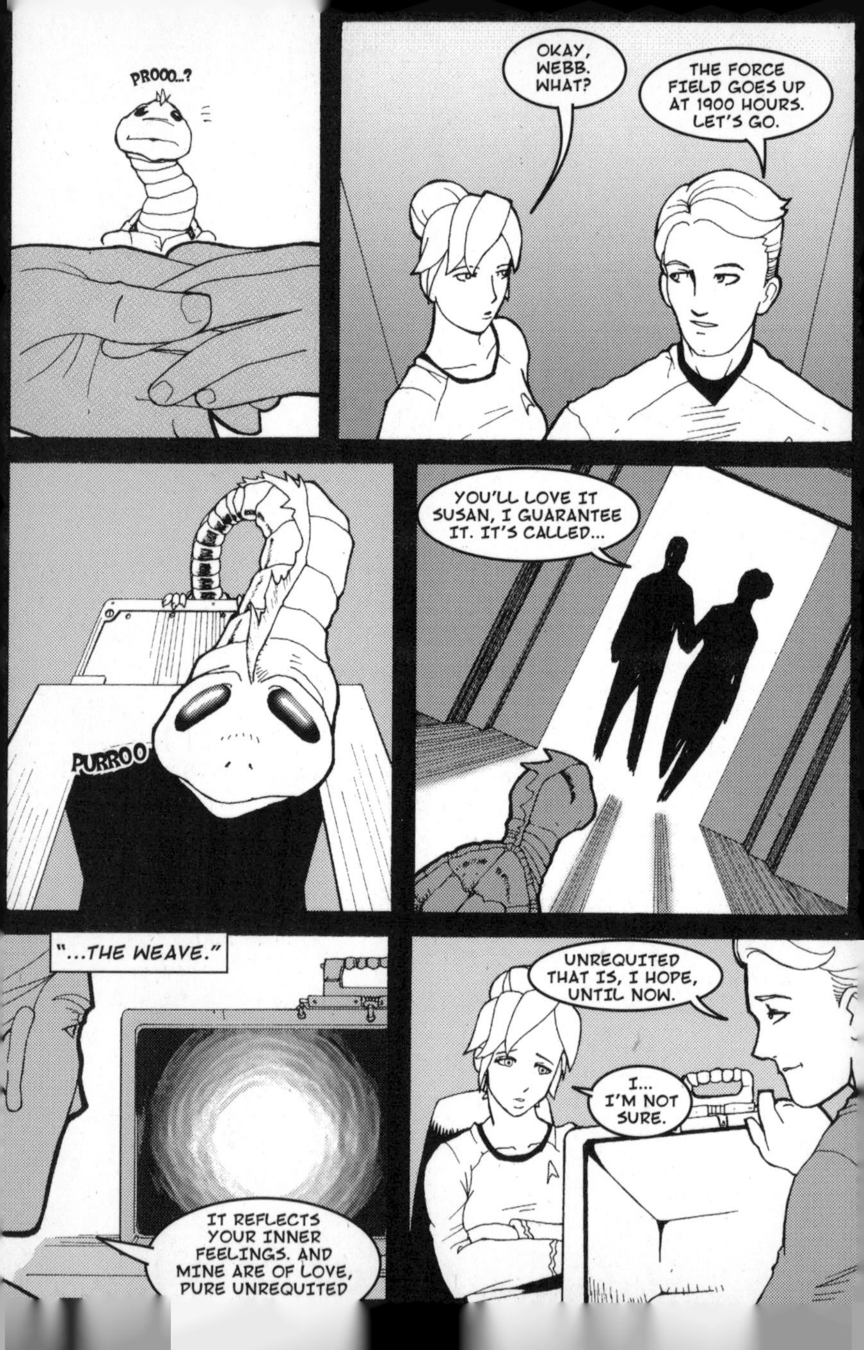
PROOO...?
OKAY, WEBB. WHAT?
THE FORCE FIELD GOES UP AT 1900 HOURS. LET'S GO.
PURROO
YOU'LL LOVE IT SUSAN, I GUARANTEE IT. IT'S CALLED...
"...THE WEAVE."
IT REFLECTS YOUR INNER FEELINGS. AND MINE ARE OF LOVE, PURE UNREQUITED
UNREQUITED THAT IS, I HOPE, UNTIL NOW.
I... I'M NOT SURE.

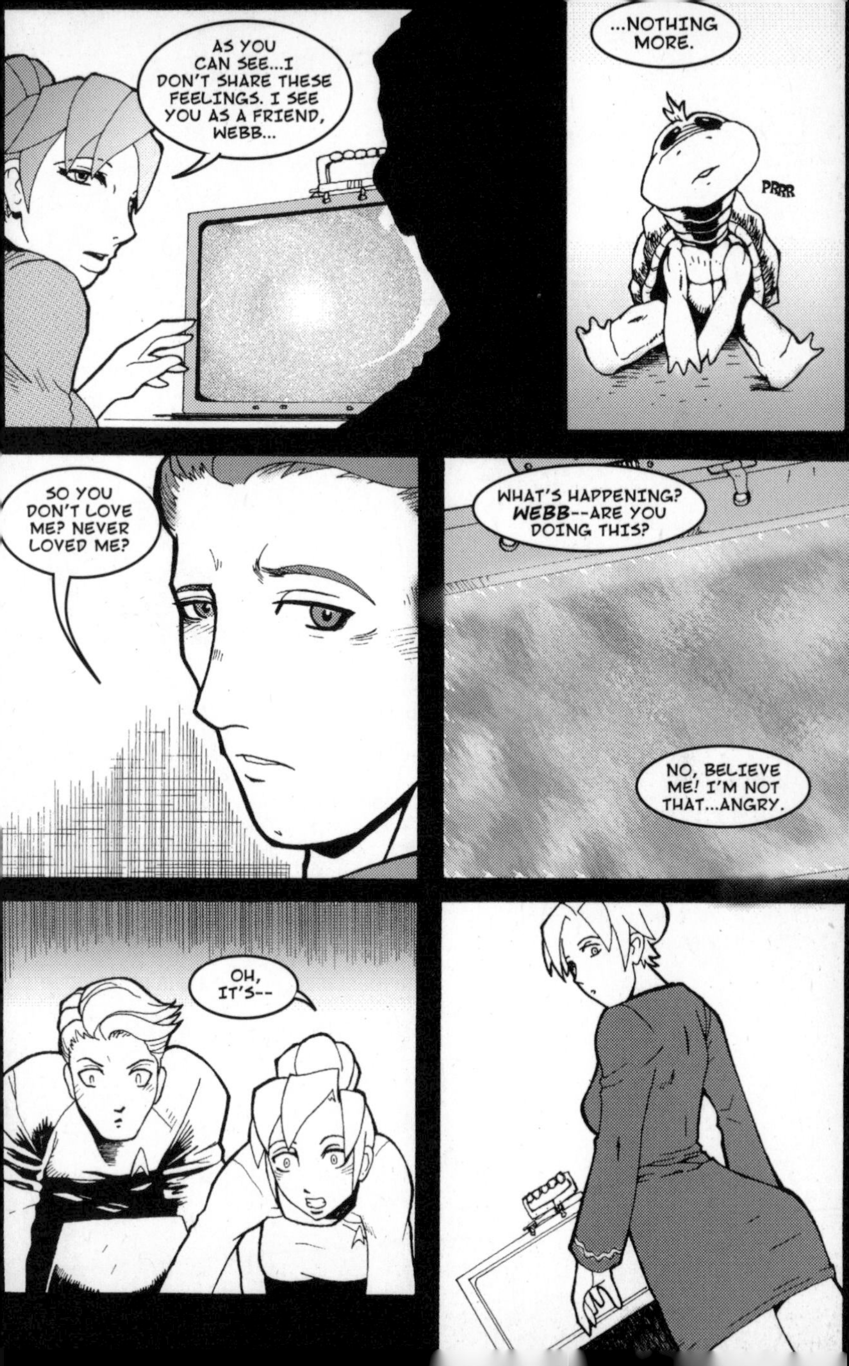
AS YOU CAN SEE...I DON'T SHARE THESE FEELINGS. I SEE YOU AS A FRIEND, WEBB...
...NOTHING MORE.
PRRR
SO YOU DON'T LOVE ME? NEVER LOVED ME?
WHAT'S HAPPENING? WEBB--ARE YOU DOING THIS?
NO, BELIEVE ME! I'M NOT THAT...ANGRY.
OH, IT'S--

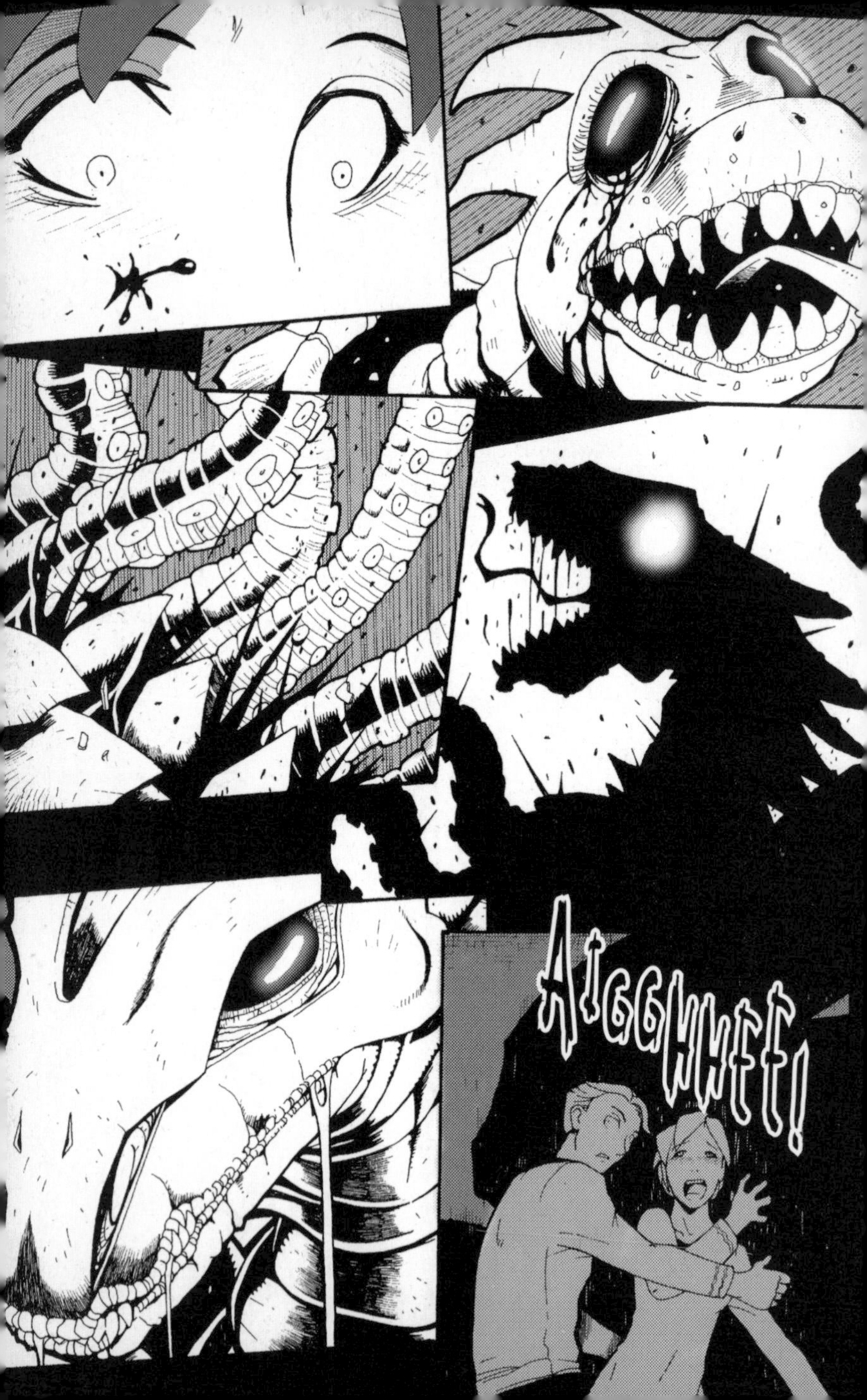
AIGGHHFF!

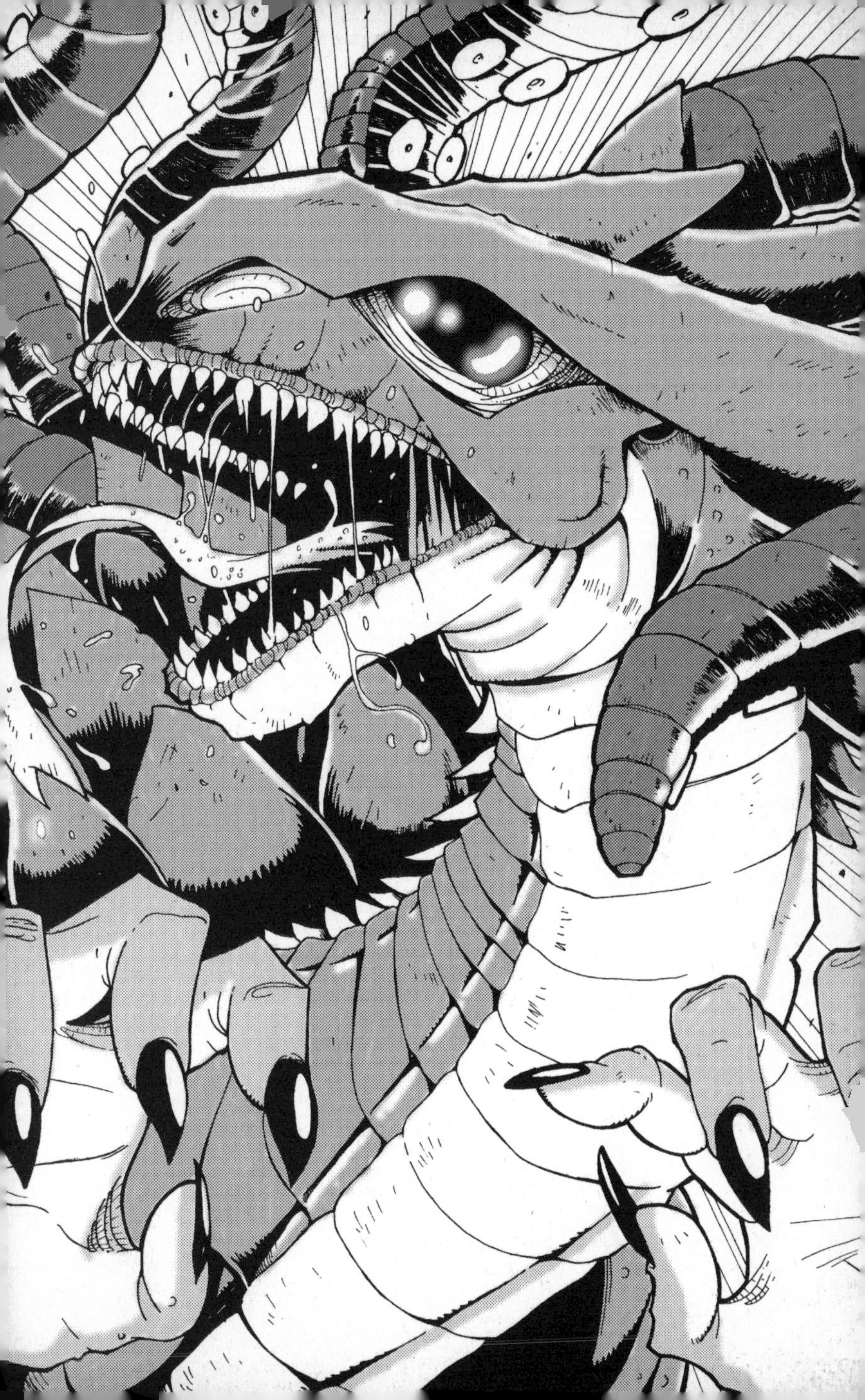

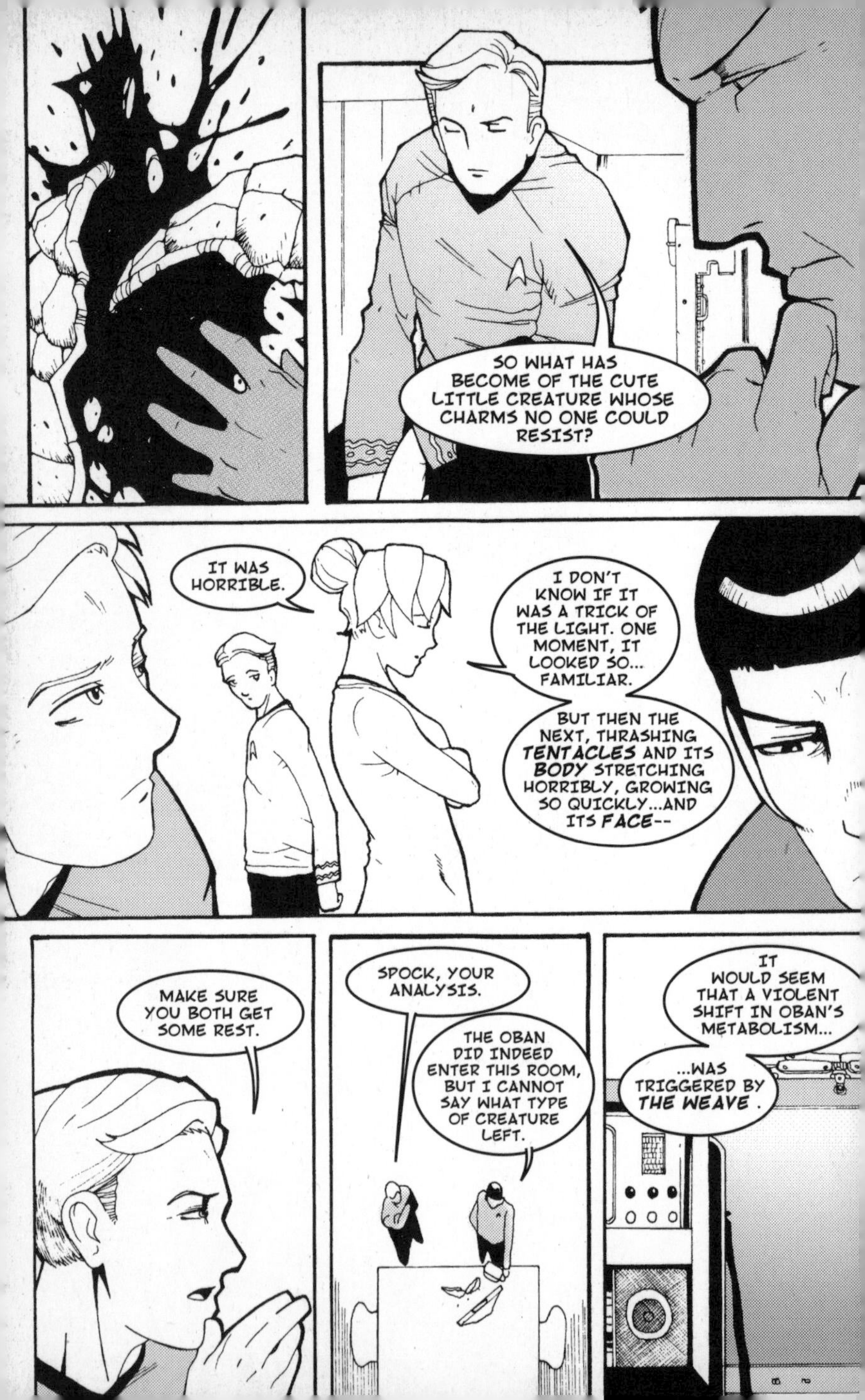
SO WHAT HAS BECOME OF THE CUTE LITTLE CREATURE WHOSE CHARMS NO ONE COULD RESIST?
IT WAS HORRIBLE.
I DON'T KNOW IF IT WAS A TRICK OF THE LIGHT. ONE MOMENT, IT LOOKED SO... FAMILIAR.
BUT THEN THE NEXT, THRASHING *TENTACLES* AND ITS *BODY* STRETCHING HORRIBLY, GROWING SO QUICKLY...AND ITS *FACE*--
MAKE SURE YOU BOTH GET SOME REST.
SPOCK, YOUR ANALYSIS.
THE OBAN DID INDEED ENTER THIS ROOM, BUT I CANNOT SAY WHAT TYPE OF CREATURE LEFT.
IT WOULD SEEM THAT A VIOLENT SHIFT IN OBAN'S METABOLISM...
...WAS TRIGGERED BY *THE WEAVE* .

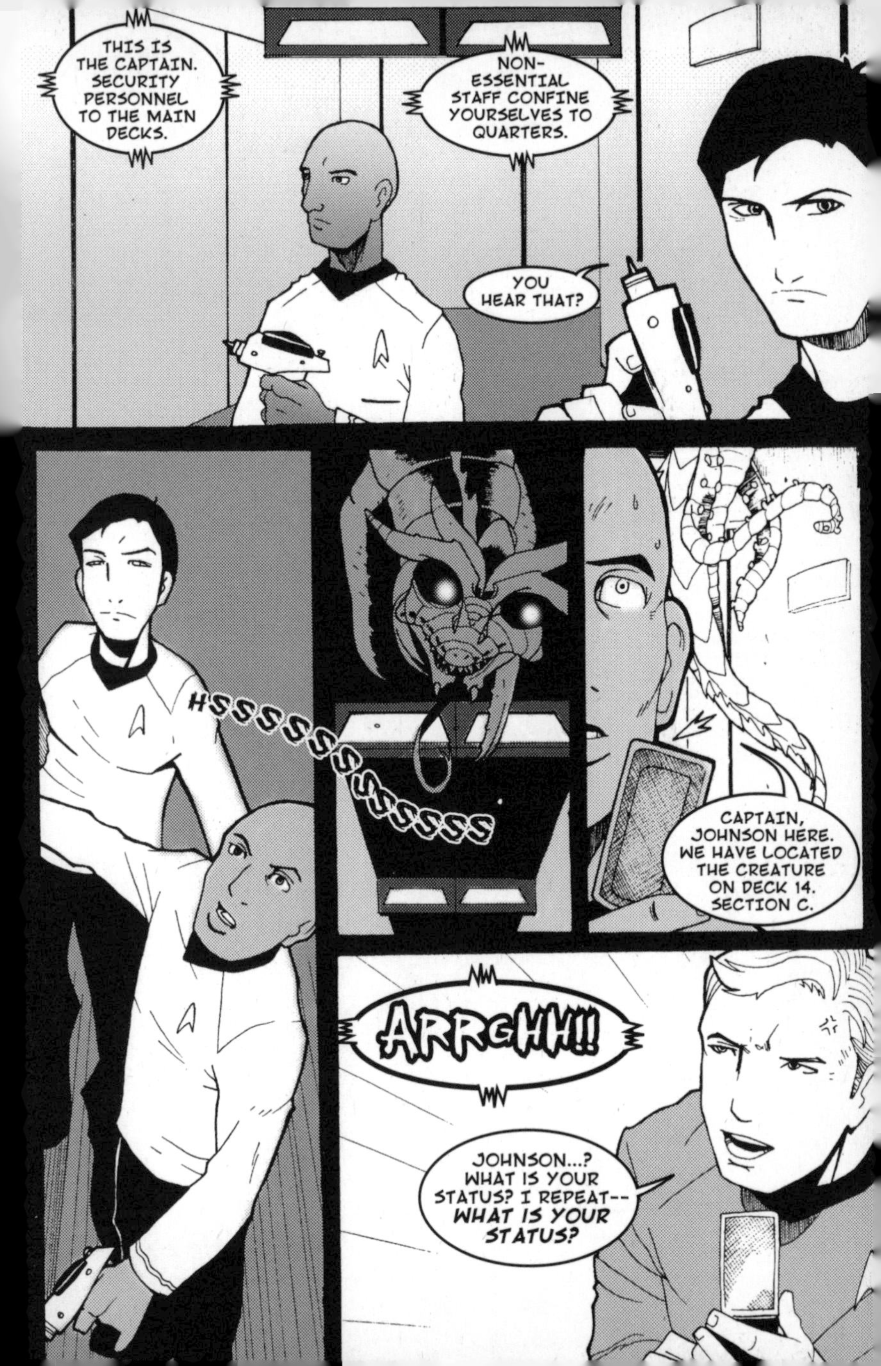
THIS IS THE CAPTAIN. SECURITY PERSONNEL TO THE MAIN DECKS.
NON-ESSENTIAL STAFF CONFINE YOURSELVES TO QUARTERS.
YOU HEAR THAT?
HSSSSSSSSSSSSS
CAPTAIN, JOHNSON HERE. WE HAVE LOCATED THE CREATURE ON DECK 14. SECTION C.
ARRGHH!!
JOHNSON...? WHAT IS YOUR STATUS? I REPEAT-- WHAT IS YOUR STATUS?

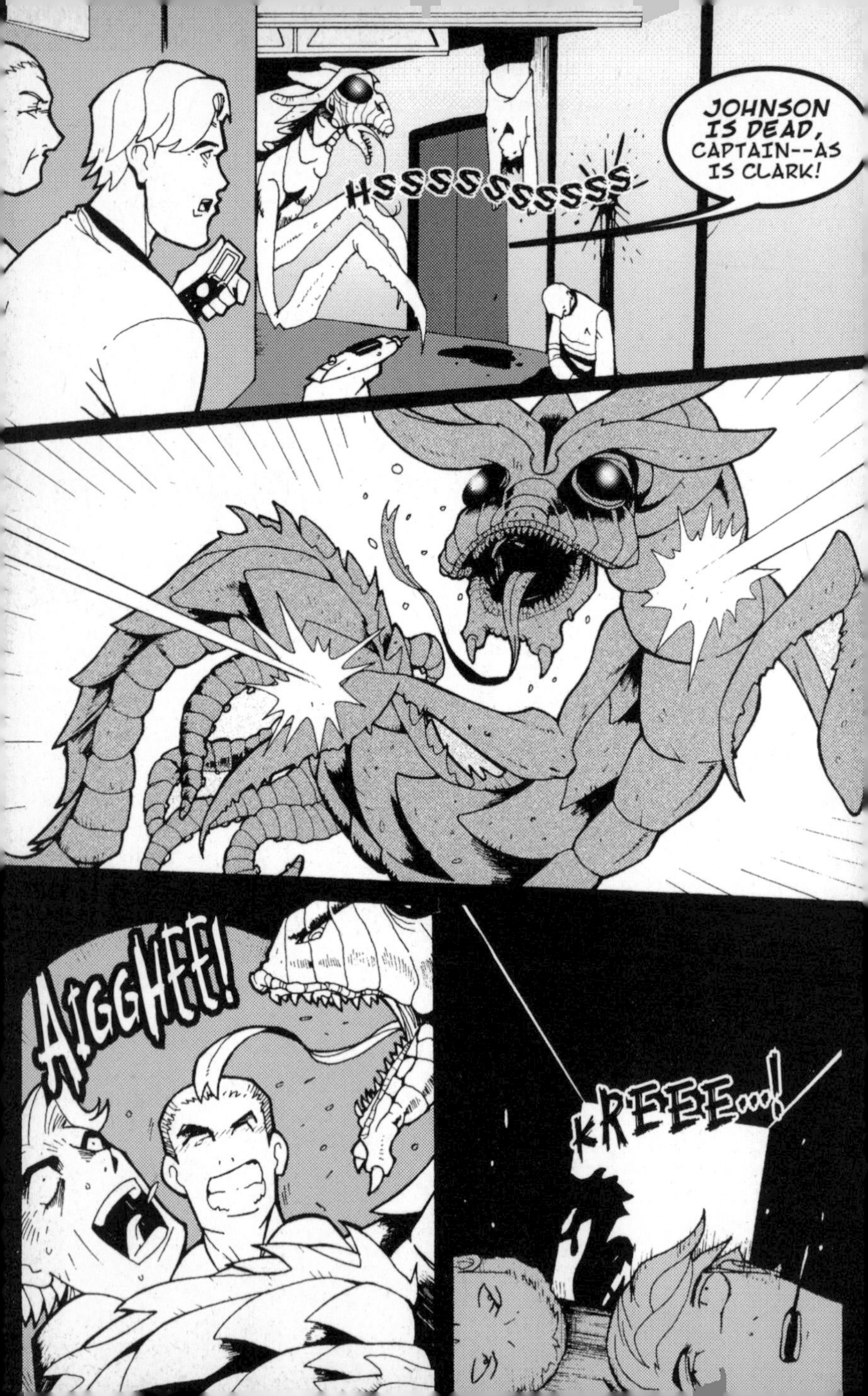
JOHNSON IS DEAD, CAPTAIN--AS IS CLARK!
HSSSSSSSSSSS
AIGGHEE!
KREEE...!

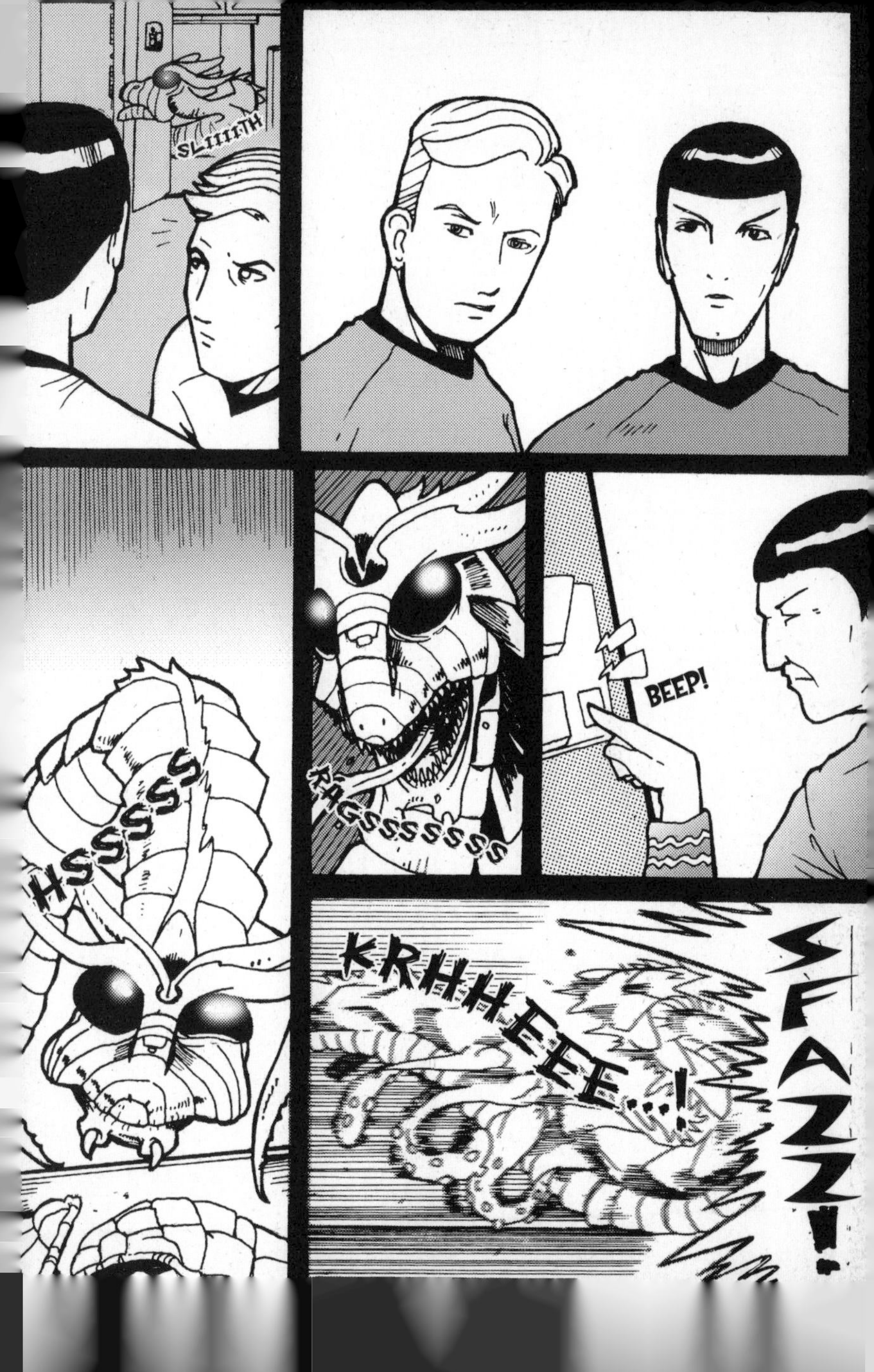
SLIIIIITH
HSSSSSSS
RAGSSSSSSSS
BEEP!
KRHHEEE...!
SFAZZ!

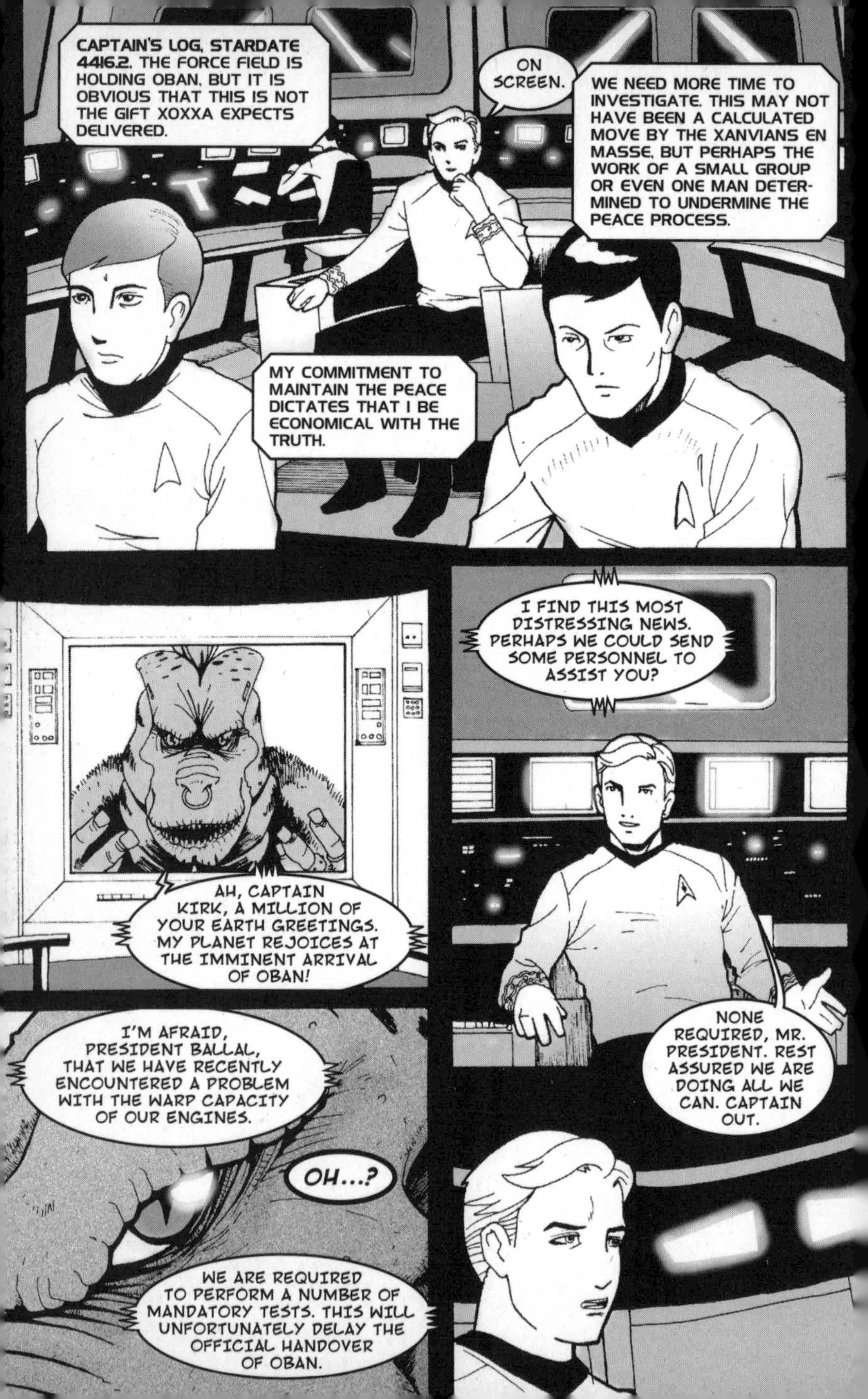
CAPTAIN'S LOG, STARDATE 4416.2. THE FORCE FIELD IS HOLDING OBAN, BUT IT IS OBVIOUS THAT THIS IS NOT THE GIFT XOXXA EXPECTS DELIVERED.
ON SCREEN.
WE NEED MORE TIME TO INVESTIGATE. THIS MAY NOT HAVE BEEN A CALCULATED MOVE BY THE XANVIANS EN MASSE, BUT PERHAPS THE WORK OF A SMALL GROUP OR EVEN ONE MAN DETERMINED TO UNDERMINE THE PEACE PROCESS.
MY COMMITMENT TO MAINTAIN THE PEACE DICTATES THAT I BE ECONOMICAL WITH THE TRUTH.
AH, CAPTAIN KIRK, A MILLION OF YOUR EARTH GREETINGS. MY PLANET REJOICES AT THE IMMINENT ARRIVAL OF OBAN!
I'M AFRAID, PRESIDENT BALLAL, THAT WE HAVE RECENTLY ENCOUNTERED A PROBLEM WITH THE WARP CAPACITY OF OUR ENGINES.
OH...?
WE ARE REQUIRED TO PERFORM A NUMBER OF MANDATORY TESTS. THIS WILL UNFORTUNATELY DELAY THE OFFICIAL HANDOVER OF OBAN.
I FIND THIS MOST DISTRESSING NEWS. PERHAPS WE COULD SEND SOME PERSONNEL TO ASSIST YOU?
NONE REQUIRED, MR. PRESIDENT. REST ASSURED WE ARE DOING ALL WE CAN. CAPTAIN OUT.

GENTLEMEN, WE HAVE PRECIOUS LITTLE TIME TO PREVENT THIS SITUATION FROM ESCALATING INTO A MAJOR INTERPLANETARY WAR.

I AM OPEN TO SUGGESTIONS.

WE'VE NEVER ENCOUNTERED A MONSTER SUCH AS THIS. ITS GUT PRODUCES MASSIVE LEVELS OF BACTERIA AND GAS.

WHICH IS BASICALLY HOW AND WHY IT GOT SO BIG SO FAST.

AGREED, THE OBAN WE BROUGHT ABOARD HAS BEEN RADICALLY ALTERED.

CAPTAIN, I BELIEVE OBAN'S REACTION WAS TRIGGERED BY THE XOXXAN MICROBES RESIDING INSIDE THE WEAVE.

IT WAS LUCK THAT I HAD ORDERED THE WEAVE TAKEN AWAY FOR FURTHER TESTS.

AFFIRMATIVE. THE CREATURE, INITIALLY VULNERABLE, NEEDED TO FIND A SAFE LOCATION IN WHICH TO COMPLETE ITS METAMORPHOSIS--

--BEFORE RETURNING TO DESTROY THE WEAVE AND KILL THE MICROBES--ONLY TO FIND THE WEAVE GONE.

A 'SLEEPER' BIOLOGICAL WEAPON DESIGNED TO DESTROY INDIGENOUS XOXXAN LIFE.

ENMITY BETWEEN THE TWO PLANETS IT WOULD APPEAR IS ALIVE AND WELL.

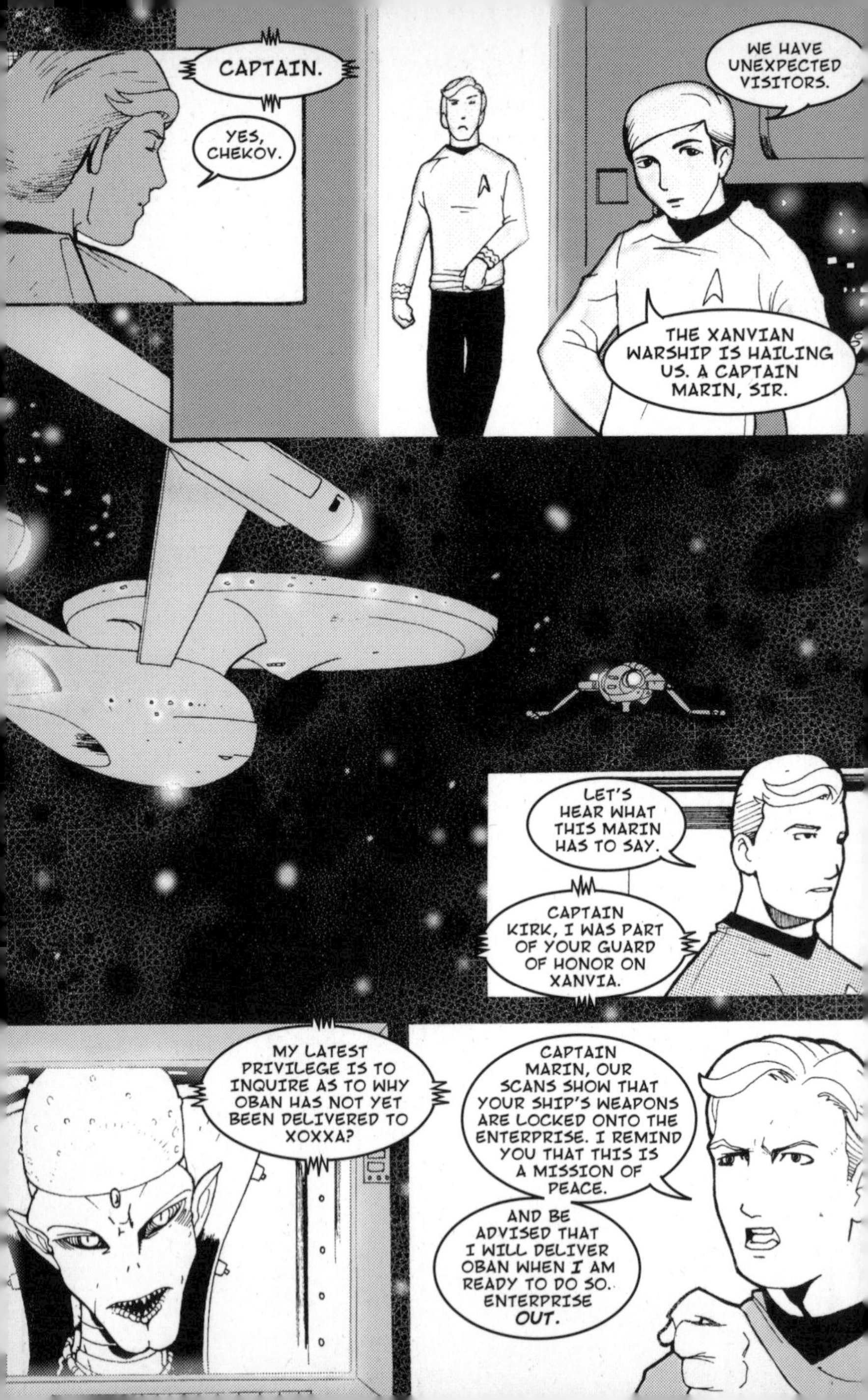
CAPTAIN.
YES, CHEKOV.
WE HAVE UNEXPECTED VISITORS.
THE XANVIAN WARSHIP IS HAILING US. A CAPTAIN MARIN, SIR.
LET'S HEAR WHAT THIS MARIN HAS TO SAY.
CAPTAIN KIRK, I WAS PART OF YOUR GUARD OF HONOR ON XANVIA.
MY LATEST PRIVILEGE IS TO INQUIRE AS TO WHY OBAN HAS NOT YET BEEN DELIVERED TO XOXXA?
CAPTAIN MARIN, OUR SCANS SHOW THAT YOUR SHIP'S WEAPONS ARE LOCKED ONTO THE ENTERPRISE. I REMIND YOU THAT THIS IS A MISSION OF PEACE.
AND BE ADVISED THAT I WILL DELIVER OBAN WHEN I AM READY TO DO SO. ENTERPRISE OUT.

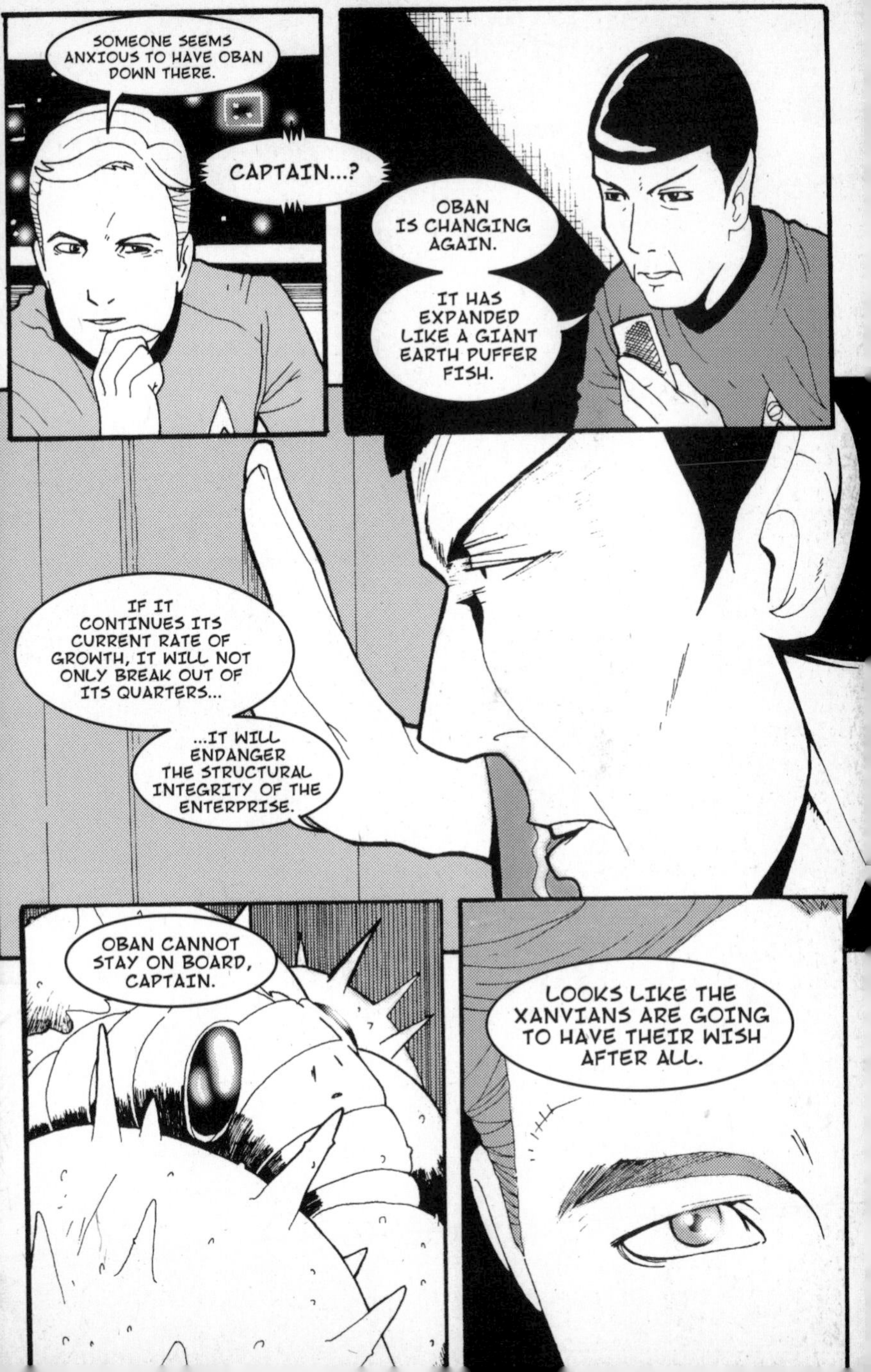
SOMEONE SEEMS ANXIOUS TO HAVE OBAN DOWN THERE.
CAPTAIN...?
OBAN IS CHANGING AGAIN.
IT HAS EXPANDED LIKE A GIANT EARTH PUFFER FISH.
IF IT CONTINUES ITS CURRENT RATE OF GROWTH, IT WILL NOT ONLY BREAK OUT OF ITS QUARTERS...
...IT WILL ENDANGER THE STRUCTURAL INTEGRITY OF THE ENTERPRISE.
OBAN CANNOT STAY ON BOARD, CAPTAIN.
LOOKS LIKE THE XANVIANS ARE GOING TO HAVE THEIR WISH AFTER ALL.

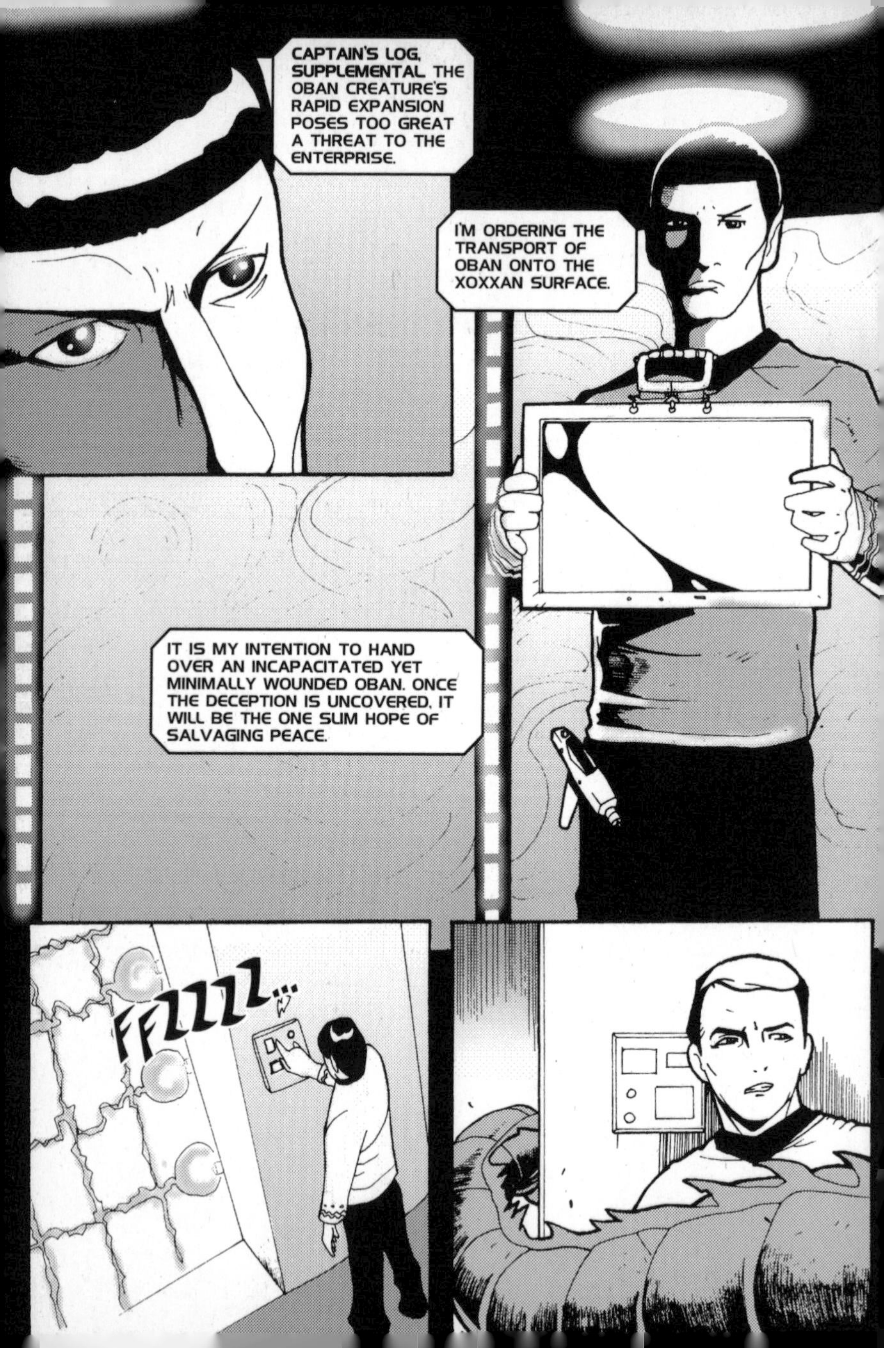
CAPTAIN'S LOG, SUPPLEMENTAL. THE OBAN CREATURE'S RAPID EXPANSION POSES TOO GREAT A THREAT TO THE ENTERPRISE.
I'M ORDERING THE TRANSPORT OF OBAN ONTO THE XOXXAN SURFACE.
IT IS MY INTENTION TO HAND OVER AN INCAPACITATED YET MINIMALLY WOUNDED OBAN. ONCE THE DECEPTION IS UNCOVERED, IT WILL BE THE ONE SLIM HOPE OF SALVAGING PEACE.
FFZZZZ...

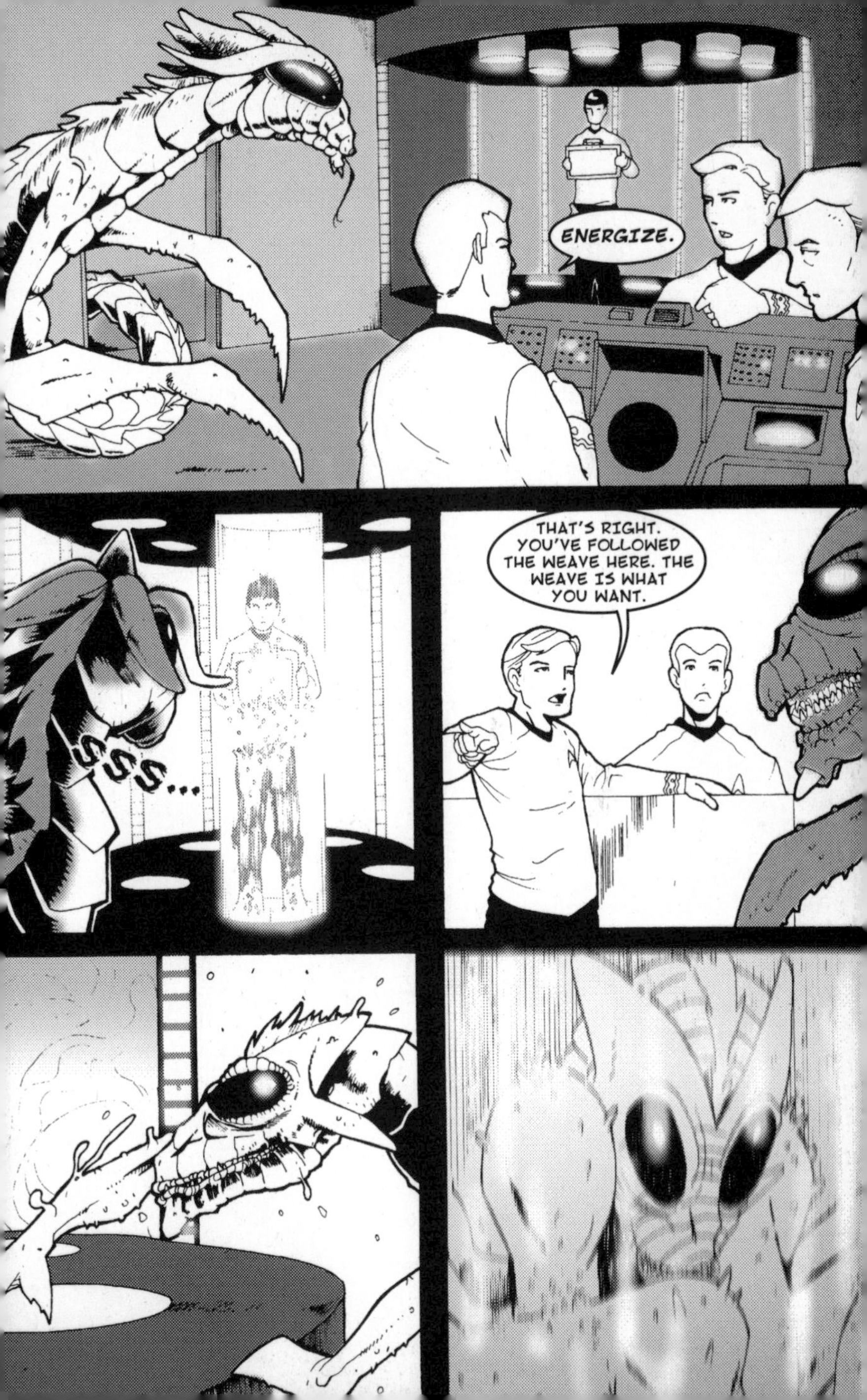
ENERGIZE.
SSS...
THAT'S RIGHT. YOU'VE FOLLOWED THE WEAVE HERE. THE WEAVE IS WHAT YOU WANT.

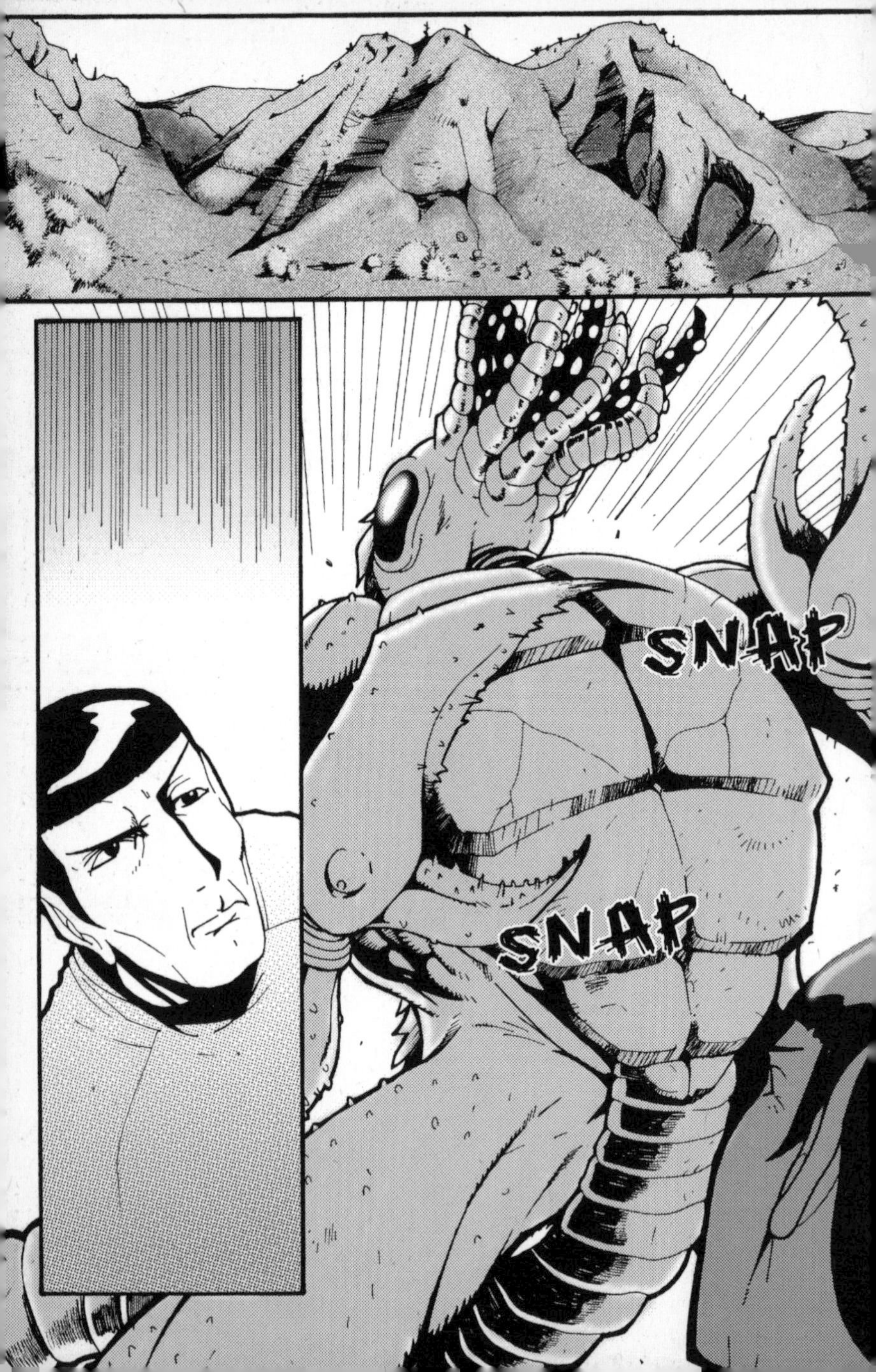
SNAP
SNAP

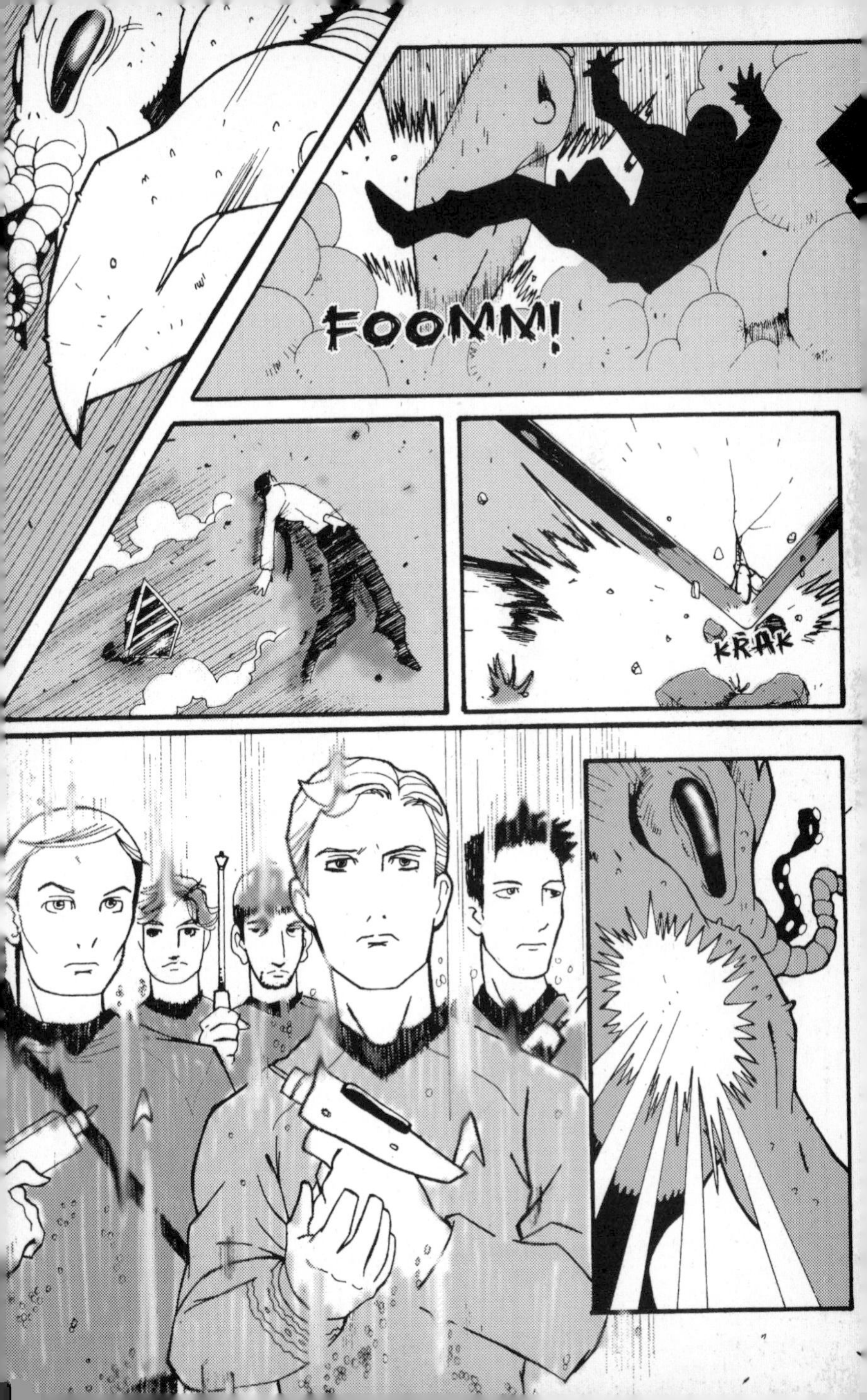
FOOMM!
KRAK

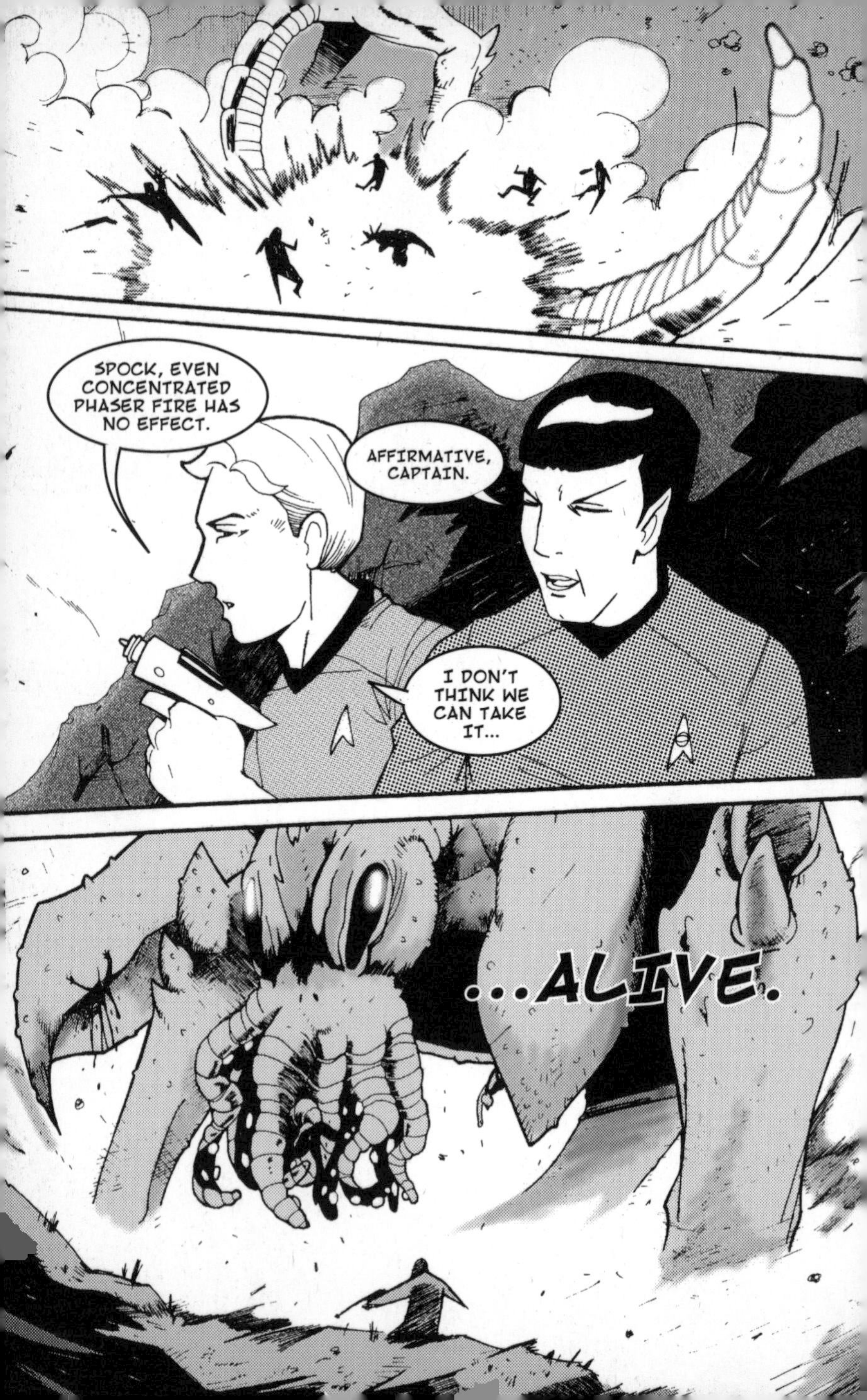
SPOCK, EVEN CONCENTRATED PHASER FIRE HAS NO EFFECT.
AFFIRMATIVE, CAPTAIN.
I DON'T THINK WE CAN TAKE IT...
...ALIVE.

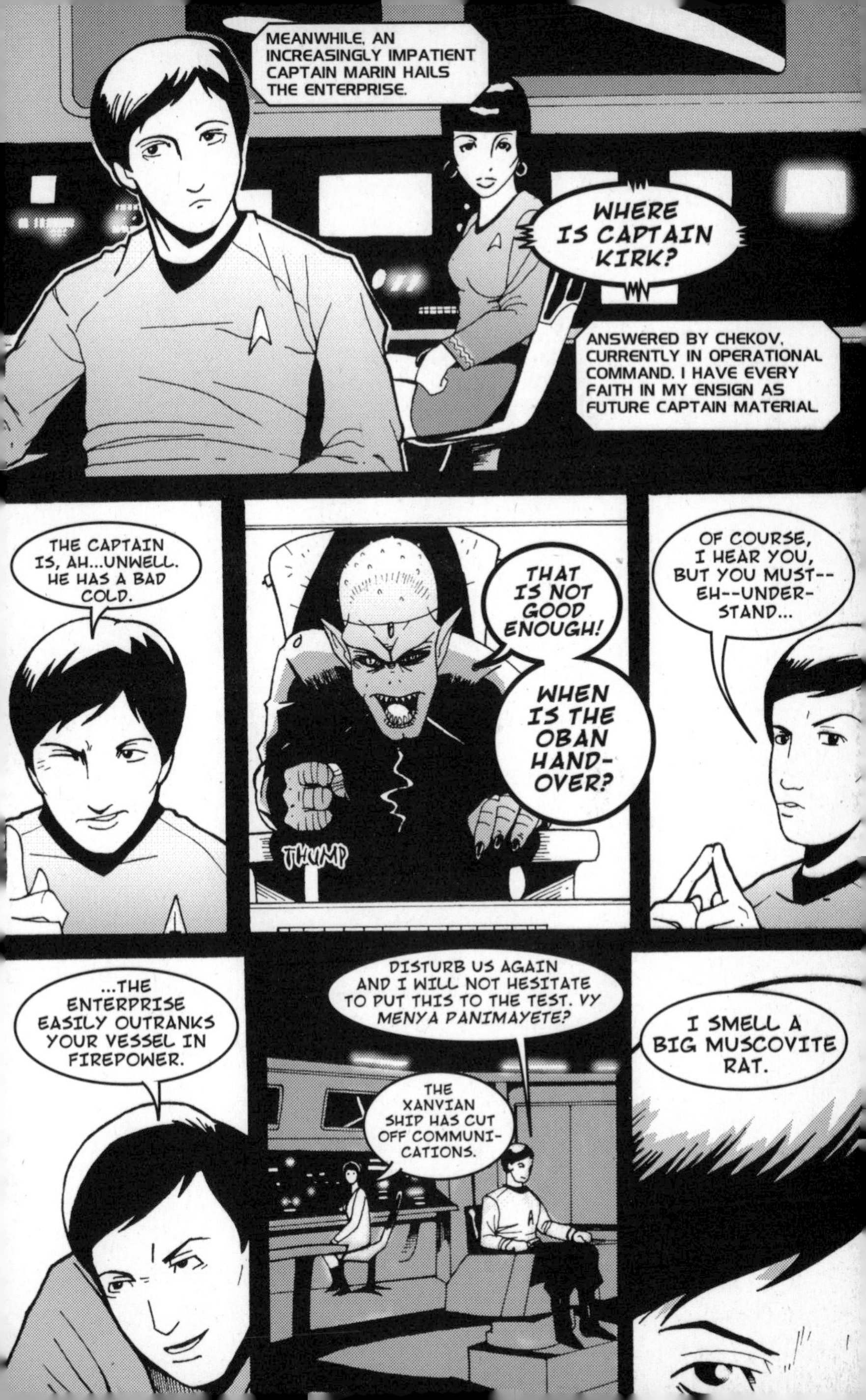

MEANWHILE, AN INCREASINGLY IMPATIENT CAPTAIN MARIN HAILS THE ENTERPRISE.
WHERE IS CAPTAIN KIRK?
ANSWERED BY CHEKOV, CURRENTLY IN OPERATIONAL COMMAND. I HAVE EVERY FAITH IN MY ENSIGN AS FUTURE CAPTAIN MATERIAL.
THE CAPTAIN IS, AH...UNWELL. HE HAS A BAD COLD.
THAT IS NOT GOOD ENOUGH!
WHEN IS THE OBAN HAND-OVER?
THUMP
OF COURSE, I HEAR YOU, BUT YOU MUST--EH--UNDER-STAND...
...THE ENTERPRISE EASILY OUTRANKS YOUR VESSEL IN FIREPOWER.
DISTURB US AGAIN AND I WILL NOT HESITATE TO PUT THIS TO THE TEST. VY MENYA PANIMAYETE?
THE XANVIAN SHIP HAS CUT OFF COMMUNI-CATIONS.
I SMELL A BIG MUSCOVITE RAT.

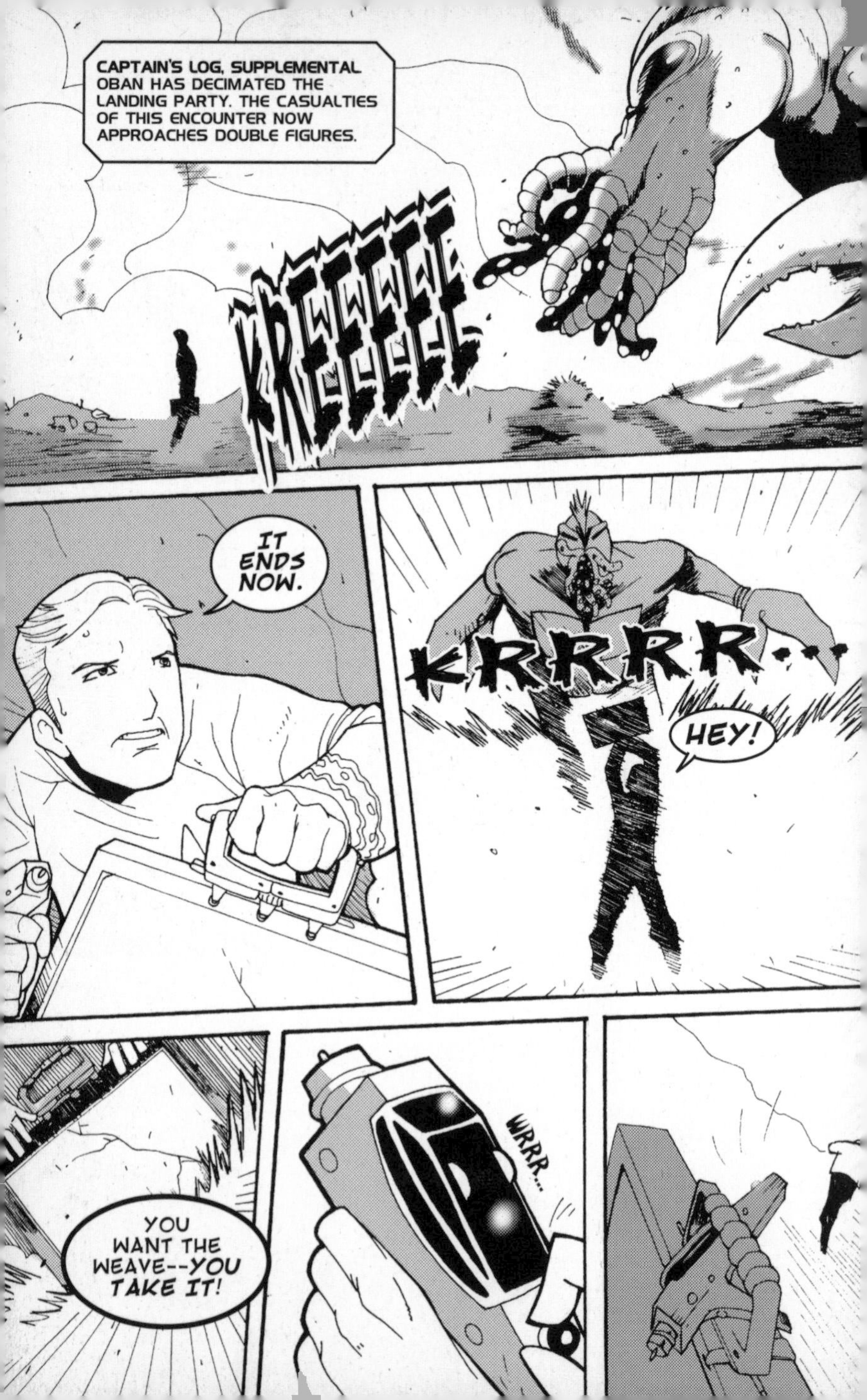
CAPTAIN'S LOG, SUPPLEMENTAL OBAN HAS DECIMATED THE LANDING PARTY. THE CASUALTIES OF THIS ENCOUNTER NOW APPROACHES DOUBLE FIGURES.
KREEEEEE
IT ENDS NOW.
KRRRRR...
HEY!
YOU WANT THE WEAVE--YOU TAKE IT!
WRRR...

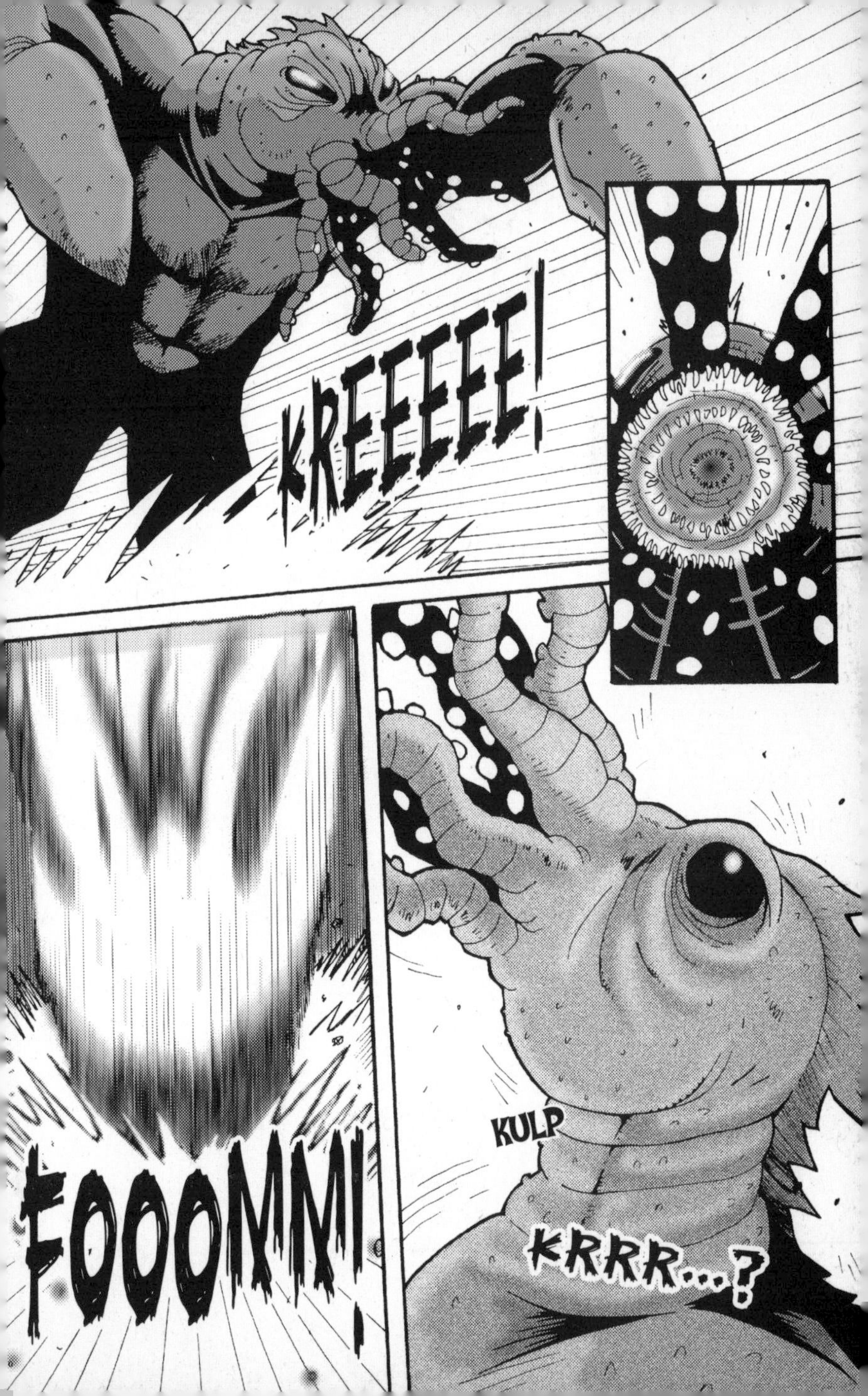
KREEEEEE!
FOOOMM!
KULP
KRRR...?

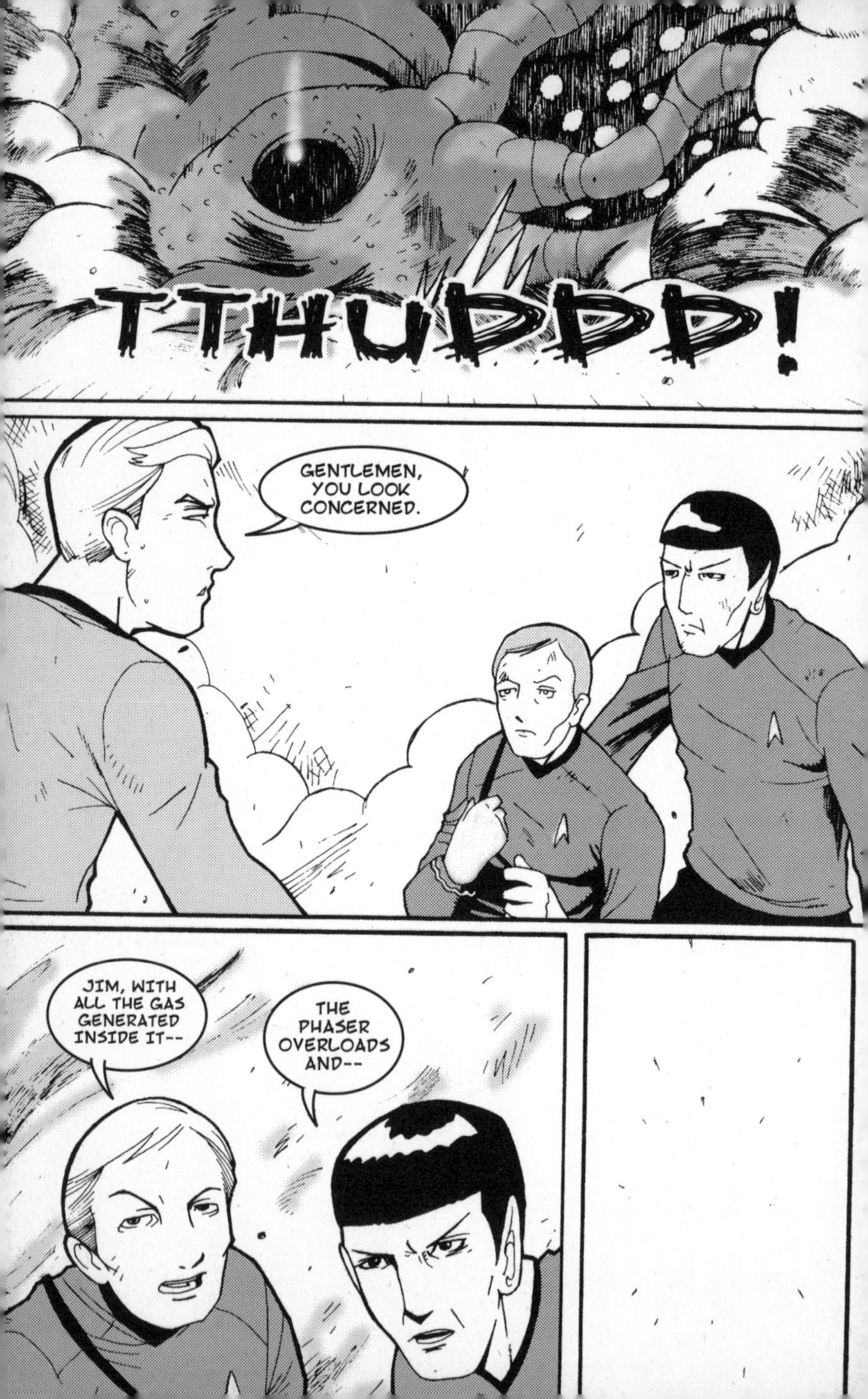
TTHUDDDD!
GENTLEMEN, YOU LOOK CONCERNED.
JIM, WITH ALL THE GAS GENERATED INSIDE IT--
THE PHASER OVERLOADS AND--

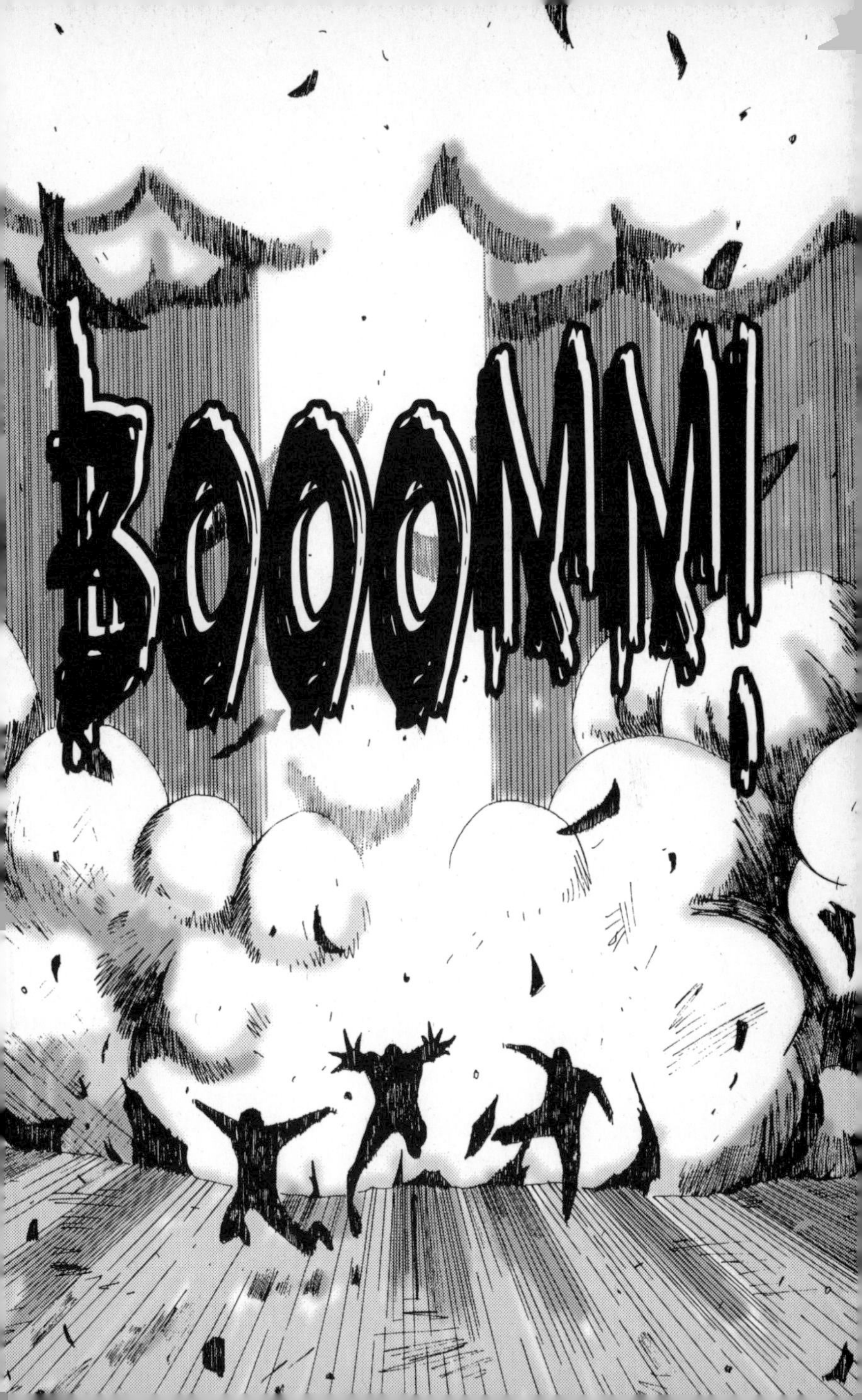
BOOOM!

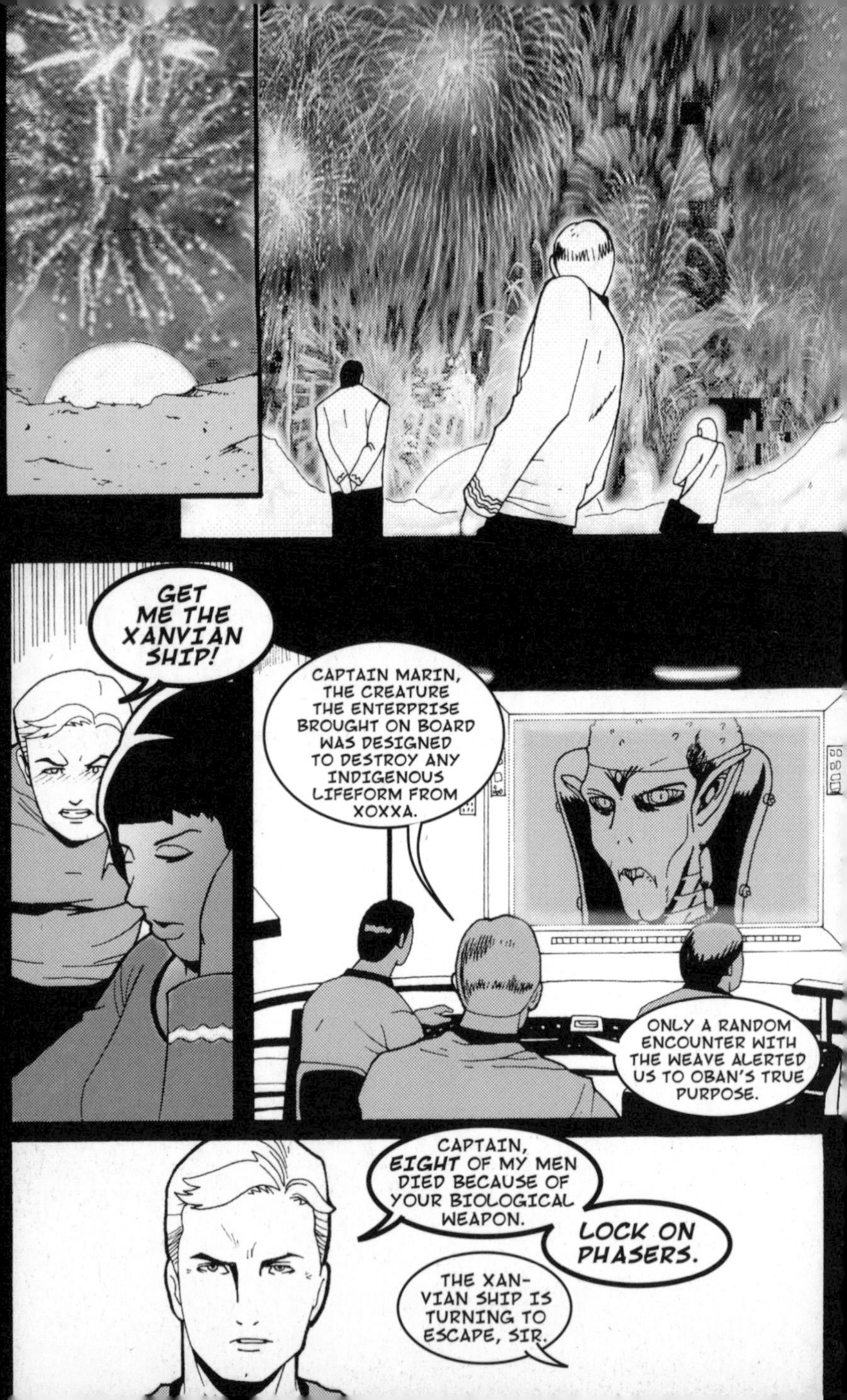
GET ME THE XANVIAN SHIP!
CAPTAIN MARIN, THE CREATURE THE ENTERPRISE BROUGHT ON BOARD WAS DESIGNED TO DESTROY ANY INDIGENOUS LIFEFORM FROM XOXXA.
ONLY A RANDOM ENCOUNTER WITH THE WEAVE ALERTED US TO OBAN'S TRUE PURPOSE.
CAPTAIN, *EIGHT* OF MY MEN DIED BECAUSE OF YOUR BIOLOGICAL WEAPON.
LOCK ON PHASERS.
THE XAN-VIAN SHIP IS TURNING TO ESCAPE, SIR.

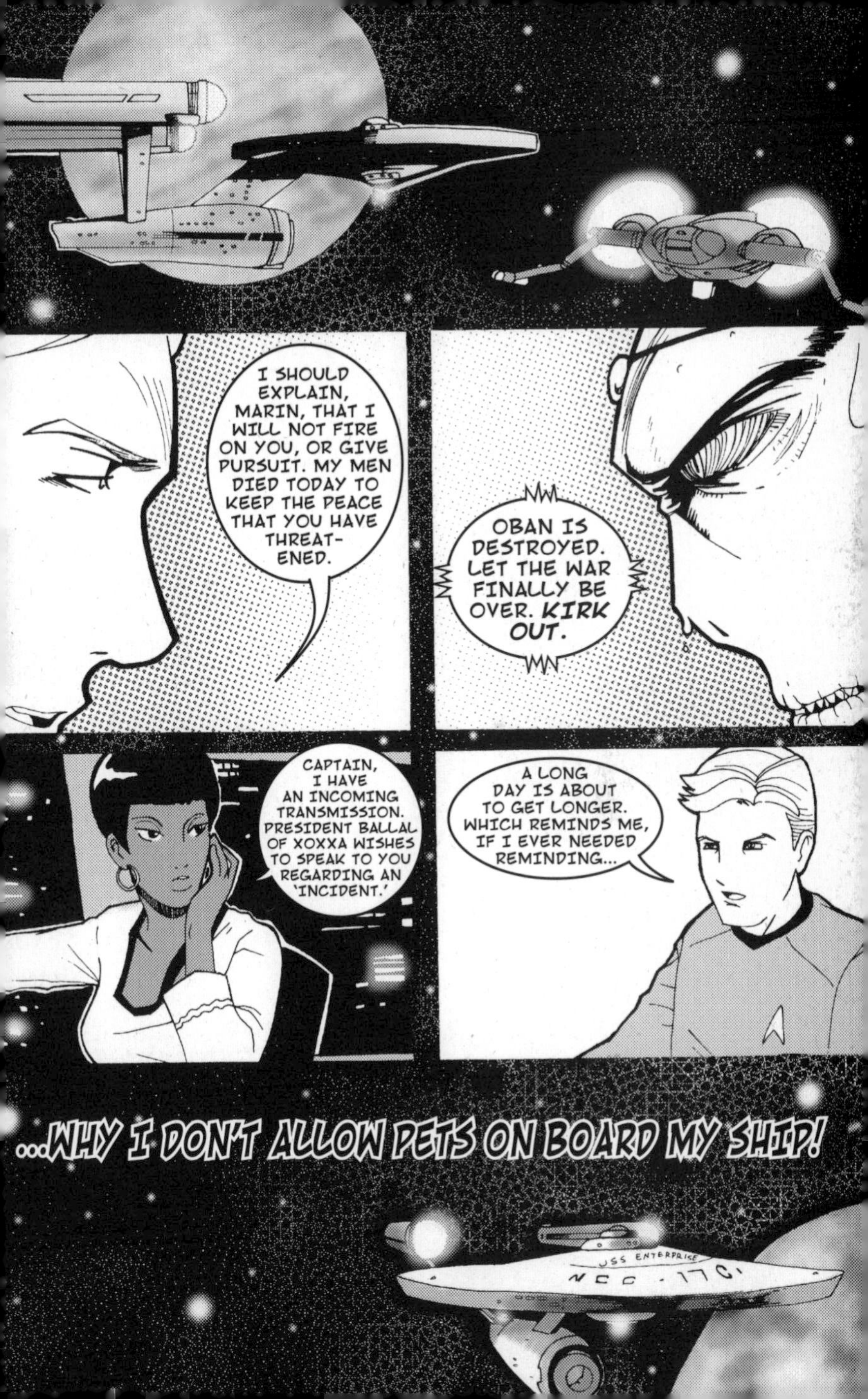
I SHOULD EXPLAIN, MARIN, THAT I WILL NOT FIRE ON YOU, OR GIVE PURSUIT. MY MEN DIED TODAY TO KEEP THE PEACE THAT YOU HAVE THREAT-ENED.
OBAN IS DESTROYED. LET THE WAR FINALLY BE OVER. **KIRK OUT.**
CAPTAIN, I HAVE AN INCOMING TRANSMISSION. PRESIDENT BALLAL OF XOXXA WISHES TO SPEAK TO YOU REGARDING AN 'INCIDENT.'
A LONG DAY IS ABOUT TO GET LONGER. WHICH REMINDS ME, IF I EVER NEEDED REMINDING...
...WHY I DON'T ALLOW PETS ON BOARD MY SHIP!
USS ENTERPRISE
NCC-1701

ORPHANS

STORY BY ROB TOKAR
ART BY EJ SU

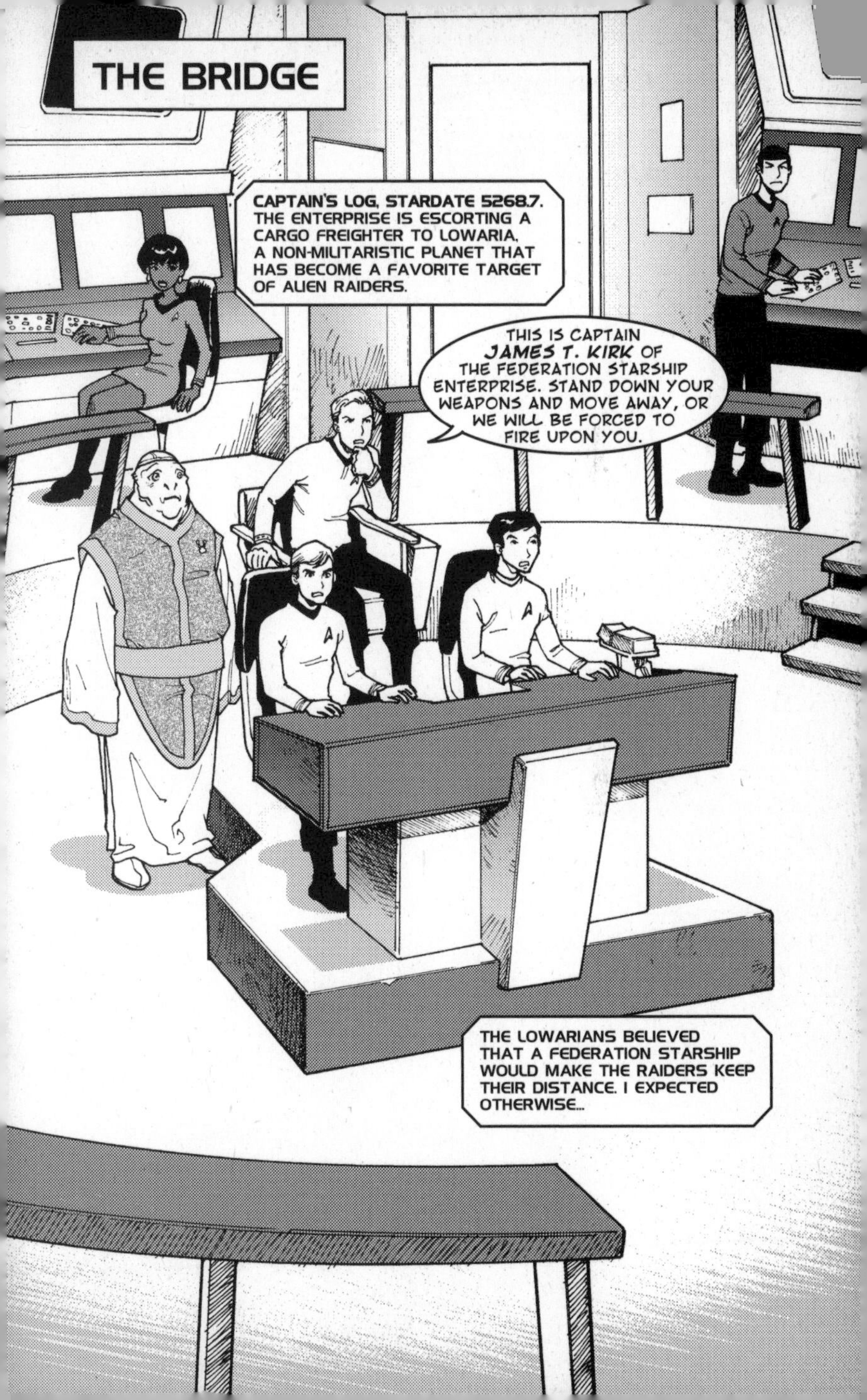
THE BRIDGE
CAPTAIN'S LOG, STARDATE 5268.7. THE ENTERPRISE IS ESCORTING A CARGO FREIGHTER TO LOWARIA, A NON-MILITARISTIC PLANET THAT HAS BECOME A FAVORITE TARGET OF ALIEN RAIDERS.
THIS IS CAPTAIN JAMES T. KIRK OF THE FEDERATION STARSHIP ENTERPRISE. STAND DOWN YOUR WEAPONS AND MOVE AWAY, OR WE WILL BE FORCED TO FIRE UPON YOU.
THE LOWARIANS BELIEVED THAT A FEDERATION STARSHIP WOULD MAKE THE RAIDERS KEEP THEIR DISTANCE. I EXPECTED OTHERWISE...

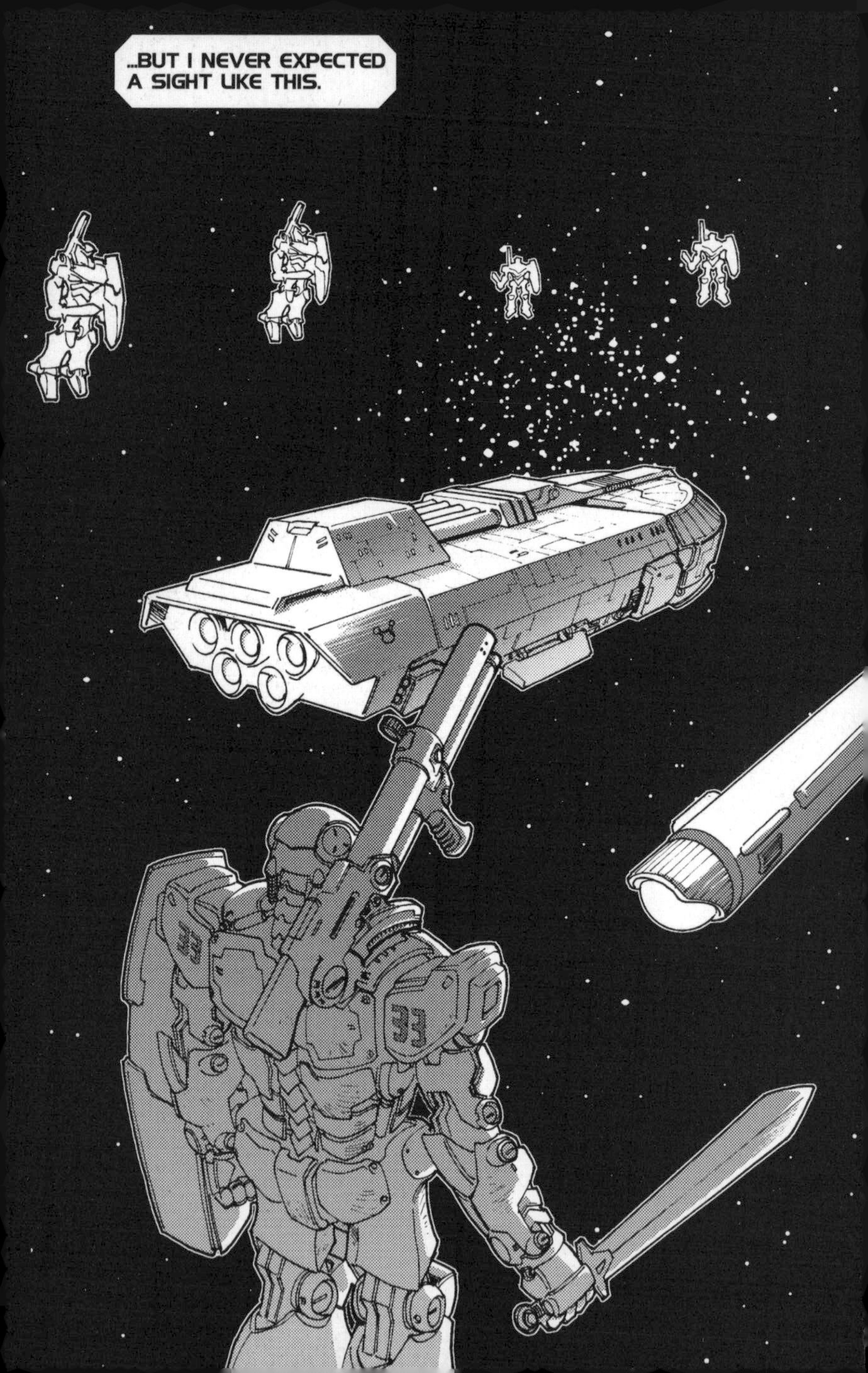
...BUT I NEVER EXPECTED A SIGHT LIKE THIS.

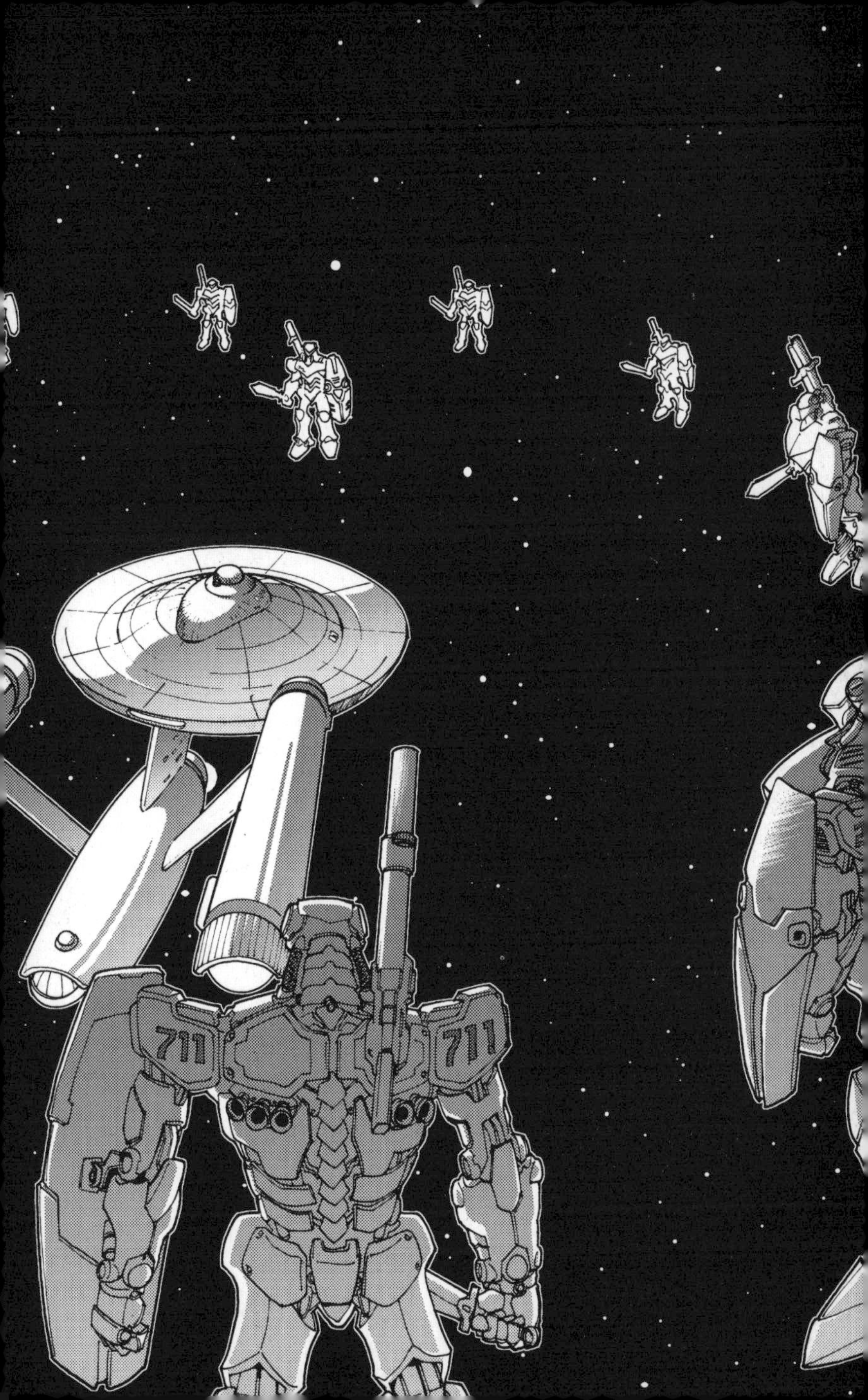
711
711

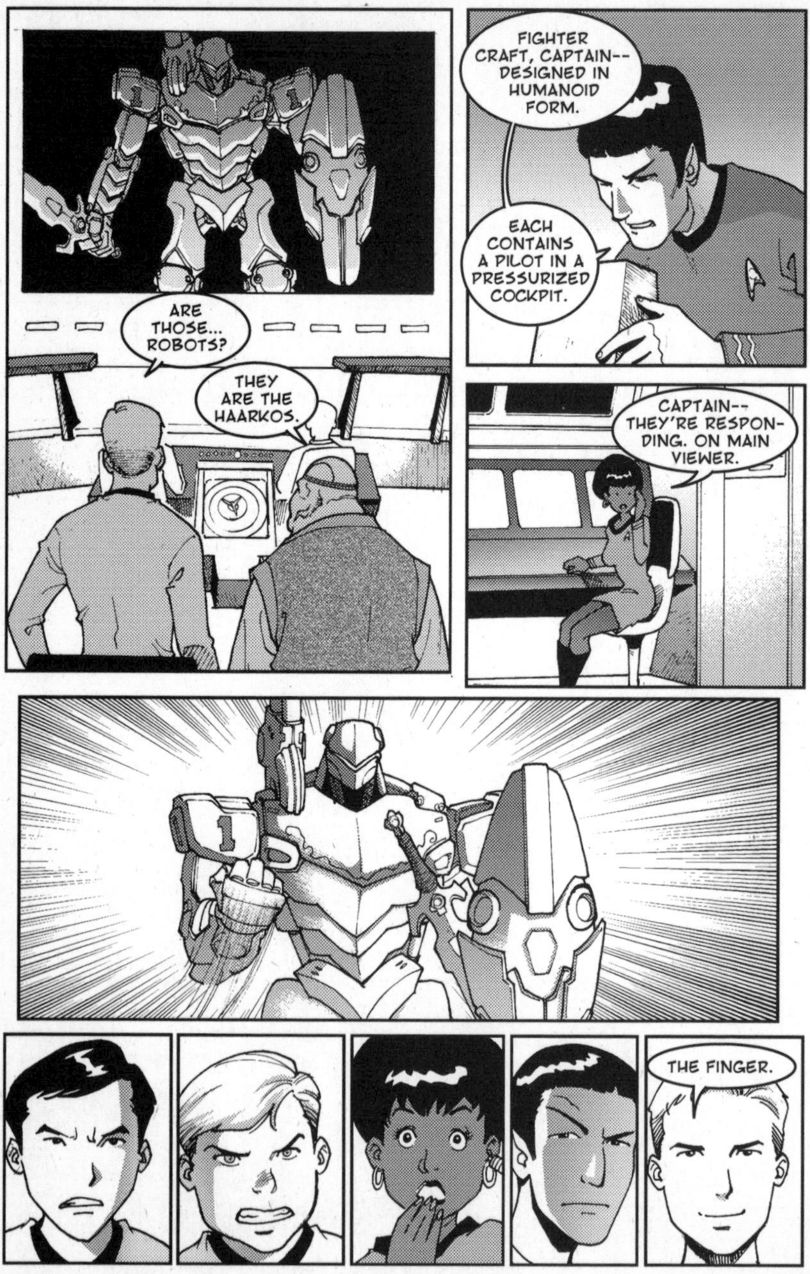
ARE THOSE... ROBOTS?
THEY ARE THE HAARKOS.
FIGHTER CRAFT, CAPTAIN--DESIGNED IN HUMANOID FORM.
EACH CONTAINS A PILOT IN A PRESSURIZED COCKPIT.
CAPTAIN--THEY'RE RESPONDING. ON MAIN VIEWER.
THE FINGER.

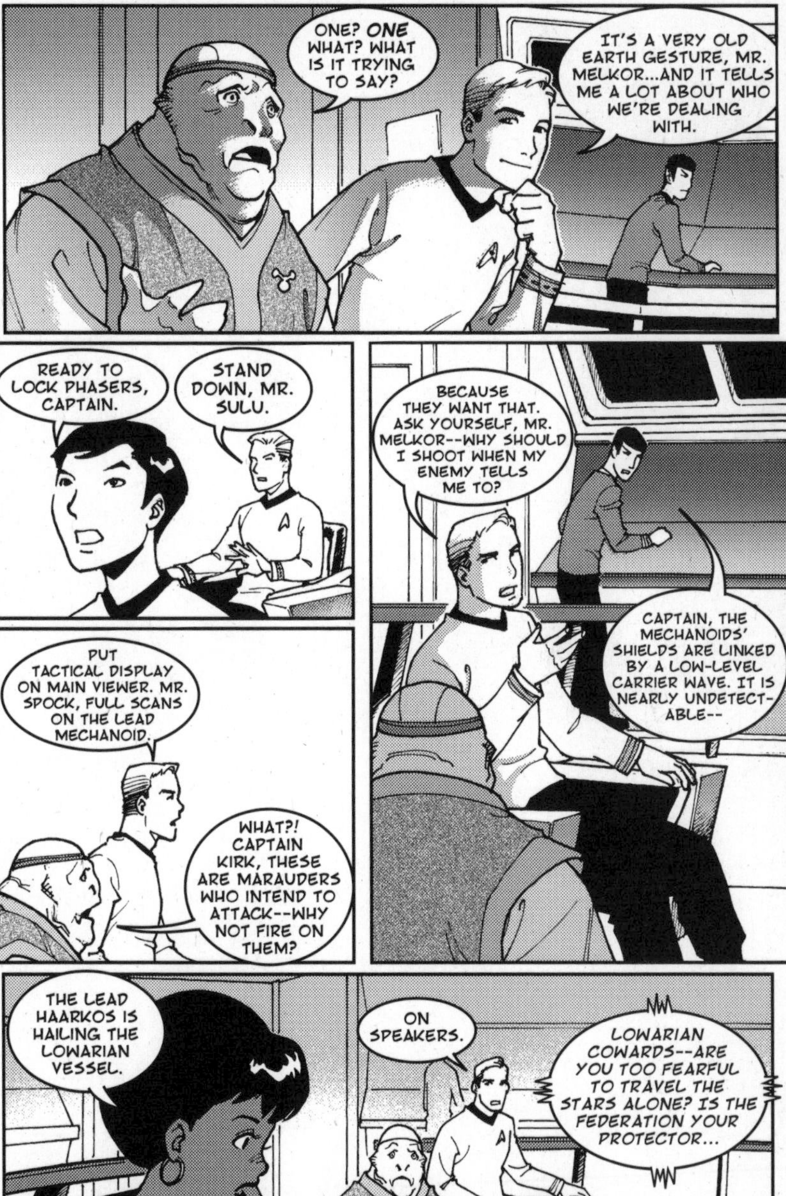
ONE? ONE WHAT? WHAT IS IT TRYING TO SAY?
IT'S A VERY OLD EARTH GESTURE, MR. MELKOR...AND IT TELLS ME A LOT ABOUT WHO WE'RE DEALING WITH.
READY TO LOCK PHASERS, CAPTAIN.
STAND DOWN, MR. SULU.
PUT TACTICAL DISPLAY ON MAIN VIEWER. MR. SPOCK, FULL SCANS ON THE LEAD MECHANOID.
WHAT?! CAPTAIN KIRK, THESE ARE MARAUDERS WHO INTEND TO ATTACK--WHY NOT FIRE ON THEM?
BECAUSE THEY WANT THAT. ASK YOURSELF, MR. MELKOR--WHY SHOULD I SHOOT WHEN MY ENEMY TELLS ME TO?
CAPTAIN, THE MECHANOIDS' SHIELDS ARE LINKED BY A LOW-LEVEL CARRIER WAVE. IT IS NEARLY UNDETECTABLE--
THE LEAD HAARKOS IS HAILING THE LOWARIAN VESSEL.
ON SPEAKERS.
LOWARIAN COWARDS--ARE YOU TOO FEARFUL TO TRAVEL THE STARS ALONE? IS THE FEDERATION YOUR PROTECTOR...

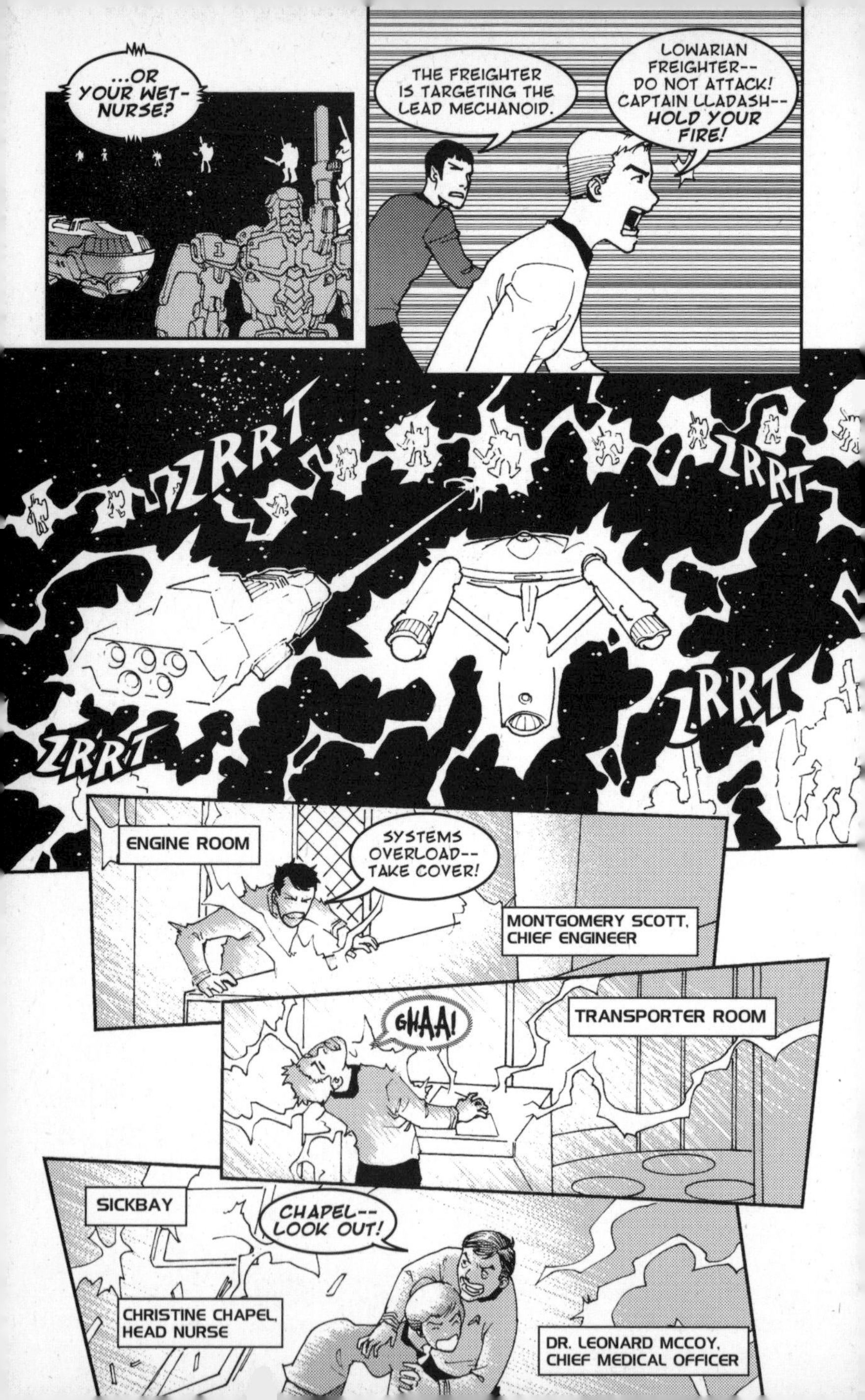
...OR YOUR WET-NURSE?
THE FREIGHTER IS TARGETING THE LEAD MECHANOID.
LOWARIAN FREIGHTER-- DO NOT ATTACK! CAPTAIN LLADASH-- HOLD YOUR FIRE!
ZZRRT
ZRRT
ZRRT
ZRRT
ENGINE ROOM
SYSTEMS OVERLOAD-- TAKE COVER!
MONTGOMERY SCOTT, CHIEF ENGINEER
TRANSPORTER ROOM
GHAA!
SICKBAY
CHAPEL-- LOOK OUT!
CHRISTINE CHAPEL, HEAD NURSE
DR. LEONARD MCCOY, CHIEF MEDICAL OFFICER

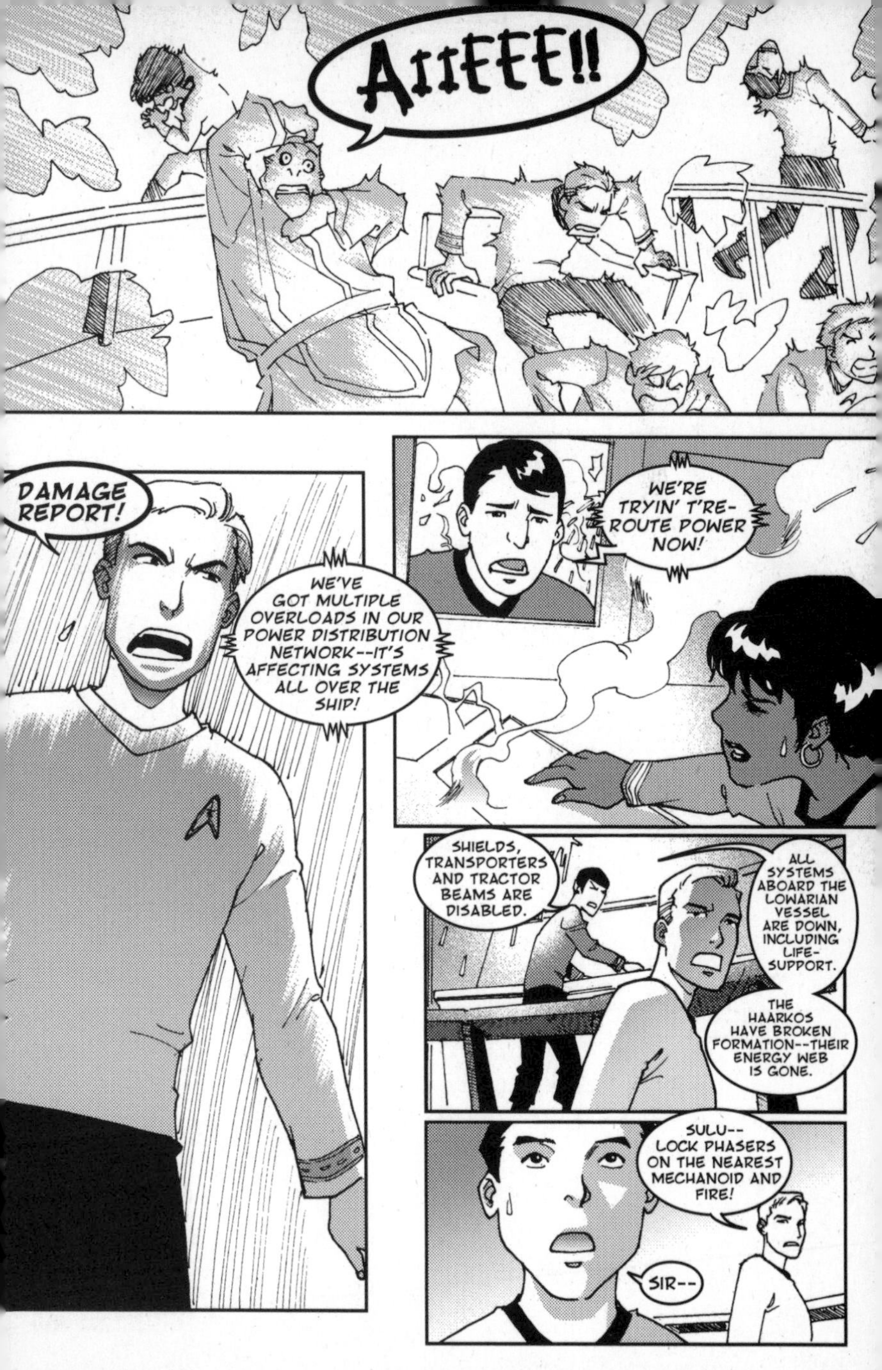
AIIEEE!!
DAMAGE REPORT!
WE'VE GOT MULTIPLE OVERLOADS IN OUR POWER DISTRIBUTION NETWORK--IT'S AFFECTING SYSTEMS ALL OVER THE SHIP!
WE'RE TRYIN' T'RE-ROUTE POWER NOW!
SHIELDS, TRANSPORTERS AND TRACTOR BEAMS ARE DISABLED.
ALL SYSTEMS ABOARD THE LOWARIAN VESSEL ARE DOWN, INCLUDING LIFE-SUPPORT.
THE HAARKOS HAVE BROKEN FORMATION--THEIR ENERGY WEB IS GONE.
SULU--LOCK PHASERS ON THE NEAREST MECHANOID AND FIRE!
SIR--

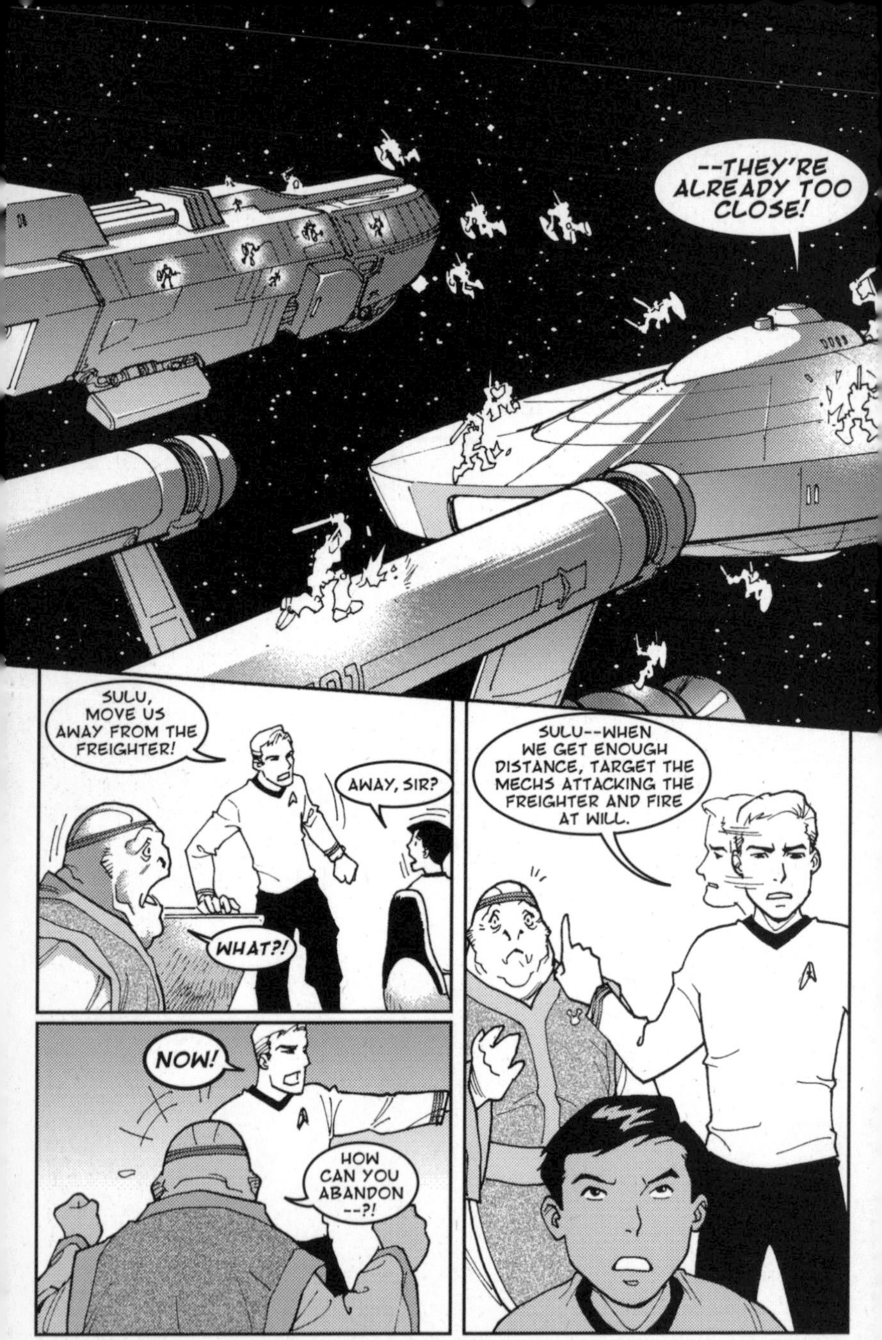
--THEY'RE ALREADY TOO CLOSE!
SULU, MOVE US AWAY FROM THE FREIGHTER!
AWAY, SIR?
WHAT?!
NOW!
HOW CAN YOU ABANDON --?!
SULU--WHEN WE GET ENOUGH DISTANCE, TARGET THE MECHS ATTACKING THE FREIGHTER AND FIRE AT WILL.

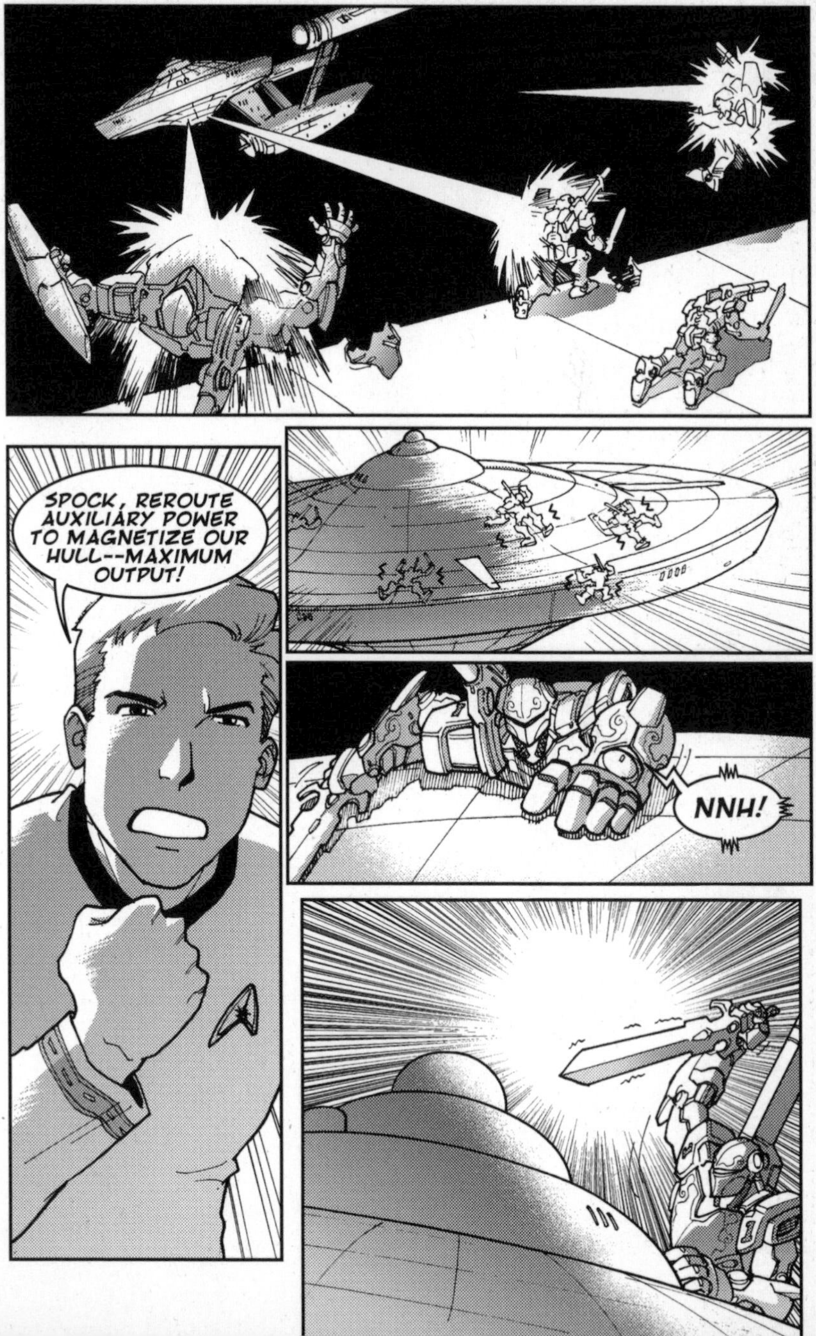
SPOCK, REROUTE AUXILIARY POWER TO MAGNETIZE OUR HULL--MAXIMUM OUTPUT!
NNH!

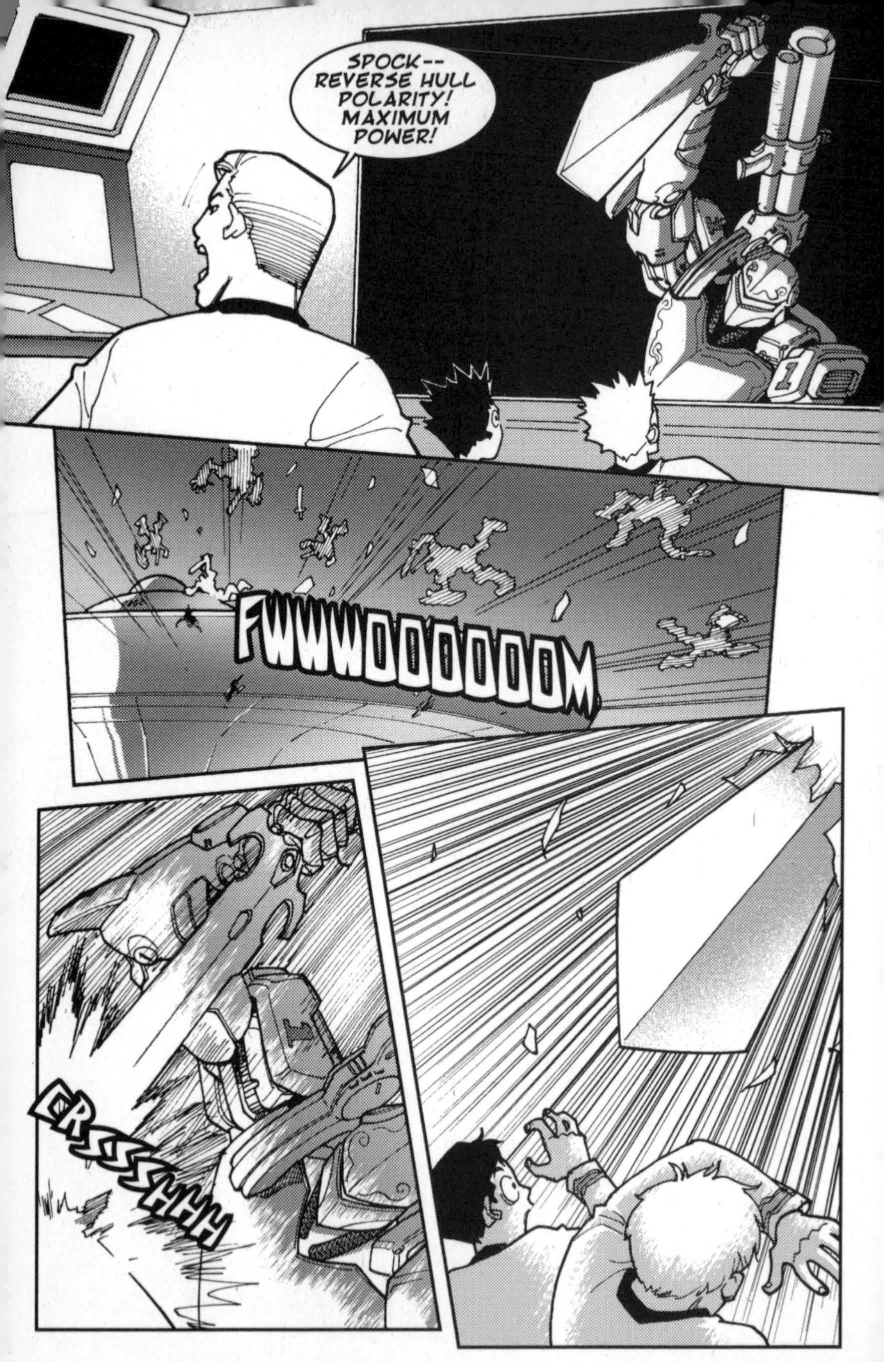
SPOCK-- REVERSE HULL POLARITY! MAXIMUM POWER!
FWWWOOOOOOOM
CRSSSHHH

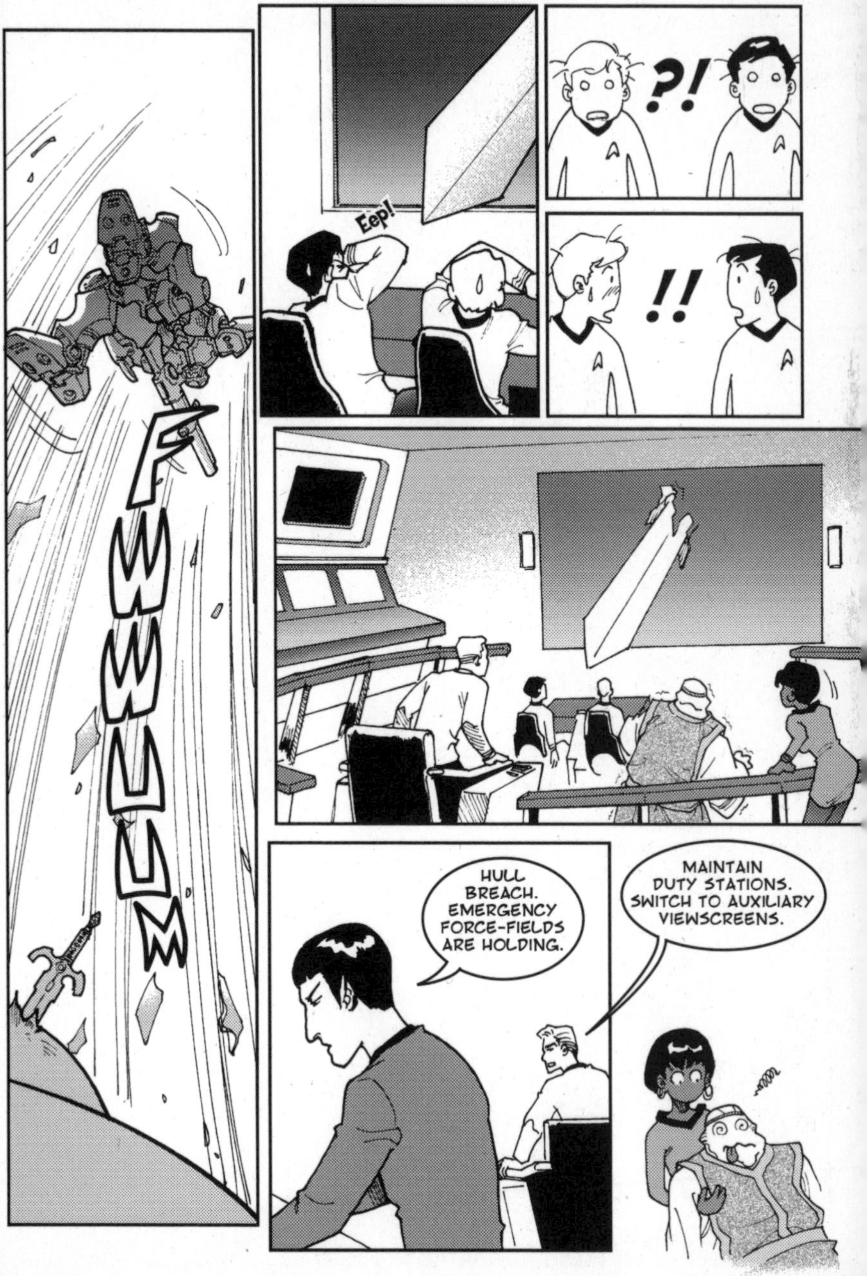
FWWWUUM
Eep!
?!
!!
HULL BREACH. EMERGENCY FORCE-FIELDS ARE HOLDING.
MAINTAIN DUTY STATIONS. SWITCH TO AUXILIARY VIEWSCREENS.

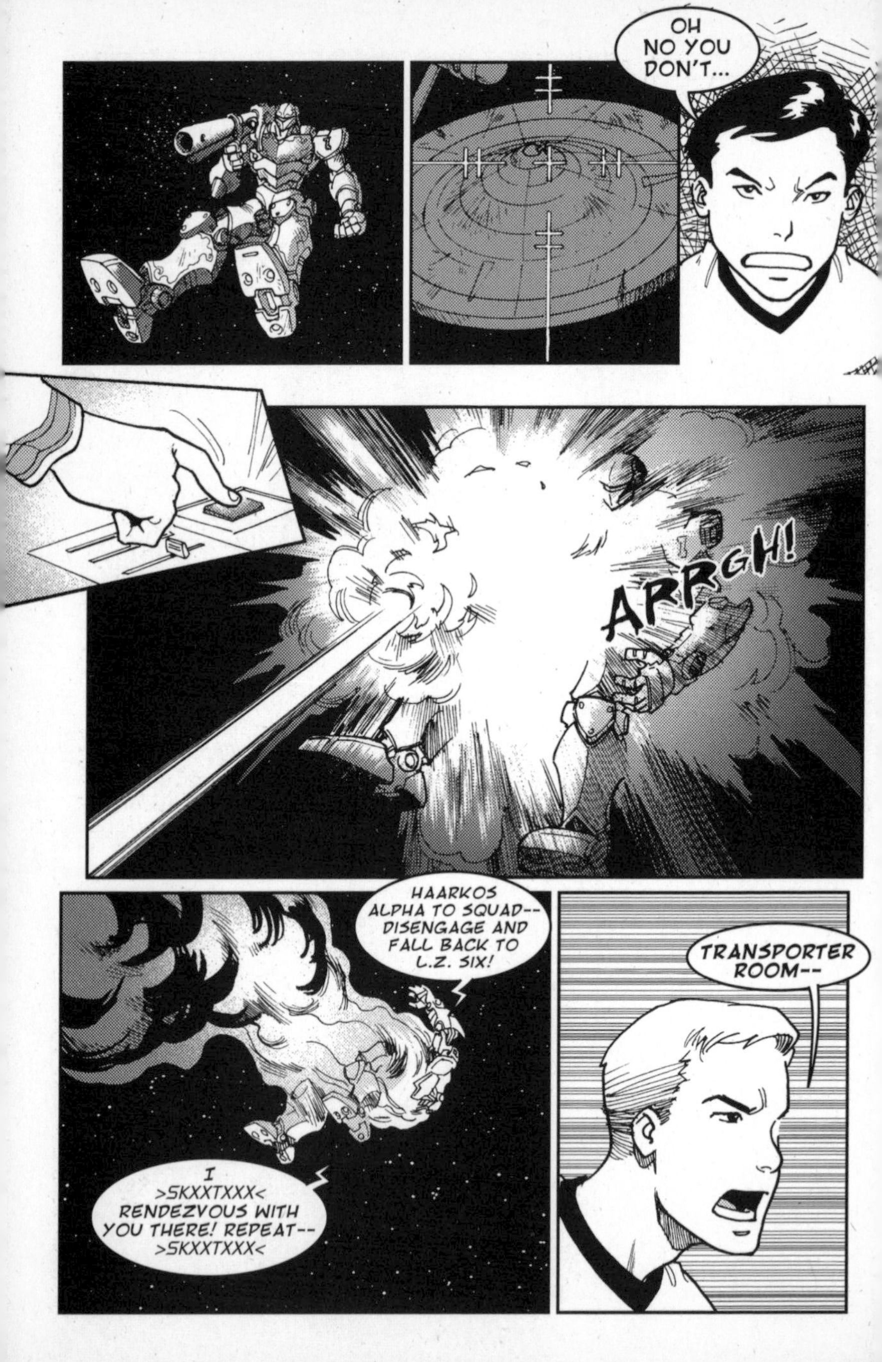
OH NO YOU DON'T...
ARRRGH!
HAARKOS ALPHA TO SQUAD-- DISENGAGE AND FALL BACK TO L.Z. SIX!
I >SKXXTXXX< RENDEZVOUS WITH YOU THERE! REPEAT-- >SKXXTXXX<
TRANSPORTER ROOM--

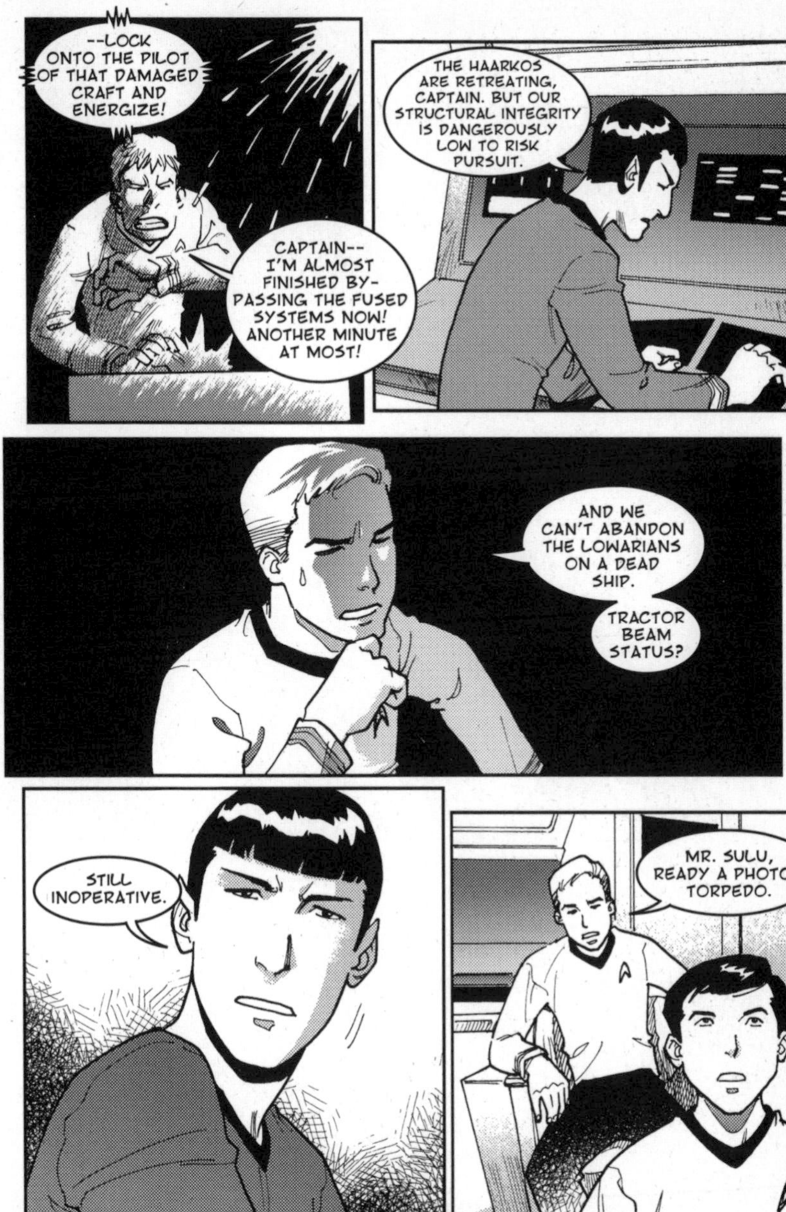
--LOCK ONTO THE PILOT OF THAT DAMAGED CRAFT AND ENERGIZE!
CAPTAIN-- I'M ALMOST FINISHED BY-PASSING THE FUSED SYSTEMS NOW! ANOTHER MINUTE AT MOST!
THE HAARKOS ARE RETREATING, CAPTAIN. BUT OUR STRUCTURAL INTEGRITY IS DANGEROUSLY LOW TO RISK PURSUIT.
AND WE CAN'T ABANDON THE LOWARIANS ON A DEAD SHIP.
TRACTOR BEAM STATUS?
STILL INOPERATIVE.
MR. SULU, READY A PHOTON TORPEDO.

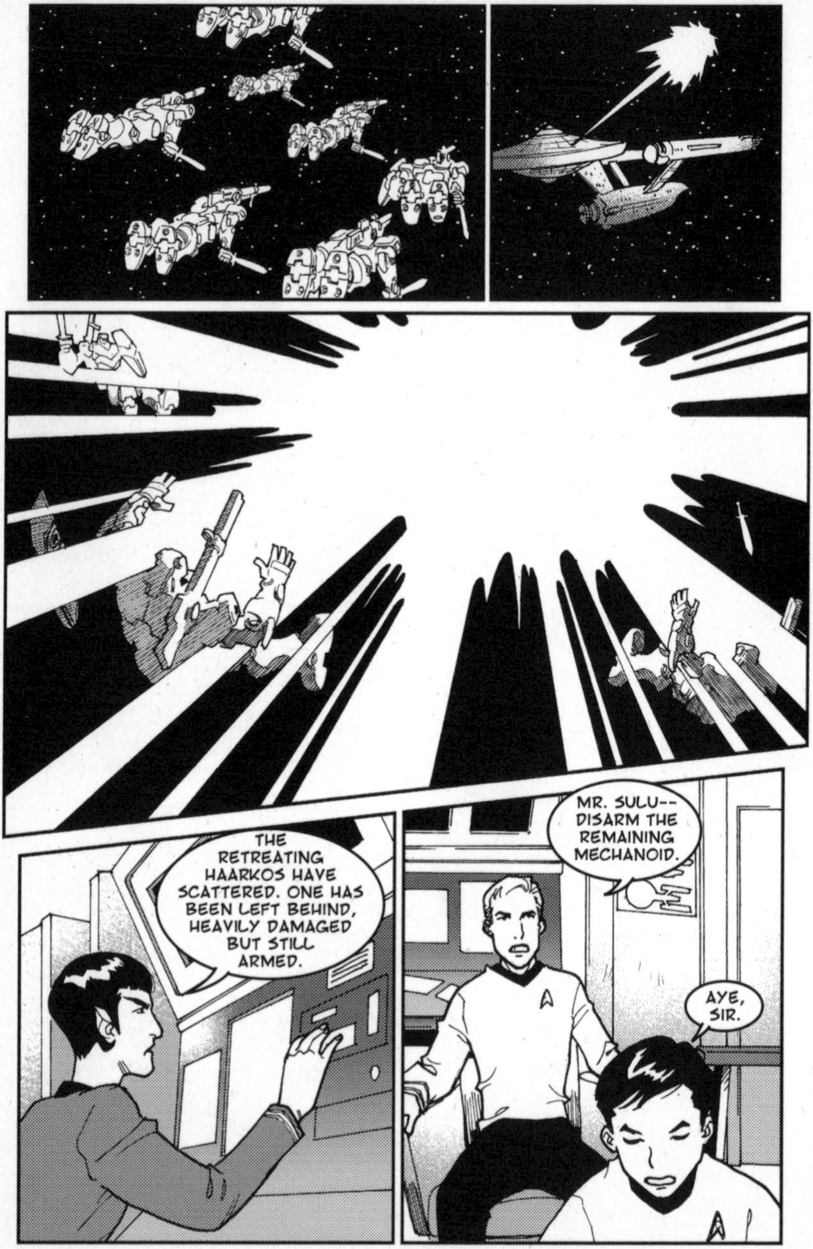
THE RETREATING HAARKOS HAVE SCATTERED. ONE HAS BEEN LEFT BEHIND, HEAVILY DAMAGED BUT STILL ARMED.
MR. SULU-- DISARM THE REMAINING MECHANOID.
AYE, SIR.

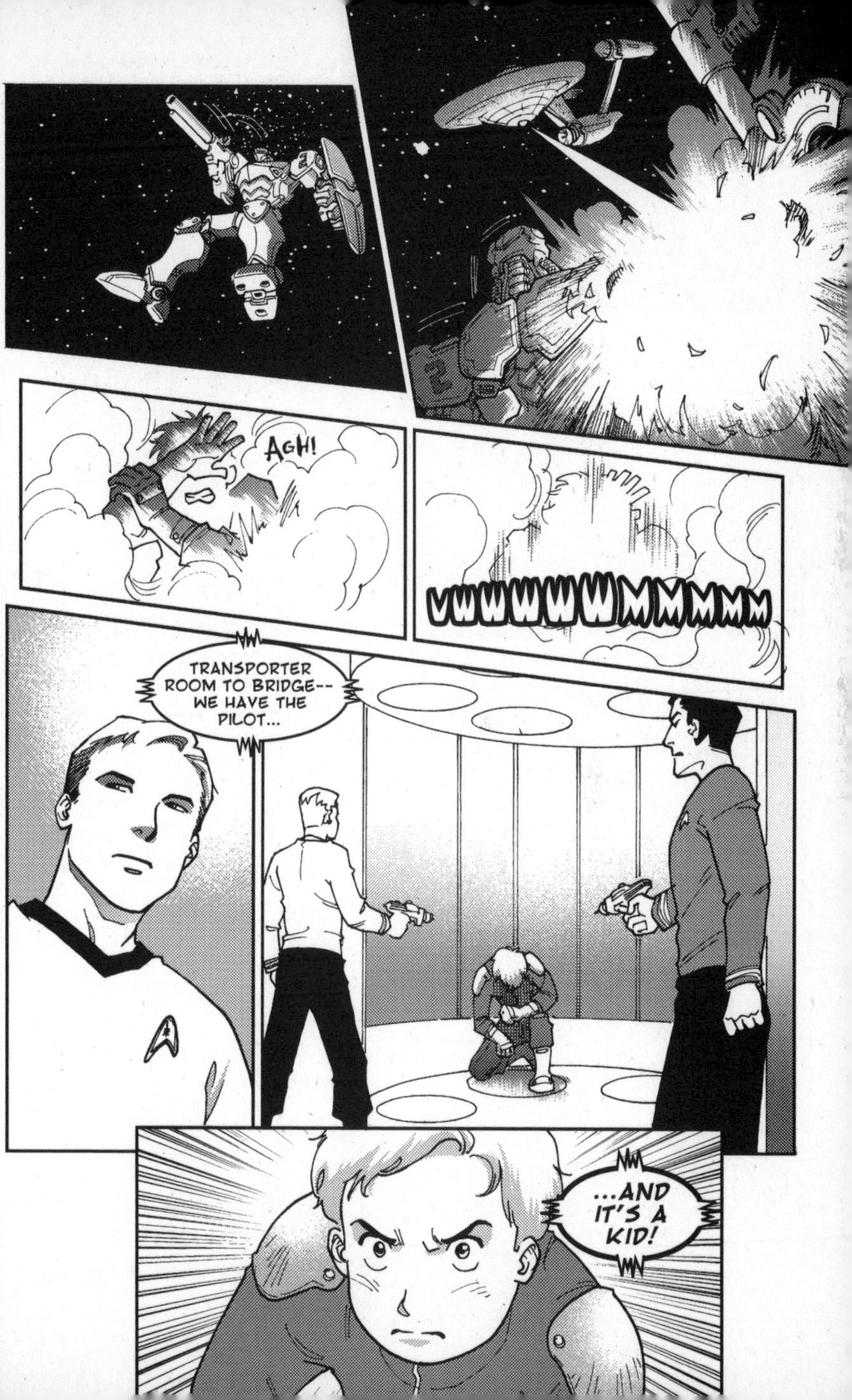
AGH!
VWWWWWWMMMMM
TRANSPORTER ROOM TO BRIDGE-- WE HAVE THE PILOT...
...AND IT'S A KID!

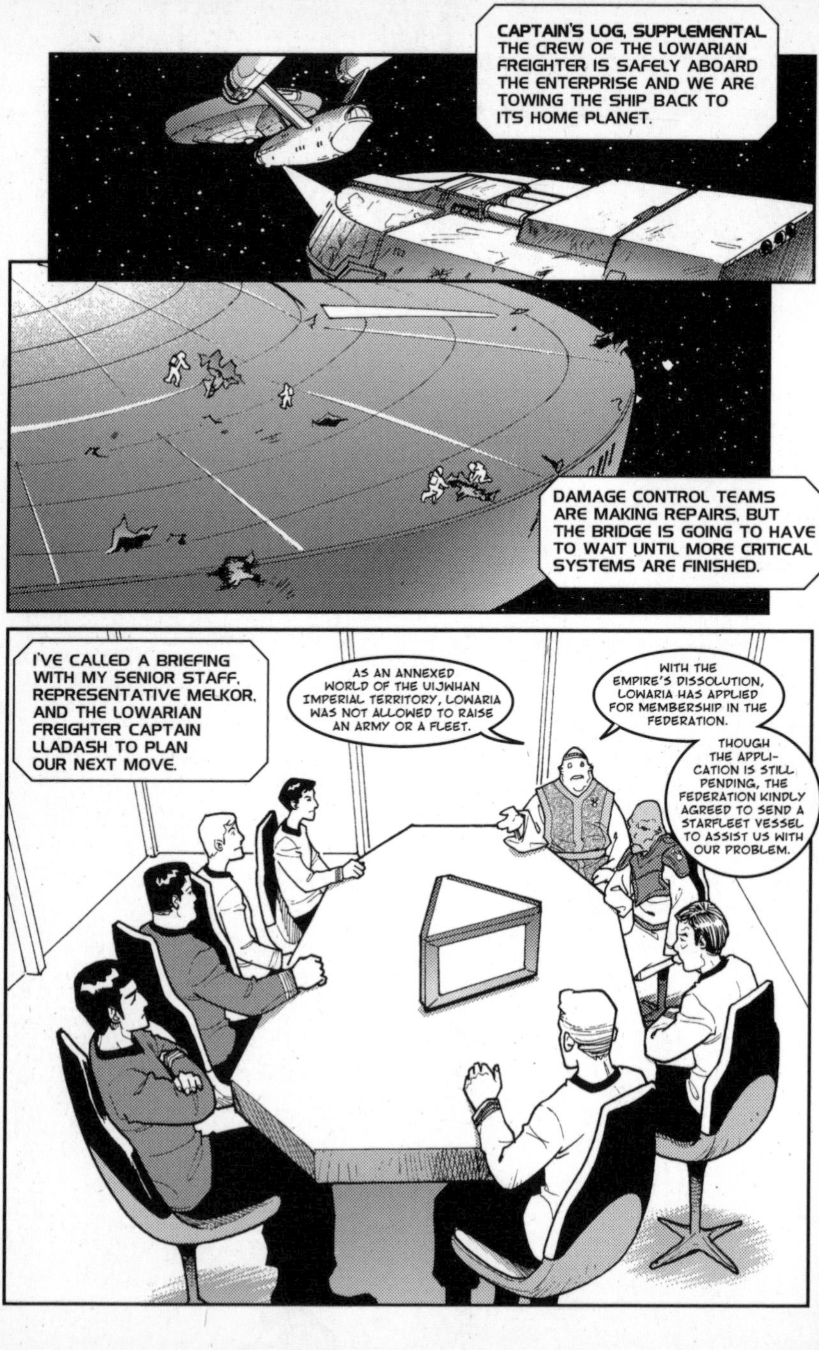
CAPTAIN'S LOG, SUPPLEMENTAL
THE CREW OF THE LOWARIAN FREIGHTER IS SAFELY ABOARD THE ENTERPRISE AND WE ARE TOWING THE SHIP BACK TO ITS HOME PLANET.
DAMAGE CONTROL TEAMS ARE MAKING REPAIRS, BUT THE BRIDGE IS GOING TO HAVE TO WAIT UNTIL MORE CRITICAL SYSTEMS ARE FINISHED.
I'VE CALLED A BRIEFING WITH MY SENIOR STAFF, REPRESENTATIVE MELKOR, AND THE LOWARIAN FREIGHTER CAPTAIN LLADASH TO PLAN OUR NEXT MOVE.
AS AN ANNEXED WORLD OF THE UIJWHAN IMPERIAL TERRITORY, LOWARIA WAS NOT ALLOWED TO RAISE AN ARMY OR A FLEET.
WITH THE EMPIRE'S DISSOLUTION, LOWARIA HAS APPLIED FOR MEMBERSHIP IN THE FEDERATION.
THOUGH THE APPLI-CATION IS STILL PENDING, THE FEDERATION KINDLY AGREED TO SEND A STARFLEET VESSEL TO ASSIST US WITH OUR PROBLEM.

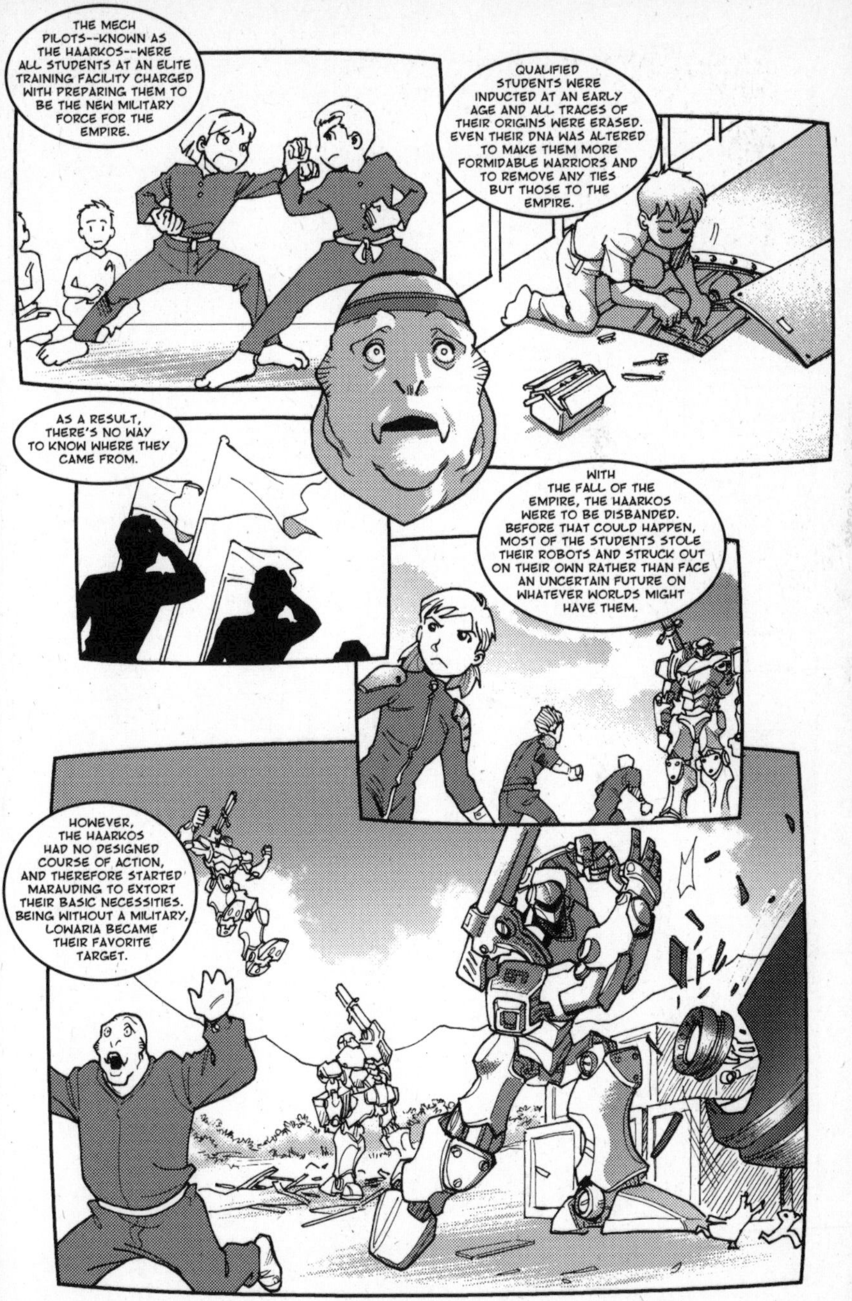
THE MECH PILOTS--KNOWN AS THE HAARKOS--WERE ALL STUDENTS AT AN ELITE TRAINING FACILITY CHARGED WITH PREPARING THEM TO BE THE NEW MILITARY FORCE FOR THE EMPIRE.
QUALIFIED STUDENTS WERE INDUCTED AT AN EARLY AGE AND ALL TRACES OF THEIR ORIGINS WERE ERASED. EVEN THEIR DNA WAS ALTERED TO MAKE THEM MORE FORMIDABLE WARRIORS AND TO REMOVE ANY TIES BUT THOSE TO THE EMPIRE.
AS A RESULT, THERE'S NO WAY TO KNOW WHERE THEY CAME FROM.
WITH THE FALL OF THE EMPIRE, THE HAARKOS WERE TO BE DISBANDED. BEFORE THAT COULD HAPPEN, MOST OF THE STUDENTS STOLE THEIR ROBOTS AND STRUCK OUT ON THEIR OWN RATHER THAN FACE AN UNCERTAIN FUTURE ON WHATEVER WORLDS MIGHT HAVE THEM.
HOWEVER, THE HAARKOS HAD NO DESIGNED COURSE OF ACTION, AND THEREFORE STARTED MARAUDING TO EXTORT THEIR BASIC NECESSITIES. BEING WITHOUT A MILITARY, LOWARIA BECAME THEIR FAVORITE TARGET.

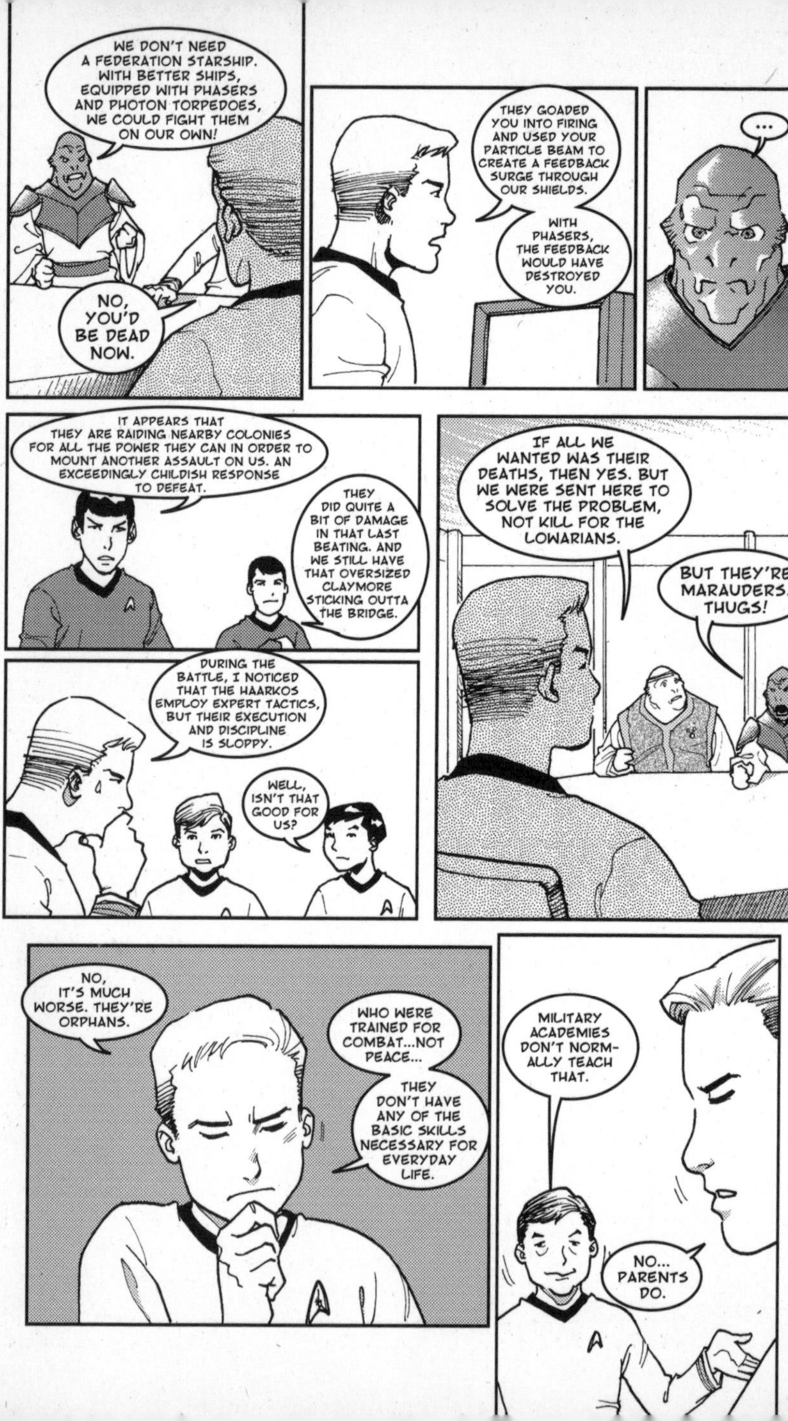
WE DON'T NEED A FEDERATION STARSHIP. WITH BETTER SHIPS, EQUIPPED WITH PHASERS AND PHOTON TORPEDOES, WE COULD FIGHT THEM ON OUR OWN!
NO, YOU'D BE DEAD NOW.
THEY GOADED YOU INTO FIRING AND USED YOUR PARTICLE BEAM TO CREATE A FEEDBACK SURGE THROUGH OUR SHIELDS.
WITH PHASERS, THE FEEDBACK WOULD HAVE DESTROYED YOU.
...
IT APPEARS THAT THEY ARE RAIDING NEARBY COLONIES FOR ALL THE POWER THEY CAN IN ORDER TO MOUNT ANOTHER ASSAULT ON US. AN EXCEEDINGLY CHILDISH RESPONSE TO DEFEAT.
THEY DID QUITE A BIT OF DAMAGE IN THAT LAST BEATING. AND WE STILL HAVE THAT OVERSIZED CLAYMORE STICKING OUTTA THE BRIDGE.
DURING THE BATTLE, I NOTICED THAT THE HAARKOS EMPLOY EXPERT TACTICS, BUT THEIR EXECUTION AND DISCIPLINE IS SLOPPY.
WELL, ISN'T THAT GOOD FOR US?
IF ALL WE WANTED WAS THEIR DEATHS, THEN YES. BUT WE WERE SENT HERE TO SOLVE THE PROBLEM, NOT KILL FOR THE LOWARIANS.
BUT THEY'RE MARAUDERS. THUGS!
NO, IT'S MUCH WORSE. THEY'RE ORPHANS.
WHO WERE TRAINED FOR COMBAT...NOT PEACE...
THEY DON'T HAVE ANY OF THE BASIC SKILLS NECESSARY FOR EVERYDAY LIFE.
MILITARY ACADEMIES DON'T NORMALLY TEACH THAT.
NO... PARENTS DO.

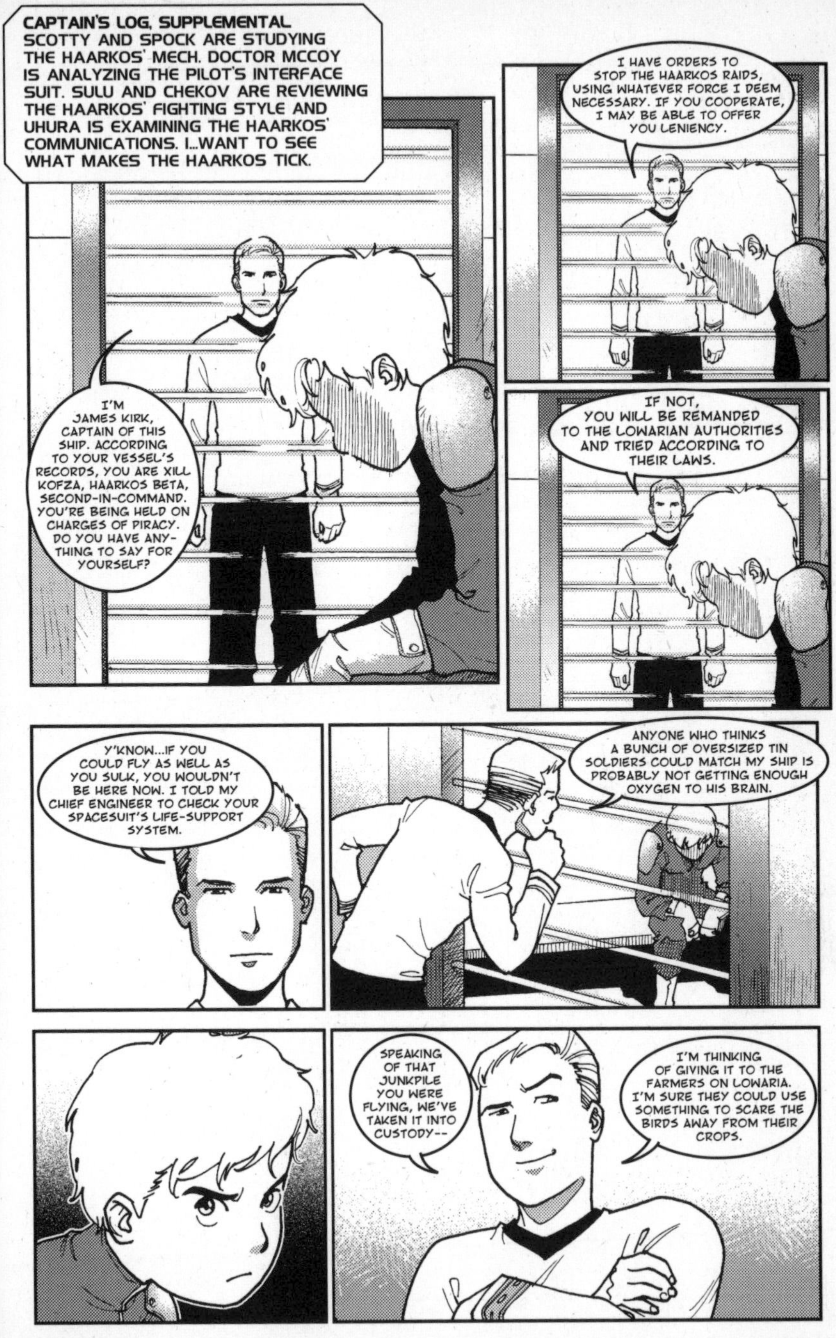
CAPTAIN'S LOG, SUPPLEMENTAL. SCOTTY AND SPOCK ARE STUDYING THE HAARKOS' MECH. DOCTOR MCCOY IS ANALYZING THE PILOT'S INTERFACE SUIT. SULU AND CHEKOV ARE REVIEWING THE HAARKOS' FIGHTING STYLE AND UHURA IS EXAMINING THE HAARKOS' COMMUNICATIONS. I...WANT TO SEE WHAT MAKES THE HAARKOS TICK.
I'M JAMES KIRK, CAPTAIN OF THIS SHIP. ACCORDING TO YOUR VESSEL'S RECORDS, YOU ARE XILL KOFZA, HAARKOS BETA, SECOND-IN-COMMAND. YOU'RE BEING HELD ON CHARGES OF PIRACY. DO YOU HAVE ANYTHING TO SAY FOR YOURSELF?
I HAVE ORDERS TO STOP THE HAARKOS RAIDS, USING WHATEVER FORCE I DEEM NECESSARY. IF YOU COOPERATE, I MAY BE ABLE TO OFFER YOU LENIENCY.
IF NOT, YOU WILL BE REMANDED TO THE LOWARIAN AUTHORITIES AND TRIED ACCORDING TO THEIR LAWS.
Y'KNOW...IF YOU COULD FLY AS WELL AS YOU SULK, YOU WOULDN'T BE HERE NOW. I TOLD MY CHIEF ENGINEER TO CHECK YOUR SPACESUIT'S LIFE-SUPPORT SYSTEM.
ANYONE WHO THINKS A BUNCH OF OVERSIZED TIN SOLDIERS COULD MATCH MY SHIP IS PROBABLY NOT GETTING ENOUGH OXYGEN TO HIS BRAIN.
SPEAKING OF THAT JUNKPILE YOU WERE FLYING, WE'VE TAKEN IT INTO CUSTODY--
I'M THINKING OF GIVING IT TO THE FARMERS ON LOWARIA. I'M SURE THEY COULD USE SOMETHING TO SCARE THE BIRDS AWAY FROM THEIR CROPS.

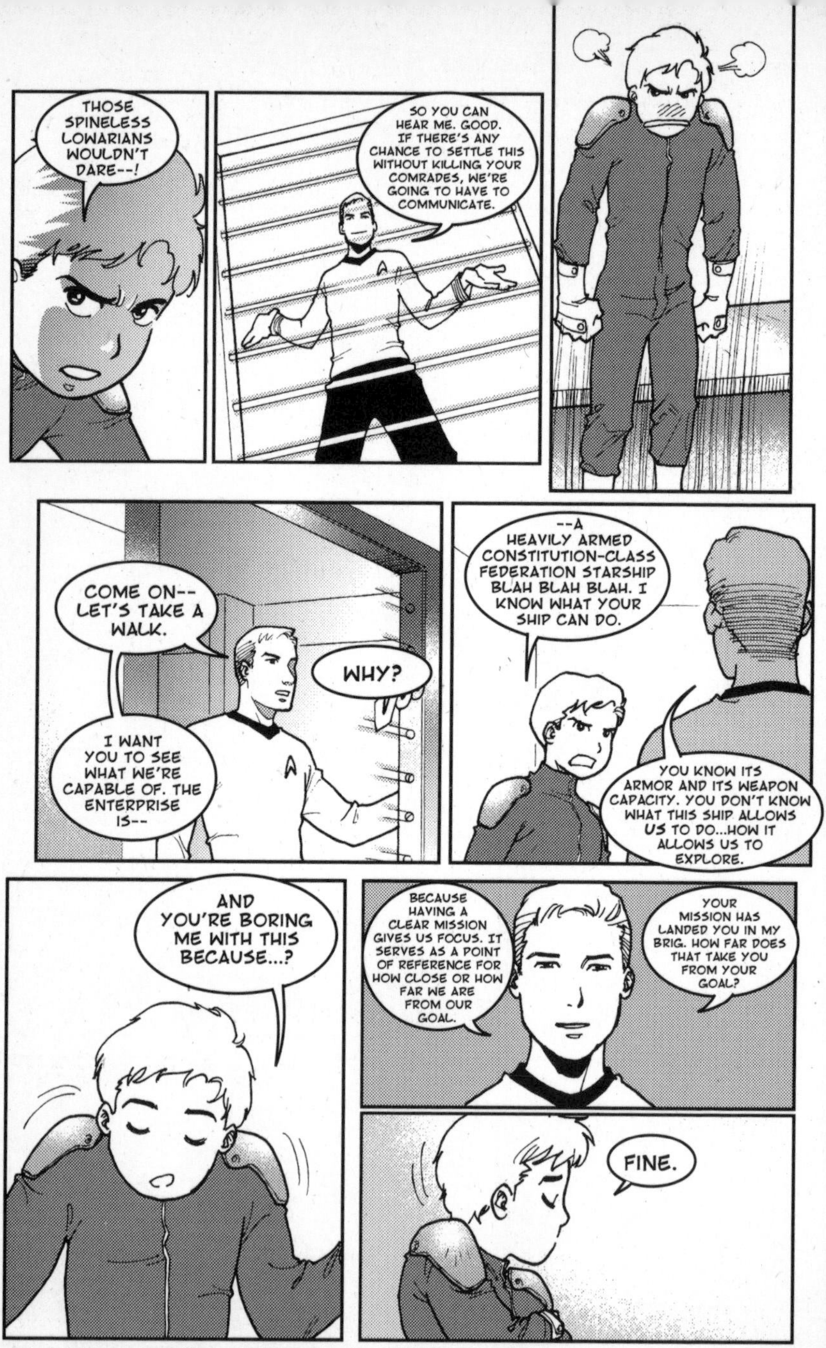
THOSE SPINELESS LOWARIANS WOULDN'T DARE--!
SO YOU CAN HEAR ME. GOOD. IF THERE'S ANY CHANCE TO SETTLE THIS WITHOUT KILLING YOUR COMRADES, WE'RE GOING TO HAVE TO COMMUNICATE.
COME ON--LET'S TAKE A WALK.
WHY?
I WANT YOU TO SEE WHAT WE'RE CAPABLE OF. THE ENTERPRISE IS--
--A HEAVILY ARMED CONSTITUTION-CLASS FEDERATION STARSHIP BLAH BLAH BLAH. I KNOW WHAT YOUR SHIP CAN DO.
YOU KNOW ITS ARMOR AND ITS WEAPON CAPACITY. YOU DON'T KNOW WHAT THIS SHIP ALLOWS US TO DO...HOW IT ALLOWS US TO EXPLORE.
AND YOU'RE BORING ME WITH THIS BECAUSE...?
BECAUSE HAVING A CLEAR MISSION GIVES US FOCUS. IT SERVES AS A POINT OF REFERENCE FOR HOW CLOSE OR HOW FAR WE ARE FROM OUR GOAL.
YOUR MISSION HAS LANDED YOU IN MY BRIG. HOW FAR DOES THAT TAKE YOU FROM YOUR GOAL?
FINE.

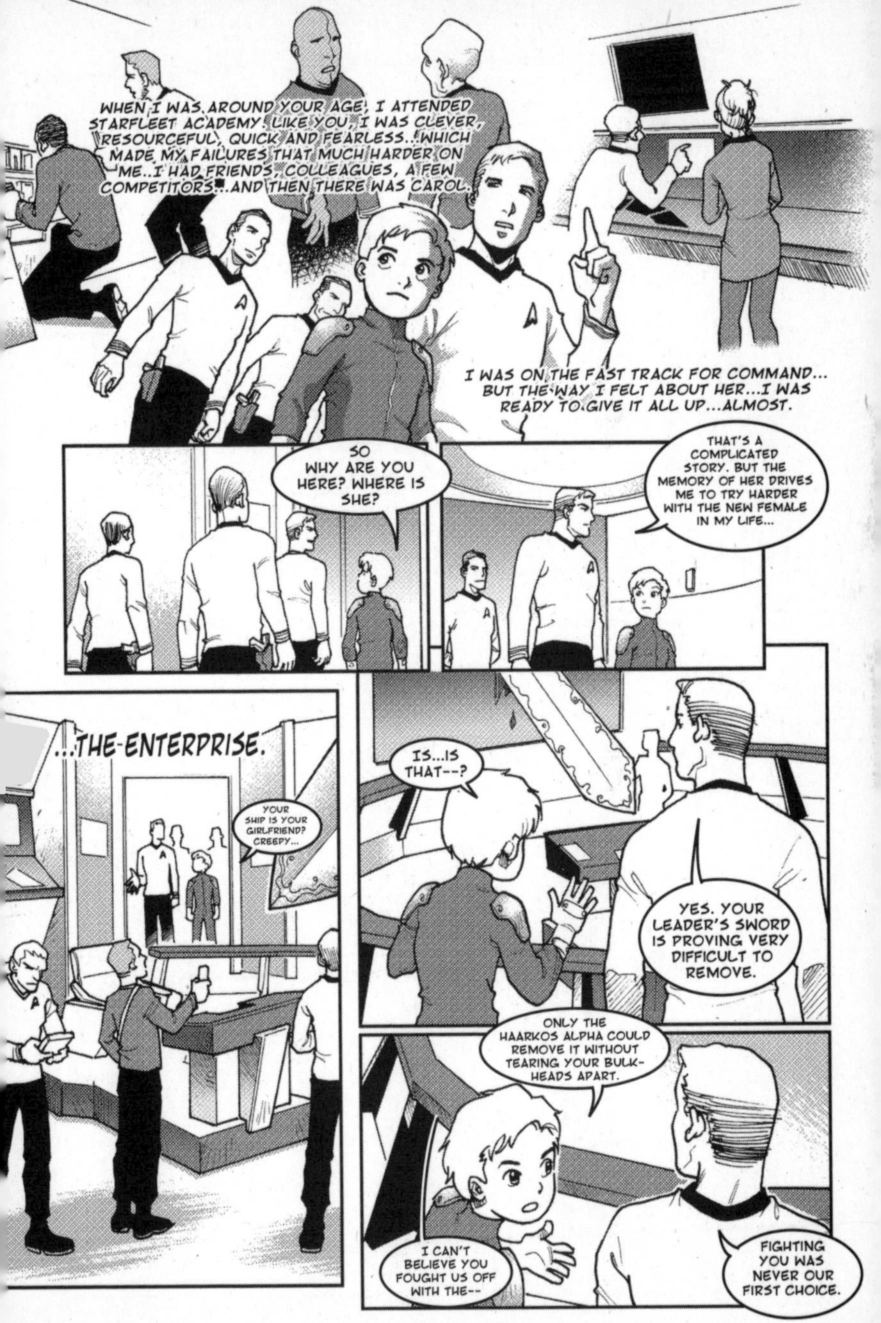
WHEN I WAS AROUND YOUR AGE, I ATTENDED STARFLEET ACADEMY. LIKE YOU, I WAS CLEVER, RESOURCEFUL, QUICK AND FEARLESS...WHICH MADE MY FAILURES THAT MUCH HARDER ON ME..I HAD FRIENDS, COLLEAGUES, A FEW COMPETITORS...AND THEN THERE WAS CAROL.
I WAS ON THE FAST TRACK FOR COMMAND... BUT THE WAY I FELT ABOUT HER...I WAS READY TO GIVE IT ALL UP...ALMOST.
SO WHY ARE YOU HERE? WHERE IS SHE?
THAT'S A COMPLICATED STORY. BUT THE MEMORY OF HER DRIVES ME TO TRY HARDER WITH THE NEW FEMALE IN MY LIFE...
...THE ENTERPRISE.
YOUR SHIP IS YOUR GIRLFRIEND? CREEPY...
IS...IS THAT--?
YES. YOUR LEADER'S SWORD IS PROVING VERY DIFFICULT TO REMOVE.
ONLY THE HAARKOS ALPHA COULD REMOVE IT WITHOUT TEARING YOUR BULK-HEADS APART.
I CAN'T BELIEVE YOU FOUGHT US OFF WITH THE--
FIGHTING YOU WAS NEVER OUR FIRST CHOICE.

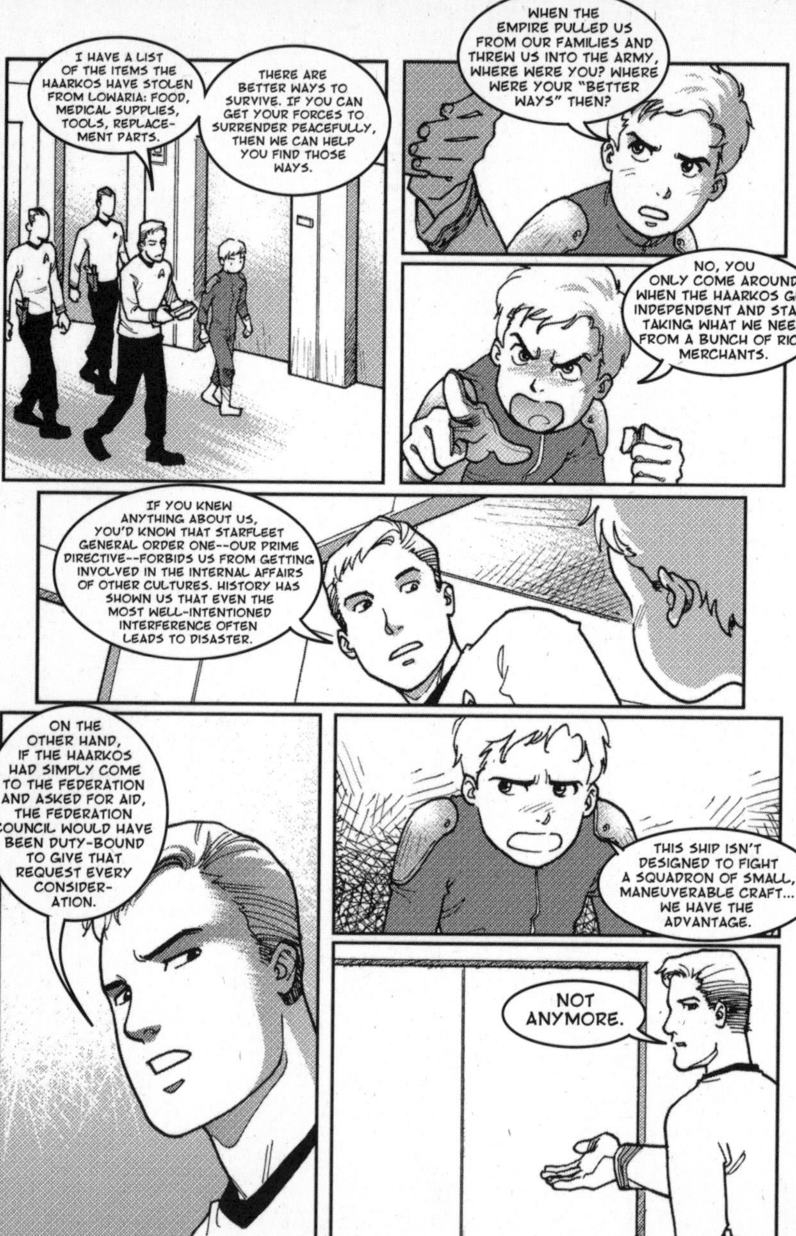
I HAVE A LIST OF THE ITEMS THE HAARKOS HAVE STOLEN FROM LOWARIA: FOOD, MEDICAL SUPPLIES, TOOLS, REPLACE-MENT PARTS.
THERE ARE BETTER WAYS TO SURVIVE. IF YOU CAN GET YOUR FORCES TO SURRENDER PEACEFULLY, THEN WE CAN HELP YOU FIND THOSE WAYS.
WHEN THE EMPIRE PULLED US FROM OUR FAMILIES AND THREW US INTO THE ARMY, WHERE WERE YOU? WHERE WERE YOUR "BETTER WAYS" THEN?
NO, YOU ONLY COME AROUND WHEN THE HAARKOS GET INDEPENDENT AND START TAKING WHAT WE NEED FROM A BUNCH OF RICH MERCHANTS.
IF YOU KNEW ANYTHING ABOUT US, YOU'D KNOW THAT STARFLEET GENERAL ORDER ONE--OUR PRIME DIRECTIVE--FORBIDS US FROM GETTING INVOLVED IN THE INTERNAL AFFAIRS OF OTHER CULTURES. HISTORY HAS SHOWN US THAT EVEN THE MOST WELL-INTENTIONED INTERFERENCE OFTEN LEADS TO DISASTER.
ON THE OTHER HAND, IF THE HAARKOS HAD SIMPLY COME TO THE FEDERATION AND ASKED FOR AID, THE FEDERATION COUNCIL WOULD HAVE BEEN DUTY-BOUND TO GIVE THAT REQUEST EVERY CONSIDER-ATION.
THIS SHIP ISN'T DESIGNED TO FIGHT A SQUADRON OF SMALL, MANEUVERABLE CRAFT... WE HAVE THE ADVANTAGE.
NOT ANYMORE.

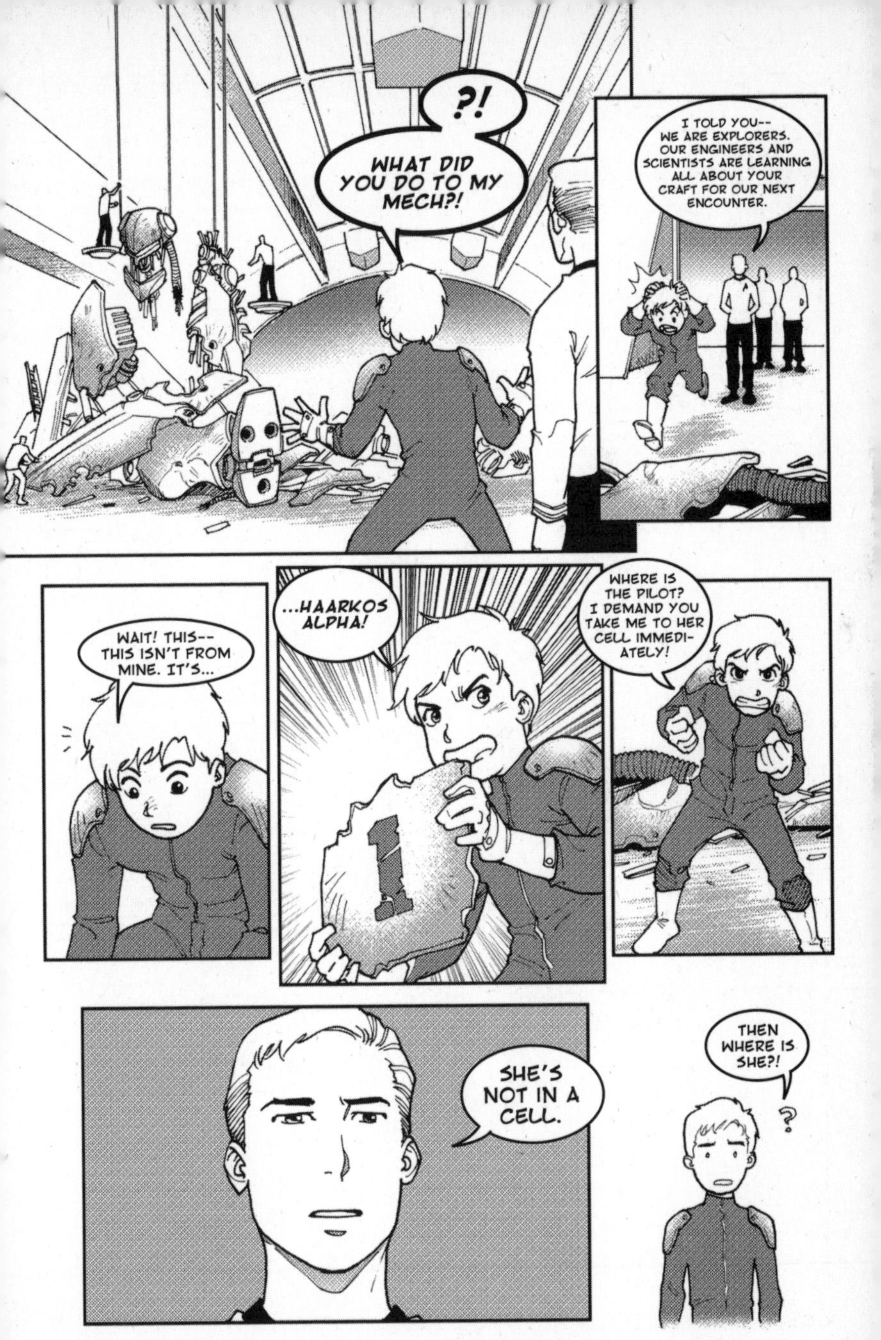
?!
WHAT DID YOU DO TO MY MECH?!
I TOLD YOU-- WE ARE EXPLORERS. OUR ENGINEERS AND SCIENTISTS ARE LEARNING ALL ABOUT YOUR CRAFT FOR OUR NEXT ENCOUNTER.
WAIT! THIS-- THIS ISN'T FROM MINE. IT'S...
...HAARKOS ALPHA!
1
WHERE IS THE PILOT? I DEMAND YOU TAKE ME TO HER CELL IMMEDI-ATELY!
SHE'S NOT IN A CELL.
THEN WHERE IS SHE?!
?

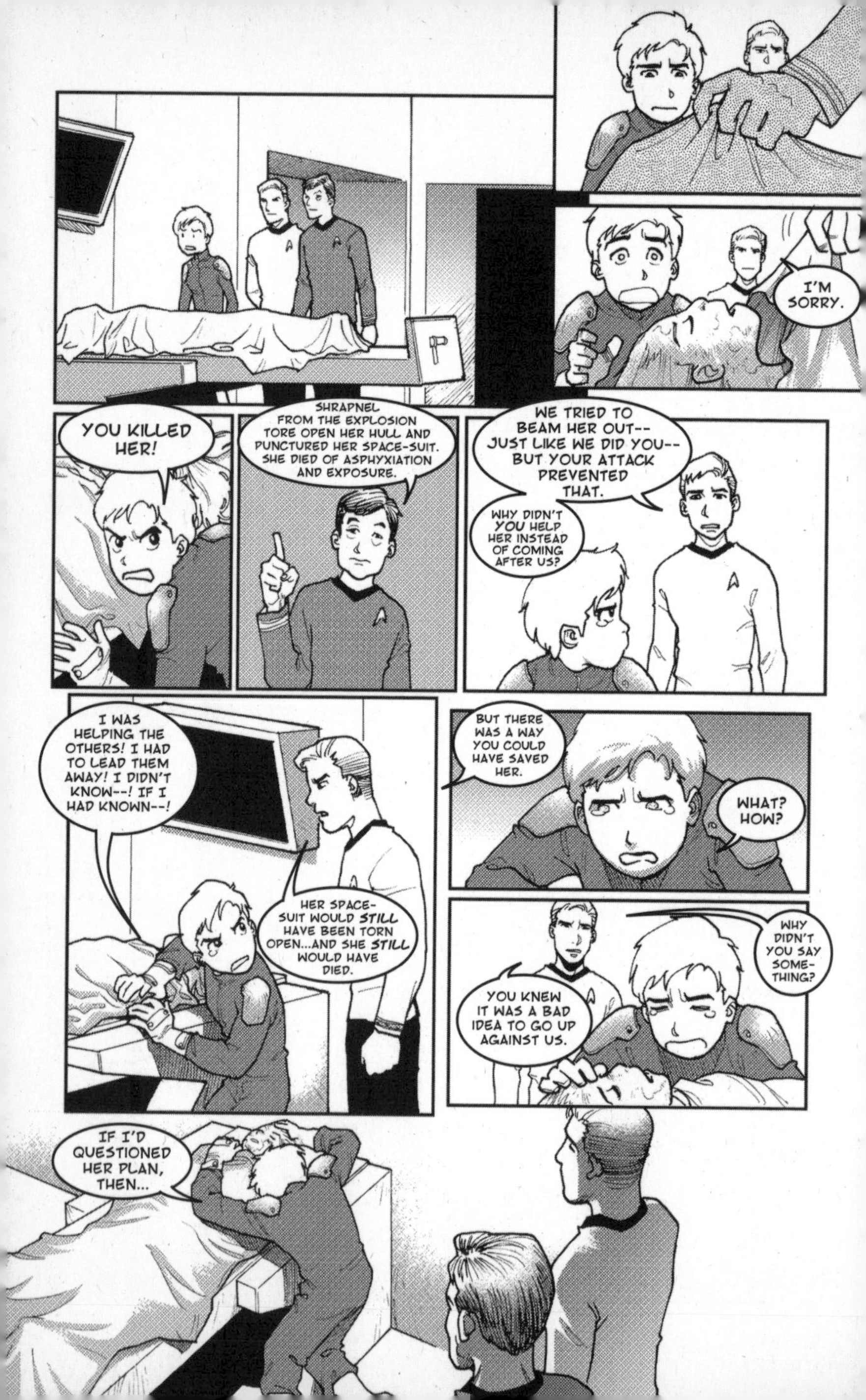
I'M SORRY.
YOU KILLED HER!
SHRAPNEL FROM THE EXPLOSION TORE OPEN HER HULL AND PUNCTURED HER SPACE-SUIT. SHE DIED OF ASPHYXIATION AND EXPOSURE.
WE TRIED TO BEAM HER OUT-- JUST LIKE WE DID YOU-- BUT YOUR ATTACK PREVENTED THAT.
WHY DIDN'T YOU HELP HER INSTEAD OF COMING AFTER US?
I WAS HELPING THE OTHERS! I HAD TO LEAD THEM AWAY! I DIDN'T KNOW--! IF I HAD KNOWN--!
HER SPACE-SUIT WOULD STILL HAVE BEEN TORN OPEN...AND SHE STILL WOULD HAVE DIED.
BUT THERE WAS A WAY YOU COULD HAVE SAVED HER.
WHAT? HOW?
WHY DIDN'T YOU SAY SOME-THING?
YOU KNEW IT WAS A BAD IDEA TO GO UP AGAINST US.
IF I'D QUESTIONED HER PLAN, THEN...

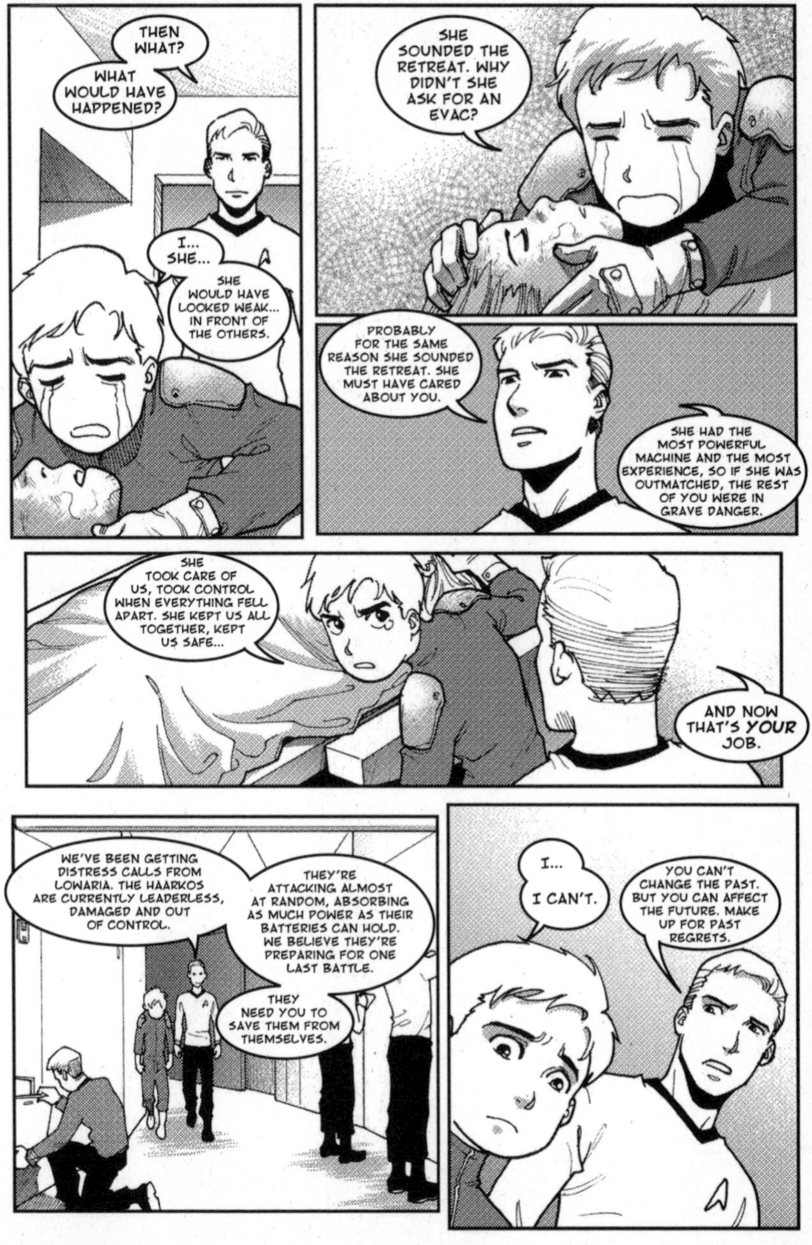
THEN WHAT?
WHAT WOULD HAVE HAPPENED?
I... SHE...
SHE WOULD HAVE LOOKED WEAK... IN FRONT OF THE OTHERS.
SHE SOUNDED THE RETREAT. WHY DIDN'T SHE ASK FOR AN EVAC?
PROBABLY FOR THE SAME REASON SHE SOUNDED THE RETREAT. SHE MUST HAVE CARED ABOUT YOU.
SHE HAD THE MOST POWERFUL MACHINE AND THE MOST EXPERIENCE, SO IF SHE WAS OUTMATCHED, THE REST OF YOU WERE IN GRAVE DANGER.
SHE TOOK CARE OF US, TOOK CONTROL WHEN EVERYTHING FELL APART. SHE KEPT US ALL TOGETHER, KEPT US SAFE...
AND NOW THAT'S *YOUR* JOB.
WE'VE BEEN GETTING DISTRESS CALLS FROM LOWARIA. THE HAARKOS ARE CURRENTLY LEADERLESS, DAMAGED AND OUT OF CONTROL.
THEY'RE ATTACKING ALMOST AT RANDOM, ABSORBING AS MUCH POWER AS THEIR BATTERIES CAN HOLD. WE BELIEVE THEY'RE PREPARING FOR ONE LAST BATTLE.
THEY NEED YOU TO SAVE THEM FROM THEMSELVES.
I...
I CAN'T.
YOU CAN'T CHANGE THE PAST. BUT YOU CAN AFFECT THE FUTURE. MAKE UP FOR PAST REGRETS.

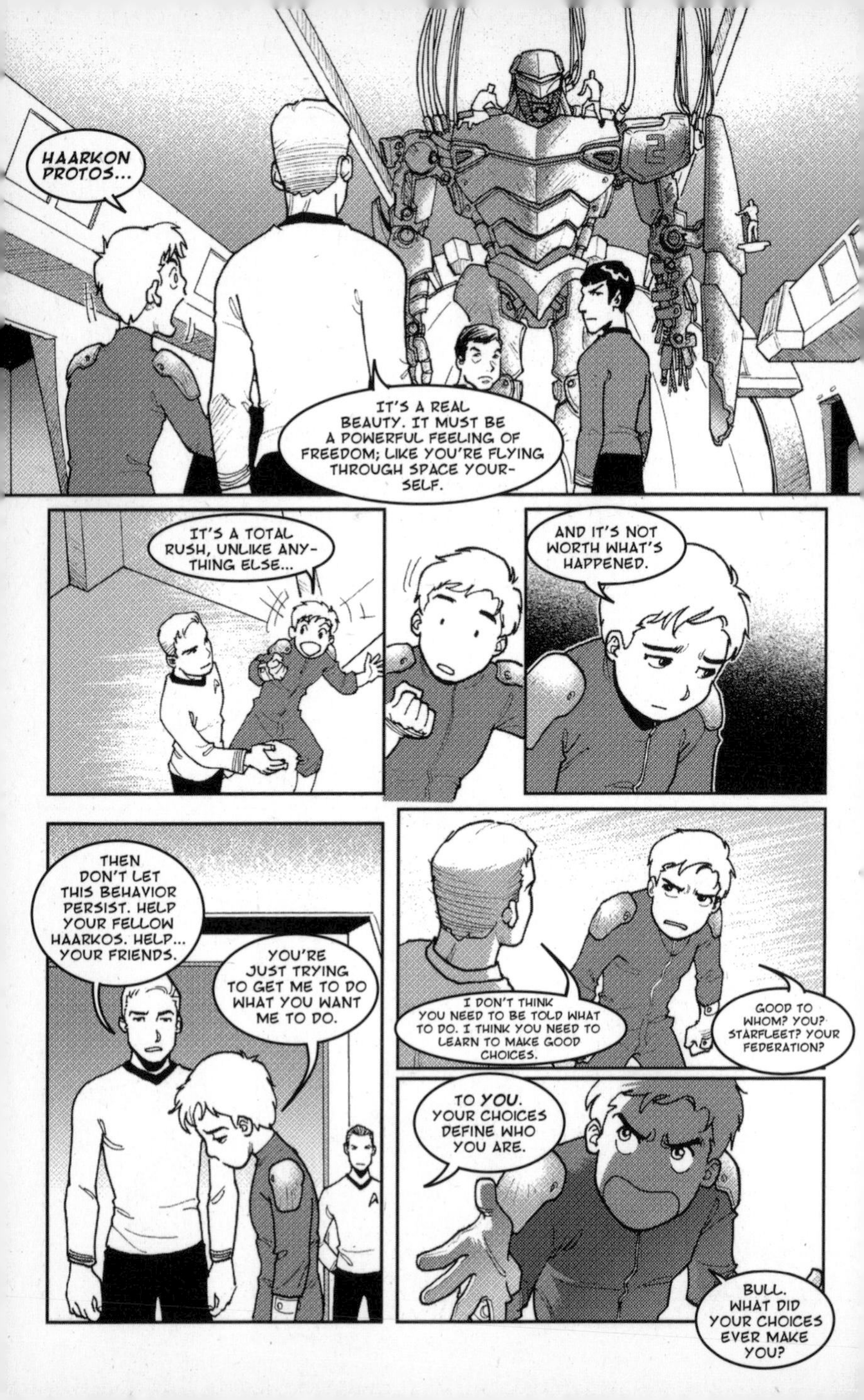
HAARKON PROTOS...
IT'S A REAL BEAUTY. IT MUST BE A POWERFUL FEELING OF FREEDOM; LIKE YOU'RE FLYING THROUGH SPACE YOUR-SELF.
IT'S A TOTAL RUSH, UNLIKE ANY-THING ELSE...
AND IT'S NOT WORTH WHAT'S HAPPENED.
THEN DON'T LET THIS BEHAVIOR PERSIST. HELP YOUR FELLOW HAARKOS. HELP... YOUR FRIENDS.
YOU'RE JUST TRYING TO GET ME TO DO WHAT YOU WANT ME TO DO.
I DON'T THINK YOU NEED TO BE TOLD WHAT TO DO. I THINK YOU NEED TO LEARN TO MAKE GOOD CHOICES.
GOOD TO WHOM? YOU? STARFLEET? YOUR FEDERATION?
TO *YOU*. YOUR CHOICES DEFINE WHO YOU ARE.
BULL. WHAT DID YOUR CHOICES EVER MAKE YOU?

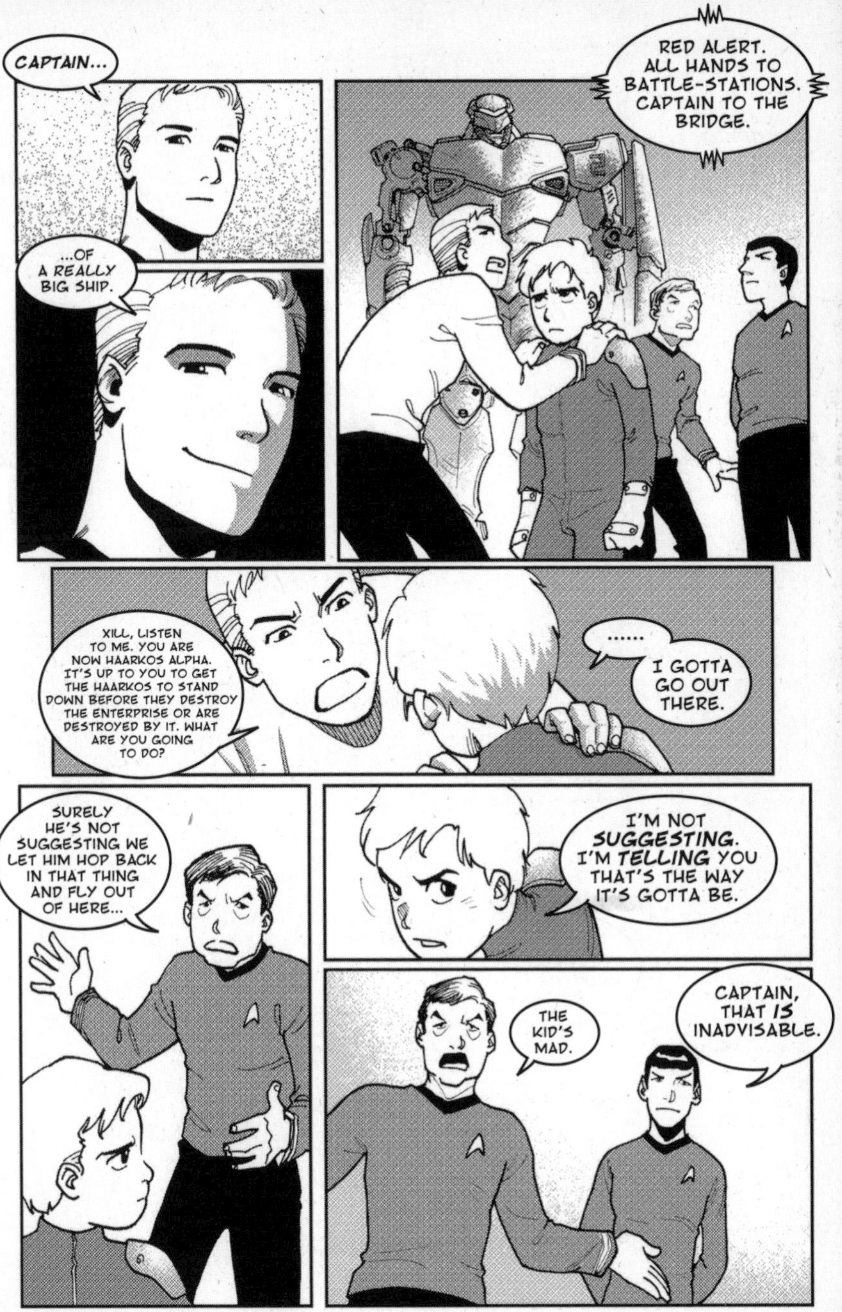
CAPTAIN...
...OF A *REALLY* BIG SHIP.
RED ALERT. ALL HANDS TO BATTLE-STATIONS. CAPTAIN TO THE BRIDGE.
XILL, LISTEN TO ME. YOU ARE NOW HAARKOS ALPHA. IT'S UP TO YOU TO GET THE HAARKOS TO STAND DOWN BEFORE THEY DESTROY THE ENTERPRISE OR ARE DESTROYED BY IT. WHAT ARE YOU GOING TO DO?
......
I GOTTA GO OUT THERE.
SURELY HE'S NOT SUGGESTING WE LET HIM HOP BACK IN THAT THING AND FLY OUT OF HERE...
I'M NOT ***SUGGESTING***. I'M ***TELLING*** YOU THAT'S THE WAY IT'S GOTTA BE.
THE KID'S MAD.
CAPTAIN, THAT ***IS*** INADVISABLE.

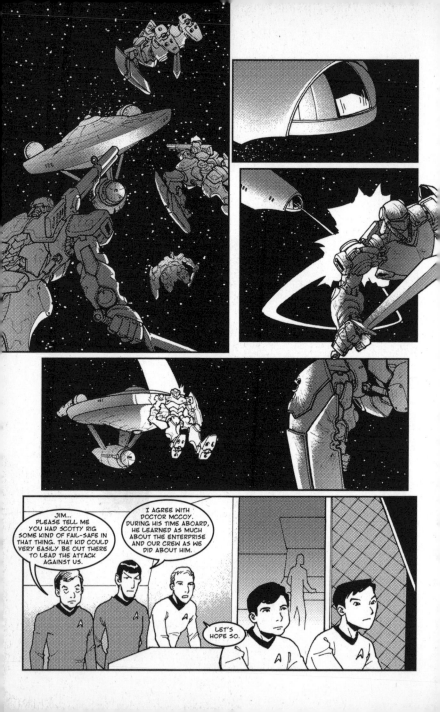

JIM...
PLEASE TELL ME
YOU HAD SCOTTY RIG
SOME KIND OF FAIL-SAFE IN
THAT THING. THAT KID COULD
VERY EASILY BE OUT THERE
TO LEAD THE ATTACK
AGAINST US.

I AGREE WITH
DOCTOR MCCOY.
DURING HIS TIME ABOARD,
HE LEARNED AS MUCH
ABOUT THE ENTERPRISE
AND OUR CREW AS WE
DID ABOUT HIM.

LET'S
HOPE SO.

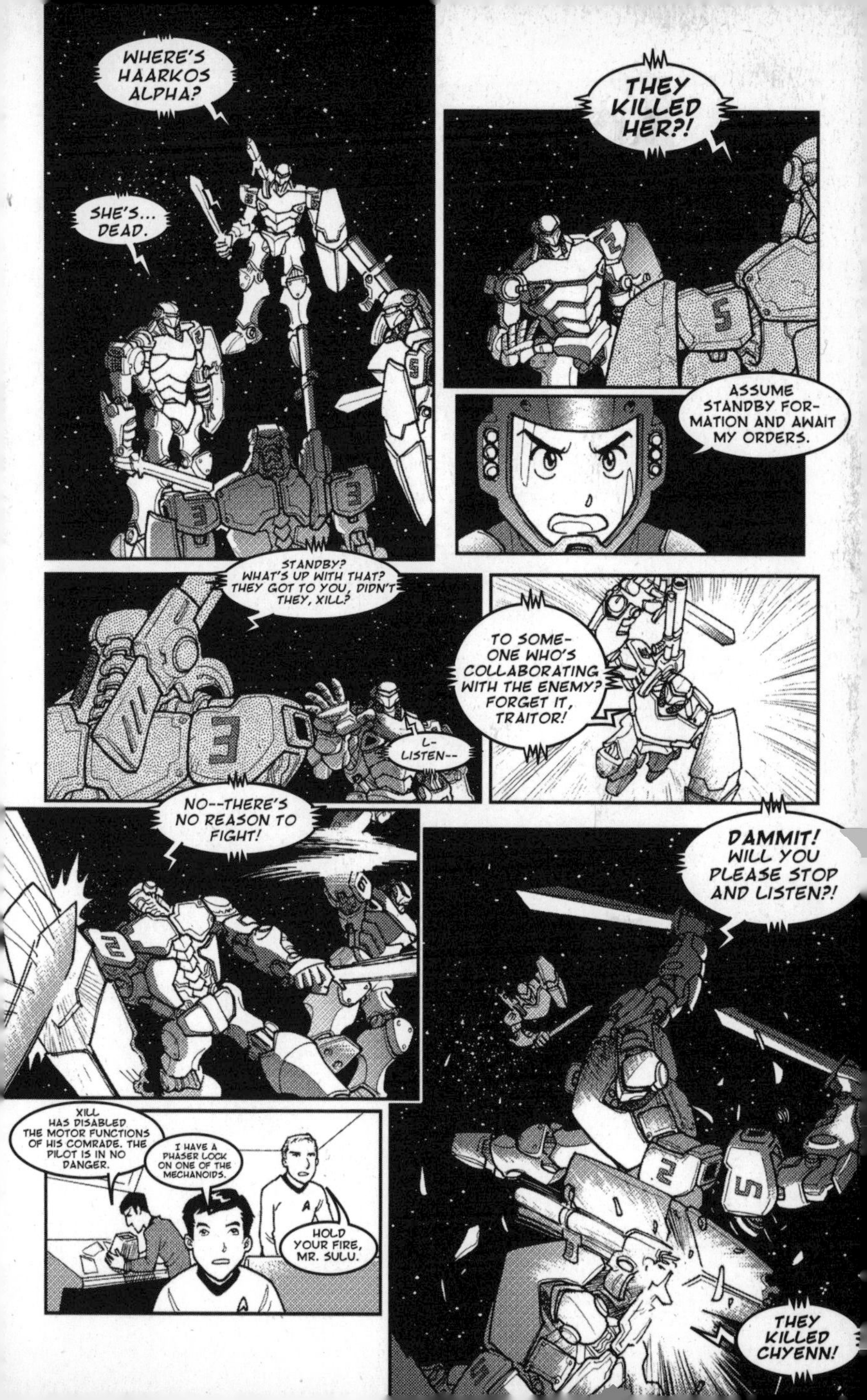
WHERE'S HAARKOS ALPHA?
SHE'S... DEAD.
THEY KILLED HER?!
ASSUME STANDBY FORMATION AND AWAIT MY ORDERS.
STANDBY? WHAT'S UP WITH THAT? THEY GOT TO YOU, DIDN'T THEY, XILL?
L-LISTEN--
TO SOMEONE WHO'S COLLABORATING WITH THE ENEMY? FORGET IT, TRAITOR!
NO--THERE'S NO REASON TO FIGHT!
XILL HAS DISABLED THE MOTOR FUNCTIONS OF HIS COMRADE. THE PILOT IS IN NO DANGER.
I HAVE A PHASER LOCK ON ONE OF THE MECHANOIDS.
HOLD YOUR FIRE, MR. SULU.
DAMMIT! WILL YOU PLEASE STOP AND LISTEN?!
THEY KILLED CHYENN!

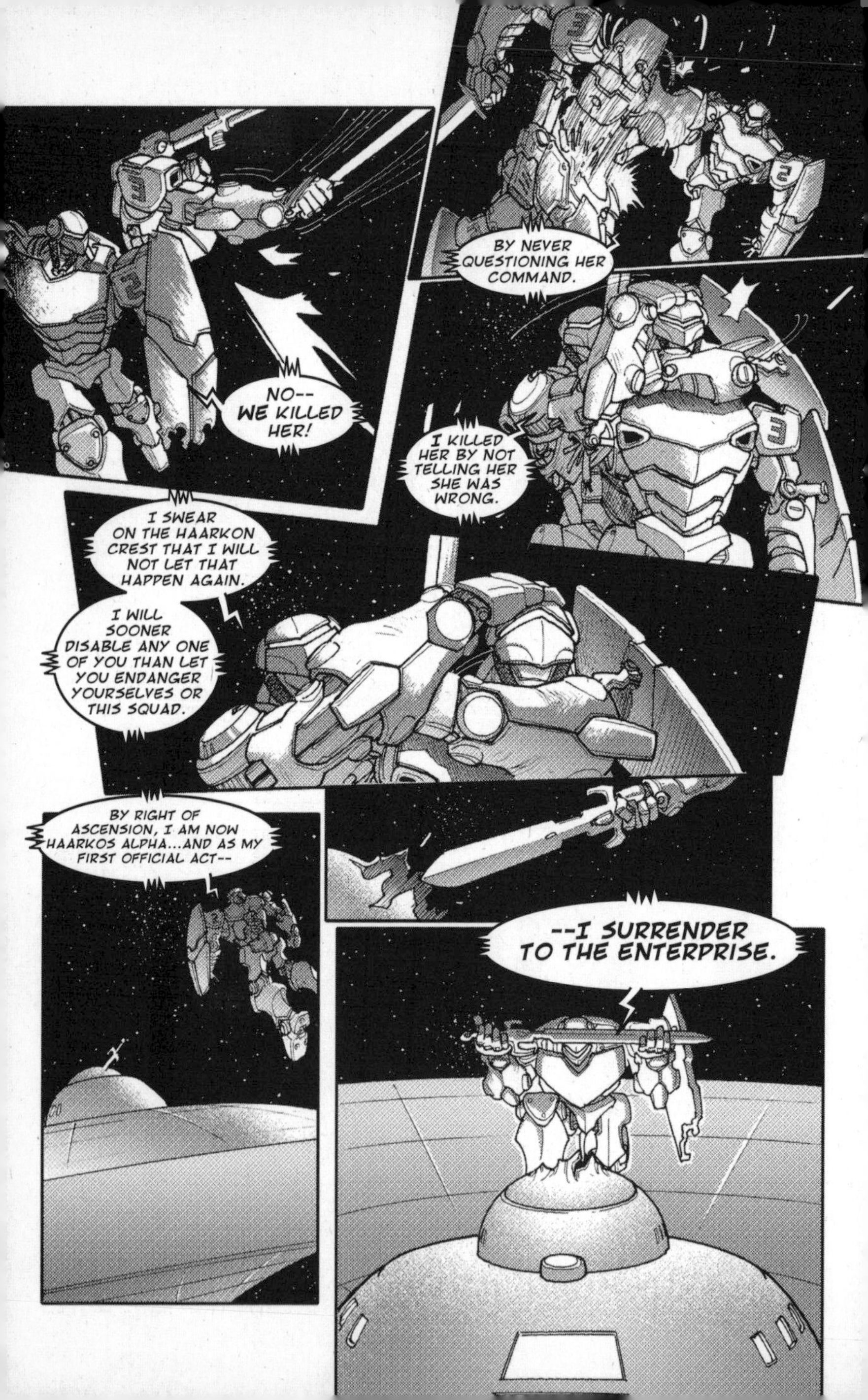

NO-- WE KILLED HER!
BY NEVER QUESTIONING HER COMMAND.
I KILLED HER BY NOT TELLING HER SHE WAS WRONG.
I SWEAR ON THE HAARKON CREST THAT I WILL NOT LET THAT HAPPEN AGAIN.
I WILL SOONER DISABLE ANY ONE OF YOU THAN LET YOU ENDANGER YOURSELVES OR THIS SQUAD.
BY RIGHT OF ASCENSION, I AM NOW HAARKOS ALPHA...AND AS MY FIRST OFFICIAL ACT--
--I SURRENDER TO THE ENTERPRISE.

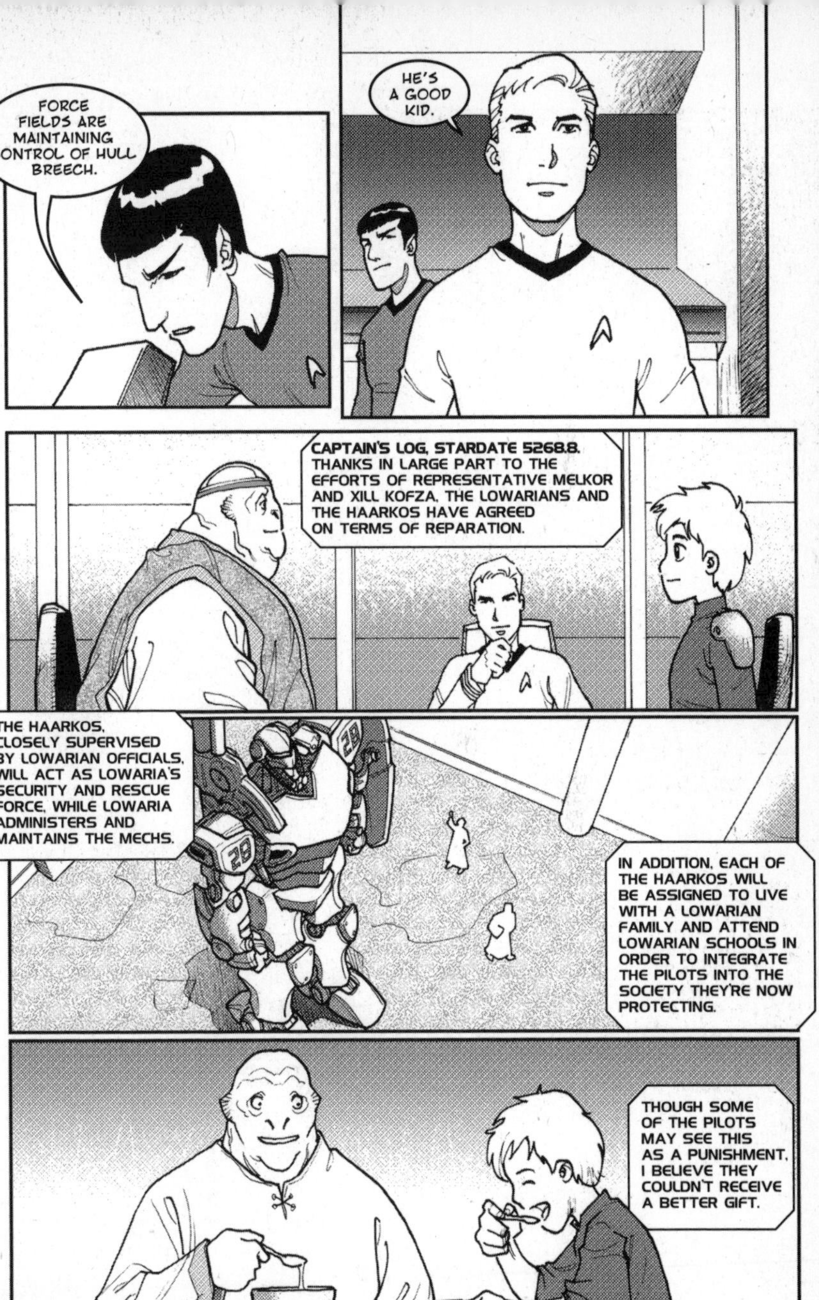
FORCE FIELDS ARE MAINTAINING CONTROL OF HULL BREECH.
HE'S A GOOD KID.
CAPTAIN'S LOG, STARDATE 5268.8. THANKS IN LARGE PART TO THE EFFORTS OF REPRESENTATIVE MELKOR AND XILL KOFZA, THE LOWARIANS AND THE HAARKOS HAVE AGREED ON TERMS OF REPARATION.
THE HAARKOS, CLOSELY SUPERVISED BY LOWARIAN OFFICIALS, WILL ACT AS LOWARIA'S SECURITY AND RESCUE FORCE, WHILE LOWARIA ADMINISTERS AND MAINTAINS THE MECHS.
IN ADDITION, EACH OF THE HAARKOS WILL BE ASSIGNED TO LIVE WITH A LOWARIAN FAMILY AND ATTEND LOWARIAN SCHOOLS IN ORDER TO INTEGRATE THE PILOTS INTO THE SOCIETY THEY'RE NOW PROTECTING.
THOUGH SOME OF THE PILOTS MAY SEE THIS AS A PUNISHMENT, I BELIEVE THEY COULDN'T RECEIVE A BETTER GIFT.

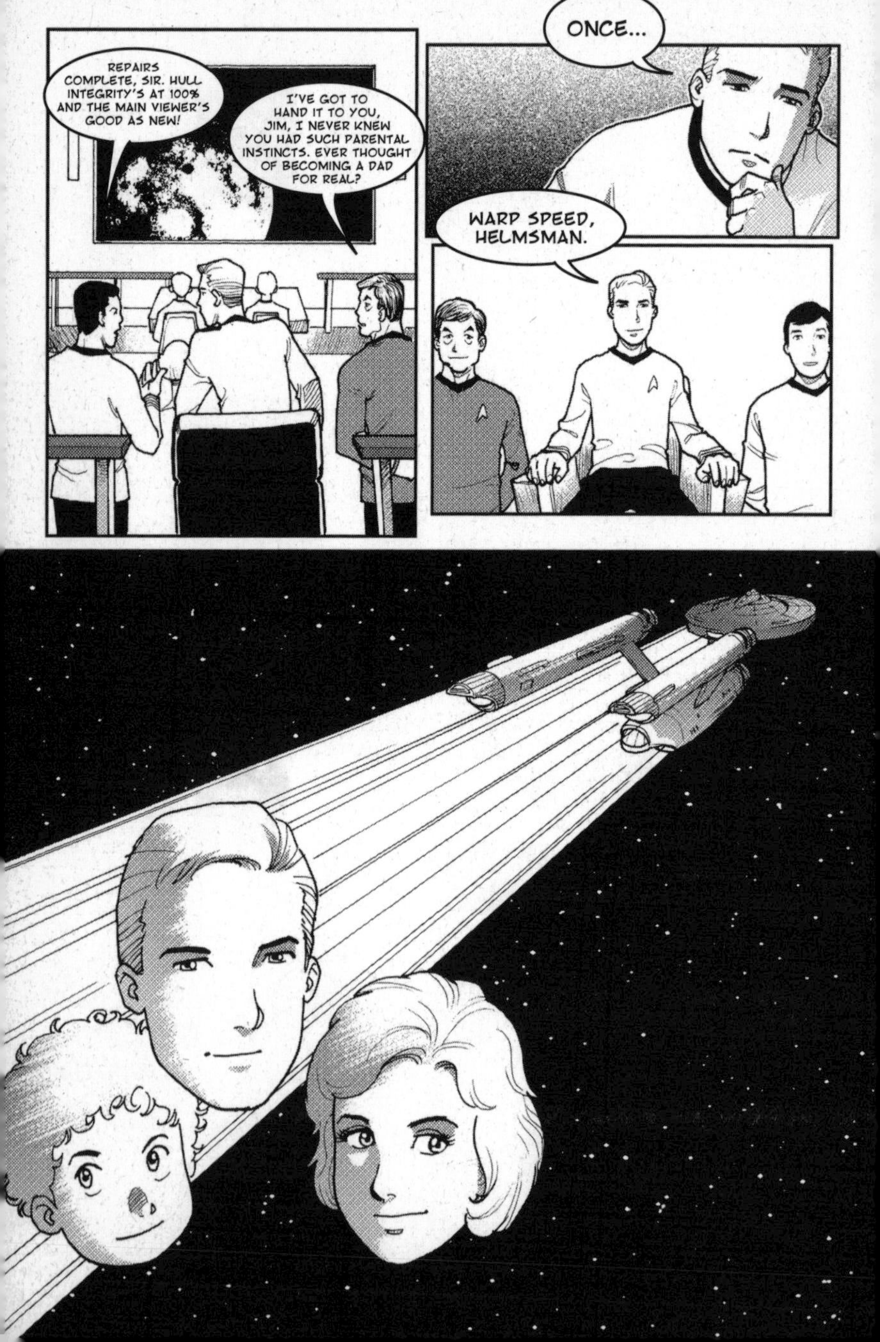

REPAIRS COMPLETE, SIR. HULL INTEGRITY'S AT 100% AND THE MAIN VIEWER'S GOOD AS NEW!
I'VE GOT TO HAND IT TO YOU, JIM, I NEVER KNEW YOU HAD SUCH PARENTAL INSTINCTS. EVER THOUGHT OF BECOMING A DAD FOR REAL?
ONCE...
WARP SPEED, HELMSMAN.

FIRST, DO NO HARM

BY
DAYTON WARD & KEVIN DILLMORE
A story from the collection CONSTELLATIONS

CELEBRATING FORTY YEARS

STAR TREK®

CONSTELLATIONS

A new anthology from Pocket Books

with stories by
Christopher L. Bennett • Steve Bond
Dave Galanter • Allyn Gibson • Robert Greenberger
Jeffrey Lang • Kevin Lauderdale • William Leisner
Stuart Moore • Jill Sherwin • Dayton Ward & Kevin Dilmore
Howard Weinstein

and an introduction by
David Gerrold

Available wherever books are sold

TURN THE PAGE TO READ
"FIRST, DO NO HARM"
BY DAYTON WARD & KEVIN DILMORE

www.startrekbooks.com

First, Do No Harm

Dayton Ward & Kevin Dilmore

Blood was *everywhere*.

Revati Jendra knelt before the young male's motionless form, fighting to bring her breathing back under control after the harried sprint from her clinic to the village's small ironworks. Coughing as she inhaled some of the building's sooty, metallic-tasting air, she pried open the injured adolescent's eyes to see that his large, black pupils remained sensitive even to the dim, orange-hued light within the metal shop. That was a good sign, at least a somewhat better sign than the pale pink blood staining his chalk-white hair and widening into a disturbingly large pool where his head rested on the bare, dirty floor of the shop.

"He just fell, *Beloren*," said a voice from the crowd, addressing her, as nearly all of the villagers did, by the Grennai term for "healer." It was a name to which she'd grown accustomed during the year or so she had lived and worked among them. "He started shaking and then just let go of the ladder."

A growing crowd of concerned friends and co-workers—all of them, Jendra thought, appearing too young to be working in such a place—began to encircle her as she lowered her ear to the injured male's lips, listening and feeling for even the faintest breath.

If only they weren't hovering over me, this could go so much more damned quickly.

Spasms abruptly wracked the young man's body, and Jendra

reached down to support his head with one hand while rolling him to one side in case he started to vomit. "I need help to move him," she called out to no one in particular as he continued to tremble. "We have to take him to the white home right away." Though possessing only rudimentary facilities, the Grennai hospital and its staff would probably be able to see this young man through most of his injuries. As his seizure started to fade, however, Jendra began to suspect that the man's fall had been no mere accident.

In a practiced move, she reached into the pocket of her frayed, homespun overcoat and retrieved a small, light-colored cloth. Hoping her actions appeared to the onlookers as trying to staunch the flow of blood from her patient's wound, Jendra activated the small Starfleet medical scanner concealed within the cloth. Pressing it against the dark skin of the man's head and watching as it turned pink with his blood, she manipulated the hidden, silenced device in order to determine the extent of his injuries. While his neck and spine were undamaged, the scan had detected a small tumor within the man's brain, and Jendra recognized it as the likely culprit behind the man's seizures.

"Step aside," said a strong, deep voice, that of Crimar, the ironworks supervisor. Jendra looked up to see the burly Grennai and one of his workers carrying a makeshift stretcher. Sweat matted their stark white hair to their heads and soot stained their rough, woven clothing. "We will carry him, *Beloren.*"

"Just a moment, Crimar," she said as she searched through her worn, leather medicine satchel. While she knew the bag did not contain what she needed to eliminate the tumor, which under Grennai medical standards would be undetectable and eventually fatal, Jendra was sure she could cure the young man given a little time and privacy. Unable to administer a hypospray in the midst of the onlookers, Jendra opted for an oral dose of trianoline. She slipped the small strip into his mouth, where it dissolved instantly on contact with his tongue. Within moments, the medication would begin to relieve some of the trauma the fall had inflicted upon his brain.

After taking an additional few moments to wrap the man's head in a thick bandage, Jendra pointed to one of the workers and had him kneel next to her. She handed him an another wad of cloth, instructing him to hold it against the victim's wound.

"Keep pressing here until you get to the *beloren* at the white home," Jendra ordered as she rose and waved to Crimar. "Take him now. I'll follow after you." She stepped back, allowing the supervisor to direct two workers to load their comrade onto the stretcher.

After directing the rest of the workforce to return to their respective tasks, Crimar turned to Jendra. "Thank you for coming so quickly, *Beloren*," he said. Though normally she found his accent as he spoke in his native language to be fluid and almost musical, on this occasion his tone was flat and emotionless. "But he has lost much blood. Surely he will die?"

"Not if I can help it," Jendra replied, the resolve in her voice abruptly shattered beneath the force of a ragged cough that hunched her aging, slender form. Seeing the look of concern in Crimar's wide eyes, she offered a weak smile as she wiped her mouth. "I'm fine, my friend. It's merely the soot in here. Maybe you could tidy up for me the next time I pay a visit?"

A wide smile creased Crimar's dark features. "I hope that is not for some time, *Beloren*."

Jendra patted his shoulder as she suppressed what would have been another coughing fit, then gathered her meager medical bag and headed for her home. As she walked down the village's main thoroughfare with its dual row of one- and two-story wooden frame buildings, she hoped she would not have any patients awaiting her return. Still, she knew that as the villagers became more accustomed to her presence, they would come in a steady stream even for the most minor of ailments. That seemed to be the way of the Grennai as she moved from settlement to settlement, this one her fifth since her return to this planet more than a year earlier.

While her personal mission of medical duty on this decidedly primitive world—catalogued in Starfleet databases only as NGC 667—had not gone precisely as she originally planned, Jendra managed to allow herself some small measure of satisfaction in her accomplishments this afternoon as well as what she would do for her latest patient at the first opportunity. Thanks to her, with an admitted assist from her borrowed Starfleet-issue medical equipment, one young man's life would change for the better.

The least I can do for these kind people, and we should be doing a damn sight more.

Hoping to catch a little rest before following up with her patient, Jendra opened the door to the clinic that doubled as her home. Moving shadows in the hallway leading to her examination room caught her by surprise, though, and she stopped. Hushed voices—she could not make out any words—carried from the far room.

Making her way down the hall, minding her steps so as not to clatter her hard-soled shoes against the wooden floor, Jendra peered into the exam room and saw three cloaked figures searching through her belongings. They seemed to know exactly what they were looking for and were gathering specific items atop her worktable: two Starfleet medical tricorders, a communicator, assorted surgical instruments, a hypospray kit, and other equipment that was at extreme odds with the room's comparably primitive trappings.

Her temper flaring at the violation, Jendra burst into the room, hoping to catch the intruders off guard. "Just what the hell do you think you're doing here?" she shouted.

Three Grennai males looked up at her with matching expressions of alarm, though none of them moved from where they stood. Instead, one of the men regarded her, his features changing from shock to what Jendra read as annoyance. In a firm voice, he said, "I've been waiting to ask you *exactly* the same question, Dr. Jendra."

The words were in Federation Standard, rather than the language native to Grennai in this region. Jendra's jaw dropped as she fumbled for her own response. She remained silent as one of the other men stepped forward, his hand reaching up to move his hood back from his head, and Jendra was startled to realize that she recognized his face.

"Revati, we need to talk."

Despite the darkened skin, white hair, and obviously prosthetic ears, there was no mistaking the voice of Dr. Leonard McCoy.

McCoy watched as Revati Jendra—cosmetically altered just as he was to resemble the indigenous Grennai—regarded him with an expression first of shock, then confusion before comprehension dawned and a wide smile creased her aged features.

"Leonard?" Jendra exclaimed, stepping forward to clasp both of his hands in hers. Smiling, she said, "I never thought I'd see you again, least of all here."

"You're not exactly the easiest person to track down," McCoy replied, relief at seeing her seeping into his voice. "I've been worried about you. A lot of people have."

Her smile fading, Jendra cast her head downward. "I can imagine." She cleared her throat before returning her gaze to meet his, and McCoy saw a hint of regret in her eyes. "Not a chance this is happy coincidence, I suppose."

"You suppose correctly, Doctor."

Even with his normal features disguised beneath the darkened skin tone and the artificial hair and ears, there was no hiding or suppressing James Kirk's command presence. McCoy saw the familiar set to his captain's jaw as he stepped forward to confront Jendra. "We're here to take you back with us."

She glanced at McCoy before offering a warm, knowing smile the doctor would have recognized regardless of the situation at hand. "You must be Captain Kirk," she said. Looking at McCoy's other companion, she added, "And Mr. Spock. Leonard has spoken very highly of you both." She held out her hand in greeting.

As if unprepared for Jendra's lack of initial resistance, the captain paused before nodding. "Thank you," he offered, his tone less rigid now. As Kirk and Jendra shook hands, McCoy noticed the slight yet obvious relaxing of his friend's stance and, yes, even the first hints of that now-familiar glint in the man's eye. For Jim Kirk, turning on the charm for a woman—any woman—seemed a reflex as natural as breathing.

"I'm sorry we have to meet under these circumstances, Doctor," Kirk said after a moment, his tone all business once again, "but I'm afraid Starfleet can't allow you to remain here."

Pulling herself up as if to meet Kirk eye-to-eye, Jendra replied, "The nature of my work here is humanitarian, Captain. I want us to be clear about that."

"Then *clearly*," Kirk snapped, biting down on the word, "you must be aware that your presence here is a violation of the Prime Directive and poses a risk to these people and their natural course of development. Your knowledge, your equipment, all of it is centuries ahead of these people and their level of technology."

McCoy saw the anger in Jendra's eyes, but she held her tone in check as she glared at Kirk. "I'm well versed in the Prime Directive." She held her hands out and away from her body. "As you can see, I've taken steps to prevent any cultural contamination. I'm also no stranger to the Grennai and how they live."

"Indeed," Spock said, moving to stand beside Kirk. "Three years ago, you were assigned as a medical officer to the initial Starfleet cultural observation detachment on this planet."

Jendra nodded. "That's right, Mr. Spock. We were tasked with covert study of the Grennai's preindustrial development, which we believed very closely mirrored that of your own people on Vulcan. We were here for nearly a year, during which we spent a great deal of time among the Grennai. So, you see, I've become quite adept at blending into the indigenous population."

"Your mission was terminated prematurely," Kirk said, "due to issues stemming from atmospheric irradiation and planetary conditions deemed potentially harmful to the research team. According to your own report, the planet was deemed unsafe to anyone but the local population."

"It is safe," Jendra corrected. "The rings of radiation encircling the planet constantly bombard the atmosphere, yes, but the indigenous population is immune to the radiation's effects."

Spock nodded. "*Enterprise* science teams have been studying the phenomenon since our arrival."

"Then you also know that it was part of the reason for our research here," Jendra said. "Trying to learn about the Grennai's natural immunity. Outsiders can only be exposed for short periods without protection. My team and I received regular inoculations of a hyronalin derivative to protect ourselves. I'm able to synthesize a version of that compound with the equipment I have and with raw ingredients I collect as I need them."

McCoy said, "After you returned to Earth, you were involved in some kind of research for a while, but then I get a message from you saying you're leaving Starfleet, and you just disappear." The words came out harsher than he had intended, and he swallowed the sudden lump in his throat. Looking around the crude examination room and its array of equally primitive medical and surgical implements— for all intents and purposes a medieval torture chamber when compared to his own sickbay aboard the *Enterprise*—he shook his head. "It was Starfleet Command that eventually suggested you might have come back here, but why?"

Looking away for a moment as if considering the weight of her response, Jendra finally sighed. "I have my reasons, Leonard."

The answer was vague, but her eyes spoke volumes, McCoy thought, reminding him of what he remembered most about the time they had spent together as colleagues—her drive to heal, the strength she drew from confidence in her abilities, her sense of doing right by her patients regardless of any personal toll it might exact upon her—all of that shone through her expression with startling clarity.

What the hell have you gotten yourself into, Revati?

In response to her words, Kirk stepped forward. "I'm sorry, Doctor, but you'll have to explain your reasons to Starfleet Command."

Jendra smiled once more, a tired, resigned smile. "I can imagine they're quite upset with me, but that doesn't change anything. I can't go. Not now."

Casting a glance toward McCoy that the doctor understood as the first hint of true irritation with the current proceedings, Kirk said, "It's not a request. You can come voluntarily, or I can carry you out of here."

"Such a tactic might prove unwise, Captain," Spock said, his tone and demeanor unflappable and—to McCoy, anyway—almost comical in its seriousness. "We would almost certainly attract attention during our attempt to return to the shuttlecraft."

At that, Jendra's eyebrows rose. "Shuttlecraft? Oh, that's right. I'd almost forgotten what the radiation bands do to transporters and communications." Shaking her head, she made a *tsk-tsk* sound through pursed lips. "A shame, that."

McCoy saw Kirk open his mouth to reply, no doubt with the intention of playing some kind of bluff, but Spock beat him to it.

"Our chief engineer has been researching the problem since our arrival," the Vulcan said, "but at last report he had not succeeded in recalibrating the transporter's annular confinement beam to work within this planet's atmosphere. I calculate the odds of his completing that task before we can return to the *Columbus* at seven thous—"

"*Thank* you, Mr. Spock," Kirk snapped.

Sighing, McCoy shook his head. "Spock, one of these days we need to have a long talk about that nasty habit of yours."

Spock's right eyebrow, artificially whitened and thickened in keeping with typical Grennai facial features, arched in the manner that always characterized his curiosity or skepticism. "What habit is that, Doctor?"

"Your mouth runneth over."

"That's enough," Kirk said, his tone and the expression on his face clear indications that he was in no mood for his friends' latest round of verbal jousting. To Jendra, who was still smiling as she observed the exchange, he said, "You seem to think this is funny, Doctor. I assure you it isn't. My orders are to return you to Starfleet Command, in restraints if necessary."

No sooner did the words leave his mouth than McCoy heard the sound of the door at the front of the building being thrown open, followed as quickly by a series of rapid, almost frantic footsteps on the hardwood floor. He felt his pulse quicken as he heard pain-wracked sobs from what could only be a child, all but drowned out by a louder, more adult voice echoing down the passageway.

"*Beloren! Beloren, kono nata!*"

Whatever enjoyment Jendra might have been feeling at Kirk's expense vanished. "This'll have to wait, Captain." Waving her arms toward the worktable and the array of Starfleet medical equipment lying atop it, she hissed, "Hide that, *now!*" Without waiting for a response, she grabbed her worn satchel and hurried from the room.

Leaving Kirk and Spock to tend to the sanitizing of the room—which involved both men stuffing various articles into the pockets of their robes or the large bag Spock wore slung over his shoulder—

McCoy followed after his friend. He found her kneeling beside the body of a young Grennai female, a child, whose clothing was stained with what his gut told him was far too much blood. Standing nearby was a Grennai woman, obviously the girl's mother, whose clothes also sported blood. He reached for her in an attempt to help.

She only waved him away, her expression pained as tears ran down her cheeks. "It is not my blood," she said, his universal translator filtering the native Grennai language into Federation Standard. "Please, help my *tundato!*"

"I'm trying to do just that," Jendra snapped, also in the local dialect, and McCoy looked down to see her hand clamped around the girl's right arm just above the elbow. To him, she said, "Help me get her to the examination room." It took only seconds to transfer the young patient to an exam table at the rear of the clinic, after which Jendra waved him out of her way as she set to work. Kirk and Spock hung nearby, watching intently.

McCoy could see a large gash in the girl's arm and pale blood running liberally from the wound. Jendra reached for a nearby clay pitcher with her free hand and began to pour water over the blood-covered wound. The girl screamed as the water hit her olive skin.

"Looks like a vein was hit," Jendra said before whispering something McCoy could not hear to the still-squirming child. Looking at the mother, she asked, "What happened?"

"We were working in the fields near our home," the woman replied. "Litari was clearing brush when she slipped in the mud and fell on the blade." Holding a hand to her mouth, she trembled for a moment. "Can you help her?"

Rather than answering the question, Jendra said, "Leonard, bring me the tray on the middle shelf." She nodded toward a set of wooden shelves to her right.

Glancing toward Kirk and Spock before doing as instructed, McCoy moved the tray near Jendra's left hand. "What can I do?" he asked.

"The dish with the green paste," Jendra replied. "Take some and rub it on her upper lip, just under her nose." As she continued to work at cleaning the struggling girl's wound, she added, "Don't inhale it yourself."

"Bones," McCoy heard Kirk say, the captain's tone one of caution, but he ignored it. Instead, he reached for what appeared to be nothing more than an earthen petri dish and—without thinking or even checking to see that his hands were clean—dipped his right forefinger into the viscous, emerald-colored substance it contained. Leaning forward, he applied the paste beneath the girl's nostrils even as Jendra kept working.

Almost immediately, the child's movements grew weaker and she began to relax. Less than ten seconds after he had applied the ointment, the girl's breathing slowed and she went limp on the examination table.

"I'll be damned," McCoy breathed.

Reaching for what he saw was a rudimentary version of a hemostat, Jendra looked up from her work. "It would be better if the mother waited outside." Her gaze locked with his for an instant before she glanced in the direction of her ever-present satchel, the meaning behind her words now quite plain.

She needs her equipment, and doesn't want to use it in front of the mother.

"We should all make room for the . . . *beloren,*" Spock said, taking the initiative and stepping toward the girl's mother.

When the woman did not budge from where she stood, Jendra looked to her and offered an encouraging smile. "Don't worry, Walirta. She's going to be fine."

Walirta allowed Spock to escort her from the examination room, with Kirk following after them. McCoy reached for the door, intending to give Jendra and her patient some privacy, and before exiting the room nodded encouragement to his friend.

"I'll be outside if you need me," he offered, and in that instant saw the determination in her eyes. Jendra's calling as a healer of body and spirit had led her to this place and to these people, and no person or regulation was going to hold sway over her.

But what are you trying to prove here? What do you think you can change?

Closing the door, he turned to find Kirk waiting for him, his jaw set in an expression of determination that the doctor knew too well.

"She's committed herself to this place, Jim," he said, "and to these people. I don't think I can convince her to leave, at least not until I know more." Frowning, he added, "Assuming I can get it out of her."

Looking over his shoulder as though to ensure Spock had taken the Grennai woman out of earshot, Kirk said, "Bones, she's appointed herself their caretaker. She's using her advanced medical knowledge and equipment to treat them in clear violation of the Prime Directive. It's not that I don't sympathize with her desire to help, but . . ." He shook his head, his brow furrowing as he pondered the situation. "It's as if she feels responsible for them somehow, as though she can save them, but why? From what?"

McCoy had to admit that the same questions were troubling him, as well.

"What do you mean, *classified?*"

Feeling his temper flare as he listened to the open communicator channel, Kirk rose from his chair and began to pace the small room at the front of Dr. Jendra's clinic.

From the communicator in his hand, the voice of Ensign Pavel Chekov replied, *"I am sorry, Captain, but all attempts to access the mission logs of the NGC-667 survey team are being rejected. Starfleet Command has flagged them off-limits except to authorized personnel."* Static eroded the quality of the transmission, despite the signal-enhancing effects of channeling the connection through the larger and more powerful communications system of the shuttlecraft *Columbus,* which sat concealed in a wooded valley three kilometers distant.

It had taken a bit of digging by the resourceful ensign—with Spock helping him to create an A7 computer specialist's rating and access key—just to discover that there was more to Jendra's mission to NGC 667 than was recorded in the official file Kirk had already reviewed prior to the *Enterprise*'s arrival in the system. Still, even the Vulcan's formidable prowess with Starfleet computer technology had proven insufficient to penetrate the security apparently surrounding the information Kirk now sought.

"Captain," came another voice from the communicator, this one belonging to Lieutenant Hikaru Sulu, *"Lieutenant Uhura has just informed me that she's received a subspace message from Admiral Komack. He wants to talk to you as soon as possible, and Uhura says the admiral doesn't sound very happy."*

From where he sat near the window at the front of the room that overlooked the village's main street, McCoy said, "Komack upset? That's a surprise."

"Not now, Bones," Kirk snapped. To his communicator, he said, "Stall the admiral, Mr. Sulu. What's the status on transporters?"

The *Enterprise* helmsman replied, *"Mr. Scott reports he's made some progress, but he's still running safety tests. He thinks he can certify it safe for biomatter within three hours, sir."*

It was not the best news, the captain thought, but it would have to do. "Keep me informed, Lieutenant. Kirk out." As he closed the communicator and returned it to an inside pocket of his robe, Kirk shook his head. "I knew something about this wasn't right." He looked to McCoy. "She came back here for a reason, Bones, and it has something to do with whatever Starfleet has classified about her first mission here."

"She's a doctor, Jim," McCoy replied. "It's what she does." He waved through the window. "Can't say I blame her. Lord knows how many primitive cultures we've visited where I wished I could stay longer, help them in some lasting way."

Clasping his hands behind his back, Spock said, "Even with the advanced technology and pharmaceuticals at her disposal, one physician cannot hope to make a lasting impact on any society by treating random incidents of illness and injury. The risk Dr. Jendra poses toward adversely affecting this culture's development should any of her advanced equipment be discovered is exponentially greater than any help she might offer. Logic suggests that—"

"Logic is probably the last thing on her mind!" McCoy barked. "Can't you drop that damned Vulcan stoicism and just try to connect with someone's feelings for once?"

"Actually, he's right, Leonard."

Kirk whirled toward the voice behind him to see Jendra standing in the doorway, regarding him with an expression mixed of equal parts amusement and resignation.

"I heard you in contact with your ship," Jendra said as she entered the room. "You should take better care to conceal such conversations as well as your equipment. Wouldn't want to disrupt the indigenous culture, after all."

Kirk ignored the gentle verbal jab. "How's the girl?" he asked, hoping to soften the doctor's demeanor.

"She'll be okay," Jendra replied, following that with a small cough. Clearing her throat, she reached up to rub the bridge of her nose. "I had to repair the severed vein, but don't worry, I did so in a manner that's undetectable to the Grennai *beloren*. I've had her taken to the local hospital." Releasing a sigh, she regarded Kirk with tired eyes. "So, ready to haul me away in irons?"

"Revati," McCoy said, "please. Jim's not the enemy."

A raspy, humorless chuckle pushed past Jendra's lips. "Doesn't look to be my friend, either."

"This isn't personal, Doctor," Kirk said, once again feeling his irritation growing. "I have my orders, and my duty, just as you once did."

He saw the tightening of her jaw line as she regarded him in silence for a moment, and he thought he almost could sense the struggle taking place within her. What secrets did she harbor? What burden did she carry? Why was she so driven?

"Maybe that's the problem," Jendra said after a moment, her gaze hardening. "It's not personal for you."

Kirk shook his head, "I don't understand." Even as he spoke the words, however, something told him that her passion and focus went far beyond even the absolute commitment typically displayed by the most dedicated physicians.

She'll accept help, his instincts told him. *Let her ask for it.*

"What hasn't Starfleet told us?" he asked. "What happened during your mission that made you come back here?"

Crossing the room to the chair next to McCoy, Jendra coughed again as she sat down and spent a moment fussing with the hem of her woven shirt before drawing a deep breath. "Our primary task was to learn about the Grennai's inherent immunity to the planet's radiation in the hope of learning ways to perfect protection against similar hazards."

She indicated her face and clothing with a wave of her hand. "Our disguises allowed us to interact with the indigenous population, but our actions were in keeping with the Prime Directive. We did *not* interfere with these people's societal development." Her features clouding into what Kirk recognized as an expression of guilt, she cast a glance toward the floor before sighing and shaking her head. "At first, anyway."

McCoy leaned forward until he could take her left hand in both of his. "Revati, what happened?"

"It was Roberts," Jendra replied.

Kirk knew the name only from the report he had read during

the transit to NGC 667, but that was why he had Spock. A single glance was all that the first officer required, and he nodded in reply.

"Prior to his retirement," the Vulcan said, "Dr. Campbell Roberts had a noteworthy career spent almost entirely within the xenosociology field. He participated in the concealed observation and study of more than two dozen developing cultures, including a solo endeavor where he spent over a year embedded within a tribe of primitive humanoids who had not yet discovered fire. It was revolutionary research—something never before attempted by any pre–first contact team."

"That's what I call dedication," McCoy remarked.

Jendra nodded. "He had a reputation as a bit of an eccentric, of course, particularly after that mission, but no one could ever argue with his work or most of his recommendations. When our passive research and observation of the Grennai failed to turn up anything useful about their apparent immunity to the radiation, it was Campbell who made the decision to take additional measures. He began collecting tissue and blood samples, first from the bodies of dead Grennai but later from living specimens."

"I take that to mean he didn't do so within the guise of a local doctor?" Kirk asked after she paused again.

"Correct," Jendra replied. "He and his assistants enacted a program where they would select a promising candidate, tranquilize them while they were sleeping, then move them to one of our secure locations where the patient could be subjected to a full battery of tests, all noninvasive except for the collection of samples. The patients would be returned to their homes unharmed and none the wiser."

Kirk said nothing, but instead watched as McCoy's expression turned to one of horror and disbelief.

"Revati," the doctor said, his voice low and solemn. "He abducted innocent people for medical testing without their knowledge?"

Coughing again, Jendra reached up to wipe her forehead before replying, "Yes, and I helped him." Before McCoy could respond to that she pressed forward. "I didn't accept his reasoning at first, but after a while I became convinced it was the only way to learn about the long-term effects on their physiology, to track how the radiation worked in concert with the Grennai's normal growth and aging cycle. We gathered samples from children as well as adults, even babies, but at no time was anyone in any danger. At least, that's what we thought."

She stopped to clear her throat, and Kirk could see that recalling the mission was evoking what could only be pain the doctor had been only partially successful at suppressing.

Then she collapsed.

McCoy caught her as she fell forward from her chair, with Kirk and Spock both lunging across the room to offer assistance. The captain saw that Jendra was unconscious, her body limp in McCoy's arms as he lowered her to the floor.

"What's wrong with her?" Kirk asked.

"How the hell should I know?" the doctor growled as he reached into his robe for his tricorder. Kirk and Spock watched in silence as their friend conducted a brief, hurried examination, with the captain's attention moving from the door to the window overlooking the street and back again as the whine of McCoy's medical scanner echoed in the room. It lasted only a few seconds, after which the physician looked up and locked eyes with Kirk.

"She's dying, Jim."

After helping to move Jendra to a bed in another room of the doctor's home, Kirk and Spock could only wait while McCoy conducted a more thorough examination of his friend. The captain considered a return to the shuttlecraft *Columbus* but decided against it as darkness fell over the village, opting instead for a check-in call to Lieutenant Sulu. The status report was not promising, with

Scotty still hard at work attempting to recalibrate the transporters while Admiral Komack continued his efforts to strangle Kirk via the subspace connection linking Starfleet Command with the *Enterprise.*

Another entertaining after-action report for the admiral, Kirk mused. *It's a wonder he doesn't bust me down to second officer on a garbage scow.*

"She's got three, maybe four months at most," the doctor said thirty minutes later after inviting his friends into the room where Jendra lay in bed, asleep and resting. "If she stays here, that is."

"The radiation?" Kirk asked. "I thought she was inoculating herself to protect against that, like we are."

It was Spock who replied. "I took the liberty of examining her supply of medications, Captain, but I found no quantities of the hyronalin derivative developed for use here."

"Revati told me the synthesizer she brought with her broke down and she wasn't able to fix it," McCoy said. "She'd manufactured a reserve to get her through in case she ran into trouble procuring the raw materials to make more, but she went through the last of that a month or so ago, and once her immunity started to fail . . ." Shaking his head, he let the sentence fade on his lips.

Kirk frowned, turning to regard the still-sleeping Jendra. "The condition can't be reversed?"

"I might be able to do something for her on the *Enterprise,*" the doctor replied, "but her best chance is a Starbase medical facility."

"I'm not going."

Her voice was feeble as Jendra struggled to sit up in her bed, coughing as she did so. McCoy moved to help her and she allowed the assistance, and in a moment was sitting with her back against the headboard, still dressed in her heavy shirt but covered from the waist down by a thick woven blanket.

"Revati," McCoy began.

Shaking her head, Jendra held up a hand. "I can't leave these people, Leonard. Not now, not after what we did to them."

"Did to them," Kirk repeated. "You mean there's more to what you were telling us, don't you?"

Looking to McCoy, Jendra offered a weak smile. "You said he wasn't stupid."

"I also said he wasn't your enemy," McCoy replied. "Tell us, Revati. Tell us everything."

"It was one of our team members, Dr. Quentin Melander," Jendra said. She paused to cough once more before continuing. "He had been exposed to a strain of Ametan rubeola some years ago on another mission. According to his most recent physical, the virus was dormant in his system, held in remission thanks to a regular vaccination schedule. What no one counted on was the virus mutating once he came into contact with the atmosphere here."

"Dear God," McCoy whispered. "No."

Her expression one of sadness, Jendra nodded. "The radiation exposure altered the virus so that he became contagious." Kirk saw her eyes watering, and a single tear fell down her right cheek. "Not to us, though. Just the Grennai."

"Ametan rubeola causes dehydration, pneumonia, encephalitis," Spock said. "Left unchecked, it can decimate populations, particularly those with a level of medical knowledge and technology similar to this one."

"Children are especially susceptible to it," McCoy added. "I've seen it run through thousands of people in a month, Jim."

"The mutation accelerated even that timetable," Jendra said. "Melander died within seventy-two hours, and his exposure to just two members of the village we were observing was enough to wipe out its entire population—two hundred thirty-eight people—in less than two weeks."

"What did Starfleet do?" Kirk asked, though he felt his gut already trying to scream the answer at him.

"Starfleet Medical evaluated the situation," Jendra said, "and determined the virus in its mutated form would be immune to available vaccines. Projections for developing a new treatment were poor—far beyond the projected life expectancy of anyone exposed to the virus. Our team was evacuated from the planet, and all signs of our presence were removed. We left the Grennai to their fate."

Spock said, "According to public news sources, Dr. Roberts retired from Starfleet due to health reasons and withdrew from public life. If memory serves, he still publishes for the *Starfleet Medical Journal,* though on an infrequent basis."

Releasing a humorless laugh that was all but lost in a renewed coughing fit, Jendra replied, "Campbell was convicted of violating the Prime Directive and sent to a penal colony. The rest of us were given suspended sentences and official reprimands in our files—all classified, of course, along with pretty much everything pertaining to the mission. It was all buried." She shook her head, turning to look at a spot in the corner of the room as though to avoid making eye contact with her visitors. "In some ways I wish they would have sent us with Campbell. Instead, we were left with our own conscience to act as judge, jury, and deliverer of punishment."

"Well," Kirk said. "At least now it makes sense why Starfleet 'guessed' you might be here." As he digested the new revelations, he nevertheless found himself drifting away from disdain for what Jendra and her colleagues had done. While he could not argue that their actions were in clear, unquestioned violation of regulations—including the one upon which every Starfleet officer's oath of service was based, General Order One, the Prime Directive—the captain could see that Jendra's intentions, along with those even of Campbell Roberts, had been noble if misguided.

During his own Starfleet career, Kirk had already violated the letter of the law on occasion while at the same time struggling to uphold its spirit. Had his actions always been successful? Not at all. Several failures continued to loom in his mind, harsh lessons and hard-won wisdom he hoped would guide him toward making better decisions in the future, while at the same time allowing him to retain the humanity that had driven him to make those early choices—and mistakes—in the first place.

Because of that, he felt for Revati Jendra.

The question now was, where did he—and she—go from here?

"I don't understand," Kirk said. "Obviously there was no planetwide epidemic." He waved toward the window opposite Jendra's bed, beyond which was the darkness of early evening. "You didn't wipe out the entire population."

"Only by luck," Jendra replied. "When I came back with a new vaccine, I discovered that the contamination had spread, but only marginally."

"The Grennai's current level of societal development," Spock said, "including the limited means of travel over great distances, would have done much to offer rudimentary protection against widespread outbreak across the planet."

"Correct," Jendra said. "I was able to track the spread of the contagion from village to village, but by then the cases of infection were very widespread and infrequent. I've not seen any indications of a renewed outbreak in months, but I still move from province to province, working as a local healer—a *beloren*—and as part of my routine examinations of the villagers I very carefully administer a preventive vaccine to them in the form of tablets or powders. I tell them it's vitamins or protections against some local malady." Sighing, she looked down at her hands lying listlessly in her lap. "It's not much, but it's better than doing nothing."

"And that's what you've been doing here all along?" McCoy asked.

Sitting up straighter in her bed, Jendra replied, "That's right. We got very lucky here, Leonard. Despite that good fortune, several hundred Grennai still died who would be alive if not for our meddling."

She looked to Kirk. "It was a violation of the Prime Directive, Captain, to say nothing of my oath as a physician. There's a penance to be paid for that, and so here I am. I'll treat these people and care for them as best I can until the day I die. You can't take me away. Not now."

"For God's sake, Revati," McCoy said, moving to sit beside her on the bed. "We've been friends for twenty years. Why didn't you tell me? I might've been able to help."

"If she had, Doctor," Spock replied, "you would be as culpable in the continued violation of the Prime Directive as Dr. Jendra. Starfleet would almost certainly find you guilty of being an accessory in some manner."

"Guilty of what?" McCoy snapped. "Helping to correct a mistake Starfleet made in the first place? If I have to be guilty of anything, it might as well be that."

"Bones," Kirk started to say, but stopped when his attention was caught by a faint orange glow flickering from somewhere outside the window. An instant later a dull thump reverberated through the room's wooden walls and floorboards, followed by the momentary rattling of the window's panes and a few loose objects scattered on the bureau across from Jendra's bed.

"What the hell was that?" McCoy asked, rising from where he sat next to Jendra.

Having already retrieved his tricorder from beneath the folds of his robe, Spock activated the device, its high-pitched whine echoing within the small room. "There has been an explosion from within a large structure near the village's northern perimeter."

"The ironworks," Jendra said, her eyes widening in concern.

From outside the building, Kirk heard a horn blowing, instinct telling him it was an alert signal for the rest of the village. "Spock?"

Still studying his tricorder, the Vulcan replied, "I'm detecting a fire inside the building, Captain, spreading rapidly."

"We have to go," Jendra cried as she struggled to rise from the bed. "There may be people hurt."

"Revati," McCoy said, holding out a hand to steady her, "you're in no condition to go running down there."

"They'll need me, damn it!" Jendra shouted, appearing to gather strength as she moved from the bed toward the door. Stopping at the threshold, she turned to regard the three *Enterprise* officers. "And I could use some help, too."

Despite the rules and regulations, Kirk knew there was only one choice to make.

Komack's going to have my hide.

Even before they reached the massive, two-story structure housing the iron smelting factory as well as—according to Jendra—the village's trio of blacksmiths and also the dozen or so kilns used for brick-making, Kirk could see flames licking from inside the structure's highest windows. As he, Spock, McCoy, and Jendra drew closer, the captain noted the large gathering of people near the building's main entrance. He counted eight people lying scattered on the ground, two of them coughing and five unmoving as others hovered over them. The eighth was writhing and screaming, both of his legs scorched black. The unmistakable odor of burnt flesh assailed Kirk's nostrils, and it was a physical effort to keep from retching.

Without saying a word, Jendra moved to the burn victim. Several of the villagers saw her approach and stood aside to allow her passage, and Kirk heard a steady chorus of *"Beloren!"* as she knelt beside her newest patient.

"I'm going to see what I can do," McCoy said. It wasn't a request for permission, Kirk noted, not that he would have expected anything less from the doctor. Though worried about the potential for their exposure as outsiders here among the Grennai, the captain trusted his friend to use sound judgment even while doing everything in his power to heal those in need.

"Captain," Spock said in a low voice, and Kirk turned to see the Vulcan surreptitiously consulting the tricorder he held concealed by his robe. "I count six life-forms inside the structure, surrounded by fire. They appear to be trapped."

Looking around, Kirk took in the scene of Grennai villagers scrambling to maneuver various kinds of crude fire-fighting equipment into position, chief among them a device that he recognized as a form of hand-operated water pump set atop a wagon and drawn by a quartet of sizable, long-haired quadrupedal animals that looked to be a cross between horses and water buffalo. Members of the wagon team were already unloading spools of hose made from either canvas or leather.

There was no way, Kirk decided, that the villagers would be able to get the fire under control in time to save the trapped workers.

"Damn," he hissed through gritted teeth as he retrieved his communicator and flipped it open. "Kirk to *Enterprise!*"

"Enterprise. *Lieutenant Sulu here, sir,*" came his helmsman's prompt reply.

"Sulu, tell me Scotty's got the transporters working."

"Not yet, sir." Kirk heard the regret in the lieutenant's voice. *"They're still not safe for biomatter transport."*

There was nothing to be done about that now. "Have sickbay stand by for possible emergency triage to treat burn victims, and start prepping a shuttlecraft with the appropriate equipment and supplies."

Closing the communicator, the captain caught sight of McCoy looking over at him from where he knelt beside Jendra. The hint of an understanding and appreciative smile teased the corners of his mouth.

"Shut up," Kirk said to his friend before turning to Spock. "Where are the trapped people?"

The Vulcan pointed toward his left. "Toward the rear of the structure on the ground floor. Life-signs are weak."

"Let's go, then," Kirk said before taking off at a run down the length of the ironworks. Flames billowed from open windows on the second floor, licking at the structure's exterior wood trim. Kirk spied a dark sliver farther along the wall and was buoyed to see that it was a door, standing open and offering unimpeded access to the building.

"Come on, Spock!" Kirk yelled as he plunged through the doorway, the heat from the fire playing across his exposed skin the instant he was inside. Smoke stung his eyes and he reached up to cover his mouth with part of his hood. Inside the building, the only illumination was that offered by the blaze eating at the flammable materials around him. With Spock indicating the correct direction, the captain moved across the floor of the ironworks, dodging between equipment, tools, and burning debris that had fallen from the ceiling, all while trying to ignore the nagging feeling that the entire building was about to fall down around his ears.

"Help!" a voice called out from somewhere to his left, and Kirk turned to see a male Grennai waving in his direction, the man's frantic plea and the emotion behind it channeled through Kirk's universal translator. As he drew closer, the captain saw the panic in the man's eyes. "We're trapped in here! Help us!"

"Don't worry," Kirk said, hoping to ease the man's fears, "we're going to get you out of here." He placed his hands on the Grennai's shoulders. "Where are the others?"

"This way!" the man replied, leading Kirk and Spock deeper into the building to where a group of five other Grennai were lying beneath a set of stairs in the rear corner of the room. A quick check revealed that all of the workers were unconscious, having succumbed to either the heat or smoke inhalation.

The fire was close, Kirk knew, working its way across the structure's wooden framework. Smoke thickened the air, making it difficult to see and even harder to breathe. As he pressed a fold of his robe over his mouth, the captain was sure he heard dull groans and creaks of protest as the burning building continued to deteriorate around them.

Something cracked and snapped above and behind Kirk an instant before he felt a hand on his back pushing him forward. Struggling to keep his balance, he turned in time to see Spock narrowly avoiding a large, burning timber as it fell from the ceiling and plummeted to the cobblestone floor. Embers and ash swirled around the massive piece of wood as it came to rest less than a meter from the Vulcan's feet.

"You all right?" Kirk called out.

Spock nodded. "We do not have much time."

"We must hurry!" the Grennai cried, his voice cracking under the obvious strain.

Nodding in agreement, Kirk replied, "No time to get them all out the way we came." Reaching inside his robe, he retrieved the compact phaser from his pocket, showing it to Spock while also shielding it from the other man.

Spock exchanged a look of understanding with Kirk before stepping closer to the man. "Sir, a fragment of burning ash has landed on your clothing. Let me help you." His hand clamped down at the junction of the Grennai's neck and shoulder, and the man's eyes opened wide in surprise as his body fell limp.

"What are the odds I'll ever learn to do that?" Kirk asked as Spock lowered the man's unconscious form to the ground.

"They continue to defy my efforts at computation, Captain."

Moving closer to the wall, Kirk checked the power setting on his phaser before taking aim and firing the weapon. Harsh blue-white energy lanced from the phaser and struck the wall, washing over the crude earthen bricks and expanding outward in a near-perfect circle. Masonry dissolved beneath the glare of the phaser blast, revealing open ground outside the building. Kirk ceased firing, and smoke immediately began to filter through the newly created hole.

He set to work assisting Spock to move the stricken victims from their place of fleeting shelter to safety outside the structure. Once outside and safely away from the scene, the Starfleet officers could only stand by, administering preliminary first aid to their unconscious charges and watching as the building was slowly yet inexorably claimed by the intensifying blaze.

"Captain," Spock said after a time, "you do realize that Dr. McCoy will almost certainly find no end of humor and irony in your actions?" There was a subtle yet still wry expression gracing the Vulcan's features.

Kirk offered a stern look to his first officer. "Then we'll have to be sure not to tell him, won't we?"

I think I might actually be getting too old for this.

Jendra's entire body—her lungs and sides in particular—ached from the exertion of hiking through the thick forest and uneven terrain in the predawn darkness, and she was appreciative of the moderate pace McCoy had set. Grunting with new effort, she hitched her modest pack a bit higher onto her back, once again feeling its straps digging into her shoulders even through her thick shirt.

"You all right?" McCoy asked, looking over at her with an expression of concern.

She nodded. "I'm fine." He had offered to carry the pack more than once, but she had refused, insisting instead on carrying what remained of her personal belongings. With the *Enterprise*'s engineer having successfully recalibrated the ship's transporters, Captain Kirk had assured her that the bulk of her possessions, including what remained of the Starfleet equipment and supplies she originally had brought with her to NGC 667, would be transferred aboard. All that remained was to get her up to the starship, and she was damned if she was going to have someone else carry the rest of her things—or carry her, for that matter.

Other than the periodic offers to assist her, McCoy had said almost nothing during their hike from the village. She sensed his discomfort, and though she had said nothing to the effect herself, Jendra was thankful for the silence. Despite the way she had faced off against Captain Kirk, she had felt constantly on guard, required to justify actions that before the *Enterprise* officers' arrival she was certain were unquestionably the right thing to do, from a moral perspective if not a legal one. She knew that—on some level, at least—McCoy agreed with her, but Jendra nevertheless was grateful for a respite from having to defend herself.

"There she is," McCoy said after a moment, pointing to his right. A glint of artificial light flickered through the trees, and as they drew closer Jendra could make out the straight, smooth lines of the shuttlecraft *Columbus*. Sitting in the center of a small glade barely large enough to accommodate it, the vessel's flat gray-white hull and bright red striping contrasted sharply with the muted browns and greens of the surrounding forest.

She and McCoy emerged from the woods near the shuttle's left side, and as they approached, Kirk stepped through the craft's open hatch and down onto the ground. All traces of his Grennai disguise—the white hair, prosthetic ears, and artificial skin pigmentation—were gone, and he was now wearing his standard Starfleet captain's uniform.

"Hello, Doctor," Kirk said, offering a smile that, while guarded, still retained much of the charm Jendra had observed earlier.

If I were thirty years younger . . . I think I'd still be more interested in his first officer.

"Captain," she said, nodding her head in greeting as she slid the pack from her shoulders and set it on the ground at her feet.

"How are your patients faring?" the captain asked.

Pausing to wipe perspiration from her brow, Jendra replied, "We lost five, all told, but three others are still missing. More than a dozen wounded, but they should recover in time." Feeling the resignation creep into her voice, she added, "They've not found the foreman, Crimar. He was the most knowledgeable metalworker among them, and he was a friend to me. It's quite a setback for us . . . that is, for the whole village."

She had been surprised by Kirk's decision to let her remain at the village and oversee the treatment of the fire victims. He could have had her transported to his ship without another word on the subject, of course. That he had not done so spoke volumes about the man's character, so far as she was concerned.

Leonard was right about him, I think.

"You know these people," Kirk said after a moment. "Will they be able to rebuild the ironworks in short order? Get back on their feet?"

Jendra shrugged. "The building's a total loss. Collapsed in on itself during the fire. They'll have to start from scratch, but if I know them, they'll be just fine. I never thanked you for your help, Captain. You saved a lot of lives. It would have been easy just to stand back and let things happen without . . . interfering."

The smile on Kirk's face faded, and he seemed to take on a wistful expression for the briefest of moments before shaking his head. "Easy? Not really, no." When he spoke the words, Jendra saw for the first time that this man had encountered similar dilemmas in the past and been forced to make difficult decisions in the face of such crises. She could not be sure, but she sensed that he might even harbor guilt over the results of at least some of those choices.

More to him than meets the eye, I'll grant that.

She caught movement behind the captain and looked up to see Spock exiting the shuttlecraft. Like Kirk, the Vulcan also was dressed in Starfleet garb, all vestiges of his Grennai persona gone. "I take it the local look didn't agree with you gentlemen?" she asked.

"The need for us to interact with the indigenous population has ended," Spock said. "There was also the matter of my . . . compromised disguise."

"One of his ears melted at the fire," Kirk deadpanned, his expression remaining fixed and neutral.

"Damn shame, too," McCoy said. "I thought it was an improvement. Spock, you were almost likable."

Jendra started to laugh but was interrupted by a coughing fit so severe that it felt as though her lungs were tearing. McCoy moved to her side, maneuvering her so that she could sit on the steps leading into the shuttlecraft. After taking a moment to catch her breath, she looked up to Kirk, sighing. "All right, let's get this over with, Captain. I'm only here because I'm too damned tired to outrun or outfox you. What's done is done, I suppose I'm ready to atone for my actions, and I want to do it while I'm still breathing." She had given her word to Kirk that she would not attempt to flee the village, in return for his allowing her to tend to the victims of the fire. Despite momentary temptation, she had every intention of keeping her promise, no matter how difficult it was to do so.

Kirk regarded her in silence for several heartbeats, and Jendra thought she saw conflict behind the captain's bright, hazel eyes. His jaw line tightened, and he inhaled a deep breath before drawing himself to his full height and squaring his shoulders.

"No."

Confused by the abrupt statement, Jendra blinked several times. "No, what?"

"While waiting for you this morning," Kirk said, "I completed my after-action report for Starfleet Command. I haven't yet transmitted it, but it says that you died earlier this morning from complications due to injuries you suffered while rescuing Grennai villagers from the fire."

"Jim?" McCoy said, and Jendra was sure that her friend's expression of uncertainty mirrored her own. She found herself fumbling for something to say.

Finally, she managed to whisper, "I don't understand."

"My report will also state that your body was interred in accordance with local Grennai customs," Kirk continued, "and that your presence didn't introduce any obvious or permanent cultural contamination. Our mission here was concluded without further incident." Looking down at her, he smiled again. "It's not often that someone gets the opportunity to correct a mistake, Doctor. I wasn't sure about this until just a little while ago, but I think you should have that opportunity."

Her eyes darted from Kirk's face to McCoy's, and she saw a knowing smile spreading across her friend's features.

"I'll be damned," McCoy said, shaking his head before looking at Spock. "You're going along with this, too?"

The Vulcan nodded. "While I do not condone violation of the Prime Directive, Doctor, this situation is somewhat unique. Dr. Jendra's efforts, limited though they may be, do serve a noble purpose. It seems logical to allow her to continue."

"And you're okay with lying?" McCoy asked.

His right eyebrow arching, Spock replied, "It is not a lie to protect the truth from those who would act against it without concern for mitigating circumstances, Doctor. In this matter, I believe Starfleet to be wrong, both then and now."

"My God," McCoy said in mock astonishment. "I need a drink."

Now unable to stifle a joyous laugh even as she felt her eyes watering, Jendra reached out until she could grasp Kirk's hands in her own. "Thank you, Captain. I don't know what to say."

"It's my pleasure, Doctor." Casting a quick glance toward the approaching sunrise, he said, "It's almost daybreak, and we need to be going." He offered a look at McCoy. "But we've still got a few minutes, Bones."

The captain and Spock offered their farewells and good luck wishes before climbing into the shuttlecraft, leaving McCoy alone with her even as she wiped tears from her face. Ever the gentleman, he produced a handkerchief for her.

"Leonard," she said, "I don't believe it."

"I probably shouldn't, either," McCoy replied, "but I know better. This isn't the first time I've seen Jim wring a second chance out of a bad situation." He reached into his robe and withdrew a small pouch and offered it to her. "A parting gift, I suppose. It's not much, but you might be able to do some good with it." She saw tears welling up in his eyes as he pulled her close, his voice trembling as he planted a soft kiss on her weathered forehead. "Take care of yourself, Revati."

Jendra stepped back from the shuttlecraft as McCoy climbed aboard, turning to wave once more to her before the hatch was closed. A moment later, she felt the rush of wind whipping her clothes and her hair as the vessel's thrusters lifted it into the air and pushed it into the slowly brightening sky.

As the echo of the departing shuttle's engines faded, Jendra looked down at the pouch in her hand and opened its protective flap, only to find several vials of tablets. The labels on the vials identified the medicine as the hyronalin derivative she had lacked for these many weeks. While the medication would not reverse her condition, it certainly would allow her much more time among the Grennai than she might have hoped for.

Given the extra time, she might even find a substitute remedy, she decided.

Clutching the medication to her chest, Revati Jendra closed her eyes and offered silent thanks for the fortune that had been visited upon her.

Leonard, my friend, your captain is hardly the only giver of second chances.

READ MORE *STAR TREK* STORIES IN

CONSTELLATIONS

AVAILABLE NOW
WHEREVER BOOKS ARE SOLD

www.startrekbooks.com

TOKYOPOP.com

WHERE MANGA LIVES!

JOIN THE TOKYOPOP COMMUNITY!

Come and preview the hottest manga around!

CREATE...
UPLOAD...
DOWNLOAD...
BLOG...
CHAT...
VOTE...
LIVE!!!!

WWW.TOKYOPOP.COM HAS:

Manga-on-Demand • News
Anime Reviews • Manga Reviews
Movie Reviews • Music Reviews
and more...